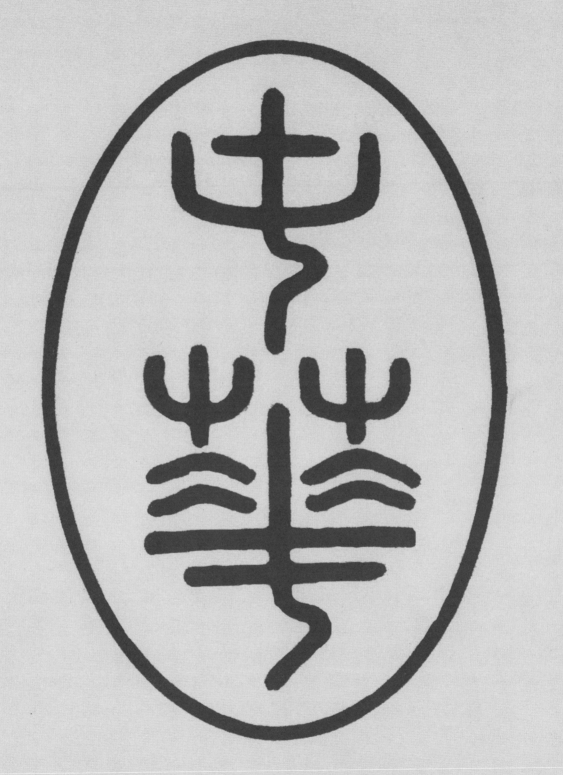

The Shopkeepers

The Shopkeepers

Commemorating

150 years

of the

Chinese in Jamaica

1854 - 2004

**A historical record of their arrival
and personal stories of their endeavours and experiences**

Compiled and Edited by Ray Chen

慶祝

華僑定居牙買加

一百五十週年紀念

序　言

2004年，我们将见证首批华人抵达牙买加一百五十周年的历史时刻。作为见证人之一，我有幸应邀在《店主》一书付梓之际写几句话，身临其境，感慨系之，故欣然援笔。

一百五十年前，我们的先民们怀着对美好生活的憧憬，在结束了巴拿马铁路上的辛勤劳作后，又经过一路漂泊，踏上了牙买加的土地，从此在这片"林水之地"上安身立命、繁衍生息，和其他族群和睦相处，与这个美丽的岛屿休戚与共。在创业初期，牙买加华人大多靠在乡村开办杂货店为生。这些店铺以经营日用百货和农业器具为主，并采用赊销等灵活方式逐渐扩大规模，成为牙买加早期商业的主要支柱。"Chinese Shops"也成为家喻户晓的"诚信、便利"的同义词。华人店主们诚实经商、与邻为善，充分体现了中华民族勤劳、朴实、诚恳、敬业的美德。正因为有了先民们的辛勤积累，今天，华人在为这个国家创造出巨大财富的同时，也为牙买加的商界、政界和文化界贡献了一大批杰出的人才。传承美德，昭示后人。我想，这是本书以"店主"为名的用意所在。

这一百五十年的历史，也是中华民族从羸弱走向强盛的历史，祖国人民与三千多万散居世界各地的华人一道，同是这部历史的主角。因此，当我们为历史教科书上那一幕幕惊心动魄的"大历史"而深深震撼的时候，也应当记取华人移民在异域创造出的平凡却同样伟大的历史。《店主》一书正是这样一种有益的尝试，它没有严格的历史考证或繁琐的史料堆砌，而是试图通过不同人物对自己家庭历史的追忆来"还原"牙买加华人的发展史。翻检这样一部"活"历史，无论是兴之所至的普通读者，还是有志于海外华人历史研究的学者，都能从中受益。

作为本书的第一批读者，我要向策划者Ray Chen先生和出版商Periwinkle出版公司致敬。Ray Chen先生是享誉牙买加和加勒比的著名华人摄影家，包括我在内的许多人都是通过他的摄影作品得到对这个美丽国度的初始印象的。我相信读者们能从本书一个个精美的故事中触摸到一个人、一个家庭乃至一个民族强劲跳动的脉搏。如是，Ray Chen先生和他领导的Periwinkle出版公司所付出的辛勤劳动就有了最好的回报。

中华人民共和国驻牙买加特命全权大使

（赵振宇）

二○○四年七月于金斯敦

Chinese Ambassador's message

中华人民共和国驻牙买加大使馆

The Embassy of the People's Republic of China in Jamaica

The year 2004 marks the 150th anniversary of the arrival of the first Chinese in Jamaica, and I am honoured to have been asked to write a few words for inclusion in the *The Shopkeepers,* a compilation of historical data and stories of the personal pilgrimages of these Han Chinese in Jamaica.

One hundred and fifty years ago they came to this 'land of wood and water', cherishing ardent hope for a better life. Their hard work, determination and self-sacrifice made it possible for their Jamaican-born descendants to succeed in achieving their goals. Their personal stories reveal the inherent qualities which are part of Chinese philosophy, and which helped these early immigrants to triumph over adverse circumstances.

Periwinkle Publishers and its CEO, Ray Chen, have produced a book which not only provides solid information for the serious researcher, but it documents in an entertaining and informative manner the varied experiences of the immigrant Han Chinese and their Jamaican born descendants.

I wish to pay tribute to Mr. Chen and his company, Periwinkle Publishers for his determination and industry in producing this historical document of our people's lives and experiences in Jamaica. He has accomplished a remarkable feat in convincing so may of them to share their life stories with the world at large. As one of the Jamaican-born descendants of the original Chinese immigrants, Mr. Chen has honoured the ancestors of all Chinese who adopted this beautiful island and contributed significantly to its growth and development.

Zhao Zhenyu

Ambassador Extraordinary and Plenipotentiary of
The People's Republic of China
Kingston, July 15, 2004

First Published in Jamaica, 2005 by
Periwinkle Publishers (Jamaica) Ltd.
7 Clieveden Avenue
Kingston 6
Jamaica. W. I.

periwinkle@cwjamaica.com

Tel: (876) 978-3408 / 978-7828
Fax: (876) 978-9101

© 2005 Periwinkle Publishers (Jamaica) Ltd.

National Library of Jamaica Cataloguing in Publication Data

Chen, Ray
The Shopkeepers: Commemorating 150 years of the Chinese in Jamaica

Include index:
        Glossary:

ISBN   976-610-638-X   Hardback
ISBN   976-610-639-8   Paperback

1. Chinese in Jamaica – History
I. Title

Published in Canada by Periwinkle Publishers Inc.
132 White Lotus Circle,
Markham, Ontario, L6C 1V8
Canada

© 2005 Periwinkle Publishers Inc

Cover and book design by Ray Chen and Andrea Blake (Jamaica)

Printed in Hong Kong, China

*This book
is dedicated
to the memory
of our
forefathers and
especially
our parents
who dedicated
their lives
to hard work and
the love of family.*

Contents

CONTENTS

Acknowledgements

This is to say thanks to all the folks who contributed so much of their time and energy in helping to see this project of love through, for I am truly indebted to you.

To the Chinese Ambassador in Jamaica, Zhenyu Zhao, for his kind words.

To my relatives, friends and colleagues:

Alexandra Lee, who at the beginning, contributed so much of her time in interviewing people and writing their stories.

Hubert Lue for sharing the tales of your journey during the earlier years in Jamaica and especially for your encouragement.

Roger, my brother, to whom I owe so much. He gave so freely of his time, his energy and his talent. His experience has allowed him to provide suggestions, illustrations, maps, charts, and the scanning of photographs. I am truly blessed to have him as a brother.

Lillian, my sister, who listened and observed as an 'outsider', before giving her opinion and advice on the church and many other subjects.

Carol Wong, 'My Toronto Connection'. Your contribution is really IRIE. Without your participation in setting up the first interviews for Alexandra, there would be no interviews or stories.

Sonia Gordon Scott. Mon amie, my friend. What would I do without you? Your talent for writing, your encouragement, your smiles and your BIG ears for listening in times of stress and especially being my 'special pen yu.'

Peggi Russell for your patience, understanding and the long, long hours you've put in while working with Maureen Lyn Sue. You are a true friend and a real trooper.

Andrea Blake, for your design talents and the long hours, accompanied by the 'reggae boy', in putting the pages of text and photographs together.

Mark Weinberger, for stepping in after the 'reggae boy' arrived. You are a true friend when the going gets tough and it was much appreciated.

Lisa Morgan and Deidre Taylor for your time and diligence in doing the final edit of the manuscript.

Carl Chang, my friend, for taking the time to source the documents of the *S.S. Prinz Alexander's* journey. *Courtesy of the National Archives of Jamaica.*

Benjamin Koo, for your assistance and for providing us with the Chinese calligraphy.

Patrick and Loraine Lee, of Huntsmill Graphic Limited (Toronto, Canada), for allowing us the use of photos from his dad's first book on *The Chinese in Jamaica,* First Edition 1957. Also photos and maps and the story on the Air Force from their two books, *The Canadian Chinese Jamaicans* published in 2000 and *The Jamaican Chinese Worldwide… One Family* published in 2004.

Norman Hew-Shue who remembers everything and in great detail. The result of pleasant memories with loving parents and long 'labrish' (chat) between Everard Hoo and himself.

Sister Grace Yap for just being so helpful with her thoughts.

Reggie Chin a friend indeed. You have been helpful in so many ways.

Juliet Lambert, a special thank you, for taking on the administration of Periwinkle during this period, thus allowing me the time to put all my energy in the production of this project. The staff of Periwinkle for faithfully 'doing their thing', and Camille Berry for assisting Andrea in all areas in the production.

Mrs. Loraine Von Strolley, a special thank you, for granting us permission to use the photographs from her mom's album, Kathleen (Kay) Chin.

My other friends who provided us with photographs of the past. They are: Clive Chen, Colston Chen, Linda Chin Yee, David Chin Yee, Ken Chung, Clive Fung, Busta Hoo, Gil Kong, Ivy Williams, Phil Young, *The Gleaner* archives and Eppy Edwards, Chief Librarian, at the National Library of Jamaica.

To our contributors, my old and new friends, for the wonderful stories and photographs you provided. You are the true heroes; it is your stories that tell the tales of our past and for this, I am truly thankful. Jamaica will always be the land of our birth and a place we call home.

Last, but by no means least, I would like to say a very special thanks to my wife Lin, whose love, patience and encouragement gave me the inspiration and the energy to see it through for our grandsons, Brandon and Jeremy. Her comments in all areas and her contribution in the final selection of words for the cover and the dedication page are much appreciated. I would also like to add a big 'THANK YOU' to Stephanie and Jerry, Roderick and Cecile for just being there for me.

Wan Luv,

Ray

Preface

Where do I begin?

At the time of my parents' passing some thirty years ago, I realized that there would be no more Chinese lessons for our children from their gung gung* and popo* (my parents). Their lessons always began with the Chinese names for the hair, the eyes and then the nose; next was the mouth, the teeth and then the hands and fingers. The legs, feet and toes were last. This was their way of bonding.

I also realized that we were coming to the end of an era. An era where we, as the first or second generation born in the island, would be the last to carry on the Chinese traditions and customs that our parents taught us when we were at the same age as our grandchildren.

With most of our generation living away from Jamaica, what was there to say that we were ever here? Apart from Mr. Lee Tom Yin's book (published in 1957), and Easton Lee's book of poems titled, *Behind the Counter*, or the occasional news item in the local papers of the time, there was really nothing else other than a brief section about the Chinese in Jamaica in the book by Sir Phillip Sherlock and Dr. Hazel Bennett, titled, *The Story of the Jamaican People.* There are other books that speak of the Chinese in the Caribbean as a region, but nothing that speaks of the Chinese in Jamaica.

The question then was…***Where to begin?***

It started with an open letter that I addressed to most of my friends, in which I wrote:

> *"It seems so long ago that I had this strong feeling about documenting the history of the Chinese in Jamaica. There is so much to be told, and it grieves me to see that 'the elders of our tribe' are taking the history of our race and their presence in the island, to their graves without passing it on for future generations to know."*

Time was of the essence, and I alone could not tell this story. The idea was to document the story of the Chinese in Jamaica in the written word, and through the memories of our international community. We were looking for folks from all walks of life to contribute their memories – be it of having grown up in the island, or of their parent's or grandparent's experiences. We wanted stories from the city folks plus those who lived in the rural areas. The folks that I asked to contribute are people just like you and me. I wanted stories that told the tales of love, laughter, disappointment, and if there was sadness too, so be it.

This would allow us to have a better over-view of how we lived, how we played, learned, loved, socialized and grew. Most importantly, it would allow us to show what effect the Jamaican culture had on our growing up years and vice versa.

It has been my dearest wish to produce this book for our future generations for, as I mentioned at the beginning, there is not enough documented evidence to represent our presence here. What pages do we refer to when we wish to tell our grandchildren the story of how we came to be from Jamaica, and where their forefathers came from before ending up in Jamaica? I feel that this generation, our generation, has a responsibility to document our time in the island. We are now the OLDER GENERATION and we must act before it is too late, for soon we will all be forgotten as we take our own little store of memories to the grave.

One hundred and fifty years ago our forefathers landed in Jamaica. The pages of this book tell the tales of generations of Jamaican-born Chinese, of what it was like for them growing up in the island. The stories themselves are sometimes of sadness, of hardship, but also of many happy times.

In closing, I would like to say that I find within the stories many similarities in all the families and even the way we were taught to behave and to have respect for our elders. Any other story could have been a part of my story or part of another contributor's story, for it is from our parents' teaching that we learnt from an early age the discipline and worth of being responsible, especially while we were in the shop.

But the 'silken thread' that is common throughout all the stories is the sacrifice and the love that our parents showered on us. We are truly a very privileged generation and we are equally proud to be the children of *"The Shopkeepers"* - Wan Luv and 'nuff IRIE.

Ray Chen

* See Glossary

Foreword

I have known Ray and his wife Lin from our days in Montreal, Canada more than 20 years ago. I have also had the pleasure of working with him on other projects, but none as ambitious or as personal as this has been. I was therefore both honoured and stunned when Ray asked me to write the foreword to **The Shopkeepers**.

Collaborating with him on this book has been challenging and deeply interesting, exhausting yet exhilarating. The book is well documented and is an excellent source of reference material. I have learned much about the culture, customs and food of our Jamaican-Chinese brothers and sisters and have even learned a smattering of the language!

Anyone who grew up in Jamaica between the end of World War 1 and the beginning of the '70s will recognise the images of the country in more peaceful times; bygone days when simple courtesy and human kindness were the stuff of everyday life, not occasions so rare as to incite comment. That is not to suggest that there were no problems or that the hydra-headed monster of racism, cruelty, oppression and dishonesty did not rear itself. Time, however, has preserved the memories of happy times shared with good friends which generally override the darker side of life. Many stories are certain to be read several times.

Producing *The Shopkeepers* has been a cooperative effort involving many persons who worked hard and long hours, but no one has put in as many hours, or been more dedicated to producing the finest possible work, than Ray has. He epitomizes the qualities which have made the Hakka [the Han Chinese] so successful. It has been my pleasure and privilege to have worked with him on this unique piece of Hakka and Jamaican history.

Sonia Gordon Scott

Jamaican Chinese Surnames

Jamaican Hakka Surname	Character	Mandarin Pin Yin	Meaning	Jamaican Hakka Surname	Character	Mandarin Pin Yin	Meaning
Cha	謝	Xie	express gratitude, thanks	Fung	馮	Feng	to ride a horse to cross the river
Chai	蔡	Cai	banish	Hoo (Hoe)	何	He	what; when; which; who; why
Chang	鄭	Zheng	serious, solemn	Hugh	丘	Qiu	Hill or mound
Chen (Jen)	曾	Zeng	has already been; great grand (father or child)	Kong (Gong)	江	Jiang	large river
Chin	陳	Chen	to arrange; exhibit; narrate; old	Kok (Gok)	郭	Guo	second wall of a city
Chin	程	Cheng	regulation; formula; a journey	Lai	賴	Lai	depend on; trust in; rely on
Chong (Jong)	張	Zhang	magnification; to establish	Lee	李	Li	plum
Chou	鄒	Zou	name of an ancient state in China	Lee	呂	Lu	ancient state in China; a musical tone
Chow	曹	Cao	A company; a class; a generation	Leung	梁	Liang	a beam, bridge or elevation
Chuck (Juck)	卓	Zhuo	distinguished; high; prominent; outstanding	Lim	林	Lin	forest or grove
Chue	周	Zhou	delicate; considerate	Lowe	羅	Luo	a net to catch birds; display
Chue	朱	Zhu	red, scarlet	Lue (Liu)	劉	Liu	Chinese surname
Chung (Jung)	鍾	Zhong	bell	Lue	盧	Lu	Chinese surname; colour black
Fong	房	Fang	room, house	Luk (Look)	陸	Lu	land; continent; the shore
For (Foe)	賀	He	congratulate	Lye Lai	黎	Li	many; multitude or host
Fou	胡	Hu	reckless, blindly	Lyew (Liao)	廖	Liao	chinese surname
Fung	洪	Hong	flood; damage	Lyn	凌	Ling	ice; approach; advance

Jamaican Chinese Surnames

Jamaican Hakka Surname	Character	Mandarin Pin Yin	Meaning	Jamaican Hakka Surname	Character	Mandarin Pin Yin	Meaning
Mar (Mah)	馬	Ma	horse	Tenn	鄧	Deng	Chinese family surname
Moo	巫	Wu	clever doctor, wizard	Tong	唐	Tang	Chinese family surname
Nam	嚴	Yan	stern, strict, serious	Wan	萬	Wan	ten thousand
Ngian (Neon) (Yan)	阮	Ruan	chinese surname	Williams (Wei)	魏	Wei	Chinese family surname
Ngu	吳	Wu	name of an ancient state in China	Wong	黃	Huang	yellow
Pun	潘	Pan	water that had been used to rinse the rice	Wong	王	Wang	king, ruler
Phang (Pang)	彭	Peng	plenty; strong and huge	Woo	鄔	Wu	Chinese surname
Sett	薛	Xue	a kind of wild grass called Lai Hao	Woon	溫	Wen	luke warm & gentle
Seow	蕭	Xiao	the name of a herbal grass	Yap	葉	Ye	leaf, a period, a page
Shim	沈	Shen	investigate; analyze carefully	Yee	余	Yu	remainder, extra surplus
Sue	蘇	Su	revive from unconsciousness	Yen	袁	Yuan	Chinese surname
Sunn	孫	Sun	grandchild; all the offspring	Ying	殷	Yin	great, many abundant
Tie	戴	Dai	wear, bear or put on	Young	楊	Yang	poplar, aspen

Notes on spelling of surnames:

The preceding list was compiled with information from the Chinese Benevolent Association of Jamaica and contains most of the names used in Jamaica up to 1980. The surname "Chong" 張 is also sometimes spelled "Chung". "Williams" has been adopted in place of "Wei".

Pronunciation of Mandarin (Pin Yin)

Pin Yin is the official transliteration of Putonghua, or Mandarin, used in the People's Republic of China. For the most part Pinyin approximates the phonetic values of English with the following notable exceptions:

c	is pronounced	ts as in cats
i	is pronounced	ee, except when it follows c, ch, r, s, sh, z and zh, in which case it is pronounced er
ian	is pronounced	ien
q	is pronounced	ch as in cheese
r	is pronounced	zhr, like in treasure
x	is pronounced	sh as in banshee
z	is pronounced	ds as in cards
zh	is pronounced	dg as in fudge

Source for pronouncement guide: Modern China, J.A.G Roberts
Source for meanings of surnames: Chung Yoon-Ngan,
"The Origin of Chinese Surnames"

INTRODUCTION

The Migration of the Hakka People and Their Arrival in Jamaica

WHO ARE THE HAKKAS? We are Han Chinese who speak a unique dialect that has changed little since we settled in the fertile plains of the Yellow River, in the provinces of Shanxi, Honan and Shandong. These three provinces are recognized as the 'homeland' of the Hakkas. Today, we number about 30 million overseas, worldwide, and there are five major versions of our dialect. Meixien – or Moiyen as our parents called it – is now the major centre for Hakka culture, followed closely by Taiwan.

The label of being 'Gypsies', or migrants, is on account of the five big migrations of the Hakka People to the South. They left their homeland because of invasion from the north, or as a result of famine, which could have been caused by severe drought, flooding, or pillage by the invading armies.

THE FIRST MIGRATION

The first migration occurred during the period of The Sixteen Kingdoms of the Five Barbarians, (317 - 581 A.D). Due to the invasion of non-Han Chinese from the Siberian steppes, the Hakka People crossed the Yangtze River and settled in the provinces of Jiangsu, Anhui and Jiangxi. There were feuds between the emigrants and the native inhabitants, mostly over the squatting of lands. But because the newcomers were now powerful family groups, they established control over their new homeland. They made few attempts to return north since they were content with the fertile land they had found, and they were the ruling group. With the continuing and large influx of Han from the north, the native inhabitants were eventually assimilated.

At the same time, the ruler of another tribe, Prince Si-Ma Rui, took over a thousand families across the Yangtze River and settled in present day Nanjing city in Jiangsu province. Another eight large clans did not stop but continued their journey south, eventually settling in the area that is now the provinces of Fujian and Guangdong. These eight clans were: Lim, Wong, Chin, Chang, Zhan, Hugh, Ho and Fou… the original Cantonese.

THE SECOND MIGRATION

The second migration took place at the end of the Tang Dynasty (618 A.D. to 907 A.D.). Prior to this, there was a period of 250 years of peace brought about by Emperor Xiao Wen (471 A.D. to 499 A.D.) of the Xian Bei people. Contrary to Machiavellian rules of conquest, Xiao Wen not only allowed the Han to retain their own customs and language, but he passed an edict that all Xian Bei should be sinocized i.e. become Han-Chinese, and he decreed the following:

They were to:

1. Adopt Han Chinese surnames.
2. Speak only the Han language and adopt the Han model of administration in government offices.
3. Intermarry with the Han Chinese, and
4. Abandon their own tribal customs and costume.

This integration was so successful in bringing peace and prosperity to the region that other tribes followed suit, sinocizing themselves as Han Chinese too. However, the following century was another period of unrest, involving famine and an uprising against the administration. These conditions led to the second mass migration of the people from Honan and Shandong.

The initial exodus was led by Huang Chao around 875 A.D. He led members of his village to the coastal region of Fuzhou and Guangzhou, and installed himself as Emperor of the short-lived Qi Dynasty, after he captured the Tang capital of Chang An (Xi'an). Although he returned to Shandong province, the migration of people from Shanxi, Honan and Shandong continued. What started out as a group of family farmers grew into a formidable ad hoc army, as they moved southward and settled around the provinces of Jiangxi, Hunan and Guangdong. They never intended to stay, but with the collapse of the Tang Dynasty in 907 A.D., things became worse and they remained. However, they did not integrate with the local inhabitants and so preserved their ancient tongue (Hakka) and customs.

THE THIRD MIGRATION

The third migration started around 1274 A.D. during the Song Dynasty (960 -1279 A.D). The Songs were fighting the Jins at the time, and were losing. A Song General invited the Mongol leader, Genghis Khan, (through the Juyongguan Pass of the Great Wall – near Beijing) to help them. Together they defeated the Jins, but then the Mongols turned against and defeated the Songs, eventually starting the Yuan Dynasty. A strategy used by the Mongols was to send emissaries to the villages to ask for their peaceful surrender. If arms were raised against them, they would wipe out the entire village.

The Hakka People, who were strong supporters of the Song Court, fled from the conquering Mongolian armies. The provinces of middle and south China were already settled by the Cantonese, and the Hakka had to settle farther south. They arrived in the provinces of Guangdong, Fujian, Taiwan and North Vietnam, and settled in the coastal areas that are now Meizhou (Meixian), Chaozhou, Xiushan (in Dongguan district), Huizhou, Yashan, Dabu, Haifeng and many other places. For a period they were forced to live on boats because they had no land of their own, which is the reason they are sometimes referred to as 'the Boat People'.

THE FOURTH MIGRATION

Two events at the end of the Ming Dynasty spurred the fourth migration, which occurred after the Manchurians created the Qing Dynasty (1644-1911 A.D.). One was the involvement of the Manchurians in suppressing some rebels. The other was the sacking of Sichuan and its capital, Chengdu.

The 1628 A.D. famine in Shaanxi began the downfall of the Ming Dynasty. Two separate groups of bandits, under Zhang Xian-zhong and Li Zi-cheng, terrorized the country and, because of the famine, high taxes and corruption, many of the hungry unemployed youths were eager to follow Li Zi-cheng in his pillage of the countryside. In April 1644 A.D. he captured Beijing.

Li, however, made the mistake of kidnapping the favourite concubine, Chen Yuan-yuan, of a Ming general, Wu San-gui, who manned the Shan-hai-

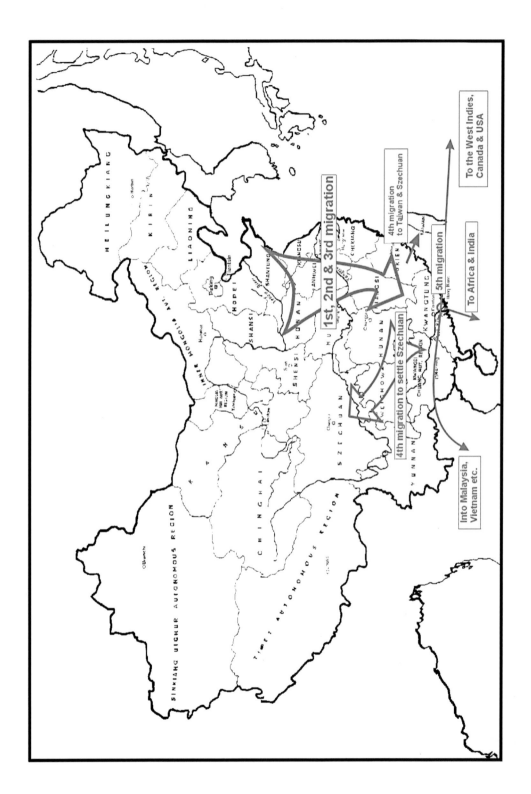

CHINA: *Showing the origin and migration of the Hakka people*

kuan pass of the Great Wall. Wu invited the Manchus through the pass to join forces with him to attack Li, and together they routed the rebels. But before Li withdrew from Beijing, he killed Wu's father and his entire family. The Manchus then took over Beijing and established the Qing dynasty.

The other rebel, Zhang Xian-zhong, settled in the province of Hubei long enough to strengthen his troops on the abundant food and wealth of the region, before he marched on Sichuan. He faced a rebuff from the Sichuanese, so he withdrew to Shanxi province to bolster his army, then returned to capture Sichuan. When he took Chengdu he killed all the citizens and went on to kill millions in the province of Sichuan.

The Manchu could not allow this to go unpunished, so they marched on Sichuan and defeated Zhang. This time it was the Manchu who razed Chengdu, killing Zhang Xian-zhong's people and millions of other Sichuanese. Sichuan was almost depopulated.

In the meantime, Zheng Cheng Gong, a patriot of the Ming Court, resisted the Qing Government fiercely. The Manchus pursued him, but he fled to Taiwan with his troops across the Straits of Taiwan. With him were many Hakkas. Other Hakkas emigrated to Taiwan to escape the miserable lifestyle and oppression on the mainland.

In an attempt to regain the support of the population and to repopulate Sichuan, the Manchu Emperor, Kang Xi, offered eight ounces of silver per man, and four ounces per woman or child who were willing to resettle in Sichuan. Thousands of Hakkas living in the regions between the provinces of Guangdong and Fujian accepted Emperor Kang Xi's offer in order to escape the poverty and hardship of these regions.

This mass migration of Hakkas to Taiwan and Sichuan was their fourth migration.

THE FIFTH MIGRATION

The fifth and last migration took place at the end of the Taiping Rebellion (1851-1864 A.D.). This was by far the most important event to affect the Hakka, and had a bearing on why our fathers and grandfathers emigrated to the Americas, the Caribbean, India, and other parts of the globe. The Rebellion was led by a Christian Hakka called Hung Hsiu-ch'üan. He had a vision that God had chosen him to liberate China from oppression and idolatry, and that he was the younger brother to Christ. He believed that the overthrow of the Manchus was the only way to bring the Kingdom of Heaven on earth.

This great peace rebellion lasted for over twenty years, during which time 20-30 million people were killed as a result of the conflicts. The Manchus appointed a Hakka general, Tsang Kuo-fan, to suppress the rebellion. Tsang claimed that although he had no admiration for the Manchus, he took this job because he saw that if the Rebellion succeeded, it would erode the Confucian values that were dear to him.

With the failure of the Taiping Rebellion, reprisals against the Hakka began. The Manchus ordered that all known families participating in the Rebellion should be killed, especially all Hakkas with the surname of Hung. Because of this, most of the Hungs changed their names and many Hakkas fled the country to other parts of the world e.g. Nanyang (what is now Malaysia), Brazil, Panama, U.S.A, the Caribbean, India and even Africa. Others would sell themselves off as 'pigs' or indentured labour. This was the start of the fifth and most recent migration.

THE ARRIVAL OF THE CHINESE IN JAMAICA

But there were other forces and world events that helped to shape this migration. There was the abolition of slavery in the Caribbean in 1834, Hong Kong became British in 1842, and in 1848 gold was discovered in California. Also, 1850-1856 saw the start of the building of the Panama Railroad.

With the abolition of slavery, there was a need for cheap labour to work the sugar plantations in the Caribbean, and to help build the Panama Railroad. Many labourers were recruited from southern China.

On 21st April, 1854, the *SS Epsom* left Hong Kong with 310 indentured labourers bound for Jamaica. It took over 118 days for the journey around India (initially stopping in Java), around the Cape of Good Hope, up the western coast of Africa to St. Helena (79 days), before crossing the Atlantic to Jamaica (29 days). By the time they reached Kingston, 43 had died, so only 267 disembarked. Later that year, a few hundred Chinese who had originally been contracted to work on the Panama Railroad arrived in Kingston aboard the *SS Gorgona* suffering from opium withdrawal symptoms. They continued to come from Panama that epic year on the *SS Vampire* (195), and *SS Theresa Jane* (10), but not many of them survived.

Those who originally came to Jamaica as indentured labourers, contracted with the Captain of the ship to work on a specified plantation for a period of 5 years, for the sum of £3 per month, after which they would be given free passage home. Some were not so fortunate. They were forcibly taken off the streets, or from prisons, and put on board ship without their consent. Shanghaied!

A series of events between 1864-1870 brought an additional 200 Chinese from Trinidad and British Guiana. Their contracts had expired, and the cane fields in which they had worked were devastated by insects and a hurricane. They took the opportunity of a three-year contract to work on large scale planting of coconuts, bananas, and sugar cane in Jamaica. Others came on their own to start small shops. These shops usually had no more than ten to twenty items of goods, and the total weekly sales averaged three to six pounds.

Events such as the second opium war (1856-1860), with the resulting loss of sovereignty to the Russian, French, British, and Americans, and the war with Japan (1875-1885) continued to drive the Hakkas away from China.

The next large-scale arrival of indentured Chinese labourers was on July 12, 1884 aboard the *SS Prince Alexander*. It boarded 681 labourers and 122 women in Hong Kong, and took 67 days for the journey around India, through the Suez Canal, stopping at Malta to replenish supplies, and then on to Jamaica. By the time it arrived in Kingston, one labourer had died, and three children had been born on board ship. They were dispersed to various plantations throughout the island.

The Boxer Rebellion (1895-1905) was an uprising against the foreigners occupying China. The citizens turned against the missionaries and those who embraced Christianity (remember the leader of the Taiping Rebellion?). This Rebellion maintained the pressure to emigrate, but emigration to the Caribbean was curtailed because of the imposition of a head tax. It eventually ceased in 1949 at the end of the Civil War, with victory by the Communists.

List of Vessels travelling to the British, French and Dutch West Indies from China between 1853 and 1884

Name of Ship	Whence	Destination	Arrived	Total Embarked	Total Landed	Females Landed	Infants Landed
Epsom	Hong Kong	Jamaica	30/07/1854	310	267	0	0
Vampire	Panama	Jamaica	01/11/1854	195	195	0	0
Theresa Jane	Panama	Jamaica	18/11/1854	10	10	0	0
Diamond/ Prince Alexander*	Macao/ Hong Kong Canada-Jamaica	Jamaica	12/07/1884	681 (694)	680 (696)	122 (109+17)	3
Sea Witch/ Gorgona	Canton/ Panama	Panama/ Jamaica	30/03/1854 ?/1854	?	?		

* Hong Kong – Port Said – Malta – Jamaica (Kingston)

Written by ©Roger Chen

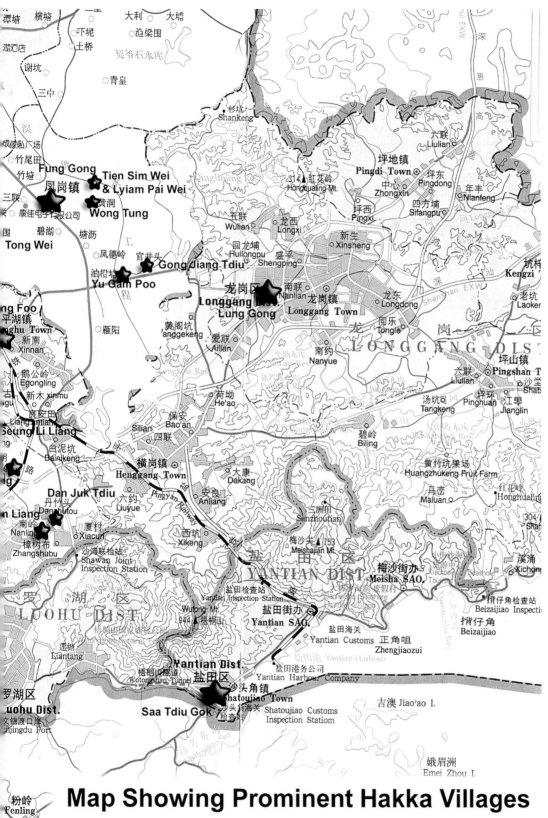

Map Showing Prominent Hakka Villages

THE GERMAN STEAM SHIP *PRINZ ALEXANDER*

As we view the historic documents of the Steamship *Prinz Alexander* we cannot help but wonder if these pages could talk, what tales they would tell.

The *S.S. Prinz Alexander,* carrying her Chinese passengers (or indentured labourers, or 'souls' as they were called), to Jamaica, was only one of the many ships that made this journey. There was also the *S.S. Epsom* which was the first, followed by the *S.S. Vampire* and the *S.S. Theresa Jane.* The *S.S. Prinz Alexander* was the fourth.

I will try to put in order the sequence of events by following the order in which these pages are presented.

NO's	DESCRIPTION
1.	Licence for the conveyance of the Chinese emigrants.
2-5.	Names of the passengers travelling on the *S.S. Prinz Alexander.*
6-7.	Special identifying marks beside the names.
8.	Regulations respecting Chinese passenger ships and the dietary scale required.
9.	Check-list of the accommodation, medical needs, food and water, etc.
10.	The Chinese translation of items 8-9.
11.	Contract passenger ticket. These were usually signed as a promissory note to reimburse the shipping line for the cost of the passage. There were instances where the demand for payment exceeded the date of expiry and the amount of money owed.
12.	A Chinese contract.
13.	A record of the number of passengers on arrival.
14-15.	Letters from the Colonial Secretary to the Government Protector regarding the immigrants.
16-21.	List showing the names of male passengers and the estate to which they are destined: Albion and Duckenfield in St. Thomas; Spring Garden in Portland; Blue Castle, Westmoreland and Llanrumney in St. Mary. Note the reference to these people as 'souls'.
22-23	Names of males, females and infants or children, and their relationship to each other.
24-27.	Payments made to the firemen, ship's officers, doctor and the dispenser of Chinese medicine on board ship.
28-32.	Contract forms for Chinese females, showing names of the estates to which they are contracted and for how long.
33-36.	Requests made to various estates for their completed paperwork and payments for their indentured workers.
37-38.	Receipts for payment for the Chinese.
39.	Letter returning Bond for £1000.00 to Messrs. Geo Solomon & Co.
40.	Letter from P. C. Cork to the Treasurer enclosing promissory notes re the Chinese ex: *S.S. Prinz Alexander.*
41.	Minutes showing the agreement between the Government of Jamaica and Doctor Telles, Surgeon of the *S.S. Prinz Alexander,* for payments for his salary and expenses for his return journey to Hong Kong.
42.	Notice from the Colonial Bank advising the Government Protector and the owner of the estate that the owner's promissory note had been dishonoured by them.
43-44.	Statement showing the cash tenth, principal and interest charged to employers of Chinese immigrants ex: *S.S. Prinz Alexander*, 1884.
45.	Map of Jamaica showing the various estate locations.

1

CHINESE EMIGRATION.

[Ordinances No. 5 of 1874, and No. 5 of 1876.]

Mis. Doc: No. *403*
                84

LICENCE FOR THE CONVEYANCE OF CHINESE EMIGRANTS.

𝔚hereas (¹) *Messrs Turner & Co Agents*
of the (²) *German Steam Ship Prinz Alexander*
have duly applied for a Licence for the conveyance of Chinese Emigrants by
the said Ship, and have furnished all necessary particulars as to the Destination of the
said Ship and as to all other matters: Now, I, Sir GEORGE FERGUSON BOWEN, Knight
Grand Cross of the Most Distinguished Order of Saint Michael and Saint George,
Governor of the Colony of Hongkong, do hereby, by virtue of the authority conferred
upon me by the aforesaid Ordinances, license the said Ship to carry any number of
Chinese Passengers not exceeding *nine hundred and seventyone (971)*
from *Hong Kong* to *Jamaica, Bristish West Indies*

This Licence is not transferable, and shall be available only for one voyage from
Hong Kong to *Jamaica, British West Indies*
and is granted upon the condition that the said Ship clears out and proceeds to sea on
or before the *twentieth* day of *May* unless I, the Governor
aforesaid, do in Council extend such period.

This Licence is granted upon the condition that, I, the Governor aforesaid, may in
my discretion cancel or revoke the same at any time before the said Ship clears out and
proceeds to sea.

Dated this *twenty sixth* day of *April* 188*4*.

G. F. Bowen
_____
Governor.

2

of CHINESE PASSENGERS per German Steam-ship "**PRINZ ALEXANDER**," Captain *R. Eckert* bound from Hongkong to *Jamaica* on *7th May* 1884 consisting of *509* Male adults, *109* Female adults, *59* Boys and *17* Girls under 12 years of age, making a total of *694* Passengers.

No. of Tickets.	Names of Passengers.	Male age.	Female age.	Occupation.	Village.	District.	Port at which the Passengers have contracted to land.
1	Chun Shue Hoo 32	335		Labourer	Hak Har	Kwoon Lan	Jamaica
2	Chun Quai Saug 25			do	do	do	do
3	Chun Ning Hoo 35			do	do	do	do
4	Cheong Fuk 28			do	do	do	do
5	Ho Cheong 25			do	do	Quai Shin	do
6	Chun Mei Fat 19			do	do	do	do
7	Chun Muk Hoo 40			do	do	do	do
8	Chun Kwon Ching 40			do	do	do	do
	...ng 25			do	do	Kwoon Lan	do

3

No. of Tickets.	Names of Passengers.	Male age.	Female age.	Occupation.	Village.	District.	Port at which the Passengers have contracted to land.
76	Wong Yeung 38			Labourer	Hak Har	Quai Shin	Jamaica
77	Wong Quai 12			Go with Father No 76	do	do	do
78	Wong Koon Hoo 22			Labourer	do	do	do
79	Mau Muk Nak 36			do	do	Tung Koon	do
80	Chue Ting Chea 18			do	do	Quai Shin	do
81	Chue Hor Chea 40			do	do	do	do
82	Lau Sze 27			do	do	do	do
83	Shing Moon 40			do	do	Sun On	do
84	Lo Ting Quai 20			do	do	Tung Koon	do
85	Chun Sze 23			do	do	do	do
86	Chan Taen 20			do	do	do	do

4

No. of Tickets.	Names of Passengers.	Male age.	Female age.	Occupation.	Village.	District.	Port at which the Passengers have contracted to land.
126	Chan Fat	23		Labourer	Hak Kar	Sun On	Jamaica
127	Ng Mong	21		do	do	Yan Ping	do
128	Ng Ngan	23		do	do	do	do
129	Ho Tsong Pang	18		do	do	do	do
130	Tsang Sang	24		do	do	Sun On	do
131	Ng Kang	30		do	do	Yan Ping	do
132	Cheong Shing	30		do	do	Kwai Shin	do
133	Yee Kum	25		Cook	do	do	do
134	Ho Kang	35		do	do	Sun On	do
135	Lee Yan	29		Labourer	do	do	do
136	Ho Mok Cha	18		do	do	do	do
137	Cheong Shin	40		do	do	Sun P	

5

No. of Tickets.	Names of Passengers.	Male age.	Female age.	Occupation.	Village.	District.	Port at which the Passengers have contracted to land
876	Jung Lum	25		Labourer no 609	Hak Kar	Wai Chau	Jamaica
877	One Koon Chai		28	go with husband no 609	do	Lai Sin	do
878	Li Kew		4	go with father no 603	do	do	do
879	Sit Tai		38	go with husband	do	do	do
880	Yip Kew		28	go with do no 625	do	do	do
881	Chow Sam Moy		26	do no 608	do	do	do
	u Sze Moy		40	do no 608	do	do	do
	Cow Kew		6	go with father no 608	do	do	do
	Li Ham		16	go with do no 608	do	do	do
	Lim boy Kew		12	do no 602	do	do	do
	Kwo Sam Mo		35	go with husband no 602		do	do
	Oe Lau			go with father		do	

continued.

6

Estate	No.	Name of Immi-grant as p contract	Name as Stated by Immigrant	Bodily marks	Sex	Age	Relationship to other Immigrants
	57	Yeung Su Stew	Chun Su Stew	Scar on rt should	♂	25	Wife of 66
	58	Chang Shau	Chun Su	Scar on rt scholt	m	28	Hus. of 57
	59	Chun Otay	Chun Oth	none	Inft	med 7	dau. of 58
	60	Chun Fig Soi			B	8	"
	61	Fong Sri Shee			♂	47	Fath. of 58
	62	Jing Fong Chia			♀	23	Wife of 58
	63	Yip Sam		Scar on lt side head	m	22	Bro. of 215
	64	Sum Strong		Face pitted with small pox		35	
	65	Chun Yuai		Scar on skull	B	11	Son of 66
	66	Chun Fong Oth		mole on chin	m	46	Fath. of 65
	67	Chun Sam		Scar on neck		25	
	68	Chun Yu		3 moles on neck		29	
	69	Chun Sor		Scar on lt temple		42	Fa. of 70
	70	Chang Fong	Chun Fong			18	Son of 69
Family	71	Chang Oth		Scar on neck		27	Bro. of 72
	72	Chun Su Moy			♂	55	Sis. of 71
	73	Chun Fos		Cuts on head	m	16	Son of 74
	74	One Sam Moy			♂	34	Mo. of 75
	75	Chun Stewie		forehead marked with Smallpox	m	19	Son of 76
	76	Sau Sam Moy			♂	41	Mo. of 75
	77	Chun Yew Cheung		Scar on lt temple & cut on back	m	50	
	78	Sai Sam Moy			♂	25	a family
	79	Chun Muk Chai			B	12	
	80	Chun Muk Yuai				4	
	81	Sp. Yuai		Scar over lt eye	m	30	
	82	Yow Fro Sri		mole on lt arm & neck	..	28	
	83	Chow Forrig		Wart on lt leg	.	22	
	84	Cisong Yu		Scar on lt leg	.	25	

Continued:

Estate	Name of Immigrant as per contract	Name as stated by Immigrant	Bodily marks	Sex	Age	Relationship to other Immigrant
85	Yau Chos		Scar on lt eye	m	28	.
86	Ng Yeung Chong		„ lt arm	.	22	
87	Yu Wah Foo	Kam Sang		. .	55	
88	Yew Ng Jai			B	6	a family
89	Yew Fat Moy			g	7	
90	Wong Sam Moy			♂	35	
91	Yu Chong		Scars on head	m	32	. . . . .
92	Chong Chong			.	26	
93	Chew Ong Chia	- . .	Scars on lt temple	.	18	nephew of 95
94	Chu Choy			..	16	
95	Chew Foo Chia			..	48	a family
96	Chu Thing			B	11	
97	Fi a Ying			♂	18	
98	Fi Ling Chai			.	44	
99	Fau Wah			m	25	
100	Thoon Chon Moy		Scars on lt cheek		20	
101	Chang Fat		„ under lt eye		31	
102	Wong Sam		Scar on lt temple	m		.
103	Wong Shoon Fin		„ over lt eye			
104	Wong Yeung		Lumps in throat	.		
105	Yi Yau	Yu a You		♂		
106	Wong Yung			g		a family
107	Wong Chau			B		
108	Yi Fong Show		Scar on cheek	m		Son of Ng
109	Fau Chat Moy			♂		m of 108
110	Yu Fum			m		
111	Kwong a Few			♂		a family
112	Yu Yung Fat			B		

8   (H. 28.)

150
20
260²

SCHEDULE (*A.*) OF THE CHINESE-PASSENGERS ACT, 1855, BEING C. 104 OF 18 AND 19 VICT.

Regulations respecting Chinese Passenger Ships.

Note.—The wilful and fraudulent Breach of any of these Regulations by the Person in charge of any Chinese Passenger Ship is punishable either by Forfeiture of the Ship, or by Fine and Imprisonment; and every Person concerned in such Breach is liable to a Fine of One Hundred Pounds for each Offence.

I.—No Chinese Passenger Ship shall clear out or proceed to Sea on any Voyage of more than Seven Days Duration without a Certificate from an Emigration Officer; and such Certificate shall be in the Form provided by the Chinese Passengers Act, 1855.

II—No Emigration Officer shall be bound to give such Certificate in respect of any Chinese Passenger Ship till Seven Days after receiving Notice that the Ship is to carry Passengers, and of her Destination, and of her proposed Day of Sailing; nor unless there are on board a Surgeon and Interpreter approved by such Emigration Officer.

III—After receiving such Notice, the Emigration Officer shall be at liberty at all Times to enter and inspect the Ship and the Fittings, Provisions, and Stores therein; and any Person impeding him in such Entry or Inspection, or refusing to allow of the same, shall be liable to a Fine of not more than One Hundred Pounds for each Offence.

IV.—The Emigration Officer shall not give his Certificate unless he shall be satisfied,—

1.—That the Ship is sea-worthy, and properly manned, equipped, fitted, and ventilated; and has not on board any Cargo likely, from its Quality, Quantity, or Mode of Stowage to prejudice the Health or Safety of the Passengers:

2.—That the Space appropriated to the Passengers, in the Between Decks contains at the least Twelve Superficial and Seventy-two Cubic Feet of Space for every Adult on board; that is to say, for every Passenger above Twelve Years of Age, and for every Two Passengers between the Ages of One Year and Twelve Years:

3.—That a Space of Five Superficial Feet per Adult is left clear on the Upper Deck for the use of the Passengers:

4.—That Provisions, Fuel, and Water have been placed on board, of good Quality, properly packed, and sufficient to supply the Passengers on board during the declared Duration of the intended Voyage, according to the following Scale:

DIETARY SCALE.

(Proclamation of 1st November, 1872.)

Rice,	lb. 1½ per diem.
Salt Beef,	
Salt Pork,	
Salt Fish,	„ ½ on alternate days.
Fresh Beef or Mutton, in tins,	
Salted Vegetables,	
Pickles,	„ ½ „
Fresh Vegetables, as Yams, Pumpkins, &c.,	
Water,	Imperial qts. 3 a day.
Firewood,	lbs. 2 „
Tea,	oz. 0½ „
Lime or Lemon Juice, and Sugar,	„ 2 a week.

NOTE.—Fresh Vegetables to be issued during the first month of the voyage only, unless the Master shall obtain a fresh supply *en route*, when these articles may be again supplied in the above proportion.

5.—That Medicines and Medical Comforts have been placed on board according to the following Scale:

1st. Remarks on the ship and its accommodations.   *Good*

9

2nd. Officers of the ship, interpreters, Sirdars and Topazes ?   *Good*

Their conduct and general behaviour towards the Emigrants ?   *Good*

3rd. Provisions and water, whether ample and good ?   *Good*

4th. Medical comforts, whether ample and good ; if not, particularize the deficiencies ?   *Good*

5th. Medicines, whether ample and good; if not, particularize the deficiencies ?   *Good*

6th. Class of Coolies ?

    (a) Where they from the Hills, or natives of the low districts ?

    (b) What number of " Junglies " or ", Santals" among them ?

    (c) Amongst what class did sickness or mortality chiefly occur ?

7th. State of health &c. of the people—

    (d) What was the condition and state of health of the people and embarkation ? How long were they in Depôt before embarkation ?   *Good* / *Don't No (sic)*

    (e) At what period of the voyage did sickness prevail, and what was the principal disease ? Did it prevail more in one part of the vessel than another ? And what in your opinion was the cause of it ?   *No particular time. Itch. Rinworm (sic) No*

    (f) State the condition and general state of health of emigrants on arrival.   *Good.*

8th. Clothing—
    (g) Were the Coolies supplied with sufficient warm clothing of a proper kind ?   *Yes*

    (h) Was there a water distilling apparatus on board and by whom made ? How much water did it produce daily, and at what consumption of fuel ?   *Good.*

洋船在香港搭載唐人規條開列

凡有搭載唐人洋船船主如有故犯開各欵條例按法可將船隻充公或將其人監罰別人同謀遞犯規條者每次罰銀一百磅

一凡有洋船搭載唐人往別處地方過於七日水程者須稟請　督理適他國搭客船隻官給發牌照方得開行其牌照要遵一千

八百五十五年所設爲洋船搭載唐人則例內所載船牌照欵式

一凡有洋船搭載唐人要預先七日稟官報明所往之地方並開行日期船中要醫生一名傳話一名候該官員驗察視其各能勝

任者然後給照

一凡該船既經稟報須任由該　督理官時到船上稽查船身梘梩繩索家伙什物火食等件倘有阻攔及不遵查閱者按例每

次罰銀一百磅

一督理適他國搭客船隻官凡查閱船隻是否遵行後開各欵方可給照

一須驗明其船堅固船戶水手人數足用梘梩繩索堅委船艙通氣船中所貯之行總勿以潮溼薰蒸或逾額滿塞或堆放雞鵝種

種不交皆於人客有礙

一船中二層櫃面搭客十二歲以上者每人至少有位高六尺長六尺闊二尺共方停七十二尺爲式一歲至十二歲之幼孩兩名

以一名計

一船面每客要留地五尺以待用

一火食柴水一俱要佳品安置妥當按行船日數照依後列欵式辦足待用

火食開列　　　　每日每人

米一磅半即十八兩　　鹹牛肉豬肉魚或鮮牛肉羊肉六兩　　鹹菜或酸菓瓜菜等六兩

水五斤四兩　　　　柴一斤半　　茶三錢三　　檸檬糖每禮拜一兩五錢

其瓜菜自行船之頭一月可能供給與各客若船主歷路可獲此瓜菜等物則照數均派與各客

一要備辦各處地道藥材船上待用

一凡有英國商船載唐人駛往別處地方過於七日水程者該船主須照依以上火食牌發給火食柴水至於以上所列床位餘地

或艙內通氣之法除因別有大益於搭客倘有改置否則不許妄意更改又毋得將搭客待薄除當緊急之時平常不得使伊等

幫做船上工夫倘搭客遇有疾病仍須發藥盡心調理須要遵依開行船照所註明應到埠頭到時經過寄錨取水及辦買各件

緊需之物必須將各客直載到之埠毋得虛將時日擔擱

一該督理官員臨期要令各家亟集查問各人是否知往何處若有與人立合約而夫者開明他是否知該合約所載之章程逐一

查明然後給照倘有合同所立該官亦宜將合同抄白或將大畧要節錄出粘附照尾倘客身有病或衣服未得足用或所立之

合約不公或疑併等是受人拐騙下船等弊該官可將其船留年，合意可着搭客不拘多少再行登岸

11

SCHEDULE *D*.

CONTRACT PASSAGE TICKET.

Under Section VI, Paragraph 5.

I Hereby Engage, that the Chinese named at foot hereof shall be provided with a Free Passage to, and shall be landed at the British Colony of, **JAMAICA,** in the West Indies, in the German Steamer called the **"PRINZ ALEXANDER,"** with not less than 72 Cubic Feet and 12 Superficial Feet for Berth Accommodation, and shall be victualled according to Schedule *A* to "The Chinese Passengers' Act, 1855," annexed, during the Voyage and term of detention at any place before its determination.

NAME AND SURNAME OF PASSENGER.	MALE. Age.	FEMALE. Age.	OCCUPATION.	NATIVE PLACE, VILLAGE & DISTRICT.
Jno. Luk	32		Head man	Shnny Chuen Hak Kar

John A. Mosely — Passage Broker.

Victoria, Hongkong, the 6th Day of May, 1884.

I Hereby Certify, that I have explained and registered the above Contract Passage Ticket.

Victoria, Hongkong, the 6th Day of May, 1884.

Emigration Officer.

寫船經紀麥加羅發單

英一千八百八十四年

五月　　　日

光緒十年四月　　日

為式立此單為據

長行或停留別處地方

華人搭客律例內所載

十二尺安置其食用照

英一千八百五十五年

停七十二英尺橫直以

收水腳銀在船上以方

西印度占架上岸不

山打前往英屬地方之

國火船名庇連士亞力

縣　　　　省

事業係　　村人准搭普

之搭客姓即名六

人係十歲做頭

船位紙　茲以下所列

12

I, *Suu yee* ——————————————— a native of Kwangtung and whose name or mark is appended hereto, undertake and agree, in consideration of receiving a free passage food and clothing, to embark on board the German Steam-Ship "Prinz Alexander" of Hamburg and to proceed in her without delay to the Island of *Jamaica* in the British West Indies; and I further agree that on arrival at Jamaica I will on demand enter into such contract or indenture of service as a labourer, as the Government Protector of the Chinese in the Island shall direct or approve of, for a term not exceeding five years from the date of my arrival there.

Dated at Hongkong, this 4 May, 1884.

Witnessed and approved,

立懇字人 井二 係廣東省人卽在下簽押名號者今因領到船位伙食

衣服搭大德國堤布城火船船名逵師亞立山大者卽日開行前往大英西印

度島名渣美嘉為此立字應承一到渣嘉日任由吩咐我卽甘願另立僱工

約夯遵照該島

國家安撫華民官定意比准另立該僱工接紅孫俾卽至謝屋之日起計囫

以五年為期滿不得踰限

香港一千八百八十四年 四月五日 立

香港管理華民出洋官署

允准見證

SURGEON'S REPORT OF ARRIVAL.

Place *Kingston. Jamaica*   **13**

Date *12° July — 1884*

To be sent to England by the first opportunity,
A Duplicate to be Lodged with the Immigration Agent.

Sir,

    Subjoined is a Classified Summary of the Principal Events which occurred on board
the Ship *Prinz Alexander* Captain *R Eckert*   bound from *Hong Kong*
To Jamaica, and of the Observations which I have to bring under the notice of the Commissioners

Place of Departure.	Date of Sailing.	Date of Arrival.	Tonnage.	No. of Statute Adults the Ship can Carry.	No. of Statute Adults Embarked.	Port at which the Vessel Touched.
Hong Kong	*7 May*	*12 July*	*2000*	*971*	*656*	*Port Said & Malta*

EMMIGRANTS.	Men.	Women.	Children between 1 and 10 years of age.		Infants.		Total Souls.
			M.	F.	M.	F.	
Embarked............................	*509*	*109*	*59*	*17*			*694*
Born on the Voyage..............					*1*	*2*	*3*
Died on the Voyage,.................	*1*						*1*
Landed.	*508*	*109*	*59*	*17*	*1*	*2*	*696*
Sent to Hospital after Arrival.......	*1*						*1*
Causes of Death.........................	*Diarrhea (Sic)*						

S. WALCOTT, Esq.

    8, Park Street, Westminster, London, S. W.

14

000
,84.

Colonial Secretary's Office,

Jamaica, 25 July 1884

CASE OF REPLY PLEASE QUOTE
THE DATE OF THIS LETTER & THE
FOLLOWING N° 5196.

Sir,

In reply to your memorandum of the 24th instant respecting the allotment of the Chinese immigrants, I am desired by the Governor to say that it must be left to you to make whatever allotment you consider most equitable within your power.

I have the honor to be,
Sir,
your obedient Servant

J. Allwood
Apt. Colonial Secretary.

The Protector

15

600/84.

Colonial Secretary's Office,
Jamaica: 26th July 1884

IN CASE OF REPLY PLEASE QUOTE THE DATE OF THIS LETTER & THE FOLLOWING No. 5079 / 3754

Sir,

I am desired by the Governor to request that you will furnish your report of the arrival of the "Prinz Alexander" with Chinese Immigrants, for transmission to the Secretary of State for the Colonies, with as little delay as possible.

2. As the allotment of the Chinese was expected to be completed this week the report

The Protector

16

IMMIGRATION PROTECTION AND REGULATION LAW, 1879,

AND THE LAWS SUBSEQUENTLY AMENDING THE SAME.

Schedule B.

NOMINAL ROLL of *Chinese, Male* Immigrants ex Ship *"Priny Alexander" R Eckert* Master from *Hong Kong* landed at *Kingston* and Indentured to *James Simpson Carson* as Agricultural Labourers on *Albion* Estate in the Parish of *Saint Thomas.*

Distinguishing Marks.	Ship's Name and Date of Arrival.	Names.	Age.	Sex.	
1		Lee Sing. *alias Lea Sang.*		Male	
2		Li Yik. *alias Lee Yet.*		do	
3		Li Koon Tong. *alias Li Foong.*		do	
4		Lee Hong. *alias On Sarong.*		do	non adult.
5		Lee Tam. *alias Ah Tem.*		do	non adult.
6		Li Loong.		do	
7		Leong Hu Yuin. *alias Chong Tat.*		do	
8	Steam Ship "Priny Alexander" 12th July 1884.	Li Loy.		do	
9		Sew Sag ynng. *alias Fok Sien*		do	
10		Li Fatt.		do	
11		Li Wah.		do	
12		Leong Song Wy. *alias Foo Che.*		do	
13		Yp Yu. *alias Le Ge O.*		do	
14		Tsong *alias Wong Keow.*		do	
15		Ng Yu Yung. *alias San Pat.*		do	

Carried forward 15 Souls

300—12.7.84.

IMMIGRATION PROTECTION AND REGULATION LAW, 1879,   **17**

AND THE LAWS SUBSEQUENTLY AMENDING THE SAME.

Schedule B.

NOMINAL ROLL of *Chinese Male* Immigrants ex Ship *"Prinz Alexander" R Eckert* Master from *Hong Kong* landed at *Kingston* and Indentured to *Edward Frederick Dawkins* as Agricultural Labourers on *Duckenfield* Estate in the Parish of *Saint Thomas.*

Distinguishing Marks.	Ship's Name and Date of Arrival.	Names.	Age.	Sex.	
		Brought forward	38	Souls	
39		Ng Leung Yee.		Male	
40		Leong Man Chee.		do	
41		Wan Hoy Leung.		do	
42		Chu Foo.		do	
43		Chow Lang.		do	
44		Wang Lang.		do	
45		Chow Foo.		do	
46		Chow Fat.		do	
47	Steam Ship "Prinz Alexander" 12th July 1884.	Chow Lang (alias Cha Luk Moy)		do	non adult.
48		Ching Chaw.		do	
49		Ching Moon.		do	
50		Ling Koon Wing.		do	non adult
51		Ling Koon Yaw.		do	non adult
52		Chin Tok Loy.		do	non adult.
53		Yaw Tong On.		do	
54		Yew Lin Young.		do	non adult.
55		Choy Yeung.		do	
56		Chang Fat.		do	
57		Joung Poo.		do	
		Carried forward	57	Souls.	

18

IMMIGRATION PROTECTION AND REGULATION LAW, 1879,

AND THE LAWS SUBSEQUENTLY AMENDING THE SAME.

Schedule B.

NOMINAL ROLL of *Chinese Male* Immigrants ex Ship *"Prinz Alexander"* *R Ckert* Master from *Hong Kong* landed at *Kingston* and Indentured to *William Bancroft Espeut* Agricultural Labourers on *Spring Garden* Estate in the Parish of *Portland*

Distinguishing Marks.	Ship's Name and Date of Arrival.	Names.	Age.	Sex.
1		Wo Lang.		Male
2		Wo Fat.		do non adult
3		Li Kang Show.		do
4		Wong Koon Koo.		do
5		Wong Yeung.		do
6		Wong Quai.		do non adult
7		Lii Kum.		do
8		One Yung Fat.		do non adult
9		Chan Kun.		do
10		Lee Kow.		do
11	Steam Ship "Prinz Alexander"	Loo Ning.		do
12	12th July 1884.	Wong Lam.		do
13		Leong Yew Shue.		do
14		Chow King.		do
15		Yew Lan.		do
16		One Yun.		do
17		Young Ling Cho.		do
18		Yaw Lin.		do
19		Ng Chun.		do
20		Chun Kum Fuk.		do
		Carried forward 20 Souls		

IMMIGRATION PROTECTION AND REGULATION LAW, 1879, ·   **19**

AND THE LAWS SUBSEQUENTLY AMENDING THE SAME.

Schedule B.

NOMINAL ROLL of *Chinese Male* Immigrants ex Ship *Prinz Alexander, Eckert* Master from *Hong Kong* landed at *Kingston* and Indentured to *Eustace Grey* as Agricultural Labourers on *Blue Castle* Estate in the Parish of *Westmoreland*

Distinguishing Marks.	Ship's Name and Date of Arrival.	Names.	Age.	Sex.	
	"Prinz Alexander" 12 July 1884	Laong Chin		m	
		Tamshin		m	
		Lumjin		m	
		Aungee		m	
		Lumjon		m	

20   IMMIGRATION PROTECTION AND REGULATION LAW, 1879,

AND THE LAWS SUBSEQUENTLY AMENDING THE SAME.

Schedule B.

NOMINAL ROLL of *Chinese* Immigrants ex Ship *Prinz Alexander Eckear*
Master from *Hong Kong* landed at *Kingston* and Indentured
to *Thomas Hamilton* as Agricultural Labourers on *Llanrumny* Estate
in the Parish of *Saint Mary*

Distinguishing Marks.	Ship's Name and Date of Arrival.	Names.	Age.	Sex.
1		Lan Hing		m
2		Cheong Look		m
3	Steamship "Prinz Alexander" Arrived 12 July 1884	Yew Wa Ching		m
4		Chin Quen Kew		m
5		Yew Show		m
6		Chun Ynik		m
7		Liu Fat		m
8		Lai Wah		m
9		Wong Fat		m
10		Lao Qui		m
11		Chung Lee		m
12		Choy Tung		m

NOMINAL ROLL—(Continued.)   **21**

Distinguish-ing Marks.	Ship's Name and Date of Arrival.	Names.	Age.	Sex.	
		Brought forward	57		Souls
58		One Sow		Male	
59		Hong A Loy.		do	non adult.
60		One A Choy.		do	non adult.
61		Lau Lin.		do	
62		New Fat.		do	
63		Chun Yue Koo		do	
64	Steam Ship Prinz Alexander.	Li Yam.		do	
65	18th July 1884	Yew Sing Young.		do	non adult.
66		Lo Chung Man.		do	"
67		Tsang Loy		do	non adult.
68		Lou Tong Mow.		do	non adult.
69		Tsang Poo.		do	non adult.
70		Ngan Ching Quat.		do	"
71		Lu Sun Quat.		do	"
72		Man Lin Fat.		do	"
73.		Man Loi Fat.		do	non adult
		Total	73		Souls

JAMAICA SS.

This Indenture witnesses, that from this 15th day of July 188 4 , the Immigrants Scheduled above have been duly indentured by the Protector. to Edward Frederick Dawkins for owner, on Duckenfield Estate, for five years, subject in all respects to the Immigration Laws, 1879. and the Laws subsequently amending the same.
As witness our Hands and Seals.

Philip C Cork
Protector of Immigrants.

David T Davis
attorney for E&F Dawkins

22

12 - 3 w.

DISTRIBUTION ROLL of Immigrants ex _____ from

_____ Landed at _____ on the _____ 18___

and Located on *Trinity* .

Number.	Ship's No.	NAME OF IMMIGRANT.	Age.	Adult.		Non Adult.		Infants.		Date of Certificate.	Whether accepted Bounty or Return Passage.	REMARKS.
				M.	F.	M.	F.	M.	F.			
1		Chun Yuen Chung		1	.					F. of 2		
2		Lai Sam Mony		.	1					Wife of 1		
3		Chau Muk Chia				1	.			Son of 1.		
4		Chin Muk Quai				1	.	.		"		
5		Chun Quai		1						Son of 6		
6		Lau Sam Moy		.	1					W. of 5	old & infirm not to be charged for
7		One Sam Moy			1					W. of 8		
8		Chun Foo		1	.					Son of 7		
9		Chin Tung		1	.					Son of 10.		
10		Chin X Coo		1	.					F. of 9		
11		Chun Koon Fuk		1	.					This man did not arrive	
12		Lum Kang		1	.							
13		Chun Tong Fuk		1	.					F. of 14	Cook in Kingston
14		Chun Quai		.	.	1	.			Son of 13.		
15		Chung Yee		1						Br. of 13.		
16		Chung Sam		1						Br. of 13.		
‡17		Chun Fuk		1						Br. of 18		
18		Chin Lee Moy		.	1					Sister of 17.		
19		Yip Sam		1							Cook

10

DISTRIBUTION ROLL of Immigrants ex _____ from   **23**

_____ Landed at _____ on the _____ 18___

and Located on *Lysious 21/7/84*

Number.	Ship's No.	NAME OF IMMIGRANT.	Age.	Adult.		Non Adult.		Infants.		Date of Certificate.	Whether accepted Bounty or Return Passage.	REMARKS.
				M.	F.	M.	F.	M.	F.			
28		*Over*	27									
28		Lee Kew			1					Reg.		wife of No 26
29		Hong Loy	4			1						Son of No 26
30		Luk Iam		1								Husband of 31
31		Lau Quai You			1							
32		Hong Moon	5	1								Husband of 33
33		Wong Quai Kew			1							
34		Yee Moon	45	1								Headman
35		Lau Poo	30	1								Husband of No 36
36		Jung Ng Moy			1							wife of No 35
37		Lau Chin	35	1								Bro of No 35
38		Lau Quai Kew	4				1					Child of No 35
				32	4	1	1			38		
39		Chang Luk Moy	46		1					1/39		mother of Chem Quai chin
										1		
40	16/85	Hi Sek		1		1	1			4		
				33	5	1	1			40		

2 of H trail
21/7/84.

9.84

24

Hong Kong
7th May 1884

Sir,

"Prins Alexander" Str

We beg to inform you that there are three Chinese Firemen shipped at $15.00 each per month & that they have already received an advance of $30.00 or two months' wages —

They are further to each receive $45.00 each in Jamaica over & above their pay due.

We have the honor to be
Sir
Your Most Obed.t Humble Servants.

Turner &

To His Excellency
The Governor of Jamaica

25

Hongkong 7th May 1884

Sir

We beg to inform you that
we have agreed that
the Chief Officer shall
receive a gratuity of
Twelve Pounds (£ 12) &
the Third Officer a gratuity
of Eight Pounds (£ 8) for
attending to the Emigrants
p St. "Prinz Alexander",
and we request you will
pay the same on the arrival
of said Steamer.

We are, Sir
Your obdt Servts
Turner & Co
p McCulloch
Charterers

26

Duplicate

Hongkong
6/5/84

The Undersigned Chang Leok Oan agrees to go as Chinese Doctor on board the German steamer "Prinz Alexander" bound to Jamaica at a salary of Forty Dollars for the voyage- one half of this or Twenty Dollars to be paid to him before leaving.

張
國
安

27

Duplicate

Hongkong
6/5/84

The Undersigned Chung Ping Cheong agrees to go as dispenser of Chinese Medi=cines on board the German steamer "Prinz Alexander" bound to Jamaica at a salary of Twenty Dollars for the voyage one half of this- or Ten Dollars to be paid to him before leaving.

陸
平
章

714

rec'd 20·9·84

28

IMMIGRATION.

200—10.0.84.

FROM	SUBJECT.
Protector of Immigrants	Contract forms for Chinese females.
DATE. 9th August 1884	
LAST PREVIOUS PAPER NO.	MINUTES.

716/84

Mr MacKenzie.

I enclose a supply of forms for Contracts of Chinese Females. On your next visit to the Estates on which Chinese are located, please see that the women execute their Contracts in duplicate in accordance with the Law 23 of 1879 Section 33. One copy to be handed to the Manager of the Estate and the other to be forwarded to this office.

Philip C. Cork
Protector of Immigrants
9. 8. 84

Mr Cork
I beg to forward the Contract papers executed by the Chinese female immigrants in this District

W.H.H....
10: 8: 84

29

Contract with Chinese Female.

I, _Chup Heng_ _____ being a Chinese Female
Immigrant within the meaning of The Immigration Law, 1879, having been allotted
to _Louis Francis Verley_ _____ of _Bushy Park_
Estate, in the Parish of _Saint Catherine_ as my Employer, do hereby agree with
the said _Louis Francis Verley_ _____ to reside upon
the said Estate for the full period of _five_ _____ years from the
date hereof.

Witness: _Cheng Heng_   her
                                             ✗ mark
           Ahmee   200—17.6.84.

30

Contract with Chinese Female.

I, _Ateen Sam Moy_ _____ being a Chinese Female
Immigrant within the meaning of The Immigration Law, 1879, having been allotted
to _Sir John Pringle_ _____ of _Trinity_
Estate, in the Parish of _St Mary_ as my Employer, do hereby agree with
the said _John Pringle_ _____ to reside upon
the said Estate for the full period of _five_ _____ years from the
date hereof.

Witness: _Ateen Sam Moy_   her
                                               ✗ mark
     R. Bayly   200—17.6.84.

Original.

31

No. 1ᵃ

Contract with Chinese Female.

I, _Chung Sam Moy_ being a Chinese Female Immigrant within the meaning of The Immigration Law, 1879, having been allotted to _D. J. Davis Esqr_ of _Duckenfield_ Estate, in the Parish of _St Thomas_ as my Employer, do hereby agree with the said _D. J. Davis_ to reside upon the said Estate for the full period of _Five_ years from the date hereof. **15ᵗʰ August 1884**

Chung Sam Moy ✕ her mark

Wm C. H. Hastings Inspector of Immigra... 200—17.6.84.

Witness: Robert C. Norris Sub Insp⁰ Constabty

32

Contract with Chinese Female.

I, _Lee Loy Kue_ being a Chinese Female Immigrant within the meaning of The Immigration Law, 1879, having been allotted to _John Sawers_ of _Constant Spring_ Estate, in the Parish of _Saint Andrew_ as my Employer, do hereby agree with the said _John Sawers_ to reside upon the said Estate for the full period of _five years_ years from the date hereof. **12ᵗʰ day July 1884.**

Lee Loy Kue her ✕ mark

200—17.6.84.

Witness: AHnee

33

600 / 84   I. O. №. 372
                  25 Sep 84.

L. Verley Esqre: ✓

J.g. D. Broughton ✓
Dr. Pringle   + not written
E. G. Levy   +   ✓
R. J. Sadler   ✓
I. H. Demercado   + not written
I. C. Melville (with respect to   me
        Llanrumy Notes –
        Cash Tenths paid 787/84)

Sir,

    I have the honour to
request that you will with
out further delay sign
the P. Notes for the Chinese
allotted to .   Estate
and transmit the same to
with the Cash-Tenths
(£   ) as I cannot, any
longer, permit the matter to
lie over.

        I have &c

Wm ... 82

Calcd. MD 27.9.84

.7: Cash Tenths rec? (See 929/82.)

34

600 10   I.O. №. 277
                8th August 1884

H. J. Ronaldson Esq,
    May Pen P.G.

Written to Ento
MD 9.8.84

                Sir,
                    I have the honour to annex five Promissory
£. 8. 0   Notes for past expenses in connection
1st Note 64. 7. 10   with the introduction of Chinese allotted
2nd do 136. 1. 6   to Constant Spring Estate, which notes
3rd do 143. 7. 4   I shall feel obliged if you will sign
4th do 150. 13. 2   and return to me by first post.
5th do 157. 19. 0   I have also to request that you will be
                so good as to remit to me the amount
                of Sixty Pounds fifteen shillings being
                one tenth of the expenses, which is payable
Cash tenth £ 60. 15. 0   in Cash under Law 18 of 1879 sec 9.

                        I have &c
                        Signed P.C. Cork

600

L. Verley

Written by Mr Ripoll

Entd MD 25.8.84

21 augt
No 297

Sir,

I have the honour to request that you will be so good as to let me have the Indentures duly executed for the Chinese allotted to B. Park Estate which was sent to you for execution under cover of my letter No 286/600 dated the 16 instant.

600/84.

Geo: Solomon Isaepe

Wm ——
24.9.84

Ret'd MD 24.9.84

I.O. No 365
24 Sept 84.

Sir,
I have the honour again call on you to sign the Indentures and Promissory Notes for the Chinese allotted to Burlington Estate and to forward these documents with the Cash-tenths (£27.15.0) without any further delay as I cannot permit the matter to lie over any longer.
I have &c
K.

37   1 R/16q/9.4.84.

Immigration Office,

Jamaica, 6 October 1884.

IN CASE OF REPLY PLEASE QUOTE
THE DATE OF THIS LETTER AND
THE FOLLOWING No. 395
600

Sir,

I have the honour to acknowledge the receipt of the Promissory Notes and Cash Instalments in respect of Chinese indentured on the following Estates:

Iter Boreale Estate:
Cash Instalment   £ 24 : 0 : 0
Five Promissory Notes.

Low Layton & Lennox
Cash Instalment   £ 42 : 0 : 0
Ten Promissory Notes.

I have the honour to be,
Sir,
Your obedient Servant
Philip C. Cork
Protr. of Immigts

J. G. D. Broughton Esq
Buff Bay P.O.

38

attached to 60⁰/84

Hordley Estate
28 Jan 1885

Sir

I have to apologize for
not sending the above sooner
I.O.U. earlier & have the honor
to remain Sir

Your obt Servt
Harrison

Phillip Cork Esq.
Protector of Immigrants
Kingston

20 No 34.

Jas: Harrison.
Hordley
P.G. River Pl.

Sir,
I have the hon: to acknowledge
with thanks the receipt of the 2nd Note
for Chinese on Hordley Estate.
I return you the original document
to be destroyed.
I have &c

Signed P.C. Cork

39

J.O. No 263
29th July 1884

$40/84

Messrs Geo Solomon & Co
Kingston.
Gentlemen.
Telegraphic intelligence
having been received from Hong
Kong to the effect that the
amount of £ 1000 stipulated
by the 21st Clause of the Charter
Party of the S.S. "Priny Alexander"
to be paid to the Captain at
Hong Kong had not been paid,
I have the honour to return to
you herewith your Bond for
that amount dated 21st instant
which was given by you to
secure the Government of
Jamaica from loss in the
event of the amount not having
been paid in Hong Kong.
I have &c
Signed P.C. Cork

Wm by McCork

Entd MD 5.8.84

attached to 50/84

40

26 No 508
27 December 1884

H W Livingston Esq
Treasurer
Kingston.

Sir,
I have the honour to transmit
to you herewith the Promissory Notes
as per accompanying list in respect
of Chinese ex Steamer "Prinz Alexander"
I have endorsed the Notes as is
customary, but they will form a
portion of the Assets of the
Immigration Fund until the necessity
arises for their being discounted.

I have &c
Signed P.C. Cork.

posy Mr C
—135—
Ento M2

Rks handed personally
Treasurer by me
day
RH Hy
29.12.84

Minute

41

Hon: Col Secy.

Dr Telles as Surgeon of the "Pring
Alexander" has an agreement from Mr
Ryrie guaranteeing him 4 months salary
@ 100 dollars (at 4/-) = £ 80
Less advance in Hong Kong   20
                            ——
                             60

A second class passage to Hong 70
Kong via Panama   £ 130
                           ======

He has also a letter dated 7th May last
agreeing on behalf of the Government of
Jamaica that "in addition to the
"passage money stipulated for in your
"agreement that you are to be paid a
"fair and reasonable sum ~~of £10~~
"for his extra personal expenses ~~incurred~~
~~incurred~~ on your way back" Dr Telles
claims the sum of ten pounds for his
personal expenses which I consider
a reasonable amount and which I
respectfully ask for authority to pay
I find Dr Telles was paid £ 20 in Hong
Kong and his father also got £ 20,
added to which I have given him as
an advance here £ 50 making in
all £ 90. The balance remaining to
be paid is therefore £ 40 plus any
sum allowed for his expenses

                    Signed P S. Cork
                            21. 7. 84

Payment of £ 10 authorized (Have you
not deducted ~~twice~~ the £10 awarded to
+/,

42

Von London, New York, Perth

COLONIAL BANK,

Kingston, *7th October* 18*84*

attah to 405/84

LODGED to the Credit of *The Treasurer*

the sum of *Forty two pounds*

£ *42 : 0 : 0*   *V. Hawkins* Cashier

Countersigned

Protector.

The above cheque for £24 has been refused at the Bank.

R.E.H.
7/10/84

J. G. O. Broughton Esq
Buff Bay P.O.

I. O. No 397
8 Oct. 1884

Sir,

I have the honour to inform you that your Cheque No A² 46498 *for £24* dated 6 inst which you handed to me in payment of the Cash truth due for Chinese ind? to Sterborsale Estate has been dishonoured by the Colonial Bank. I beg therefore that you will be so good as to make a sufficient lodgment with as little delay as possible to cover the amount.

Mr S Ento
MD 8/10/84

... the Detached of placed in the

R.H./110/84

43

$6\frac{v^o}{84}$

Statement showing the Cash Tenths, Principal and
Interest charged to Employers of   Chinese Immigrants
ex "Prinz Alexander, 1884.

Date			Cash Tenths	Principal	Interest	Total
1884			33 15 „			33 15 „
July	15	Constant Spring	60 15 „			60 15 „
	„	do: 1st Note		33 15 „	2 0 5	35 15 5
	„	do 2nd Note		60 15 „	3 12 10	64 7 10
	„	do 3rd Note		67 10 „	8 2 6	75 12 6
	„	do 4th Note		121 10 „	14 4 6	136 7 6
	„	do 5th Note		67 10 „	12 3 1	79 13 1
				121 10 „	21 17 4	143 7 4
				67 10 „	16 4 2	83 14 2
				121 10 „	29 3 2	150 13 2
				67 10 „	20 5 3	87 15 3
				121 10 „	36 9 „	157 19 „
	„	Spring Garden	42 15 0			42 15 „
	„	do 1st Note		42 15 „	2 11 3	45 6 3
		do 2nd Note		85 10 „	10 5 2	95 15 2
		do 3rd Note		85 10 „	15 7 9	100 17 9
		do 4th Note		85 10 „	20 10 4	106 0 4
		do 5th Note		85 10 „	25 12 11	111 2 11
	„	Burlington	27 15 „			27 15 „
		do 1st Note		27 15 „	1 13 3	29 8 3
		do 2nd Note		55 10 „	6 13 2	62 3 2
		do 3rd Note		55 10 „	9 19 9	65 9 9
		do 4th Note		55 10 „	13 6 4	68 16 4
		do 5th Note		55 10 „	16 12 11	72 2 11
	„	Llanrumny	22 10 „			22 10 „
		do 1st Note		22 10 „	1 7 „	23 17 0
		do 2nd Note		45 „ „	5 8 „	50 8 „
		do 3rd Note		45 „ „	8 2 „	53 2 0
		do 4th Note		45 „ „	10 16 „	55 16 „
		do 5th Note		45 „ „	13 10 „	58 10 „
		Dover	20 5 0			20 5 0
		do 1st Note		20 5 „	1 4 3	21 9 3
		do 2nd Note		40 10 „	4 17 2	45 7 2
		do 3rd Note		40 10 „	7 5 9	47 15 9
		do 4th Note		40 10 „	9 14 4	50 4 4
		do 5th Note		40 10 „	12 2 11	52 12 11
			442 „ „	1323 „ „	253 15 2	1725 12

Continued

Date		Cash Tenth	Principal	Interest	Total
1883	Brot forward	147 . "	1823 . "	25 5/8 19/8 2/7	1725 6 2
July 15	Albion	59 5 "			59 5 "
	1st Note		50 5 "	3 11 1	62 16 1
	2. Note		118 10 "	14 4 4	132 14 4
Richards	3.d Note		118 10 "	21 6 6	139 16 6
	4th Note		118 10 "	28 8 8	146 18 8
	5.th Note		118 10 "	35 10 10	154 0 10
.	Bushy Park	30 15 .			30 15 .
	1st Note		30 15 "	1 16 11	32 11 11
	2nd Note		61 10 "	7 7 6	68 17 6
	3.d Note		61 10 "	11 1 3	72 11 3
D. Verley	4. Note		61 10 "	14 15 .	76 5 .
	5 Note		61 10 "	18 8 9	79 18 9
"	Hordley	13 10 "			13 10 .
	1st Note		13 10 "	.16 2	14 6 2
	2. Note		27 " "	3 4 10 / 1 12 3	30 4 10 / 28 12 3
	3.d Note		27 " "	4 17 3	31 17 3
S. Harrison	4. Note		27 " "	6 9 8	33 9 8
	5. Note		27 " "	8 2 1	35 2 1
.	Amity Hall	18 27 15 .			27 15 "
	1. Note		27 15 "	1 13 3	29 8 3
	2. Note		55 10 "	6 13 2	62 3 2
S. Harrison	3. Note		55 10 "	4 19 9	65 9 9
	4. Note		55 10 "	13 6 4	68 16 4
	5. Note		55 10 "	16 12 11	72 2 11
"	Gibraltar	17 25 10 .			25 10 0
	1st Note		25 10 "	1 10 7	27 0 7
E. Westmoreland	2nd Note		51 0 0	6 2 4	57 2 4
	3rd Note		51 0 0	9 3 6	60 3 6
	4th Note		51 0 0	12 4 8	63 4 8
	5th Note		51 " "	15 5 10	66 5 10
		303 15 .	2733 15 .	5 2 4 18 11 9 4 / 5 2 8 8 4	3504 5 4 7 4 / 35 6 5 18 4 / 5 4

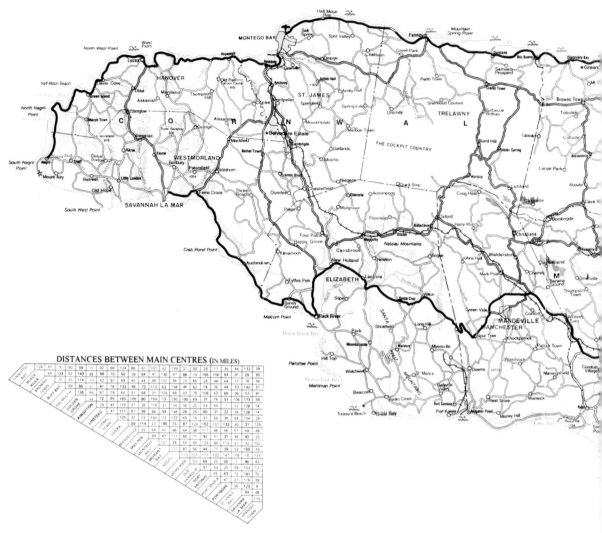

DISTANCES BETWEEN MAIN CENTRES (IN MILES)

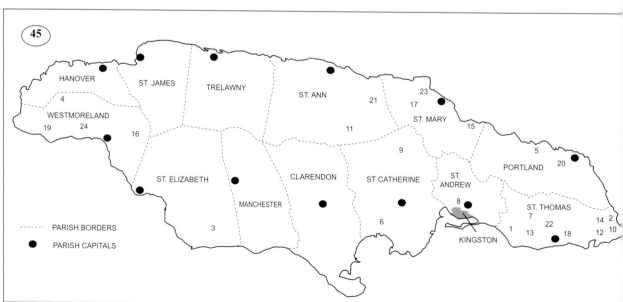

PARISH BORDERS

PARISH CAPITALS

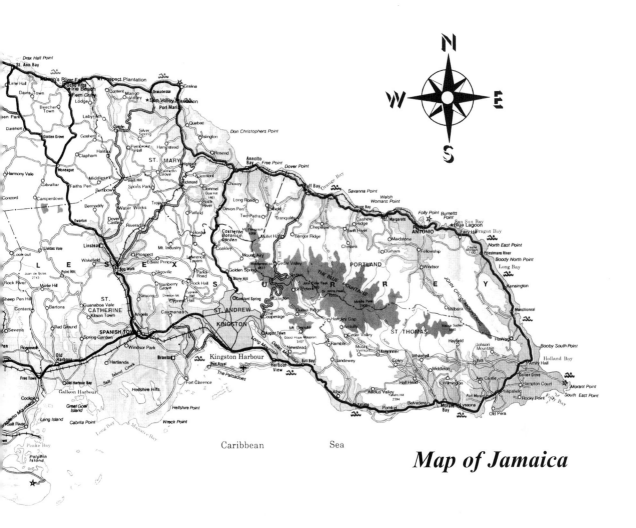

Map of Jamaica

Map of Jamaica showing the various estate locations.

Names and locations of towns

1.	Albion	9.	Dover	17.	Llanrumney
2.	Amity Hall	10.	Duckenfield	18.	Lyssons
3.	Ballard Valley	11.	Gubraltat	19.	Maylessfield
4.	Blue Castle	12.	Golden Grove	20.	Nunsuch
5.	Burlington	13.	Hall Head	21.	Orange Hall
6.	Bushy Park	14.	Hardley	22	Spring Garden
7.	Coley	15.	Iter Boreale	23.	Trinity
8.	Constant Spring	16.	Lenox	24.	Wakefield

Parishes and Capitals ●

HANOVER	Lucea	PORTLAND	Port Antonio	CLARENDON	May Pen
ST. JAMES	Montego Bay	ST. THOMAS	Morant Bay	MANCHESTER	Mandeville
TRELAWNY	Falmouth	KINGSTON	Kingston	ST. ELIZABETH	Black River
ST. ANN	St. Ann's Bay	ST. ANDREW	Half-way Tree	WESTMORELAND	Savanna-la-mar
ST. MARY	Port Maria	ST. CATHERINE	Spanish Town		

*Map of Kingston
and a portion of St. Andrew,
Jamaica*

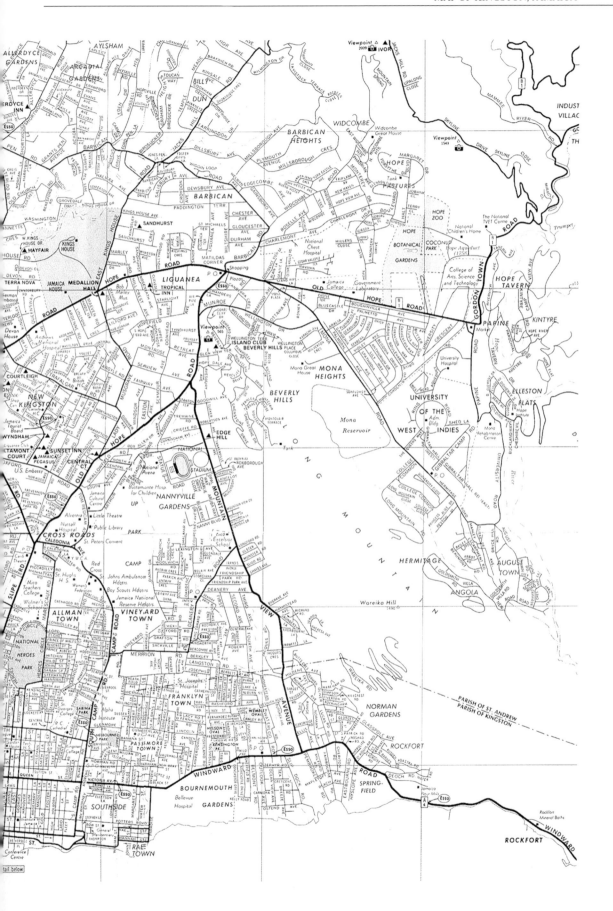

Hubert Lue
THE STORY OF THE LOCAL BORN

INTRODUCTION

I was flabbergasted when Ray Chen approached me to co-author this book. He wanted me to collaborate with him because, as he said, the Jamaican Chinese experience has not been told, especially the impact the Chinese have had on the job of nation building and the significant contribution they have made. In one hundred and fifty years of history of the Chinese in Jamaica, several generations have passed on without any kind of comprehensive record or documentation of these people who first came to this land as indentured labourers.

Ray's proposition was an interesting and challenging one. I had my misgivings about taking on this job. I am in my seventies, retired, enjoying good health, playing tennis with my old buddies four to five times a week. But with a lot of time on my hands, a good portion of this is spent at the library broadening my knowledge and expanding my horizons. At the times when I am in a sober, contemplative mood, I would think of taking up writing in a serious way, not so much for the money, but for the sheer joy of it. It is one of the activities that I have enjoyed for some time.

Strange how, in the senior years with more time on hand to reflect on the past, one can find a host of things to think about ... unfulfilled dreams, missed opportunities, friendships not treasured while good friends have passed on, the promised trip one should have made, or the caring and affection for loved ones neglected. I have often thought of my grandchildren, who are distantly removed from the life I knew as a child in Jamaica. They were born and are growing up in North America, some three generations and nearly a century removed from the young couple from far away China, who ventured forth and first planted the seed in foreign soil. That they will not know their past, pains me. And so, for them, I have taken up the challenge and opportunity that Ray has offered. It is funny how sometimes things seem to fall in place. A few months prior to Ray approaching me, I had enrolled in a three-year creative writing course.

Ray was enthused and determined that the story of our people – as he puts it – must be told. Whether or not I co-joined with him, he was adamant that the history of our people must be recorded out of respect for their magnificent courage. He is a great motivator, intensely focused and, above all, I share his grand vision. He is no stranger to the publishing world. The recent production and publication of two successful books of pictorial essays have been well received and acclaimed. They are a tribute to Ray's creative, artistic talent, and a demonstration of his professional photographic acumen. In these two editions, he excelled in capturing, at the precise moment, the finest of human emotion and expression. The natural beauty of this tropical country – Jamaica – gave full expression to his imagination. With his camera he paints scene after scene of a tropical paradise, recording in his style the colours and the beauty of God's creation.

I considered the content of this book very carefully, and tried to think through what it is that we wish to convey to the reader. What kind of stories we want to tell, what kind of pictures we want to paint. Should it cover our trials and hardships, challenges and disappointments, successes and progress? Frankly, without these all-encompassing facets, the stories would not be complete. Ray's approach was to send out a form to a number of people, with certain specific query guidelines, to enable the writers to tell of their experience living and growing up in Jamaica. This collection of stories he would chronicle in a book to reflect the Jamaican Chinese experience. I agree that nothing gives a more accurate picture than personal experience. To expand, however, on these experiences, there is a need to include a setting of place and time and by extension the political, economic and social conditions existing within those time frames. Bearing in mind the changing situations over the period is a given. Undoubtedly, these conditions have influenced people's lives significantly.

Jamaican born Chinese like Ray and I, grew up from the 1930s and '40s through colonial times of the British Empire. The Bustamante and Norman Manley eras of internal self-government leading to independence were interesting times; we witnessed a colonial territory achieve statehood, after 300 years of British rule. Drunk with the jubilation and euphoria of independence we, as new Jamaicans, started off with British style socialism and, of course, new pride in our domestic nationalism.

"Out of many, one people." This motto, composed especially to mark Jamaica's independence, was unifying in its objective and adequate to unite the many nationalities that make up the Jamaican population, at that time numbering some two million plus souls. The leadership of Bustamante and Norman Manley respectively, graduating from under British tutelage, brought much needed stability and engendered great hope for the populace.

The Chinese, as they adjusted and adapted to these changes are a study in accommodation and compromise. The Hakkas (the large clan to which Jamaican Chinese belong) are well known for this survival "live and let live" attitude. Chinese, like weeds, sprout wherever they take root and always seem to gravitate and cluster together for the survival of the clan. Chinese indentured labourers, from the first landing in the mid-eighteen hundreds through to the twenty first century, have learned to keep pace with changing times and to take advantage of opportunities as they arose. The Jamaican Chinese Hakkas have developed that uncanny trait of resilience which allows them to overcome hardship and difficulties. They are a united people of strong bonds, independent in outlook and spirit. They are courageous, never showing fear in the face of adversity.

I sincerely believe that our task is to take the reader back 150 years. We need to visualize the many, almost insurmountable, trials and hardships suffered by these early generations. Think of it – landing in an alien environment of extreme language and cultural differences, adjusting to the climate and unfamiliar types of food, recovering from tropical ailments and diseases, suffering loneliness, being deprived of spouse and family support. This had to be the nearest thing to a hell hole. Until the local born know of this history, we will not find our roots; by acknowledging and actually feeling the pain, we will better respect our heritage, treasure and appreciate our origins.

CHAPTER 1

What was the compelling reason to leave family and loved ones, to venture into the unknown? To understand, we must retrace our steps to eighteenth - century China where life, at best, was year after year of bare subsistence. The only means of livelihood was off the land; periods of famine, pestilence and severe drought were not uncommon, when land became parched earth and people were reduced to boiling tree bark for sustenance. You will recognize the pangs of hunger and know our parents have been there. The hopelessness, the unrelenting poverty. Therein lay the motivation – the compelling reason. The desperation to leave that environment was not a matter of choice, for there was none, only one of urgent escape.

A comparison is the experience of East Germany during the height of communism in Eastern Europe and we also read of the East Germans at that time: how they risked their lives crossing the Berlin Wall to escape poverty and oppression. It is the universal human spirit in us that fuels the desire of people to escape bondage, oppression and suffering.

The Hakkas* are a unique stock of the Han Chinese from the Han dynasty. That's who we are. There are differences in culture and heritage between us and the other clans – the Cantonese, the Teochius, the Mandarins, the Fukienese and the myriad of smaller clans. Our Hakka language, customs, cuisine and traditions are what define us as a distinct group. The Hakkas, centuries ago driven from the northern part of the country by barbarians like Gengis Khan and other plundering murderous war-lords, knew suffering in the extreme. Their very existence as a distinct people was continuously being threatened, and they were forever being pushed south in an exodus of mass migration. In every new province or area where they sojourned, they were emasculated and victimized by the host population when they sought a foothold to put down roots. The end of the exodus, spread over centuries, found our people settled in the most southerly of China's coastal provinces, Kwangtung, Fukken and Kwangsi. Our people were identified as "guest people", hence the word "Hakka" – a people without a home. The very exploitation and victimization of the Hakkas caused them to develop among themselves a bond and loyalty equal to that of the Jews in their suffering and persecution. It also made them uniquely identifiable with deprived and oppressed people.

Contrary to common belief, the Hakkas had a highly advanced culture of language and education. Their survival is a reflection of their industry and ingenuity. Their value of education and civilization is in direct proportion to the many great leaders in Chinese history who are Hakka. There is a powerful body of overseas Chinese (Hua Keow)*, numbering some 30 million worldwide. Hakkas form a large percentage of these millions, and control vast wealth in territories like Jamaica, the Far East nations of Singapore, Malaysia, Indonesia, Thailand, Borneo, and Sarawak and, to a lesser degree, Japan and Korea. The Hakkas in these south-eastern nations (Lam Yong)* dominate in every sphere of activity – from industry and commerce to mining, agriculture, politics and government. Their accomplishments are well documented and it goes without saying that their contributions to development in these host countries are significant. Jamaica is a good example; so are the other territories in the western hemisphere where Hakkas have established roots.

China, in the eighteenth century, was a poor nation of hundreds of millions of people, ruled by a weak, spineless Manchu Emperor. He and his government could not prevent the invasion, aggression and greed of the British and the Europeans. The Chinese were coerced, and succumbed to every exploitation and unreasonable demand of the white man. Defenceless, powerless and poor, every unequal treaty was imposed on the compliant, suffering nation of China. This was the condition and environment of the country in which our parents were born. Government administration and social services, schools and medical services were non-existent in the villages. Every conceivable service had to be provided by the people of the village. Our parents described education, even at the elementary level, as a luxury unless the child was reasonably bright. Scarce funds for school fees were diverted to encourage the brighter siblings, and slow learners were automatically streamed into "Jung Nu"*, the cowboy regime. It was cause for a big dinner and celebration when a youth graduated from elementary school. Consequently, most poor Chinese were untutored and deficient in education.

In 1999, I went to visit my parents' village in Guangdong, China, for the first time. Having entertained the desire for many years, I needed to accomplish this unfulfilled wish before it was too late. The fulfillment and satisfaction of finding my ancestral roots evoked an emotional sense of connection, of belonging, a feeling of the presence of their love and kinship, despite their departure from this homeland many eons ago. Where my parents lived, the poverty and the squalor from which they fled, is reminiscent of the long bar-rack-like, ramshackle building I grew up in on the banana plantation in rural St. Mary, Jamaica, in the 1930s. It is these experiences that taught them the virtue of frugality, perseverance and determination to better their lot, and the strength to overcome difficulties. Failure was never an option. This reminds me of a Korean businessman whom I once asked, "You open your variety store seven days a week?" He replied, "No – eight days". We laughed. To my question "what happens if you get sick?" he responded, "Me – I can't afford to get sick." This exemplifies the mindset of the Oriental – he cannot countenance the luxury of failure. The Hakkas demonstrate an indefatigable industry and intelligence honed by and through centuries of oppression and persecution. To put it subtly, we are a tough breed of people. Is it any wonder, then, that we are a successful clan?

We began our journey from the mid-1800s when Chinese immigrants to the new world arrived, not as imported indentured labourers, but as free persons in search of economic opportunities, a better life and the dream of wealth. They were attracted to the "Gold Mountain" (Gim-San)* of the American West. They became the commercial traders and shopkeepers in the colonies of Guyana, Trinidad, Jamaica, Panama, Cuba, and many countries in Latin America.

Success stories usually filtered back to the villages of the old country. This stimulated an increase in migration to overseas areas of employment and opportunities. Brothers sent for brothers, cousins invited other relatives, friends induced friends, and so on. Now we get a clearer understanding of why, in Jamaica, we have so many extended families. Of course the same pattern existed in other colonies as well.

In my father's family, there were five sons and one daughter. The eldest, Uncle Tom, was the first to leave the village and migrate to Jamaica. The second boy, Uncle Lieuw-Choy followed but ended up in Suriname. My father, Lue-Quee, went to Jamaica. The fourth and fifth boys, Fah Shueck and Ah-kquay-Shueck, also went to Suriname. The question is how come, or why did the brothers split up with some in Jamaica and the others in Suriname. The explanation, as it was told to me, goes like this: whatever the destination of the ship in Hong Kong harbour at the migrant's chosen time of departure, that was the country in which the migrant most likely ended up. Another explanation I heard is that, if there were temporary problems of restricted entry into a colony, these would naturally have a bearing on the movement of emigrants. A common thread among these migrant Chinese, however, is that folks would go to the places where they had family or friends.

At age 28, my father arrived in Jamaica. He was as old as the calendar years, meaning he was born in 1900. His father was a schoolmaster in the village of Liang Pai Wee, Guangdong province. Father was the third child and, being the brightest of the brood, naturally got the highest level of education available in the village. As far as the sixth child and only daughter in the family is concerned, details of her life were never mentioned to me but I suspect that she was either drowned at birth (a method of discarding unwanted girls), or given away to a childless family. According to the prevailing custom of that period, boys were treasured and valued as an economic asset, while daughters were of lesser importance and counted for nothing. An absolute paternalistic society, this attitude evolved from the time of the dynastic emperors in early Chinese history. We need to recognize also that village communities had, at the beginning, a feudal component and the background of a closed and tightly knit society, comprising generations of family members with the same surname, like the Chins, Wongs, Lees, Chens – all blood relatives concentrated in separate, individual communes. This family structure and the commune environment, conditioned by poverty and the emasculating absence of economic opportunity of employment, bred a strong bond of closeness among the families. Foreign-born Chinese like us cannot understand or comprehend the nature of communal life imposed by poverty. Members of the commune depended greatly on each other for survival and support. Every problem or social issue in that closed community was addressed co-operatively. Disputes among families were resolved by the elders within the commune, to the exclusion of external interference.

It should be noted that the more economically independent a family member became, the greater the degree of individuality he or she enjoyed. Within the framework of a commune, economic independence promoted detachment from the commune, thereby weakening the social cohesiveness and unity. This detachment was also aggravated by migration and the availability of opportunities outside the village. What we have then is an individual's leap from being a member of a closely-knit village commune, who would normally behave as a member of a group, to one of an individualistic character. In a sense, similar to western cultural life patterns, this condition is considered economically progressive, but conversely has a negative impact on family unity and closeness. Foreign-born Chinese are grossly affected by this detachment from family and, in the process, become less caring.

CHAPTER 2

FROM SLAVERY – A NEW BEGINNING

The history of colonial Jamaica is one where every facet of life was controlled, patterned, and developed according to the British model. The imprint of their religion, their customs and traditions, their history, their mode of government and other institutions, used as tools for total domination, achieved the desired result. It was so pervasive and effective that former African slaves were thoroughly made over into replicas of the Englishman. They saw themselves through the eyes of the Englishman. African-Jamaicans, consistently denied their history, experienced another type of psychological enslavement and further loss of their identity. This is a major stumbling block for building a new society. The Rastafarian brethren are the only section of modern day Jamaica who openly and consciously reject the white man's dominance.

Marcus Garvey, William Gordon, Bogle, and, in more recent times, Bustamante, Marley, and Martin Luther King, are the heroes who sought to awaken Africans' consciousness of their culture and heritage, and encouraged them to take pride in their African origins. We can see signs of the growth today of this consciousness and awareness in the society. As the memory of slavery recedes into history, a new generation of African-Jamaicans will emerge. Unburdened by the mental baggage of slavery, they will rise to redeem their heritage and build the new society.

Jamaican minority people – the Jews, Syrians, Lebanese, Indians and Chinese – although not having suffered the stigma of slavery, nevertheless experienced the same make-over due to the pervasive British influence. In the case of local-born Chinese, we are best described by our China-born brothers as 'bananas' (yellow on the outside, and thoroughly white on the inside), meaning, white oriented in thought, culture and language, but clothed in Chinese skin. I can only concede we were also victims of history.

In *The Story of the Jamaican People* by Philip Sherlock & Hazel Bennett, there is a chapter about the Chinese in which Professor Sherlock said: "*The Chinese constitute a separate racial group which serves as a cushion between the whites and the blacks.*" Chinese indentured workers first arrived in Jamaica in 1854 and continued to arrive in different batches up to 1949. Like the Indians, the Chinese came on contract to plantation owners for a fixed number of years. The Chinese workers on an estate in Duckenfield, St.Thomas, protested the poor working conditions, laid down their tools, took strike action and refused to work. *This was recorded as the first strike to have taken place in the island.* Concessions and other improved working conditions were granted to them, including the reduction of a 12 hour working day to 9 hours.

The Chinese indentured workers, at the end of their contract period, decided to branch out into the retail trade as shopkeepers, which was much more lucrative than working for the white man on his plantation. The large number of Chinese engaged in the retail trade, over time, led to their eventual dominance in this sector of the economy. Their success attracted the unfavourable attention of the colonial government, and the envy of other members of the population. This gave rise to restrictive red-tape and taxation, designed to limit the progress of the shopkeepers.

On the imposition of the Government's *Shop Assistance Law,* Professor Sherlock in the *The Story of the Jamaican People* made this observation: "*For a long time the colonial Government continued to discriminate against minority groups by introducing laws restricting daily opening hours of business places, compelling them to curtail their operations. Although the businesses were operated by family members and were therefore not affected by the law, Chinese and Jews were singled out for additional taxation.*" This was a most unfair law, designed primarily to control hardworking shopkeepers. It forced shopkeepers to use huge cloth screens to cover sections of the retail area at 4:00 p.m. This was the section where haberdashery, patent medicine, fabrics and ready made garments were stocked, leaving only the grocery and provision areas open for business. Of course, you and I know these oppressive and restrictive measures could not deter our parents. The spiteful envy of sections of the local population was also a matter of great concern to the community. The cultures of the minorities living in Jamaica were not acceptable to them due to ignorance, e.g., the traditional clothing of a Chinese person, made from the finest Chinese silk, could not be appreciated as a thing of beauty but was ridiculed as a Chinaman wearing "oil-skin". Our language was also an object of mockery and racial slurs. Ignorance and intolerance were not confined to the illiterate and the uneducated. I recall in the late 1940s the well known trade unionist and PNP politician of the day, Wills O. Isaac, disparaging the Chinese for practising their cultural traditions in Jamaica. It seemed the exposure and addition of different cultural experiences to the Jamaican society could not be seen by these ignoramuses as enrichment of the Jamaican experience. This was the sort of one-dimensional view encouraged by the white man by means of which the African-Jamaican population was programmed to admire and worship only things European.

The pioneering Chinese persevered, worked hard, adapted to their local surroundings, were respectful of the communities in which they lived, established roots, raised their families, suffered all kinds of difficulties and all manner of indignities brought upon them by the spiteful, discriminating white government. We Hakka Chinese know how to endure; we are no strangers to hardship. We survived because we are single minded in our pursuit and never lose sight of our objective. The African Jamaican people, although resentful in the beginning, came to acknowledge the contributions and appreciate the lessons of the minorities in their midst.

This, then, is the background to the country to which my father migrated in 1928.

CHAPTER 3

CHILDHOOD MEMORIES

I remember it well, just a little room, but to my sister and I it was like a prison because it had one small window, two feet by two feet, placed high up and almost touching the ceiling. This room suited our parents very much; ideally it was a store-room where provisions were kept to replenish stock in their little country village shop. It was also a lock-up for misbehaving kids. If we were naughty, we would be locked away for half an hour or so as punishment. At the tender ages of three and four, this seemingly dark dungeon loomed large, fortress-like in the uncluttered minds of bawling toddlers.

My earliest memories of childhood… huge banana plantations, many acres and acres of bananas being grown for the American and British markets. Those were the days of the giant United Fruit Company, during the era of British colonial rule (1930s). I was born in Jamaica, British West Indies, to parents who were Chinese immigrants from that far away land of old Cathay. My sister and I were too young to comprehend the complexity of being aliens in the ocean of a majority black population. The innocence of childhood kept our young minds from adult prejudices. Our differences did not detract from our childhood fantasies, and hide-and-seek or a good round of chevy-chase. I knew the colour of our skin and our hair was unlike that of our playmates, the offspring of slaves not yet one generation removed from the emancipation of slavery by the British colonial masters. We were so engrossed with fun and laughter that the world was what we made of it.

Growing up in Albany, St. Mary, and attending Mrs. Kennedy's one room school restricted my exposure to just those four walls and the many children's stories which Mrs. Kennedy read to us, molding our young minds. She was a Quaker missionary, a white American lady, and probably the only educated person in the whole village, who also dispensed charity and Christian teaching. My parents, on Sundays, would dress us up and pack us off to Mrs. Kennedy's church and Sunday school. It is a funny thing, my parents were never exposed to Christianity; more, I suspect, to Confucianism and Daoism. Yet, they saw in Mrs. Kennedy's teaching the goodness of humanity and the universality of man.

The village had a population of approximately 4,000 to 5,000: all farm hands and labourers employed to work the banana plantations. There were some small land owners who worked the land, barely eking out subsistence. Do you remember those almost primitive and austere times of rural Jamaica, where there was no community centre, no high school, no electricity, no piped water, and one district constable to maintain law and order, no radio, medical service restricted to half-a-day every two weeks by a medical doctor provided by the parish council? The post office and the train station were some two miles away. Such a spartan environment robbed the inhabitants of some of the barest necessities for a reasonable standard of living, and was a sure way to breed country bumpkins. The British colonial government was much to be blamed for the lack of basic social services.

This was the environment in which my father operated his little grocery shop. A poor neighbourhood naturally produced a low volume of business. It could be said that dad was equally as poor as the customers he served. In an effort to increase business, he expanded by opening another shop not too far away and had mother run that business. Poor mom, knowing not a word of English or patois, solved her language problem by employing the aid of a long stick, which was made available to customers to point to the shelf and the can of sardines or milk that was required. Although short on language skills, mom was no fool when it was time to handle money and make change. She was skilled in dealing with the pounds (sterling), shillings and pence of the local currency.

My parents, like all Chinese immigrants of that period, were hard workers. Opening shop at six in the morning to 'catch' the early morning workers going to work, continuing throughout the day to nine or sometimes ten on Friday and Saturday nights, was quite the norm. Long hours in any Gulag, this regimentation became their whole life. As they toiled year after year, bringing a much needed service to the country folks, a certain kinship and beneficial rapport developed between dad and his customers, to the point where a great degree of trust was established. Dad became a confidant to many families. He acted as mediator for their disputes, and advisor on matters requiring greater insight and wisdom. He was a friend to everyone in the village, extending credit to families in hardship, helping out in dire situations, and even contributing money and kind for the burial of poor family members. In fact, dad became the unofficial 'elder' of the village. I am sure this human interaction and experience was repeated all over Jamaica during my father's generation.

In summer, the country folks would bring baskets of fruits and vegetables for us. This was their way of showing their appreciation and thoughtfulness. Although poor in a material sense, they were rich in their humanity, generous in their kindness and proud of who they were. Being poor did not diminish their integrity, neither did it rob them of their self respect. This is the Jamaica I love to remember and cherish. Prejudice and discrimination had no place in their psyche or wisdom. These proud people, hard working and God fearing, steadfast in their religion, never entertained any complex of inferiority. They saw each other and anyone else as a brother human being, equal in the sight of God.

Speaking of God, I would like to share an experience with you. It is a funny story but true, and it proves the ingenuity of man as a creative being. While growing up in St. Mary as a young man, there was a man called Preacher Singh, of above average proportions and a gentleman of East Indian stock, who was the village preacher who rented the one room school house for his weekly Sunday church service. The major problem was, Preacher Singh couldn't read. But did I say Preacher Singh was not intelligent and not smart? Solution – he employed the services of a student from the local school to read verses and chapters from the Bible. So on Sundays, with the Church filled to capacity, Preacher Singh would be at the pulpit, his Bible reading student at his side, much like an interpreter in other such situations. The student would read a verse or two from the Bible and, Preacher Singh, ever the dramatic showman, in his fire and brimstone stentorian voice, would pick up and repeat the words after the student. Student: "And the Lord said to Moses on the mount". Preacher Singh: "AND THE LORD SAID TO MOSES ON THE MOUNT". It was a performance worthy of a skilled and experienced actor. Needless to say I was truly impressed; it was a first class lesson in dramatics and acting. Preacher Singh succeeded in bringing the words of the Lord to his equally illiterate congregation. The bottom line is that the members of his church were illumined and inspired by the words of the Lord, while Preacher Singh benefited richly from the collections on Sundays. Of course he was also showered with chickens and eggs, provisions, fruits and vegetables. After all, a stout champion of the Lord must be kept trim and in sound health, to continue his missionary work. Back in those days, the peasantry was far more fervent in their religious practice, God-fearing and respectful of authority; untarnished by excess materialism, proud and independent in their moral uprightness, caring and loving in a compassionate way.

The grocery shop in which my sisters and I were born was also the birth place of Ray Chen's father, Samuel Chen. Uncle Young, Samuel Chen's father, and Ray's grandfather, was the owner of the shop. Uncle Young and my father's mother were brother and sister, hence the relationship. My dad arrived in Jamaica in 1928 without my mom. In those days, the reality was that a young man had to first 'learn' business and save up his paltry income over a long period of time, with the sole purpose of sending for his wife and children. To acquire a business, the young apprentice had to prove his diligence and capacity for hard work, possibly over two or more years. If his employer was satisfied with his performance and was convinced that the young man was capable of managing his own business, the employer (usually a friend or relative) would then recommend the graduate to his wholesale suppliers to supply goods for the new venture he proposed starting. This arrangement was usually facilitated by the employer acting as guarantor for the new businessman.

There were other methods of accessing funds to start new businesses. One of the best known was the Chinese 'Fui'. This is similar to the Jamaican 'Partner', but with a difference. The late Mr. Lowe Shue San, a respected and successful merchant on Princess Street in Kingston's Chinatown, was the best known operator of Fui. To start a Fui, Mr. Lowe would select fifty people to contribute 100 pounds sterling, weekly. To participate, each member had to first pay the sum of 100 pounds to Mr. Lowe as head of the Fui for his management, and as guarantor of the Fui for fifty weeks – which was the life of the Fui. Any of the fifty members who wished to realize funds from the Fui had to make a sealed bid to have an opportunity for the 'draw'. There could be any amount of bids for a draw in any given week. All bids were opened on a Sunday. If, for example, my bid one week was 2 pounds sterling then when the bids were opened on Sunday of that week and if mine was the highest bid I would get the draw, and the other 49 members would have to pay 98 pounds into the Fui. Mr. Lowe would then draw me a cheque for 49x98 = 4,802 pounds. My repayment to the Fui would be 100 pounds for the next 49 weeks. Members who were not in need of funds and did not need to bid for a draw could earn a handsome interest on their capital.

It is important for us to know how our parents realized startup capital in those early years. My dad was apprenticed to a few businesses in Manchester and later Portland. One of the groceries where he worked in Port Antonio was Sang Hing & Company, owned by the Lee Sang family. When dad was ready to venture out on his own, his Uncle Young (Ray's grandfather) offered him the business in Albany, St. Mary. He then sent for mom, and that's how we happened to be born in the same shop as Ray's father. Mom didn't spend much time with us – after bearing four children (my three sisters and myself), she died from malaria (a tropical disease prevalent during that period) on October 18, 1938 at the age of 37. She was a relatively young woman, healthy and strong. She would take me and my sister, during the summer time when the river was drying up, to catch 'janga'*. And during the mango season she would take us up into the mountain to a farmer's property to pick mangoes.

In 1938 (I was about seven years of age at the time), an event of national importance and significance took place in the island, which was to mark a historic change in the life of the Jamaican people and the British colonial administration that governed the island. The 1938 riots and civil disturbance was of such magnitude that the whole country was shut down. It began with the workers at the sugar estates in Westmoreland going on strike for better pay and improved working conditions. The striking workers, helped along by agitators, got out of hand, and the disturbance spread rapidly, engulfing the island and all sectors of industry, Government-workers included. Police and soldiers were called out in great numbers to deal with the disturbance, but rioters, criminals and ruffians had a field day. Civil authority lost control of the situation, and a state of emergency was declared by the then British Governor. This major civil strife lasted over a week and there was much looting of business places. The fire brigade personnel in Kingston, the capital city, went out on strike, and there was serious concern that rioters might use the opportunity to burn down the city. Many Chinese shops were looted and some were burnt to the ground. The loss to the Chinese shopkeepers was tremendous, and created extreme hardship. I remember, during the time of the disturbance, my father made preparations for my mother and the maid to take us down to the river to hide, fearing that rioters would continue their march to our district of Albany and loot and burn down the shop. Fortunately, my father's worst fear was never realized.

Although the 1938 riots affected the Chinese shopkeepers in a big way, with many suffering great financial loss, none of the books or items of news that I have read dealing with this epoch making event, carried the slightest bit of information about the huge loss suffered by this group of people. Lee Tom Yin's book *The Chinese in Jamaica* written and published first in 1957 and again in 1963, did not even mention the riots. I am almost sure the Chinese Benevolent Society must have protested to the colonial authorities and pressed for compensation for their members but I am unable to confirm whether any form of compensation was paid.

The suffering of the Chinese community at the hands of criminal elements in the Jamaican society goes back many years. Ever since they started to ply their trade as shopkeepers from the 1890s, the frequent murder of Chinese shopkeepers was commonplace. Many of these criminal elements were caught but never severely punished. The courts and the police were openly prejudiced against the Chinese. In one glaring case in the 1920s, a shopkeeper was closing up his shop when he was set upon and murdered by a criminal who had entered the shop. The accused person was caught and charged with the capital offence. At the trial, the judge reduced the charge and declared the death of the Chinese shopkeeper 'an accident'. This was the kind of injustice suffered by our people. Many robberies and murders were committed against our people during that early period. One of my grand-uncles, Thomas Lue, was murdered around 1942-1943 in Albany and, a few weeks later, the postmistress was also murdered. Many of these murders went unsolved, including these two.

In 1941, at the age of 10, I was shuffled off to the Chinese Public School to be immersed in the culture and, hopefully, to acquire a Chinese education. Not having left home before, I am a little reticent to tell you that I cried buckets the first two days. The following few weeks I came to realize that there were other country bumpkins like me at the boarding school, so I began to make new friends, and over the next five years we developed life long friendships. In the free for all, rough and tumble world of boarding school, one grew up real fast. Life was rough, regimented, exceedingly enjoyable, plenty fun, full of caning by the teachers, much bullying, too much sports and plenty, plenty friends. This was to be one of the happiest times of my life. Do you want to meet some of the bad dudes who made life good for me? Reggie (Colonel) Chin from Skibo, Wallace Nam from Chapelton, Leslie R. Chin from Fellowship. Victor Chung came from Port Antonio. Louis Lee, Albert and Nelson Chin, Alphanso Chin, all from Morant Bay. Vincent Chen from Snowhill, Ronald and Cecil Hew from Claremont. I was among my peers, genuine country bumpkins from some of the most remote parts of Jamaica. I know I have left out many others, but this is not intentional. I treasure the memory and the friendship of all my school buddies.

Our teachers were dedicated people who played a big role in influencing our lives, sometimes with the assistance of the ever present cane. Headmaster Chen Kung Yee, for example, was a stern disciplinarian and grudgingly known to us as 'Hitler'. Long before Bruce Lee was born, 'Hitler' was already teaching us the ancient Chinese martial art of Kung Fu. The regulation issued from the office of the 'Furher' - that only Chinese must be spoken on school premises – greatly assisted us in becoming fluent in the language. Of course, the language police were invisible, but you knew you had been caught when names were called out at the end of the school day.

With fond memories, we all remember teachers like Vernon Chen, Ruben Young and George Wong (St. George's College old boys) who taught us English and Math. Neon Sen-Sang, Mrs. Chong (I was one of her favourite students) spoke Hakka and Cantonese. Miss. Lily Ho taught us music and art. With Neon Sen-Sang in charge of the boarders, in the nights after supper, he would gather us around and tell us exciting Chinese legends of flying heroes – a-la Chow Yung Fat's Crouching Tiger – battling the bad guys with swords and Kung Fu.

Oh, for the magnificent imagination running wild, of children whose fantasies knew no bounds. I am grateful for having attended this school and to the

Jamaican Chinese community that made it possible. I am also grateful for the exposure to the language and culture, an enriching experience that influenced my life.

I was most surprised to discover that my five years spent at the Chinese Public School in Kingston in the 1940s learning Chinese, afforded me a better education in the language than a lot of my friends had had in China. Some of the women cannot read a word of Chinese. I consider myself truly fortunate to have had the opportunity to learn the language. In those early years – '30s-'40s – the prevailing rationale with Chinese parents in Jamaica was that learning Chinese was of no economic benefit. In other words, the student could not get a job by learning Chinese. English was required in the Jamaican society. This reasoning appears very logical. My father, for whatever reason, had a different opinion but I never did get around to questioning his decision. My only reasoned rationale is that he placed a higher value on cultural immersion than on the white man's language. I regret not having attended one of those name brand high schools like St. George's, Kingston College, Jamaica College, Wolmers or Munro. I am, nevertheless, quite happy and comfortable with the Chinese language, and I function very well in this multicultural environment of Toronto. The Chinese menus in the restaurants do not confuse me. The guy who cannot recognize a word is at a terrible disadvantage. I have friends who agonize over the missed opportunity of knowing the language. Other cultures place a very high value on their language. An Italian who can't speak Italian is not considered to be 100% of the race. This is the reason we are termed by our China born brethren "Ship Yit Diam". We are number eleven (11), one point short of the maximum twelve.

What improved and further enhanced my education and cultural awareness was the opportunity I had to work at the Chinese newspaper company as a compositor for a few years. I not only learned more Chinese and spoke the language more frequently but, most importantly, I gained a good amount of knowledge and insight, observing the Jamaican Chinese society from that vantage point, to see how it functioned, and to know the leaders and major players in the community. At one point during my tenure, when the battle between the Kuo Min Tang and the Chinese Communists was raging big time (early '50s), the war carried over from the Far East was no less fierce in Kingston's Chinatown, and was just as divisive and factionalized as it was in, say, Malaysia or Kuala Lumpur. The old guards were very pro-nationalist Kuo Min Tang. People and names that return to memory are community fathers like Lee Tom Yin, Chang Hon Gin, Wong Chew Onn, Tai Kee, Ernest Ho-Tai, my past headmaster Chen Kung Yee, Lim Hing, Yap Sam, Lee Chit Chong, Wong King and many others. Pro-communist defenders were people like Lee Fah Funn (a scholarly gentleman who used his pen to his advantage), Chin Chung Yee, Lue Biang Fah, Cam Hugh, Young Hon Lee and a battalion of freshly returned (from China) young men from Marxist propaganda schools who had been immersed and fired up in the teachings of communist ideology. It is of interest to note that, at that time, the KMT Nationalist Government of China provided printing equipment and funds to the local community purely for propaganda purposes in an effort to win the minds of the overseas Chinese. Even in today's Toronto (2003), the battle of the mind continues with the Taiwanese Government and the People's Republic of China heavily supporting factionalism through propaganda and financial funding. These are some of the realities of most Chinese societies. Because of my closeness to the community I have been privy to all these happenings.

CHAPTER 4

ENTREPRENEURS AND BUSINESSMEN

From indentured workers progressing to successful traders and retail merchants, our parents were true pioneers. Although small in number (the 1954 census recorded the Chinese population at approximately 14,000), the many organizations they created to protect and look after the social needs of the community and to safeguard their commercial interests, have to be seen as farsighted, commendable and noble. Their commitment to the Jamaican society is a sign of permanence in their adopted country.

From the earliest times the Chinese entrepreneurs and businessmen continued to grasp every opportunity to increase their involvement and build their wealth in the commercial activities in the island. Their contribution to the

The Old Guards. Standing l-r: Fung Sang, Ho See Hong, Ying Fie Ying, Chen Hen Yee, K F Young, Mr Charley Yee, Lee Sin Siak, Mr Lue, Chin Bak Leung. Sitting l-r: Lee Tom Yin, Wei Jun Fen, Wong Chew On, Milton Wong, Lyn Mew See, Chung Koon Pen, Chen Kung Yee.
Chung Fah Fui Gon, 1964.   Photo courtesy of Clive Chen

development of Jamaica is priceless, a fact both the people and government of Jamaica have acknowledged. Local born Chinese, integrated into the Jamaican society, have become a major stabilizing force today in a much troubled Jamaica.

The names of the original group of Chinese that I can recall, and often read about, seem to come up very frequently in the formative years in the late 1800s and early 1900s. They were a hard core group of community fathers who gave their all to the community. Their financial assistance, their help in support of family and friends to set up new businesses, established a solid foundation for first and second generations who have benefited enormously from their foresight, as will future generations. To those forefathers, we give praise and thanks for their selfless contributions and for setting the foundation for who we are today. Lest we forget, I want to remember giants like Albert Chang, Alexander Tai Ten Quee, Wong Chew Onn, Yam Sam, Lee Tom Yin, Lee Chit Chong, Lim Hing, Ernest Ho Tai, Albert Chin Yee, Cecil Chin Yee, Joe Wong, Arthur Chin Lenn, Chin Chun Yee, Daniel Lee, Chang Shin Shue, Chang Gin Sang, Chen Kung Yee and many, many more. In every new organization that was established for the betterment of the people in those pioneering days, these men were involved. Their legacy is something to be treasured and emulated.

An interesting personality of the period was Mr. Alexander Tai Ten Quee, a gentleman of imperial bearing. The first three piece suit I ever laid eyes on was worn by Mr. Tai Ten Quee. The only time we got to see the honourable gentleman was when he attended Board meetings at the Chinese school, always well dressed in his three piece suit, driven by liveried chauffeur, in his beautiful Packard (or was it a large Buick?) The epitome of wealth and elegance, good manners and gentleness were his trade mark. As the Second World War continued and gasoline became more scarce and rationed, Mr. Tai Ten Quee was forced to convert one of his smaller cars to animal horse power. The engine and front fenders of the small car were removed and, because in those days cars were built with a separate chassis, a horse was positioned between the two protruding ends of the chassis and hooked up with the required harness – voila! Mr. Tai Ten Quee was still being driven in style except at a much slower pace. Mr. Tai Ten Quee was well ahead of his time. He was the first Chinese industrialist in the island, establishing Caribbean Products Company, which manufactured edible oils, margarine, soap products and toilet articles, detergents etc. His daughter was the first British trained Chinese doctor in the island, but returned to England where I understand she married a Cambridge University professor. Mr. Hubert Tai Ten Quee, an only son, inherited his father's vast fortune and continued his philanthropic work for the community and Jamaica.

Chinatown came to be established in Kingston at a time when there were no mechanical trucks and the only means of transporting goods was by the dray carts (horse drawn carts). When the merchant ships arrived in Kingston harbour from Halifax and the western prairie provinces of Canada, the nearest streets to the wharves were Princess, Barry, Orange, Tower, Harbour, Beckford and Pechon Streets and many smaller lanes in between. The Jamaica Government Railway was also located very near to this area of commerce, and was the only mode of transportation to carry goods and passengers to the interior of the country. Other country towns, like Spanish Town, Ocho Rios, Mandeville, Montego Bay, Port Antonio, Port Maria, Savanna-la-mar, Black River, Falmouth and many others had their fair share of Chinese groceries, restaurants, rum bars, dry-goods and hardware stores. As these one-main-street towns grew in size and population, so did the Chinese entrepreneur in tandem with that progress.

Here are some of the firms that were located in Chinatown – Lee Tung Kee, Tack Sing, Tung On Tong, Man Chun Tong, Tai Sang Tong, Wong Pow Hong, Henn Shin Min Tai, Nuke Chong Co., Henn Fah Co., Yuen Hing Fah Sang, Chin Yee & Co., Chin Yee's Travel Service. Lowe Shue San Co., Royal Cremo Ice Cream Co., Diamond Mineral Water Co., United Grocery, John R. Wong, Hubert & Harold Chen Co., Lyew Quee Onn., Cyril Ying Co., Wong Chew Onn Co., Joe Wong, O'So Grape Co., Lue Fook Barbers, Chung Yin Restaurant, Fook Chong Restaurant, Cathay Restaurant, Wing Shing Restaurant, Golden Bowl Restaurant, International Restaurant, Hong Kong Restaurant, Dudley Hosang Co., Shing Aha, Get For Co., Tai Tung, Yap Man Fung, Kong's Commercial Agency, Fah Shing Co. All these were traders and merchants dealing in a great variety of products, mainly food provisions and some commission agency operation, importers of Chinese goods from the Far East. Mostly on Mondays, the country shopkeepers would converge on Chinatown merchants to replenish their stocks. There were times when these shopkeepers would take a shot at 'Pai-Q',* a Chinese game that is played with numbered tiles – much like Dominoes – at Lee Tung Kee, to see if lady luck would smile on them. Many returned home with neither stocks nor cash!

CHINESE ORGANIZATIONS IN THE NEW SOCIETY

The earliest Chinese organization – The Chinese Benevolent Society (later changed to Association) – was established in 1891. The objective of the CBA was to look after the affairs of Chinese nationals. Any problems affecting its members were addressed, whether these were of a governmental nature or problems of robbery and attacks on Chinese by the local people. The appearance of a unified organization like the CBA carried much weight in the forum of Government and in the courts of the land.

Many of the aforementioned organizations were controlled, funded and operated by the Chinese Benevolent Association (CBA).

The Nationalist Government of China began the process of establishing consular service overseas to protect their nationals after the revolution which overthrew the Manchu Government in 1911.

List of Organizations

Chinese Old Folks Home	Established by CBA	1877
Chinese Freemason Society (Chee Gung Tong)	Established in	1887
Chinese Benevolent Society	Established in	1891
Chinese Benevolent Society's Kuan Kung Temple	Established by CBA	1897
Chinese Cemetery	Established by CBA	1904
Sin Min Association	Established by New Citizen	1904
Yi Yee Tong	Established by Group of Chinese	1905
Chinese SANITARIUM	Established by CBA	1922
Chinese Public School	Established by CBA	1928
Chinese Public News	Established by CBA and Albert Chang	1930
Chinese Athletic Club	Established by Local Born Chinese	1937
Wholesalers' Association	Established by Members of the Trade	1938
Bakers' Association	Established by Bakery Owners	1938
Pagoda Magazine	Established by Charles Chang	1940
Jamaica Branch Chinese Aviation Construction Association	Established	1942
Chinese Retailers' Association	Established by Retailer merchants	1942
Chinese Consulate in Jamaica	Established in	1943
Chung San News	Established by Kou Min Tang group	1952
Soda Fountain & Restaurant Association	Established by Members of the Trade	1953

THE CHINESE OLD FOLKS HOME established by the CBA in 1877, provided refuge for destitute Chinese who could no longer support themselves and who were without any family support. CBA purchased four or five properties in the old Chinatown area over a number of years with donations from members of the community. Some of these properties were used to house destitute persons. The accommodation was minimal. It was the custom to collect donated food from nearby grocery merchants for the inmates and each occupant was also given a stipend of 10 shillings per week by CBA.

CHINESE FREEMASON SOCIETY – CHEE GUNG TONG. This is one of the many secret societies (Tongs) whose origin stretches back to 1644, the time of the Ching Dynasty in Chinese history. The Fung Munn Movement – the original name of the Tong – was founded to protect its members from social upheavals and banditry during the Ching Dynasty. The Jamaican Branch, founded in 1887, celebrated its 100th Anniversary in 1987 with a gala function attended by Government ministers, and many dignitaries from China.

Chinese Publications: *Chinese Public News*, published twice per week. *Min Chi Weekly, Chung San News,* twice per week, and the *Pagoda Magazine,* a fortnightly English news magazine.

Mr. Albert Chang saw the need for a newspaper to keep the community informed, especially those compatriots who couldn't read the local newspapers and were cut off from the outside world because they lived in the remote parts of the island. So he went abroad, bought a complete set of equipment, recruited a technician from Cuba and started publication in 1930. Mr. Lee Tom Yin was the first editor. The paper was first known as *The Chinese Commercial News,* and later changed its name to the *Chinese Public News* when Lee Tom Yin and Lewis Chang bought out the business from Albert Chang. The newspaper was subsequently sold to the CBA, which continued its operation until 1956. Falling advertisement revenue, along with reduced numbers of subscribers, were the reasons for the closure. In 1947, three of us Chinese Public School graduates, Wallace Nam, Byron Kong and myself, joined the *Public News* as compositors. The editor was Mr. Chang Hon Gin, the manager,

The Chinese Commercial News

Mr. Winston Chen, and Ray's father, Samuel Chen in charge of finance. The paper contained local and international news. Local news was selected by Winston Chen from the *Daily Gleaner* and translated into Chinese for publication. International news came in the form of news clippings from Chinese newspapers like *The World Journal* based in New York, and would arrive by mail. Hong Kong was also a main source of news of the Far East and mainland China.

CHINESE BENEVOLENT SOCIETY'S KUAN KUNG TEMPLE. An interesting aspect of early Chinese society in Jamaica is the many customs and traditions the immigrants brought to this new land. The Hakkas – devout Confucian people with Taoist up-bringing and way of life brought with them the tradition of ancestor worship. From the earliest times of the Chinese Benevolent Society, the revered statue of the deity Kuan Kung – the patron saint of Hakka people – was enshrined in a temple created by the CBS for him in the CBA building on Barry Street in Kingston.

It was common practice in those early years for the China-born generation to visit the temple to pay homage to the deity Kuan Kung, as a sign of respect and devotion. The ceremonial visit involved the burning of incense followed by bowing three times in front of the Kuan Kung statue, and chanting of words symbolic of respect and

The CBA building at 129 Barry Street and on the third floor the Kuan Kung Temple.

obedience to the ancestors. The employment of the joss-stick by devotees seeking guidance from the deity was another common practice. The CBA temple was a busy place on Sundays and public holidays when families usually visited Kingston's Chinatown, and a visit to the temple was always a part of their activities.

THE CHINESE CEMETERY was established in 1904. A twelve acre property in the Waltham Park area of the city was purchased by Chin Lien Kao, Chang Shen and a few other generous business people, who donated the property to CBA for use as a cemetery. In 1937, a wall was built to enclose the property; a pavilion and a terraced area along with a monument were also built. The cemetery was used at "Gah- San"* in April of each year, for the

ceremonial function of blessing the graves. When I was a kid my father always took us for "Gah-San". I recall many families bringing food and placing it on the tombs of their loved ones for their spirits, as is practised in China. In more recent times, this practice has been discontinued. I believe they assumed the ceremonial whole roasted pig, laid out at the pavilion when the ceremony was performed, was enough for all the spirits to partake. What do they do with the roasted pig after the ceremony? In my days this was usually sent to the Old Folks

Home for the inmates to enjoy. Today, I am not sure how they dispose of it.

YI YEE TONG* was a short lived community organization founded in 1905 by Lyn Ah Woo, Albert Chang, Alexander Tai Ten Quee and other prominent members of the community, very much off the order of the CBA. This Tong came about because the CBA, at its earliest inception, was managed and controlled by one notorious Lyn Biang, who behaved like a mafia godfather, and engaged in unscrupulous dealings with the criminal elements. If one crossed his path during his reign, he would have his goons break a leg or two. He conducted gambling on the CBA premises, which made a lot of money for him. The members of CBA became disenchanted with Lyn Biang, so they formed the Yi Yee Tong as a competing organization to the CBA. After Lyn Biang died, the CBA was cleansed of his wrongdoing. At that time, Yi Yee Tong discontinued its operation, liquidated its assets, bought a property and donated it to the CBA. The CBA, over time, came to own many properties which appreciated handsomely in value, and provided much rental revenue for the CBA to carry out its numerous tasks and responsibilities in the community.

THE CHINESE SANITARIUM was established by the CBA in 1922. Its purpose was to accommodate members of the community who became ill, and who were not comfortable in a government hospital setting because of cultural and language differences. Other sick patients, from the rural parts of the island where medical attention was not always readily available, were also greatly assisted by the convenience of the SANITARIUM. My mother, who became ill with malaria, went to the SANITARIUM and died there a few weeks later.

THE CHINESE PUBLIC SCHOOL started its operation in the late 1920s on the CBA premises on Barry Street, and later moved to 3 North Street, when the student population outgrew the downtown space. Mr. Alexander Tai Ten Quee, successful merchant and industrialist, bought No. 5 North Street and donated this property to the CBA to be used as a girls' dormitory and headmaster's residence. From its inception, the school went through much change, with different teachers coming and going. It wasn't until 1940 when a new headmaster, Chen Kung Yee, took over the running of the school – he was a trained teacher who previously taught in South East Asia – that the school

Above: First graduation of the Chinese Public School. Dec. 1945. Headmaster Chen Kung Yee seated, students standing, L-R: Robert (Mackie) Lue, Byron Kong, Doris Chin Lenn, Vincent Lee, Ivy Lyew, Daniel Kong and Louis Lee.   Photo courtesy : Clive Chen.
Next: Class of 1940.

flourished with a student body of over 300 and a full complement of teachers. Mr. Chen's tenure, from 1940 to 1945, was the best period in the 30-odd year history of the school.

THE CHINESE ATHLETIC CLUB (CAC) was established in 1937 by the sons and daughters of the successful merchant class who were born in Jamaica. People like Horace Chang, (son of Albert Chang); Hubert Tai Ten

Quee (son of Alexander Tai Ten Quee); the Leahongs, Donald (7 times Jamaica singles tennis champion) and Bertie; the Chin Yees, Lennie, Cecil and Ferdie; the Ho Sangs, Headly and Lloyd; The Chang Brothers from Valentine - Purity Bakeries; James Chin and Brothers from Pow Hing Company and Lane Supermarket; the Chin-Loys from Cremo Ice Cream manufacturers. From that era of the '40s we can see where a new class of local born began to emerge in the community, from well-off families, many with university educations. The club was well appointed with facilities for football, tennis, badminton, billiards, cricket and basketball. It was first located on Deanery Road in the Vineyard Town area and was the venue for many weddings and social functions, including the first Miss Chinese-Jamaica Beauty Contest. In 1951, the club house was destroyed by Hurricane Charlie. Mr. Alexander Tai Ten Quee, then purchased 4 acres on Derrymore Road and donated it for a new CAC

At top: The Chinese Athletic Club, Molynes Road. Above: Hubert Tai Ten Quee and Horace Chang

club. A new sports complex was built and the CAC resumed its operation on this site.

THE PAGODA MAGAZINE was a fortnightly English news magazine which focused mainly on the local born Chinese and their activities. The magazine was established by Charles Chang in 1940. The breezy content was mostly social news of weddings, births and deaths, anniversaries and birthday celebrations, young adults graduating from overseas universities etc. Charles Chang was both publisher and editor until Thomas Ho-Lung took over the editorship. Ho Lung remained in the post until 1954, when he resigned, at which time Leslie R. Chin became the editor. Leslie did a great job, increasing the content to include editorial articles on matters of current events, be they social or of government policies, or even of economic matters affecting the country. After Leslie left *The Pagoda,* Eddie Young became the new owner and his brother Aubrey Young took over as editor.

THE CHINESE CONSULATE IN JAMAICA was established in 1943 and the first Consul General, Mr. Wong Chat Kong, a career diplomat with an M.A. degree from Oxford, was seconded to Jamaica from Mexico, accompanied by his Spanish wife and two young sons. A gentleman of short stature, about 5ft., he was fluent in Mandarin, English and Spanish and was well received and welcomed by the Chinese community. The CBA rented office space to house the consulate and even furnished the offices. An office building in the New Kingston area was later purchased with donations collected from the community. Consul General Wong visited the smaller Chinese communities all over the island, served the community well and was very much liked. However, the Consulate was closed in 1949 when the communists came to power. It was to be many years later, after Jamaica's Independence in 1962, that the People's Republic of China would establish their first Embassy in Kingston.

CHUNG SAN NEWS, a twice weekly publication, was organized by followers of the Kuo Min Tang political party, which was the official political arm of the Nationalist Chinese Government. This newspaper was to be the political propaganda medium of the Chang Kai Sheik government in Taiwan, which was fiercely anti-communist at the time.

The Min Chi weekly was organized by the Chee Kung Tong* (Chinese Freemason Society) to counter the *Chung San News,* as this group was very pro-communist and pro-Mao Tse Tong. Such was the Chinese political environment in Jamaica in the 1950s. This

created a rift in the community, and there was much political debate between the two newspapers.

The other Chinese organizations such as the Retailers Association, the Wholesale Merchants Association, the Bakers Association, and the Soda Fountains & Restaurants Association, were all commercial organizations created to look after the business interests of their members. There were many problems affecting commerce, such as quotas imposed by Government, price controls and import restrictions, price fixing by members of one group to deter unfair competition; labour and union problems affecting the bakery industry, the Shop Assistant Law, which restricted opening hours etc. I don't recall any organization for the aerated water (soft drink) industry. Chinese businessmen were also very active in this area of commerce: the Yap-Sams – Diamond Mineral Water Company, the Chin Yees – O-So Grape and Liquid Foods, the Shims Commercial Liquor Store. Their products were household names in Jamaica. The ice cream and frozen products manufacturing sector was dominated by the Chin Loys' Royal Cremo, Stephen Yap's Jamaica Ice Cream Industry, and many small operators making Popsicles for the trade. These were top quality products that captured the domestic market.

During the Second World War, because of import restrictions and a shortage of rice, many Chinese went into rice farming, and although they were able to grow the grain, many problems arose from unsuitable soil and water drainage problems which led to poor yields, and less than satisfactory quality. After the war ended, importation resumed and the rice farmers abandoned the industry.

If the Chinese were left to their own destiny, and without the assistance of Michael Manley's socialist policy and his *"seven flights daily to Miami"* diatribe, the contribution of Jamaican Chinese to Jamaica's development would have been even greater. The economic loss to the country of this vast pool of skill, talent and a well educated professional class is immeasurable. How many Lee-Chins, Hendricksons, and Ray Changs, might Michael Manley have driven from the island? No one knows. What we do know is that those who left, they and their children are today making enormous and valuable contributions to the societies in which they now live and work. And these countries are richer for their contributions.

Written by Hubert Lue and edited by Sonia Gordon Scott.

* See Glossary.

Photographs taken from
'The Chinese in Jamaica, First Edition 1957' ©Lee Tom Yin

Raymond Lodenquai
MAKING THE CONNECTION WITH THE
S.S. PRINZ ALEXANDER

I WAS DETERMINED to find out the facts of my family's history in Jamaica, so I went about asking my older cousins, who were from China, or other relatives who were sent back to live in the ancestral village named Nu Foo, in the district of Gun Lan, in Kwangtung Province, Southern China.

My two cousins who lived in China, Luo* Bit Fan & Luo Sui Fung, were very helpful. I was told that there were six Lo* brothers and the eldest had been sent to Jamaica as a youth. He came as an indentured worker and his name was *Lo Den Quai*.

The timing of the story corresponded with the voyage of the *SS Prinz Alexander* and, searching the ship's log, we found the name LoTing Quai, belonging to a young male passenger who arrived in Jamaica on board that ship. We believe that the name was misspelled by the recorder on arrival, like so many other Chinese names at the time.

These two pictures still hang in one of the houses in Niu Fu, Gon Lan built by the Lodenquai family. It shows the great grandparents of Raymond Lodenquai and many of the other Lowes (Luo, Lo) living today in Jamaica, Canada and USA. They had six sons and the eldest, Lodenquai went as a labourer to Jamaica on the Prinz Alexander in 1884. He helped four other brothers to come to Jamaica and today many of his relatives are surnamed Lodenquai.*

The story continues that he worked and paid for his freedom and then sent for two of his brothers, Lo Chong Quai and Lo Min Quai. At a later date, they put their resources together and brought two more of their brothers, Lo Shu Leong and Lo Shu Bin, my grandfather, to Jamaica. One brother, Lo Shu On, stayed back in the home village of Nu Foo.

At one point in time, the laws of Jamaica would not permit wives to join their Chinese husbands, so Lo Den Quai (the first to arrive), returned to his wife in China. Their children later migrated to Scotland.

My connection to this group is that my grandfather is a brother of Lo Den Quai.

ANSWERS FROM THE PAST

As young adults we often wondered how our parents started out in such rural areas of the country. My assumption is taken from the documents presented and from tales that my great-grand uncle told when I was a boy.

Luo Shue Bin   Mary Chung

Egbert Lodenquai   Lily Chong

Raymond Lodenquai Beverley Chin

Lauren Lodenquai   Megan Lodenquai

Above, members of the Lodenquai family. At top Raymond Lodenquai's grand parents, followed by his parents then Raymond and his wife and two of his daughters at bottom.

Documents from the National Archives in Spanish Town show that the *S.S.Prinz Alexander* was commissioned to take passengers to Jamaica. On arrival they were dispatched island wide. The documents list the estates they were destined for. Estates such as Amity Hall in St. Thomas, Orange Hall in Portland, Gray's Inn in St. Mary and Lenox in Westmoreland. There were no proper roads then. Those who were destined for estates in the western part of the island were sent by boats, either to the town of Black River or Savannah-la-mar, and then to the various estates in those parishes.

My immediate family were in the district bordering the parishes of St. Elizabeth and Westmoreland, namely New Market and Hopeton.

I recalled my great-grand-uncle, Lo Shu Leong, telling me how difficult it was at the start of opening a shop in New Market. He had to take a horse or mule cart all the way from St. Elizabeth to Kingston to buy those huge barrels of salt fish, and it took them several days to travel both ways.

Looking back, I am sure they did not do a feasibility study or market survey to determine if these were the right places in which to build a shop. It must have been a very important reason for them to have decided to remain in these areas.

I feel that they decided to stay on whichever estate or plantation they were first placed, and it became a starting point in that they knew others in the surrounding districts and may have started small trading while they were still working on the estates.

Now, as I view the information from the Log, I realize that most of the cluster of Chinese businesses were around these estates. The estate closest to my family in New Market was Dillon Big Woods.

Written by Ray Lodenquai and edited by Sonia Gordon Scott.

Charles Chong-Young
A JOURNEY OF 23,000 KM

IT IS DAWN ON May 17, 1932. Kong Sook Yin (left) sets out from Yu Gam Boo for the train station, a 3 mile walk down the dusty roads. She is carrying two cloth bags and she cries all the way to the train station.

Grandmother was crying too when she left. She had been crying for days. For seven years, Sook Yin had been her constant companion. She had depended on Sook Yin even more in the past two years as blindness set in. Now 16 years old, her youngest granddaughter is beginning her journey to start a new life in Jamaica.

On the eight hour train ride to Canton, Sook Yin consoles herself with her grandmother's advice. Go to Jamaica. Life in China is too hard. You will have a better life there. Grandma spoke about the warring between the Nationalists and the Communists, and four months earlier, just before Sook Yin's 16th birthday, the Japanese had attacked Shanghai.

On arrival in Hong Kong, she goes straight to the shipping company to

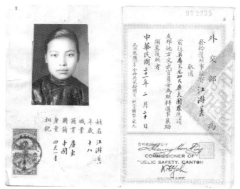

Kong Sook Yin betrothal certificate and passport showing her age as 18 when in fact she was only 16.

present her documents. Her passport and betrothal certificate are in order – born February 4, 1914, authorized to emigrate to join her fiancé. She has rehearsed her birth date should she be asked. She knows that grandmother had submitted a false birth document showing 1914. That made Sook Yin 18 years old, eligible for a passport and emigration to marry.

Sook Yin stays for two nights at a hostel run by the shipping company. The first day, she is taken by a servant boy to buy a few articles of clothing, a blanket, and a suitcase. The money she saved from weaving baskets and embroidering wedding slippers came in handy. She needs to be presentable to her new family.

The night before the ship sets sail, Sook Yin reads her father's letter again. Her brother had come to take her place with grandmother and had brought the letter with him. Father tells her how to behave and show respect for her new family. He wants her to serve them well. He says her mother has been crying all day – she will never see her youngest daughter again. It will take too long and cost too much to make the 2,400 km trip from Malaysia to Yu Gam Boo to see her before she leaves.

Sook Yin thinks of her father and mother whom she last saw 4 years ago when they visited from Malaysia. It was then that her father sent her to school for the first time. She loved school. She will miss going to school.

Ship No. 2 (there were four ships, Nos. 1-4) set sail the next morning for the first leg of the trip – 2,800 km to Japan. When the ship reaches Japan, it does not go into port but stays out in the harbour, and all passengers are taken in boats to a building on the dock.

They are told to hand over their clothes and take a shower. The passengers are terrified of the yellow water. Sook Yin takes the gown provided and wets it with the yellow water. The guards think she has taken a shower. After a few hours, her clothes are returned with a funny odour. She would learn later that the yellow colour and the odour were due to sulphur. A passenger had died on board and the Japanese were disinfecting everyone before Japanese passengers boarded.

The second leg of the trip is 6,200 km to Hawaii. Sook Yin is looking forward to seeing Hawaii. Her grandfather had died there. Grandmother told her the story of her grandfather going there to work and sending money home for her. She had been pregnant with Sook Yin's father at the time. Then the money stopped coming. A few months later, a villager returning from Hawaii came to see her. Her husband had died and she never remarried.

San Francisco is foggy when the ship docks as she says goodbye to her bunk mate of the past 17 days at sea. She thanks the old American couple who had taken her to the upper decks of the ship many times and shown her around. It was so much nicer than the dormitory in the lower deck where she could hear the engine throbbing all the time. Sometimes it was better to hear that than some of the passengers being seasick. The food had been so strange, especially the 'raw' eggs.

It isn't difficult to get to the train – just follow the crowd. A number of other passengers are on their way to Jamaica as well. It is hard carrying the suitcase and the bags of food. The shipping company had advised her to buy rice and dried and canned food in Hong Kong for the train trip to Montreal.

The very first day, two older men in the same coach approached her: "What do you have?" She turns over her food to them and they cook for her for the entire trip. Meals are not regular – the whole coach shares one 2-burner stove and you had to wait your turn. There seemed to be cooking going on 24 hours per day. Sleeping is okay, once you figure out how to deal with the thick seam in the middle of the pullout bed.

The train stops only to let off and take on passengers. At some stops, food vendors are on the platform selling dried goods and vegetables. There is no fresh meat. But, it doesn't matter – the two older men are good cooks!

On day five, 5,000 km later, the train pulls into Montreal. Carrying her suitcase is a little easier now since there is no food to carry. She goes with a group of others to a warehouse where they will spend the night; It is cold, but she has her blanket. The next morning, they walk a distance to the dock where the ship is waiting to take her to Jamaica. It is a much smaller ship than the last one. It makes one stop (probably Halifax) before many days at sea.

The ship stops in Cuba and Sook Yin sees a black person for the first time. She and other passengers are puzzled by this, but others laugh at them – they will be seeing many more!

The sea is calm in the early dawn as the ship slips quietly into Kingston Harbour. It has been 32 days since she left Yu Gam Boo. The approach to Jamaica had been announced the night before and Sook Yin slept fitfully, fearful of the next day but weary from her travels. As she descends to the dock, she keeps her eyes down with anxious glances into the waiting crowd.

She is approached by two men, one of whom she recognizes as Kenneth Chong Sow Gen, her future husband. Kenneth's brother drives her to the family she will stay with until the wedding day, and explains that her name will be Annie Young. Without the distraction of travel, she becomes terribly homesick. The wedding was to have been in a few weeks but it is postponed a few months because Kenneth is sick.

On the morning of September 18, 1932 Kenneth's aunt arrives to help her dress. Kenneth's brother takes her to Holy Trinity Cathedral where Father Fox is waiting at the altar with Kenneth. Annie walks slowly down the aisle to start her new life, completing the last 30 metres of her 23,000 km journey.

Annie Young's wedding to Kenneth Chong Sow Gen.

Annie's honeymoon is brief – a drive around the city in Uncle Freddie's motorcar. Herself and her husband, Kenneth, are returned to the United Saloon at Beckford St. and Luke Lane. The rooms above the bar would be Annie's home for the next 25 years.

The first year Annie is terribly homesick and frequently in tears. In this foreign land – which, compared to her local village, is as night to day – she thinks constantly of the life she left behind. It had been a hard life; her family had left her with her grandmother and aunt when she was nine years old. Between cooking and cleaning, there had been straw to collect and prepare, hats and baskets to weave, thread to hand-roll and dye, slippers to mark and embroider.

When her father visited 3 years later, he observed that Annie did not stand straight. Three years of weaving on the ground had caused a permanent stoop. He cut down on the weaving by sending her to school for the first time. Annie had loved school.

Annie Young with her first son and daughter.

In her new life, Annie is expecting her first child within the year. She has been working 6 days per week in the bar and, by the time the child is due, she has saved £5 from her work allowance. She sends it to her grandmother with a long letter full of stories about her new life in Jamaica.

Delivery of her first child is a near-death experience. After 24 hours of labour in her bedroom above the bar, and with the help of a midwife, Annie bears the first of her three sons. By the end of that same year, 1935, Annie is expecting again. This time, the first of her three daughters is born. The other four children arrive between 1941 and 1949.

With a nursemaid to help with the two toddlers and a growing command of the Jamaican dialect, Annie settles into a routine of working, cooking, and mothering. There is the food market up the lane, the craft market down the street, and the park in Parade square. Her favourite activity is to catch 'mudfish' at the docks for dinner. She enjoys the little outings.

In 1938, Annie has a vivid dream of her father hugging her mother in bed. Shortly after, she receives word from a traveller that her mother had died of a stroke. She is inconsolable.

Soon after the war starts in 1939, goods become scarce. The Chinese shopkeeper next to the United Saloon decides to shut down. Annie has been frustrated with her husband's poor business habits, and sees an opportunity.

There isn't much available to sell, but Annie takes over the shop with no name (there was no shop sign). The days are busy selling 3 pence or a shilling's worth of groceries, and the nights are busy weighing and wrapping small amounts of flour, cornmeal, sugar, and coarse salt in scrap newsprint paper. The persistent knocking of customers on Sundays when the shop is closed turns the business into a seven day per week operation.

For the next 15 years, Annie proves her mettle. The tiny shop on Luke Lane is a hive of activity. It offers hot saltfish fritters and hardough bread for breakfast, fresh cornbread and butter for lunch, and cold sardines and bully beef for dinner. On Saturday mornings, the market women crowd the shop to get their groceries for the bus ride back to the country.

By the mid 1950's Annie is an established Jamaican Chinese woman. After 20 years of serving customers, raising a family, and mingling with the growing Chinese community, she has overcome language barriers and emotional burdens and has become a feisty "Miss Chin", the shopkeeper. She travels out of Jamaica for the first time and visits her family in Kuala Lumpur, Malaysia. In light of the hardships that would arise after that time, including the death of her husband in 1973, these would be Annie's golden years.

Written by Charles Chong-Young and edited by Sonia Gordon Scott.

Down Memory Lane

Passport issued by the Chinese Government to local born Chinese Jamaicans for travelling to China.

Passport courtesy of Kathleen (Kay) Chin .

Easton Lee
MATCHMAKER'S HAND IN MARRIAGE

MATCHMAKING WAS STILL in vogue up to the 1940s and '50s, and my father was apparently an expert matchmaker. I can identify a couple of prominent individuals today who are a product of his efforts.

My father (right) was born in Guangdong, China as Lee Sen Fah. In Jamaica he became Henry Lee. Papa died young, so I really only recall one match he made in any detail. We were living in rural St. Elizabeth, and there was this fellow who lived about 12 miles down the road from us; my father's friend. They met once a month over mahjong with other friends – I think they gathered the last Sunday of each month. All men, you know?

Anyway, this fellow had a very prosperous business going, so one Sunday, my father and his group of friends were playing mahjong and bantering, when the argument got around to marriage and women. The married ones turned to the fellow and said it was time for him to marry. He turned to my father and said, *'then find me a wife'.*

Now at the time my father had this other friend with two very pretty daughters. They lived some 15 miles *up* the road from us so we were sort of in the middle. One Sunday morning at half past five, my father tells me, *'don' go church today. I wan' you go somewheh wid me'.* The 'somewhere' was to the friend with the daughters. The bachelor friend picked us up in his car, and we headed to the house. On that day, over a generous meal and light conversation, he met the daughter, gave her a ring, and began the association. They also discussed arrangements for her to stay with another Chinese family near to him. That was for the trial period, as was the custom and they married soon after.

My father always thought that every young girl and boy should marry. He felt that marriage, family and children were where you should put your energies. Well since matchmakers couldn't match their own children, my father didn't quite have his way when it came to his daughters.

I remember when my eldest sister reached 20, then considered almost late for a girl to marry… and incidentally, there is a custom in parts of China that says if a girl has had three consecutive periods without problems, then she can marry because, for the Chinese, that *is* the reason for marrying. Child bearing.

Anyway, someone was attempting to match Violet with a gentleman who lived in Portland. He was from China and had just come to Jamaica two years previously. So she was sent from our house to his. During that time they lived together in separate rooms, the purpose again being to test their compatibility. He was the younger brother of two, and lived with his brother, his brother's wife and children. But after a few weeks, Violet returned. Her description of the trial period made it clear. There would be no union.

Well my father was extremely annoyed, because they were supposed to have been well off. They had a big wholesale shop and lived upstairs, which was a thing of course. Needless to say for months the old man didn't speak to her. The same fellow eventually married a Jamaican girl. Today, one of their sons is a prominent doctor.

As for my own parents, they were a good example of a compatible mixed marriage. Mama was a 'red' St. Elizabeth lady. Whenever she and my father had a quarrel, you heard them mumbling. But not shouting. Then afterwards he'd say, *"yuh madda is a haad woman, you know"*. That was his way of trying to get my sympathy, being the only son and all. He'd do the same to the sister that I followed, Gloria. He complained to her because she was the intelligent, wise one. But my mother never quarrelled with him for us to hear. You heard voices, but never the arguments.

Easton Lee's mom.

Of course, the old man had his own plans for me. I was promised to a wealthy girl in Hong Kong, whose family needed her to marry someone proficient in English. The plan was that I would go to Hong Kong, meet her, enroll in university in mainland China, and eventually marry. But by then it was 1947 or so, and my cousins Noel, Dudley and Lucien had just returned from China. The Revolution hadn't yet happened, but the turmoil was building and my mother was dead set against it.

She said no way was her one boy child going anywhere. The whole ordeal even drove her to cigarettes. To make matters worse, she had also heard a few stories of Chinese stepmothers dishing out bad treatment to mixed kids like me. My father's first wife was still in his house in China. In the end, my mother put her foot down and convinced him to let me stay. Shortly after that came his illness, the Revolution, and all the horror stories about communism.

I'd say my parents had a good marriage. They respected each other. If she was talking to us about him, she'd say 'your father'. To a stranger, she'd refer to him as 'Mr. Lee'. If my father was speaking to us about her, he'd say 'mama'. To a stranger, 'mi wife' or 'mi lau po'*. They focused on common ground. Didn't dwell on differences. For instance, my Buddhist father was very supportive of our Christianity. He found that it taught many of the same principles as did the Buddhists, old Taoists and Confucians. He was quite steeped in the ways of the Tao – the old ethics. I remember once trying to memorize a bible verse. The one that says, *there's a time under the sun for everything...a time to be born, a time to die....* So there I am memorizing out loud, when he comes in. *"Wheh you geh tha' from?"* And he goes to his

Chinese book, finds a similar verse, and translates it. Different words, of course, but same thought. So I wondered aloud which came first. To which he replies, *'No matta! Is de truth!'* He was very forthright.

My mother was no docile wife either. She stood up for her rights. As parents they were usually united in our upbringing. If mama scolded us, we couldn't go to our father, or vice versa. In fact, they defended each other. She'd say, *'Your father would be very vexed with you.'* And he'd say, *'you make yuh madda cry.'*

When it came to marriage, my father did try to influence my sisters' choice of husbands, but without success. Mama had her say too. She maintained that respectability was what we were into. She often said that when she met my father, she didn't love him, but eventually grew to. To her daughters she'd say, *'maybe at the start you don't love him, but it can still work.'* That said, when my sister returned from Portland after her trial period, mama defended her decision to my father. *'It's her choice,'* she argued. *'You can't force someone to love you.'* But on another occasion she stepped in with another sister of mine, saying, *'Nuh nuh! Not that one!'* I guess she didn't like the guy. As for me, I ended up choosing my own bride, Jean, with whom my father was most pleased. He knew her family well and approved.

So matchmaking worked for the times. It had merit. The Chinese are very, very strong on family. Some cultures say *it's the person you're marrying, not the family*. But that is wrong. You do marry into a family… The very last Chinese marriage I know of to be arranged was my sister-in-law's. And that took place in 1971.

I can just see my father's face now, if he knew there was no more matchmaking. Oh he'd rue the fact that we're not adhering to the old traditions!

Written and edited by Alex Lee as told by Easton Lee.

* See Glossary

Blanche Lodenquai
GETTING MARRIED THE CHINESE WAY

LYN SUE FUNG is her Chinese name and she remembers making notes everyday in her diary during the time she was growing up in Hong Kong. Getting married never entered her mind as she was still going to school, and there was still enough time before her parents chose a husband for her. This was the custom at that time in China.

Her dad was born in China in the village of *Lee Lum* in *Bow Onn* district in *Guangdong* province, while her mother was from the city of Hong Kong. After they were married, her mother did not like the life in the village, so she persuaded Lyn Sue's dad to live and work in Hong Kong where she felt more at home. Lyn Sue Fung was born in Hong Kong, a city girl.

She remembers her annual visit to her grandparents in China in the summer and how, at the age of eight or nine, her father built a house on a property that he'd bought in the old city of *Can jun* (also called *Chim Jun* which is located on the border of the New Territories), near *Sen Sang*. They moved in after completion, and she later enrolled in a school in the city.

Lyn Sue Fung was among the few women who, at that time, were fortunate to have gone on to college and university. Perhaps it was because her mother, being from the city, knew the value of having an education and wanted her daughter to go on to higher learning.

While she was still in university, she accompanied her mother to the wedding of one of her cousins. The groom was from her mother's family while the bride was a Lodenquai. It was here that Lyn Sue met a young man, a cousin of the bride, Wilfred Lodenquai, who attended another university. Unknown to her, he approached her mother telling her of his younger brother, Felix, who was living in Jamaica, and who had requested that Wilfred find him a wife. Would she consider a match between her daughter and his brother?

Wilfred and Felix were born in Jamaica and they were among many who were sent to China "to learn the culture." Because of the war with Japan, Felix returned to Jamaica before finishing high school.

It was to be months of exchanging letters and photos between the two families before a mutual understanding was arrived at. Soon after, Lyn Sue Fung was on her way to a far off land, never to return to the land of her birth.

She travelled on a Canadian Pacific ship to Vancouver, Canada, then by train to New York City. The last leg of the journey was on a banana boat which arrived in Kingston, Jamaica, in October 1939.

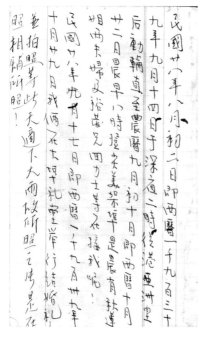

民國廿八年八月初二日即西曆一千九百三十
九年九月十四日于深夜二時在香港乘坐
后勤輪直至農曆九月初十日即西曆十月
廿二日晨早八時提岸美茱埠是有諸親
姐兩夫婦及諸甚兄四力士夫在接我呢…
民國廿八年九月十七日即西曆一千九百廿九年
十月廿九日我倆在大厚礼拜行結婚礼
重拍照幸此
照相舖所照！
無拍照蓋是在
天通不大而攸所照之事是在

From a page in her note book (left) where she recorded details of her journey, from the time of her departure from Hong Kong to the time she arrived in Jamaica, she wrote:

- Left Hong Kong on 14th September 1939 at midnight on Canadian Pacific vessel bound for Vancouver.
- Landed 22nd October at Victoria Pier (Kingston) at 8 a.m.
- Met at pier by Mr. and Mrs. Willie Lyn Ah Woo, Gilmore and Felix Lodenquai.
- Married 19th October 1939 in Kingston Parish Church.
- Travelled to Lluidas Vale for reception.

Being a city girl, she was not impressed with Jamaica. Compared to the modern buildings and cars of Hong Kong, Jamaica was a backwater, filled with old buildings and horse drawn carriages. She did not like Jamaica.

These feelings were soon put aside as this was not the purpose of her journey. She first stayed with her cousin, Lyn Ah Woo. It was the kindness extended by himself and his wife that made her feel at home. Their every effort to comfort her was appreciated as preparations for her wedding day went ahead.

One morning, a week after her arrival, Willie Lyn Ah Woo walked her down the aisle of Kingston Parish Church and gave her away. This was only the second time she'd met her husband, Felix, since their first meeting at Victoria Pier.

The ceremony was originally planned for the afternoon, but she and another bride arranged to switch their times. The wedding party had a long journey before them as they headed for home right after the ceremony … all the way to Lluidas Vale in Clarendon… to a small reception with family and friends.

According to *Blanche* (her given English name) it was a rainy day so the wedding pictures were taken at the photographer's studio, Morris' Studio.

The Lodenquai's business was located in Lluidas Vale, Clarendon, just south of Worthy Park. Worthy Park, if you remember, was the name of an estate where some of the passengers from the *S.S. Prinz Alexander* were sent. It was here that she was introduced to the Jamaican way of life. Everything was new to her.

Blanche and Felix wedding portrait.

Like so many other girls who came to Jamaica to marry, their culture did not allow personal feelings to come into play. Blanche missed her mother and

China very much. She was homesick. All that had to be put aside after the children were born, as the task of being a shopkeeper's wife and a mother was overwhelming. She had very little time for herself.

The business in Lluidas Vale consisted of many sections. There was a dry goods section, hardware, a grocery shop and a rum bar. It was growing quite rapidly and so were the families that operated the business. They were running out of living space.

Blanche was a gifted musician who could play quite a number of instruments. The harmonica (mouth organ) and the banjo were her favourites. Occasionally, while she was in Lluidas Vale, she would get together with members of another Chinese family who owned another shop in the village and, in today's language, "they would rap". She enjoyed doing this.

Blanche's father had earlier immigrated to Jamaica when she was six years old and he first opened a shop in Chapelton, Clarendon. He returned to China for a time but returned to Jamaica before any wedding plans were arranged. He opened his second shop in Spaulding, Manchester, and passed away shortly after he opened the second shop.

It was at the suggestion of his *Jah-Gung** that Blanche's mother came to Jamaica to help with the children. The little Chinese that her son Peter remembers comes from the days when his *Jah-Po** taught them the language.

Blanche was tutored in English by a special teacher who taught at the school in the area. She remembers attending classes with many small children.

After ten years in Lluidas Vale, she and Felix ventured out and started their own business in the city of Kingston. Windward Road was to be their home for the next 25 years.

Her sons, John and Peter, went to Holy Rosary Prep. School and then on to St. George's College, while her daughter Jean went to Alpha Prep, and then to Alpha Academy.

Kingston was so different from life in the country. There were more cousins and other Chinese families to visit, and there was the Annual Chinese Garden Party at the Chinese school on North Street. Jung San Beach was close by where Chinese Garden Parties would sometimes be held. Then there was Chinatown, where the language was openly spoken and the shops were filled with goodies from the Orient. It was a good time for Blanche.

She can read her bible and her missal and she says that she has no desire to return to China. Blanche and Felix are now retired and Jamaica is now her home.

Above: Lodenquai's family portrait, l-r John, Jah po, Peter, Blanche, Felix and Jean.

Written on behalf of Blanche Lodenquai and edited by Sonia Gordon Scott.
* See Glossary

Joan Moses (née Lee)
FROM A RIVER IN CHINA

THERE'S A LITTLE STORY that we like to tell in my family. It goes something like this. *One day in a small village in southern China, a young man sees a grief stricken girl trying to drown her newborn infant in a nearby river. Without thinking, he jumps into the deep water and rescues the crying baby girl. Many years later, that baby becomes his wife.*

The story is a favourite because the hero and rescue victim are my maternal grandparents.

That young mother by the river, my great-grandmother, my Japo-tai*, would eventually come to live in Haining, St. Thomas with my grandparents, who owned one of the only two shops in the tiny village. I was still a little girl when old age and retirement brought the three to live with me and my family in Port Antonio. That changed our family dynamics somewhat. My grandfather, to put it mildly, didn't like his mother-in-law. Maybe he hadn't forgiven her for that day at the river. Maybe it was just a personality difference. No one ever asked. All we knew is that the two rarely exchanged a kind word. Not that we understood what was said between them since Japo-tai spoke absolutely no English. But their two modes of communication – stony silence or venomous rage – made clear to the rest of us the state of their relationship. Well it only worsened when my grandmother died. She had been Japo-tai's only true companion. With her gone, Japo-tai's only link with the rest of the world was her son-in-law. But he refused to translate. My mother (right) struggled with her minimal Hakka* to help out.

Ironically, it was the language barrier that drew me to my Japo-tai. I think it made me observe her more. For instance, every day, sometimes even twice per day, I'd watch as she carefully pulled out an old trunk from under her bed and remove treasures of jewellery and other small objects. Each was wrapped in some kind of wrinkled tissue that she'd tenderly open. Then she'd slowly run her fingers over each item, sometimes smiling, sometimes staring blankly. She'd be just as careful when returning each item to its original place in the old container. My mother would eventually tell me that Japo-tai had left everything behind in China. Everything but what lay in that trunk. But there was more. Japo-tai had apparently once been a second wife in China. Her husband had deserted her after she gave birth to a daughter, and fled to the mountains. She and her baby fought to stay alive on the meagre wages she earned mining fool's gold from sun-up to sundown. The day grandfather found her at the river was the day she had scraped her last ounce of hope.

Grand-mother

There was one particular pair of gold earrings Japo-tai wore more than any other. They were so heavy that her ears were almost torn from the weight. I had always wanted to ask her what sentiment they held. Maybe the babies in our house knew her secrets. They were the only ones in the house she spoke to until the day she passed away.

Grand-father

Grandfather, Harold Lue Tenn, survived his mother-in-law by a few years. He was also a curiosity for me. Never one for conversation, he'd relax in our front yard for hours in the lotus position, smoking his pipe and watching people go by. At other times he'd bury himself for days non-stop in some building project or other. But his resourcefulness didn't end with woodwork. That man could make a chicken go a long way. The meat he would use for food, the blood he would allow to gel and then put into soups later, and the feathers he would dry for pillows. Nothing was wasted.

Grandfather was tall for a Chinese man, and my siblings and I kept a respectable distance from him. We thought we had good reason to, given the colourful stories we'd all been raised on about his legendary temper. But as he was happiest when active, we accommodated his indulgence in his many projects, including the board slippers he made by hand. Not the most attractive in footwear, we all had to wear them. My siblings and I at first stopped at nothing to destroy the stubborn things. But it didn't matter. Grandfather would have a replacement pair waiting for us each and every time. I am convinced that he was secretly glad whenever we needed another pair.

Drinking was another favourite pastime of his. And Black Seal rum was his undisputed vice of choice. For grandfather this was a two-stage activity. In stage one he'd drink for three weeks straight. In stage two he'd eat like a horse, also for an amazing three weeks. It was always easy to know when grandfather had hit stage two. You'd be awakened in the middle of the night by a steady *chop-chop-chop* sound coming from the kitchen. And just like the drinking, he'd eat and cook non-stop until he declared himself satisfied.

One particular stage two will forever remain in our family's treasure trove of stories. At the time, my brother Tony, had a pet turtle that lived in the garden. I remember our parents warning Tony on several occasions to keep his turtle outside. But the water in the trough we had built for it was stagnant, so Tony often sneaked the little guy under the kitchen sink, where he could enjoy fresh running water and treats of lettuce and other vegetables. Well one night we heard grandpa chopping as usual, but this time with a bit more ah… vigour. We got up the next morning to find Tony in a quiet but frantic search for his turtle. Of course, we never found that turtle, nor did we ask grandpa about it. We didn't want to know. To this day the official story is that the turtle just wandered off.

Grandfather died quietly in his sleep in his late seventies. To this day I can't look at a turtle without breaking into a smile.

Written and edited by Alex Lee as told by Joan Moses.

* See Glossary

Down Memory Lane

Black River in St. Elizabeth
Photograph ©Ray Chen

Lillian Chen
MOTHER'S JOURNEY

PEOPLE REMEMBER my mother, Violet or Chun Lan, for her quick smile, her friendly manner, and her gentle, husky voice. She was very sociable, welcoming friends and relatives who dropped by to visit, or who stayed with us when they came to town from the countryside. As a young girl, I fell asleep to the chatter and laughter of women, as my mother and visiting aunts or cousins whiled away the late evening, my father retiring to another room for the duration. She also enjoyed seeing local relatives and friends at weddings or other functions. My mother enjoyed these visits as they were a welcome break in the routine of hard work that made up the life of my parents.

Six days a week, from seven to eleven: the life of a shopkeeper's family. Growing up, I observed certain things, and overheard fragments of conversations which made me wonder what circumstances had brought her to that life. For one thing, mom's calligraphy was beautifully consistent, elegant and well formed; and dad always deferred to her knowledge of calligraphy. I also knew that she missed her older brothers very much. From time to time, a package would arrive from 'abroad'. The contents of these packages would be given a place of honour in our home: two pairs of ivory chopsticks; a set of black and red lacquer bowls, tray and chopsticks from Asia; a bottle of French perfume which stayed forever in mom's top middle dresser drawer, never moved, never opened; a gold watch, rarely worn. I learned that these were gifts sent by her eldest brother, Uncle KC, from his various postings as a Taiwanese ambassador abroad, possibly Cambodia or Paris. These things seemed to have so little to do with our day-to-day life. Then there were the rumours of the matchmaker's mistake. The story goes that the matchmaker who arranged my parents' marriage approached the wrong family, and by the time the error was recognized, it was too late to be reversed. The difference it made was that my grandmother had intended the match to be made with a family of more comfortable means

1 Mom and Jah-Po* in the garden, taken when mom was leaving her family home.

than my father's family had. Consequently, the family story developed that mom's life was harder than Jah-Po had intended for her youngest child and only daughter.

My mother was the youngest of five children, and the only girl. Her father, who died shortly after she was born, had been a schoolteacher, and he died young. Jah-Po raised the children on her own, and was progressive for her time. She sent her eldest son (Uncle KC) to be educated in Paris; her second son (raised by her brother as his son) went to Tahiti; her third son stayed in China; and her fourth son went to Vietnam. She valued education for all her children, and when mom was married and moved to dad's family home, Jah-Po sent along a dowry of black lacquer and marble chairs and table; she also sent a personal attendant who would fulfill mom's share of work in the fields, so that mom could continue her education. Mom continued her studies, while dad taught elementary school.

My mother and father were nineteen and seventeen years old, respectively, when they were married in 1932. Two years later, they departed China with Ah-Gung (dad's father) bound for Jamaica. Mom never saw Jah-Po again.

Mom had a faded red double-breasted wool coat that hung on the far side of her wardrobe as long as I can remember. She explained it was what she wore against the chill on the deck of the ship that brought them to Jamaica. The most memorable part of the journey for her was the passage through the Panama Canal, the new engineering and architectural marvel that allowed waves of adventurers and migrant workers easier passage between Asia and the West Indies.

Dad had volunteered to take his bride to Jamaica (where he was born), to work to repay a family debt that Ah-Gung had incurred during a previous trip to Jamaica. Ah-Gung returned to China three years later, and the young couple

2 Mom, seated second from the right, with dad's family, after they were married.

stayed in Jamaica. With the debt repaid, they started to make their own life the best they could. They tried their hands at a number of occupations. Eventually they had two businesses simultaneously: Dad was a partner in a printery downtown, while mom ran the grocery store (with barely any English or patois) and raised the four boys and later on, me.

Running a grocery store in those days was far less profitable than it is today. The mark-up on staples such as milk, sugar, flour, salted fish, cornmeal, and cooking oil, which were the basic commodities, was strictly controlled by the government: inspectors were sent out to check that merchants were not overcharging. These inspectors sometimes demanded kickbacks or threatened to report shopkeepers who were trying to eke out a living on less than 10% mark-up. Imported 'luxury' goods such as canned peaches and pears, and apple juice were allowed a higher mark-up, but these items were rarely purchased. Dad used to say that if we used a tin of condensed milk from a case of forty-eight, we had already lost the profit. The Chinese Retailers Association was formed to confront the distributors and the government on price control. However, major changes in the pricing system would not occur until after the exodus of Chinese during the 1970s, when the majority of shops came under non-Chinese ownership, and the new owners demanded a change in pricing policy to allow greater profit.

The typical store in our parents' time was designed so that a counter separated the goods and shopkeeper from the customer. The rate of business depended on how many people were behind the counter, and how fast they moved. With the advent of the supermarket, shopkeepers were pressured into modernizing to attract customers. The more open plan meant more opportunities for shoplifting, which ate away at profits.

3 and 4   Mom and dad with "Big Roy and Little Roy" inside the shop

My brothers Ray and Washington both dropped out of school before they turned fourteen, to work with mom in the shop, to provide more hands and eyes. It is difficult to know how much profit was lost from customers and helpers helping themselves to goods, and from what dad lost at the mah jong tables in Chinatown, after the printery closed for the day. That was a world that we were not privy to, but it was a source of frustration while it lasted. Mom would put away a little at a time for the future, knowing that the profit would easily disappear or be turned back into the business.

Dad's partnership in the printery meant that he was away from the shop and home most of the time. His partner was his cousin, and the company was based on a combination of their names: Uncle Winston's name, Jen Hen Yee, and dad's name, Jen Hen Fen; hence Yee Fen. They printed invoice books for most of the Chinese businesses islandwide. They also printed the Chinese newspaper, *Jung San Bao*, at the premises on Princess Street. Dad sometimes took me to his workplace, where I was impressed by the large black printing press, the huge bales of newsprint, and cardstock, and the bins with many compartments that held the individual letters or Chinese characters that had to be assembled one by one to make up the typeset. Eventually dad sold his share in the printery to his partner, and returned to the family business. I believe this was a loss for him, of something he had enjoyed, but he never spoke of it.

Mom advocated for the wishes and desires of the boys, even in the face of dad's resistance. Dad had no interest in the automobile, content to take public transportation, or cabs when necessary. However, mom persuaded him that even if he were not interested, it was in Ray's interest to have a car. So she facilitated the purchase of the first family car. Even when it was totalled in an accident shortly after it was purchased, she again lobbied for another vehicle. When Washington expressed his wish to study dancing abroad, it was mom who encouraged him to find a way to do that, over dad's objections, and helped dad to come to terms with it. Just as her brothers had left their family home to pursue their careers, so also did her own children leave, one by one, to pursue education or careers in far away places. I watched my mother grieve the departure of each of my brothers while she hoped for a better future for them and, through them, for the family. I was the last to leave.

When asked what it was like to live in an arranged marriage, dad invariably responded by comparing it to the Western notion of romantic love. The western romance, he said, was like a firecracker, a big bang that was dramatic and finished quickly. On the other hand, the arranged marriage was like a pot of cold water put on the fire: it started out cold, and gradually grew warmer until eventually it reached a rolling boil.

My father's personal sacrifice in repaying his family's debt shaped his ideas and expectations for us, his children. The theme of filial piety was constantly emphasized through stories of family loyalty and duty and responsibility to family and relatives. Even with our scarce means, he continued to send support to family members who remained in China. When people wonder how my parents managed, under such demanding circumstances, to raise and educate five children, I acknowledge that it was through their extreme self-denial and through their lessons to us in perseverance, hard work, creativity and resourcefulness.

Throughout all those years, I never heard my mother complain. What I remember is her laughter as she told stories about going out with the boys when they were young, two on either side, holding hands; and stories of returning from a musical performance and the boys recreating the performance, taking curtain calls from behind sheets and blankets draped above their beds. She loved us wholeheartedly.

Mom always spoke Hakka, and spoke very little English or patois, relying on dad or us when necessary. I was sent to Chinese summer school when I was about seven or eight years old, and from then on was able to speak Hakka, although I never achieved full fluency. So in our household we somehow understood each other; I often wonder how much we each missed of what the other was saying. Mom had difficulty pronouncing certain syllables, not unlike other Chinese speakers. We would try to teach her to say 'purple' or 'pulp', but they were indistinguishable as she pronounced them both 'prrrp'. She was able to laugh at herself. Mom did not have formal English lessons until she came to Canada. When she and dad lived with him in New Westminster, B.C., Wellie registered mom in ESL (English as a Second Language) classes in Vancouver. She would take the bus by herself into Vancouver for her classes, which she enjoyed a great deal. She sent me pictures of herself, her instructor and classmates, some of them dressed in their ethnic garments. Many years later, when Wellie came to visit me in Vancouver, I drove him past the elementary school that my son, Sebastian, had attended for years. Wellie said, "I recognize that building; that's where mom attended her English classes." I researched it, and confirmed that the school had been a community school where ESL classes were offered at that time; and it eventually became a French Immersion school in our time. Well, Sebastian was tickled to know that his Grandma (who died long before he was born) and he went to the same school! As for me, it feels good to associate mom with that site which is near to where we live.

Written by ©Lillian Chen (with thanks to Roger's family tree) and edited by Sonia Gordon Scott.

5   *Samuel and Violet Chen.*

Photographs 1 and 2 Courtesy of Roger Chen
Photographs 3, 4, 5 ©Ray Chen.

Gloria Palomino (née - Lyn Ah Ping)
MY OTHER MOTHER

I WAS BORN one of seven children in Manchester, Jamaica, in a small town called Newport. My father, William Lyn Ah Ping, came from Guangdong, China, while my mother came from what was then known as Siam (today's Thailand). Her beauty was almost legendary. In fact, when my father brought his young bride to Jamaica, the Registrar of Births and Deaths in Manchester, Ethlyn Rudder, organized a small crowd to come and see her. Mrs. Rudder told me so herself.

Gloria Palomino's mom and dad.

Mom gave birth to me in the Great House we called home. It was one of those houses you can never forget, with its thick mahogany stairs, deep rooms, high ceilings, and generous wrap-around veranda that hugged the two-storey structure. But despite the relatively privileged lifestyle, my siblings and I were still expected to do our part in the family wholesale store. We served customers, ran the red credit book and delivered groceries to our customers, many of whom were English nationals seeking refuge in Manchester's near perfect climate. One of my godmothers was an English spinster, Miss Lettice King, who lived across from our shop on a tiny hill. She was tall and thin, always kept her hair in a perfect bun, wore her collar up to her neck, and ensured that each button on her long sleeves was properly fastened. A poet laureate of Jamaica, who wrote under the pen name Lena Kent, her weekly column in the *Jamaica Gleaner – "For the Thoughtful Reader" –* was quite popular then.

Gloria with three of her siblings.

Growing up, my siblings and I were shaped by the influences of several cultures. At home, mom cooked Thai and tended daily to her garden of cucumbers, *pakchoy*, snow peas, mustard and tomatoes, and always in long sleeves. Pale skin, of course, was a sign of nobility in China.

Whenever dad grew tired of Thai food, he had his turn in the kitchen and cooked Chinese. Our *nurses* cared for neither cuisine and cooked Jamaican for themselves. I used to sneak out sometimes to try their cooking – treats like *saltfish* and yellow yam, mackerel with onions, tomatoes and St. Vincent yam mashed together. I'd begin indulging at about 5 o'clock, one hour before the family's evening meal, but the pre-dinner snacking often got me into trouble with my mom for two reasons. She didn't want me depriving our nurses of their dinner and, secondly, I'd barely have room for my own. Our meals were eaten with chopsticks, accompanied by *cha* and soup. Soda was never an option.

We had cousins in Newport, more family in nearby Mandeville, Malvern and Black River, and we were a close-knit family. As the token Chinese at school, my siblings and I bore the brunt of the racial slurs being hurled at the Chinese in those days. The problem was that I was never one for the passive approach, and usually ended up in a fight. *'Go back to China,'* they'd shout, *'and wear your oil skin clothes!'* The 'oil skin clothes' were, in fact, silk, as Miss Lettice explained when I ran to her complaining one day. I'll never forget the morning a classmate began assaulting me with the ever-popular: *'Chiney nyam dog! We don't want you here!'* That fight had us rolling down the hill and into the pond, but it didn't end there. Later that day, my little brother got such a bad beating from his teacher, he became swollen and had to be taken home. My dad attempted to sue, but in those days no attorney would take such a case against a teacher. My anger turned into bitterness, even hatred, but over time, my resentment turned into tolerance, thanks to Miss Lettice. Her deep religious faith saw me through many such struggles. It was Miss Lettice, in fact, who shaped my spirituality. My mother would eventually convert to Christianity, while my father remained Buddhist.

My English godmother fascinated me and each day after school I'd rush home to do my homework with her. On Thursdays we'd have high tea in her well appointed and sprawling garden, where she'd teach me how to serve the traditional beverage amongst her pink crotons and other beautiful blooms. If I did it incorrectly, she'd knock me on the knuckles. She was a lady of simple elegance and I remember running up the hill to get her the day I finally got my own room. The first comment she made when she saw it was, *'Something is missing. Flowers,'* she decided, and promptly went to her house and arranged some flowers in a simple blue vase for my new room. Today, flowers are my passion because of her.

My mother also influenced me greatly. Never one to display anger or raise her voice, she was generous with her time, and often helped the older Chinese ladies from surrounding towns to read their letters from China, and replied on their behalf by writing letters in their native tongue. She did this with grace and discretion; *despite* the fact that she was not accepted by the very women she assisted. Her handicap, in their eyes, was that she was not from China. According to my uncle, her dad (my grandfather) would dress her as a boy so that she could attend school because only boys were eligible for school in those days. The secret was exposed on the day she fell after climbing a tree and first aid was being administered. She was expelled but was reinstated at her father's insistence.

There were instances where, on her occasional visit to Chinatown in Kingston, the merchants would make embarrassing remarks about her not being Chinese. Unknown to them, she understood what was said but she never let on by trying to defend herself. She simply continued quietly on her way.

Whenever she was invited to any gatherings she would always take a gift for the hostess, sitting quietly, sipping her *cha* amid the flying gossip, (a pastime second only to gambling for which the Chinese were notorious). My mother had forbidden both from entering her house.

I was still a little girl when tradition came knocking on our door in a significant way. The time had come for me and my older brother to go to China. Miss Lettice was not happy with our plans, and on the day I left Newport she handed me a package. In it was a bible, a hymn book, flannel pajamas and these instructions: *'If you get seasick on the boat,'* she said, *'I want you to go out on deck. Don't stay in your room, and no matter what, breathe deeply. I had to do this when I came to Jamaica on a boat too.'*

We arrived in Chinatown, Kingston, on a Monday to meet our ship. I'll never forget arriving at the dock and seeing a great number of children waiting, in a perfectly straight line, to board the mammoth vessel. Mingling among them was a group of older Chinese caretakers who were to accompany us on the long voyage. Some of the younger children were crying, while the older ones were laughing. In the general hubbub you could hear whispers of *'don't cry, don't cry'*. I remember hearing my own parents quietly telling us to take care of ourselves, and that we would be fine. My mother's tears were just below the surface when, all of a sudden, the ship's captain strode hastily on to the dock. *'Attention, attention!'* he shouted. *'We have just received news that war has broken out in China! We will not be sailing for China today!'* We turned around and headed back to Newport, my parents both relieved and sad. Once home, it was pure joy for Miss Lettice.

Years later, and even after I left for Alpha Academy (High School) in Kingston, Miss Lettice and I continued to write to each other. Now older, she embarked on a compilation of her father's sermons, most of which I typed for her. Our joint effort eventually became *The Book of Sermons* by Lettice King.

I was already a young married woman when she died in Newport in 1957. I remember dreaming the night before her death that I saw my dad, although by then he had already passed away. In my dream he and Miss Lettice were on our veranda at the Newport house. They were sitting in steam-bent rocking chairs with cane backs, rocking and talking when, suddenly, dad, and then Miss Lettice, fell through the floor.

At 8:00 a.m. the next morning, a car pulled up at my house with a message from Miss Julie, her housekeeper, to inform me that Miss Lettice was gone. I hurried to Newport and buried my godmother according to her strict written instructions. Mom would tell me later that morning that she had dreamt of flowers the night before. My own beloved mother would pass away in 1982.

I didn't know it then, but the multiple influences on my life were helping me to find my own unique culture. As for the two women who helped shaped me into the woman I am today, I live each day in their honour, as the product of their joint effort.

Written and edited by Alex Lee as told by Gloria Palomino.

Tony Wong
GOING HOME

SHENZHEN, China – Mother packed her solitary bag. She carefully placed a favourite blue cotton dress inside and snapped the metal clips shut.

After a sombre breakfast of rice and porridge, she gave her grandmother a lingering hug. Her hair still in pigtails, she headed off for the 7 km walk to the train station. As she battled the July heat and dust, she stopped beneath the stone entrance to the tiny village. A final look at the only world she had known for the last 20 years.

Lily Chin didn't know it then, but it would be another 46 years before she would return. Mother had been a little apprehensive when I told her of my early Christmas gift – a trip to the village where she was born.

The excuses started to flow. There was too much housework, she had to look after grandchildren. China seemed fantastically distant.

Home was now Markham, a quiet shopping mall in suburbia on the northern edge of Metropolitan Toronto. After building a life and business in Jamaica and retiring in Canada, this was an existence free from ambiguity, an orderly progression of raising children and grandchildren. Mulling over the past was a luxury for those with an abundance of time, a wasteful penchant for looking back, not forward.

The last time Mother had seen her village was in 1950, the year after the Communists had come to power under Chairman Mao Zedong. A civil war with the Kuomintang government of Chiang Kai-shek had ended, with the general forced to flee to Taiwan. Thousands of Chinese fled from southern China to Hong Kong and to exotic places with unpronounceable names. Like Jamaica.

But it seemed she had left just in time. One year later, the land that my grandfather had toiled to earn would be confiscated in a massive land reform programme. They were tough, and at times, unpleasant years of dissipated lives and untold hardship that lingered in the back of her mind like a dim haze, her memories sometimes jolted to the fore by a chance image, a tattered photograph, a reluctant remembrance of things past.

Over the next few weeks she seemed to relent, although her excuses betrayed her fears. Suppose you really can't go back home. Perhaps the village won't be the same as it used to be. Maybe no one will remember who I am, she would say.

In Jamaica there was no time for reflection. There were the five children to raise, the seven-day-a-week grocery store downstairs, the house upstairs. You never had to leave. Going to the beach was unheard of, especially for my father. Why would you? Waste of time, waste of money. Too hot, too many mosquitoes.

Jamaica was about survival. It would take another generation to appreciate the nuances. The years went by. The children, Evelyn, followed by Victor, Cherry, Jennifer and then myself, would all be enlisted to work in the shop. Being the youngest, I invoked privilege. Most days after school I would head to the shop, open a pack of Wah-mui and chase it down with a plantain tart. Sometimes I invoked too much privilege. One year Mother rushed me off to the doctor after I ate an entire bottle of orange-flavoured St. Joseph's baby aspirin. The year before that, intoxicated with the smell, I had tried to devour a bar of Lux soap.

The other siblings ended up in Chinese-grocery store hell. One day Victor refused to work. Bad move. Fortunately he had innate Hakka survival skills and promptly raced to the roof with my father in hot pursuit wielding a thick cowhide belt.

Mother was the moderating influence. The concept of leisure time was an alien one, but she pushed for the swimming lessons, the vacations that would lead to Disney World in Miami. There I discovered colour television and caramel-flavoured Cracker Jack.

The years went by and the government changed. Michael Manley was now prime minister and Fidel Castro suddenly loomed large in the Jamaican lexicon. After escaping the Marxist revolution of Mao, the Chinese middle-class started looking for options. Canada, a member of the Commonwealth opened its doors. This time leaving was easier.

In Markham, retirement did not come easy. Self-worth was determined by work. Thankfully, there were grandchildren to raise. The years passed, becoming decades.

The issue of China would come and go. The grandchildren were old enough to have their own children. Maybe it was time to pay a visit? Finally, the day arrived when there were no more excuses. Accompanied by an uncle who acted as our guide, we set out to seek the past.

Mother in China.

The road to Mother's hometown of Chun Len Ha is far less arduous a journey than it was almost five decades ago. Then, it took more than two weeks by train, foot and boat to reach North America. On the border of Hong Kong, Chun Len Ha was now only a hop, skip, and a taxi ride away.

A journey that seemed so unimaginable in the past – a fanciful burst of imaginative story-telling – had been reduced to the mundane by the advent of technology and a slab of cement highway.

To get to the village in the district of Baoan (pronounced Bow-un) you must first pass through Shenzhen, the Chinese city closest to Hong Kong and a 40-minute train ride from the British colony. From Shenzhen, it is only 20 minutes to the village by cab.

The most remarkable thing about Shenzhen is how little difference - at least superficially - there is between the Chinese side and its British counterpart. Everywhere, from street stalls to department stores, there is the unyielding ebb and flow of commerce and an unnerving territorial dance between bicycles and automobiles for space.

The bustling frontier mentality of the city - the sidewalks pregnant with people, the congested four-lane roads - was the first clue Mother had that the tiny farming community she had known was no more. So she braced herself for the changes, for the emotional impact of seeing her town, which had weathered World War II and the Cultural Revolution, struggle to find a place for itself in the next century. Within an hour of entering her ancestral land, one of those changes, which to her came to symbolize the new China, emerged.

It arrived in the form of the familiar and the mundane. A four-storey Wal-Mart Super Centre that comprised an entire city block, so large, that the foreboding glass exterior made it appear as if it had been carved from a monstrous silver ingot.

She gave a gasp. The village she held so closely in memory was unrecognizable. The last time she felt so displaced was stepping off the plane in Jamaica after leaving China.

Shenzhen had, over the last decade, gone from being one of the most devastated areas in China to one of the richest. In its initial flirtation with capitalism, Beijing had decreed that this would be China's very first special economic zone. Throughout Shenzhen enormous buildings and infrastructure had sprung up in former rice fields. In their rush to adopt the modern, the Chinese had decided that the bigger and more garish the architecture, the better. The result was a postmodern nightmare with soaring buildings that had no relationship to the surrounding pastoral farmlands.

"To be rich is glorious," China's paramount leader Deng Xiaoping had decreed. It seemed the people had taken him at his word.

The Wal-Mart episode barely prepared Mother for her next shock. She quickly found that the rice paddy where she used to hide from the Japanese during the war was still overrun by Japanese.

She found on those same parched fields - now manicured and liberally sprinkled with water - the Japanese were swinging golf clubs, not bayonets. Inside the clubhouse, a room for the night turned out to be $225, but first you had to join - at the price of $65,000.

Mother toured the facility in wide-eyed wonder - and popped into the hairdressing salon to see if she could afford a haircut. Who would have thought that not so long ago there was barely enough rice to eat, she mused. Now, on this very plot of land, a perm could set you back $150?

Chinese people had been fleeing China for more than 100 years. Now some of them, at least, seemed to like it just fine. But while many villagers had gone on to find a greater prosperity, there was still numbing poverty. With no social safety net, the surrounding streets of Shenzhen had become the dumping ground for the infirm, the elderly and disabled. Crime had also become a major problem - many homes had become tiny fortresses with ugly steel doors and soulless iron bars.

Progress also meant that fewer of the younger generation went to traditional Chinese movies or operas. In their living room, two cousins I hadn't met before sat enraptured by an old episode of *The Bold and the Beautiful* dubbed into Cantonese and beamed by satellite television.

Ten minutes from the golf course was Mother's birthplace of Chun Len Ha. The village, although benefiting from the new prosperity, had not yet been devoured by the ravenous, encroaching development. The modest concrete block house she had been born in, we were told, was still there.

Over the course of the drive, it was almost comforting to see Shenzhen's paved streets give way to choked dirt roads as stubbly and familiar as my father's whiskers.

As we wound our way closer to the village, the familiar black-brimmed lung-mao hats traditionally worn by peasant Hakka women - the same kind my grandmother used to wear to keep the sun off her brow while working in the rice fields - started to dot the landscape. Baoan was a stronghold of Hakka Chinese, one of several Chinese groups including the Taishan and Cantonese who left China in droves over the last century. The Hakka were famous for their hard work and industry in a land known for the industrious.

Fiercely independent, the Hakkas were the highlanders of China found in the most remote parts of the world. Like others in the village before her, Mother's trip 46 years ago had first taken her to stay with relatives in Montego Bay, Jamaica, where she would eventually meet my father. The first Chinese had already arrived on that island almost 100 years earlier as indentured labourers for the cane industry.

Strong individualists, the Hakka are tenacious survivors. They didn't bind the feet of their women like many northern Chinese - because the women fought side by side with the men. Mother, never one to back down in a fight, was the ultimate Hakka woman. Kind, headstrong, fiercely protective yet relentlessly stubborn at the same time.

Eventually, the car would pull to a stop in front of a worn concrete frame that used to be the village's only entrance. The four walls that surrounded the village of 1,200 had been torn down, and inside was an amalgamation of century-old brick and concrete housing, overgrown brush and broken earthenware.

A two-minute walk and Mother soon found the house she hadn't stepped in for almost five decades. In front was an abandoned bicycle. Above the door someone had handwritten on forlorn, faded paper the words Happy New Year. But the door itself was unmistakable. It was the same splintered entrance that had been replaced after the Japanese soldiers tried to torch the village in 1939.

Because the house was made of brick and concrete by my great-great-grandfather, it never yielded to the flames.

Vacant over the last few decades, it was as musty as a tomb with anaemic light filtering through small barred windows. A solitary blue porcelain tea cup stood on a wooden table as aged as a rum cask. I wondered if it belonged to my grandfather. The house, stripped of most furniture and uninhabited for decades, was more like an anthropological dig than someone's home.

The brick stove was crumpled, but still standing. A straw basket and a clay pot smothered under dirt were in another corner. Mom pointed out in delight a massive wooden log that looked like a medieval battering ram. It was the same pestle she remembered sitting on for hours flaking off rice husks.

A woman, stooped with age, broke my mother's reverie, asking in a shrill voice who she was. After a few minutes of harried give and take, the woman, whose name was Mrs. Chia, turned out to be a neighbour who knew my grandmother, now living in Canada.

Within minutes, another neighbour, a tall haggard man in plastic sandals and a smeared tank top arrived. A few more minutes of deliberation.

"You are Yun Sinn," said the man, leaning against the wall with astonishment and using my mother's Chinese name. "How could I not have known? It's like not knowing your own sister."

The man, Afa, had been five years old when my mother had left the village. But he remembered her beauty. "You don't look like Yun Sinn now," he said, absent of guile. "Yun Sinn was taller and more beautiful." Afa, after being reminded gently that it had been 46 years since the last encounter, acted as village tour guide for the rest of the trip.

It was clear the area had been decimated over the years from emigration. Many people had also left for better jobs in one of the many foreign-owned factories making Nike and Fila shoes in Shenzhen, only 20 minutes away.

As we passed from home to home, each villager would share a nugget of information that would elicit a smile from my mother, another coin that filled a growing piggy bank of memories.

For the first time, I glimpsed the child in my mother. Her mannerisms, her laughter seemed to get younger as the day passed. Once she gave a giggle as fresh as snow off a melting marsh and lit into a Communist chant with my uncle as if belting an ABBA tune.

Later, in the cool of the evening she walked to the village burial site to pay her respects to our ancestors. The picturesque temple on a hill housed the bones of 13 generations of our village. Accompanied by the faint strains of frogs and crickets and the fragrance

Tony Wong and mother in China.

of reeds and smoke, she lit three incense sticks and bowed deeply.

At the base of the temple we found our name on a marble plaque. She was one of many overseas Chinese who had donated money to build a dignified resting place for the village founders. The donors' names were placed in order of generosity, with the most generous placed on top and the amount they had donated. Our name was last.

"You better sneak back with a chisel tonight when no one's looking so you can add some more zeroes to redeem your name," laughed my uncle, Mok Sang Wong, who had accompanied us on the trip.

Mock Sang, my father's younger brother and his spitting image down to a deep rumbling belly chuckle, was revered in the village for his philanthropy. Over the years, he, like many overseas Chinese had donated hundreds of thousands of dollars to schools and industry. At one point, much of southern China was sustained with overseas Chinese money, although it has become less important to a region now awash with foreign investment.

Mock Sang also introduced us to my aunt, my father's younger sister, the only sibling left behind after the Communists came to power. She had the same big, sad eyes and mellow, easy nature as my father. The meeting, in our hotel room the next day, was awkward and tear-filled. It had been almost a decade since my father had passed away - and there was so much to know. "I only wish your father were here," she said. "He never made the trip back. But you came in his place, and that's how it should be."

When Mother finally left the village at nightfall, there was a deep weariness in her eyes, but also a kind of elation. It's funny, she would concede later, that she had to travel so many thousands of miles to learn where her true home was. At one time that home was here. Then it was Jamaica. And now Canada. It wasn't where you were. It was what you kept inside you.

As we left, Mother looked back, but it was with a sense of happiness, not despair. She was going home.

Written by Toronto journalist Tony Wong.

Tiffany Lee
LESSONS WITH JAPO

MOST OF THE EARLY MEMORIES of the times my grandparents visited my family as I was growing up are, at best, gentle, shapeless shadows. But it is the special moments spent with my Japo* that I see more clearly, like two figures on a quiet stage. The scene was often repeated, but never rehearsed. No script guided us. No audience looked on. We simply played out our roles instinctively.

The setting was always post dinnertime. The air would still be thick with the aroma of boiled chicken and ginger. From inside the kitchen, you could hear the chaotic clanging of pots, pans and plates as my parents and Jagung busily cleaned up after dinner. All three would be chatting at the same time, their voices competing with the very noises they were generating. That was when my Japo would silently motion me into the living room and sit me down on the couch. She would then take her place beside me, always careful to turn her body so that we faced each other. Neither of us switched on any lights – I don't think it ever occurred to us that we should. And there we would sit alone together in the dim glow of the fluorescent lights that streamed from the noisy kitchen.

I guess you could describe Japo as the quintessential Chinese grandmother. Chin-length dark gray hair with a few white strands, she wore her tresses down but neatly tucked behind her ears. She usually wore simple calf-length dresses in pastel colours that buttoned in the front. Pink was her favourite colour. As she sat next to me, her hands would first smooth her dress over her lap. Then her full face would break into a gentle smile as she began speaking softly in Hakka, giving me her utmost atten-tion the entire time. Her eyes would hold me so intently in their gaze that I would try not to blink too often in case I missed some-thing. She would seem to say a lot at first, as if earnestly trying to tell me something very important. I'd sit as still as possible hoping that that would help me better understand the strange words coming from her lips. All along her hands remained fixed in her lap, moving only occasionally to gesture mildly or to point. Her voice was low and calm. It was the voice of patience.

Tiffany at age 3 years

It was the same patience that Japo had when she and my Jagung would babysit me. I was barely a year old then, and just learning how to walk. Japo used to like to give me half of an orange to eat. Within minutes, I'd be happily covered in sweet orange juice. My mother said there wasn't an inch of skin that wasn't sticky or smelling of citrus. But Japo would always be patient and gently clean me up.

Sitting next to Japo in the living room, both of us now a little older, I would listen to that same calm, gentle voice. After a while, I'd realize that she was repeating the same sound over and over again. She'd pause and look at me, and I'd try to imitate the sounds she was making. At that, she'd smile broadly, nod, and reach over to pat my knee. Sometimes if I did not pronounce correctly, she'd repeat the sound for me again, and I would try again. Then she'd continue speaking. Sometimes it would be a different sound she wanted me to repeat, and other times she just began speaking freely as if telling me a story.

Of course, while I revelled in the special attention, I'd also become bored quickly. Only seven at the time, I was far from being a prim little girl and wanted to go outside and play with my brother. I was what Jamaicans would call a *sturdy pickney*.* I was the kind of kid who, after playing and running around, would sport flush-pink chubby cheeks, with my fine, chin-length, stringy black hair plastered on my head – like a wet rat. Although I did not take my eyes off my Japo, it was at times like these that I'm sure my face betrayed me, devoid of any sign of comprehension, save for the occasional furrowing of my brow whenever I became exceedingly frustrated or tired. But Japo never got upset or frowned back. I don't remember her ever raising her voice. After what seemed to be a very long time, Japo would nod with a smile and motion that I could go. At that I would bolt off to play with my brother. As for Japo, she would just sit and watch us.

Even though she never said so with words I could understand, I knew that she loved us. And now that I'm older, I remember the unmistakable look in her eyes that told me so. I don't recall her ever trying to sit my brother down as she did me. Perhaps she thought him too young at the time, being only four. And my sister was just an infant. I was probably the only one who would sit still for any length of time.

I have often wondered what my Japo was telling me those evenings we sat together in the darkness on the couch. She had apparently learned midwifery skills in her village back in China, and apparently could tell a woman when to conceive to have a boy and how to cure sterility. Maybe she was imparting these secrets to me. Maybe she was telling me about her childhood. Or maybe she was just trying to tell me to be a good girl. I'll never know for sure. What I *do* know is that she was trying to share something of herself with me. Passing on something special to the next generation…. Now that she is gone, I hope my Japo is watching over me as I do the same.

Written by Tiffany Lee and edited by Alex Lee.

* See Glossary

Yvonne Chin (née Lee-Hing)
MEMORIES OF MAMA

(Sybil Lee-Hing, formerly Hew-Wing, née Hoo Sui Ying,
April 20, 1905 – August 15, 1988)

Sybil Lee-Hing

MY MOTHER had a beautiful smile and a wonderful sense of humour. She laughed often and was the first to admit that she was 'jokeyfy', as the country people (our customers) would say. They loved her and would comment on how 'sweet mouth' Miss Sybil was *'You're a joker'*, she would tell them when they requested credit, but she would inevitably give in.

I loved to watch her comb her long black hair. It was almost a ritual the way she did it…parting it in three, first the left side swept up and out, bobby pinned, then the right side done the same way, the front section pinned back and then the back portion brushed straight up, folded over and secured with a dark brown clip. She looked so elegant. *'Why don't you wear your gown?'* I would ask.

My mother, a hard-working shopkeeper, was well educated, spoke three dialects and had once enjoyed a privileged life as the eldest child of a barrister. She was born in Shanghai as was her younger sister, Ruby, but they came to Montego Bay, Jamaica, as the wives of two brothers, Samuel and Walter Hew-Wing, who had been sent to China to be schooled.

My mother's life was not an easy one. Even from the outset of their marriage there had been obstacles. The shop at Somerton, where she had worked so hard with Sammy, had been taken away on the death of his father and given to a nephew. Later on, the estate had been divided up and Sammy was given a token portion. She never said so, but we understood that it was because he was an 'outside' child – the half-Chinese one. A *ship-it-dam**.

In 1936, Sammy died, leaving her with four children and a fifth on the way. Family financing was not forthcoming yet she managed extremely well on her own, running a profitable business at 14 Strand Street. Up at dawn and closing shop late at night, she still made time for her children. Lloyd and Rex, the older boys, fondly remember when she bought four brand new bikes, and how they would ride out to Doctor's Cave Beach. They laughed when they reminisced about how she would chase them and even climb trees to get to them when they had done something wrong.

In 1944, my mother married my father, Frederick Lee-Hing. Not much is known about Papa, except that he was an idealist turned soldier under Chiang Kai-shek. He later became disillusioned and, subsequently, fervently believed that communism was the right route for China.

Papa was a gentle, quiet man - a spiffy dresser who wore white clothes and sported gold teeth. Papa did not try too hard to be a businessman. He gambled all night, slept in late, and yet found time to read in the day. He was an avid reader, books by the dozens! But he was very kind to all the children, and was an excellent cook. He was ecstatic when my brother, David, was born in 1948. He left us a legacy of love and the fondest memories of a happy, pampered childhood. Life revolved around the bakery, the gambling houses we frequented and fun-filled days at the beach. We had lots of pocket money, comic books and taxis to take us around. We lived extravagantly and, under my father's direction, our business soon failed. My father, who loved the good life, was spared our economic plight when he died at the young age of 50.

My mother carried on. She was the driving force of the family – the nucleus. She sent all her children to high school and was very proud of their accomplishments. She bragged about her sons Lloyd and Rex, who were not only on the Cornwall College football team, but who also broke the All-Jamaica swimming record in the 200 and 100 metres breast stroke by 28 seconds. She bragged about my older sister, Monica, about how smart she was, always achieving top marks in school, and how Wills was such a great runner.

My mother was a survivor who never stopped working or joking. When I'm particularly happy or when I see something beautiful, I think of her and say '*this is for you, Mama*!'

Written by Yvonne Chin
Re-edited by Sonia Gordon Scott.

* See Glossary

Simone Chung-Groves
MEMORIES

WHEN I THINK ABOUT my childhood I can only
smile at what I experienced until the age of eight when
we left for Canada. Growing up in Vineyard Town on
Deanery Road in Kingston with my mother and grandparents is a treasured memory. Though they are simple,
and not all that exciting, all these memories are for-
ever etched in my mind as the "good times".

*Simone Chung's younger
days with mom.*

I remember the Golden Horse Betting shop that belonged to my grandparents – the black and white checkered tile floors, listening to the horse racing
on the radio, and all the friendly, regular patrons, asking 'Miss Ruby's' grand-
daughter to choose a horse to bet on, hoping that I would bring them some
luck.

We lived above the betting shop and I remember the house vaguely, but a
few things stand out:

- The baby chicks that I used to love to play with, only to learn that in
  a few months they would be dinner. " Simone, go and catch a
  chicken." Grandma would cut the throat and the poor chicken would
  flap around endlessly.
- Many huge, vicious dogs in the backyard that would cower at
  grandma's command, but which scared me to death.
- Grandpa making delicious aromas from the kitchen, always cooking
  lots of yummy Chinese food and chasing everyone out – no one was
  ever allowed in the kitchen while he was cooking!
- Grandpa taking me to St. Theresa's Prep. School everyday, picking me
  up for lunch, cooking steamed rice and fried shrimp for lunch, taking
  me back to school and collecting me at the end of each day.
- Finding lizard eggs with my cousins in the garden and popping them
  with our fingers.
- Eating flowers with my cousins – hibiscus and another flower with a
  sweet liquid (monkey fiddle).
- At prep school there was always hopscotch traced in the dirt, and finding the best 'markers', which were just green, brown and clear bottle
  pieces to play with; finding your school pin and your house colour pin
  every morning when you dressed for school; lining up for the national
  anthem and prayers; getting the ruler from the teacher when you

talked too much in class; the dreaded machine you would be put through in the headmistress' office if you were bad.

- When it came to seeing movies, it was only to Harbour View Drive-In, and my cousins used to hide me under their legs so they didn't have to pay for me.
- Mommy's orange Volkswagen 'bug' that she used to drive – many wonderful drives and relatives we used to visit.

These are some of the more vivid memories I have and cherish.

Written by Simone Chung-Groves and edited by Sonia Gordon Scott.

Left: Simone Chung-Groves and mom Avery

Down Memory Lane

Newcastle Military Training Camp nestling in the Blue Mountains, St. Andrew. Photograph ©Ray Chen

Dr. Samuel Williams
FROM GUANGDONG TO GRANGE HILL

MY PARENTS, James and Ida Williams came from Guangdong Province. As was common then, my father married my mother, left for Jamaica ahead of her, lived common-law with a Jamaican lady in his new home and had children with her. As the story goes, my mother got tired of waiting, found her own way to Jamaica, and showed up at her husband's front door.

Home was Grange Hill, Westmoreland. I was born in 1929, the third of nine. My brother, Leslie, and sister Sadie, came before me. At the time there were only two Chinese families in Grange Hill. The Lai family, our immediate neighbours, owned a gas station and grocery store. We had the usual shop – a real country store that sold everything. We also had a rum bar, a dry goods section and, later on, a hardware section that even sold coffin handles.

Grange Hill was a small village in those days, with most of the villagers gainfully employed at the nearby Frome Sugar Estate. No question about it, our shop and bar were the main attraction. That was where everyone congregated to meet, shop, gossip and drink. The market was the town centre. There you bought your meats and provisions, and items like 'wet sugar', which was really unrefined sugar in kerosene tins. 'Jackass rope' or tobacco rope could be had for a ha'penny*, or penny an inch. And _cocoa_. You bought cocoa in balls then. It made the most beautiful tea because it had the real cocoa fat in it. We'd boil the cocoa balls, let the yellow globs of fat rise to the surface, and then top it up with cinnamon leaves. Oh the _flavour_!

I'd say ours was the life of the typical first generation Chinese Jamaican family. Life was the shop. It was simple, but we enjoyed it. And then Leslie and Sadie were sent to China and I became number one at home. A few years later when the Sino-Japan war broke out, Leslie returned while Sadie stayed behind. She was left in the care of the wife my father would take in China _after_ my mother.

Leslie was 12 or 13 when he came back. By then he had completely forgotten his English, and I teased him mercilessly for it. It was all a little strange for me because suddenly I couldn't communicate with my own brother, who was only four years older than I. Besides, my position as the eldest at home had been usurped by his return.

One time after a particularly bad teasing session, I watched him in our backyard as he vented his frustrations. He was leaning against a coconut tree, spewing rapid Chinese at the top of his voice. But the teasing would be short-lived. One day my brother reasserted his authority *and* position by giving me a seriously good beating. And so peace was restored to the Williams household.

Leslie worked in the shop from the very start, never enjoying a day's formal schooling in Jamaica. All he got was some english and arithmetic through a retired tutor, who would come by some evenings after Leslie's day at the shop had ended. But he was so exceptional that at 14 or 15 he subscribed to *Reader's Digest* and *Time Magazine*. He read voraciously and practically choked our bedroom with books. A true intellectual, my brother was. I always thought that of the nine of us, he was the brightest. It couldn't have been easy for him to watch the rest of us go to school every day.

At first, school was the verandah of a retired teacher's cottage half a mile away. Mr. James was our teacher. There were 10 or 12 of us, all different ages. We paid him *trupence** per week, wrote on slates and sat on wooden benches. He was what you'd call, no pun intended, old-school Jamaican. More English than the English. Mr. James would *not* countenance any patois at his school. As was the fashion then, he always wore black lace-up boots above the ankles. This, despite the tropical heat.

At nine I left my parents, Leslie and other siblings for preparatory school in Kingston. The trip to the big city began in Grange Hill at 10:00 a.m. I journeyed at the back of a truck with some market women, my 'grip' and I trying not to take up too much space. We stopped on Spur Tree Hill at a place called Man Bump, where we lunched on fricassee or curried chicken while waiting for the truck to cool down and stop spewing liquid. We finally pulled into Parade in Kingston by 6:00 p.m. One tram ride later I was at my uncle's house in Cross Roads. I'd make this same trip a few years in a row.

My uncle was a dapper man. He wore a white helmet, shirt, tie and white buck skin leather shoes. My cousin and I used to have to clean those for him. William, his son, was from Hong Kong and a real city slicker. He, too, was always well dressed, knee high socks and all, and sported hair pasted down with *Yardley's Brilliantine*. I was the country cousin who showed up in the standard khaki pants and shoes, no socks. But William took care of that right away. He whisked me off to E. A. Issa and Sons and outfitted me with socks, handkerchiefs - the works.

I *loved* Kingston immediately and made many friends. We hung out a lot on Barry and Princess Streets where my uncle had a grocery store. Chinatown was a busy place. It offered tens of dozens of restaurants and shops, with every sign written in bold Chinese characters. The sidewalks simply teemed with people. On the roads, the new modern taxi competed for business with the more traditional horse-drawn buggy. On a Friday, runners would sell Peaka Peow tickets and declare the winners later.

Everywhere you turned your head, your nose picked up the smells of cooking. I loved nothing more than to buy from the vendors on the streets – treats like *lopet ban**, and lychee ice cream from pushcarts – home made of course, and fritters! There's nothing like the smell of coconut oil! Then there was the cry of the fish lady *"Fresh fish! King fish! Snapper!"* You could hear her from one end of the street to the other. You'd also hear a cry for *"Booby* eggs!"* Those went for trupence a dozen or a farthing* each. They'd give you salt and pepper to sprinkle on them. Then there was the oyster man with fresh oysters from the south shore. And let's not forget the peanut vendors.

For entertainment I'd take in a Western at the cinema. Sometimes for a change of pace, I'd sit in the quietude of the three-storey Chinese Benevolent Society across from my uncle's place. Inside it boasted a lovely shaded garden.

That was our Chinatown. That's where I stayed until 1942.

I returned to Grange Hill in the summer of that year. At my mother's urging, I sat an entrance exam for Cornwall College and won a scholarship. Off we went again, my grip and I, journeying to another school in another place. This time the trips began at 4:30 a.m., and always on a Saturday, in a bus that travelled from Savanna-la-mar. You'd hear it blowing its horn as it approached Grange Hill. The route took us through tiny towns with noble names like Little London, Sheffield, Green Island and Jericho. We'd crawl into Montego Bay at noon, at which point a guy would meet me with a pushcart to take my luggage up the hill to the school. I did that trip for six years.

All this time while I was in the classroom, my brother Leslie continued life at the shop, proving to be one of the most unselfish and hardworking people I'd ever know. On visits from boarding school, I'd often complain about not having enough pocket money. Leslie would almost always hand me an extra ten shillings or pound with a sympathetic look in his eye.

He'd end up taking over as head of the family in many ways. It was Leslie who took over the business when my father died in 1949. It was Leslie who sent me to medical school in Edinburgh, so that I could become the doctor that I am today.

It's amazing. My boyhood days seem like a lifetime away. And yet sometimes they feel so close, I think I can almost touch them.

Samuel Williams with wife Mavis and children: Hilary, Andrew and David. Photo taken at the Annotto Bay Hospital - Feb. 1962

Written and edited by Alex Lee as told by Dr. Samuel Williams.

* See Glossary.

Basil Lee
MY CHINA

MY FATHER TOOK me and my sister back to China after the Sino-Japanese war. I remember looking forward to the trip because he was returning to his village, Gun-Lan-Hee, therefore I was going *home* with him. This was in 1946.

I was nine at the time, and was the son my father had with his wife in Jamaica. My mother, his second wife, had never lived with us, so leaving was not difficult. Once in China I was properly received by his first wife, my step-mother, and her sons, my half brothers. And while none of this was actually explained to me, I had an idea what was going on, because she assumed her role as mother the second we got there. Mother *and* wife. She and my father and their children would automatically become a family unit once again. Just like that. It was hard for me to fathom then, the concept of these women living like widows for 20, 30 years, and then instantly becoming unquestioning wives the minute their husbands reappeared. But my stepmother made it easy. She considered us her own. We hugged her, sat on her lap, and let her entertain us with stories like the trials and hardships of the recent war.

We were happy in the village, and I quickly adjusted to my new home. I cannot say if we were poor or well off, although I don't remember seeing my father actually work. What I *do* know is that we never starved, we were always able to buy things, and had our own rice and vegetable field. For every meal we bought the ingredients fresh. The only thing we stored up in the attic was rice. As a matter of fact, we could also pay school fees with rice if cash was short. Fortunately, for two years in succession I came first in my class, so I did not have to pay school fees then.

I *loved* my school in China. I appreciated its focus on discipline, and threw myself into the lessons we learned, the songs we sang, and the games my new friends and I played. Everyone knew that I had come from afar, but somehow they never stared or made me feel different. Soon my Chinese language skills strengthened as my Jamaican faded. That transition was briefly interrupted by the arrival of two Jamaican friends, Winston and Arthur Wong. They lived close by in their family compound at the end of the village. But they would only stay for a couple of years. When they left, my English did too.

Looking back, it's hard to believe that I can speak with such joy of a place that was then going through such pain. The time between my arrival and the 1949 Liberation was not the kind you forget. Soldiers were visible and part of our daily lives. In fact, they were billeted in my village. But we managed to work within the guidelines and go about our business without concern. For instance, within my village, soldiers blocked off sections at night, and locked the four outer gates. That meant you would have to get home by a certain time or get locked out until morning. I admit my family was worried that I might be kidnapped. The general impression then was that foreigners were wealthy. And, of course, wealthy people were good ransom victims. So they did not let me stray too far. But nothing ever happened to me.

Was I scared? Only initially. I remember one of the first times I heard gunfire at full throttle. It was night time and I was sleeping, when suddenly I was jolted awake by a sound I will never forget.

'BAM! BAM! BAM! BAM! BAM!... Ba chiiing! Ba chiiing!'

And there I was, shivering in my bed, not knowing what was happening. Well I quickly found my stepmother, who told me about these men who disappear into the hills to fight the Nationalists. That was my first introduction to the guerrillas. On this particular night they were shooting at our village. But you know, after awhile I actually got used to the sound of gun shots. I think we were more worried about the guerrillas than anything else. One of my older cousins actually ended up joining them. *I* almost ended up there too. But before he went into the hills, his younger brothers discovered his plans and warned me. Sure enough, he approached me one day.

'I'm just going for a walk outside the village,' he said. *'You want to come along?'*

I declined in a hurry. *'No, no I don't,'* I answered. Well that was the day we lost him to the hills. I would not see him again until after the Liberation.

And there were other incidents. One day my friends and I were playing at the edge of the village where the school was, when we saw the soldiers coming home. So naturally we all gathered at the edge to watch. In the distance we noticed a civilian among the soldiers carrying a bamboo stick across his shoulder, with something attached to the ends. As he drew nearer, we saw that he was carrying four human heads. Two on each end. The heads of Guerrillas, they said. In my village we had four entrance gates – north, south, east and west. The soldiers hung one at each gate. We were closest to the south gate, which I had to pass by daily to get to our vegetable garden, or to tell my sister-in-law *'dinner is ready'*. I didn't know the head's owner, but the example did the trick. We didn't fool with the soldiers.

One day they came for one of our workers. A fellow who helped us look after our rice field and cow. They accused him of being a guerrilla. There was no trial, nothing. On a separate day, they caught another guy, tied his arms behind his back, stuck something on him to show what he was charged with, and locked him up until they were ready to execute him. Well we all went to watch. They marched him to a sandy place by the river where we bought and sold cows, made him kneel in the sand, and shot him in the back. He fell. They shot him again a couple of times. It was the first time I had seen anyone being killed.

After that, I learned how to steel myself against such images, and began accepting them as part of life. So I never really feared for my safety. When the Liberation came the gates went, and we could finally come and go as we pleased. A few of us would roam around at nights for fun with a flashlight. Now *that* was a big deal.

We hardly noticed much the day the Communists took over in 1949. Most of the fighting had been done in the larger cities, so there was little difference to us in that respect. Back in the smaller villages, those who were Nationalists or supporters had already fled. They were soon replaced by a Liberation Army representative, who would live among the locals and take control. That was when certain processes began to take place, like land division. Suddenly people were calculating their entitlement based on the number of children they had. And then began the public condemnation. Gradually we heard about the torturing and public trials of landlords and people of influence and wealth. But so far nothing had happened to my father. We *did* have a firearm, however. And they let us know that they knew it. They eventually approached us one day with a proposal. With the war with the Communists still going on in Taiwan, they suggested, would we not be willing to lend them our weapon for the cause. Well, we couldn't exactly say no.

Then one day in 1950, we suddenly left for Hong Kong. I was at school, when one of my brothers walked in and told me to come home *right now*. When we got to the house, we literally packed a few things and walked to the train station. I was thinking that my father had already left for Hong Kong, because he was not at the house at this point. But my stepmother was there and she stayed behind. We got to Hong Kong without incident, and eventually my brother returned to the village. I realized afterwards that they just wanted to get me out. A few months later the Communists started closing the border. I was 13.

I remained in Hong Kong for five memorable years, where I lived the life of a slick gang member before returning to Jamaica as a young man of 18. I arrived in Kingston on a Sunday and walked into my first job the following Wednesday. The return home was difficult at first, but became easier as I reacquainted myself with English, yet again. In the end I was happy to be back. It was time to make a life for myself as a man.

As for China, I still see it through the eyes of the nine year-old that I was when I first saw it. I just can't picture it any other way. My China. And of all the things I used to love the most – from the big yellow puddings to my favourite pop songs – I miss the autumns. That is when you're surrounded by a sea of yellow and gold. And above, an endless blue sky. I still remember one particular autumn day standing in a field and staring up into the blue. I swear that day I could see right through to the end of the world.

Written and edited by Alex Lee as told by Basil Lee.

Sonia Mills
SEARCHING FOR MY FATHER

MY FATHER'S NAME was Matthew Archibald McPherson (left). He was born in Enfield, St Mary, Jamaica, on May 23, 1914. He would have been 90 years old in a few days from now, and even today I don't know what his Chinese name was. It is clear that his father, Charles McPherson (Mr. Mac), whose real name was Lee Ping Kong, having made the move to Jamaica from Hong Kong, fully intended to become a western gentleman in the New World, while retaining the life style and class habits of a Chinese laird.

My father, his first-born (he had only sons), was the Prince. And so, in 1922, accompanied by some of his retainers, Charles McPherson took his young son back to Hong Kong to be acculturated.

And acculturated he was. Although I believe that even in Hong Kong, and to anybody I've ever met who knew him, he was (Mass) Archie, a Western Prince.

My primary identity is Jamaican, and then Caribbean. I am visibly 'half-Chinese'[1] (although I am actually more Chinese than half) and I am culturally black. New World Black. What story can I tell in this book of predominantly Chinese stories?

Well, I'll tell the story of my father, for although he died in 1963, having not even reached fifty years of age, he has left behind him – unwittingly, and quite inadvertently – a very contemporary, modern legacy.

His is not a story of courage and triumph over difficulty, of hard work, honour and respect. It is a story of self-indulgence and machismo, and mis-spent charisma – and who knows what else. I daresay, of enormous frustration and great loss.

Archie was one of the first 'trans-cultural' offsprings of Chinese migration. Although he was born of Chinese parents early in the 20th century, he was the product of cultural miscegenation. Born in rural St. Mary to Charles McPherson (who was presumably still Lee Ping Kong) and his wife Hilda, his parents were married in Kingston Parish Church in 1911, but his mother died in childbirth. At some stage Charles McPherson moved to Annotto Bay and into his new identity, which he assumed when he purchased the business once owned by the real Charles McPherson. I can only assume that Archie started growing up as a regular little Annotto Bay boy, attending Miss Norton's school[2]. In 1922, Mr. Mac felt it was time for his motherless son and heir to be properly brought up and took him to Hong Kong, where he was left in the care of his relatives.

There he remained until, alarmed by news of the Japanese threat to China and atrocities in Hong Kong, Mr. Mac summoned home his Prince. Archie returned to Jamaica, by way of Ellis Island, in December 1934. By March 1935, Mr. Mac was dead. His second young wife had returned to her family and the not-yet 21 year old Archie, who had been bred for nothing but 'sweet life', was the man in charge in an environment he knew nothing about, and at a time when even for the most astute of businessmen (the late '30s), business was very difficult.

Looking back, I realize that part of my father's problem was that he was totally unprepared to be a frugal, hardworking Chinese shopkeeper in the small, already decaying town of Annotto Bay. Archie was a 'city slicker'. What's more he was a Hong Kong slicker. He was used to a free and sophisticated Hong Kong life. And it is only by talking about him later to some of the young men who had come under his thrall in Annotto Bay that we, who were when we knew him, only small children, small country children at that, understood how Archie's worldly ways entranced the young men of the town and, more importantly for our family life, the women of Annotto Bay and Kingston.

In addition, he enjoyed with the Chinese men who worked with us in the shop, a relationship more of master and serfs, not of peers. And, except from one other youngish Chinese man in town, with whom he shared his womanizing exploits, the other Chinese families were perhaps too traditional and countrified to share anything but the inevitable *mah jong*. His peers and his friends, and my mother's, were chosen from the generally upwardly-mobile Jamaican (creole) society.

To chop saltfish in a country shop in Jamaica, wrap salt and flour, sell kerosene oil, and buy produce on a busy market-day Saturday, was a far cry from the casinos of Macau and the bright lights and bridges of Hong Kong. But then what exactly was he fit to do? Except spree. That is to say – gamble and womanize.

He did try to be a shopkeeper. He did chop salt fish and buy kola nuts. I can still see him shaking a fistful of dry pimento seeds. And he made peanut brittle and popcorn and cooked chicken-in-wine and barrels full of crab. He also played *mah jong* and, from as far back as I can remember, left Annotto Bay every Tuesday morning and came back every Thursday night; off to Kingston, ostensibly to 'buy goods'. Much of that time was spent in the gambling dens of Barry Street.

My father's short but complicated life story deserves a fuller telling. For now, I merely want to trace how his trans-cultural life has left us an inter-continental family.

My parents were atypical for a Chinese couple of the late thirties, early forties. Theirs was not an arranged marriage; it was a romantic union, which went the way of many such romantic unions. And therein lie many tales! But they won't be told here.

By the week after his return home, the machinations to marry him off to eligible girls from good families in Kingston were activated. Glamourous girls arrived in Annotto Bay to be matched with the handsome young heir who had just returned from Hong Kong. But that was not to be. And in 1939, with his father dead and gone, he married the daughter of one of his father's old retainers, Lucy Lowe, the daughter of Phillip Lowe and Ella Fleming of Clonmel. Out of that union came three daughters.

I knew my father. Quite well. We were in touch until the very end. But who did I know? I knew only my perception of what a certain kind of middle-class Jamaican father should be. I was communicating with him across a very wide, unbridged cultural chasm. I neither knew nor understood anything about the Chinese Jamaican society of the '30s and '40s. (Most Jamaican families hide their secrets of survival from their children; in the Chinese Jamaican society, I think, even more so). I knew nothing of Chinese history, nor Chinese culture. I had never exchanged an intelligible sentence with a Chinese *woman* in my life (except for my father's main mistress, and even then…). I had no comprehension of the life my father had led in Hong Kong. I had no clue of the kind of courtship, nor of the relationship, between my father and my mother.

My father was not interested in acculturating his three children. First of all we were girls. He himself was a cultural orphan, so what would he draw on to teach us. Within a few months of his returning to Jamaica his father had died, leaving him adrift in a predominantly Jamaican plantation culture, among Chinese men who were not his equal, old retainers of his father for whom he felt no affinity, a Punti in a mostly Hakka culture[3] in a failing economic situation.

For one brief period in my life I had been interested in my Chinese heritage. I wanted to learn Chinese, but my mother told me that my father did not want us taught by the men who worked for us in the shop, because their Chinese was not cultivated enough; they were different – Hakka, not Punti.

My interest in the Chinese part of me may have arisen after I learnt that I had a Chinese sister! Which happened when I was about 10 or eleven. To my astonishment, I received a letter from a teenage girl in Hong Kong, whose name was June McPherson. She was my sister, born seven or eight months after my father had left for Jamaica. Her mother, Tip Wan, whom Archie had married before leaving Hong Kong, was a mid-wife. I imagine that for the time, a professional single mother in Hong Kong of the 1930s was itself quite an unusual status.

I can only imagine the consternation this revelation must have caused in our household. To us children, my father remained quite unconcerned, and, as far as I knew, took no great interest or responsibility for this branch of his family. My Uncle Albert Lee (one of my grandfather's cousins Tung Siang – came from the same village) who had always assumed the role of patriarch of the family, I believe to have been the one who was the go-between in all correspondence and communication between Hong Kong and Jamaica.

In the meantime, once the romance had cooled, the marriage revealed two unevenly yoked partners. My mother, for all her would-be worldly ways, was a country girl from Clonmel, brought up at the edges of Annotto Bay Chinese society, and very upwardly mobile in Creole society. Every weekday we ate …my father, the Chinese help and my mother at the same table…my mother's place was always set with a knife and fork and plate, while everybody else used chopsticks and a bowl. Long Man (Thomas Woo), an old Chinese man who worked and lived with us, was the main cook. (I only recently learned that Long Man had been rescued from an opium den in Cuba by my grandfather. Servitude in Annotto Bay could hardly have been regarded as such a great 'rescue'. No wonder I remember Long Man constantly saying: "Wan' fi dead and cyan' dead" – want to die and can't die.) The food for Thursday lunch was cooked by the Jamaican 'maids', as they were then called. There was country beef soup on Saturday, and chicken and rice and peas on Sunday.

But what really drove the wedge between my mother and father was not so much culture, as morality. My upwardly mobile mother, who came out of a very typical, poor rural Jamaican early 20th century culture, had been taught and fully acquired Victorian morals. As a married middle class woman she had ascended to serious status in the town. My father, for all his Western airs, was a dissolute Chinaman of a certain class and era.

I realise now, too, how much this procession of daughters must have disappointed him, how much his inner Chinese self must have longed for a son.

Eventually he did get a son. And one day, in the 1950's, when his entire Jamaican life had crashed around him (divorce, bankruptcy, many breakups and departures, fires and tragedies of one kind and another), he 'stole' his little Mongoloid son, Andrew, and took off to Hong Kong, arriving destitute, with an undocumented minor at the door of the woman he had abandoned nearly a quarter century earlier.

And Tip Wan graciously, and gratefully, received the husband and son she had waited for all those years.

I think my sister June was less sanguine about his arrival, although she too welcomed the father she had never known. His behaviour in Hong Kong was as unrepentant and blatantly profligate as ever. Visiting mistresses from Jamaica turned up at Tip Wan's door and were welcomed into her home by Archie. And when he decided to leave home to shack up with another woman, he left Andrew behind. In 1963, after an exhausting struggle with cancer, Archie died, leaving the undocumented Andrew permanently with Tip Wan (by now blind of glaucoma) and June.

However, during all this time, since the arrival of my first letter from my

Hong Kong sister, we have remained in touch. In earlier times we each received copies of every photograph June took, inscribed individually to each of her sisters. After half-a-century she has got fed up with us. ("You girls never write. I am the one who always writes!"). Over the decades we have all met, her family and ours, not all of us at one time, nor all of us and all of them, but most of us and most of them. We've met in various places: in New York and Jamaica, Hong Kong and Canada, Los Angeles and Bangkok. By design, and sometimes by chance! Andrew has no offspring, and among Archie's there is only one male. He too is childless.

Poor Archie, after all that activity there are only women to carry, not his name, but his legacy forward.

In some ways my sister June is a very stereotypical Hong Kong matron: mah jong playing, picture-taking, jewellery loving, bargain hunting. But the most special thing about her is her complete openness and ease with the other people her father brought into her life. Her attitude seems so far removed from the racism of my youth in Jamaica, when many wu-gui* children, particularly of better off Chinese men, were relegated to the back door.

Using the language of the 20th century, which is where most of my life has been and will have been spent, I defined myself as a Jamaican, phenotypically half-Chinese, and culturally Black.

The Jamaica of this era of my youth was a very racist society, (has it changed?) where all races disdained the other – except under cover.

"Chiney nyam dog" (Chinese people eat dogs).

"John (the generic name given to the Chinese shopkeeper) will dig out you yeye"
(John' will take you for every cent you've got).

"Nayga man too boasy, tief and 'trong"
(The Black man is too conceited, too much of a thief, and too strong).

"Coolie weak and lie…"
('Coolies', usually applied to those of Indian descent, are spineless liars).

And in Annotto Bay, the few white people who lived on the low hills of the surrounding plantation, disdained all the rest of us.

Presumably I did not want to be a 'Chiney nyam dog', so I chose the prevailing culture, to be one of the majority. I wish we had all realized that we were preparing a world for globalization in the 21st century. Instead of despising parts of our culture, we should have drunk deeply from all parts of it.

Archie's descendants, for the most part, range along the spectrum of colour and race.

His legacy to us has not been a solid base of material security, a moral foundation of respect for ancestors, hard work and providence… Rather it is of a multiracial family, strewn across the world.

What will be the role of race in the future? Will there ever come a time when we can celebrate all our cultural strands? Equally…?

With a billion and a half people in the land mass known as China alone, plus all the millions of second, third, fourth and fifth generations all over the planet, (like Archie's descendants, of all colours) the Han people will certainly have a say in the politics of race and culture in this century.

Will the discussions be different from the politics of the last two (few) centuries?

Written by Sonia Mills and edited by Sonia Gordon Scott.

* See Glossary

Notes:

1. *The term half-Chinese was very prevalent in my youth. It defined all people who showed evidence of SOME 'Chinese blood'. Nowadays, Jamaicans don't recognize the mixture as easily, partly because of the significant decrease in the Chinese population in Jamaica since the '70s (apart from the new immigrant workers who are - not yet - a cultural factor.)*

2. *Miss Norton's one-room school was the kindergarten/prep/and even high school of generations of Annotto Bay children. It only closed sometime in the '50s, when after giving hundreds of "duncey head pickney" a sound foundation, Miss Norton threw in the towel, and her sanity.*

3. *A hundred years before, Punti-Hakka conflicts (1854-1858) had left whole villages in China's Guangdong province destroyed, with hundreds of lives lost. These conflicts pitted the Hakka against their Punti neighbours.*

Roger Chen
BECOMING A CHINESE DOCTOR

CHINESE MEDICINE has been, and still is, herbal based. It is the distillation of thousands of years of observations, trial and error. By closely watching animals in their native environment, noting the herbs they consume when they are sick, the chinese accumulated knowledge about the nature of animals and plants, and the use of plants as medicine. This art or science was passed from generation to generation and with each generation, their knowledge increased and became exact and refined. Then around 260 B.C., China's first emperor, Qin Shi Huang-di, commissioned the *Nei-Jing**, the first recorded compendium of medicine called *The Yellow Emperor's Classics of Internal Medicine*. Even today, traditional Chinese medicine is based on this compendium.

By the end of the Tang dynasty (~A.D. 900), the practice of herbal medicine and the classification of herbs according to their usage was well documented, to the extent that formulas of various herbal mixes for specific ailments were recorded. As well, acupuncture and moxibustion* were widely in use.

"You are what you eat" is the essence of Chinese medicine. The aim is to maintain the balance of yin and yang in the physical body, in the spirit, and energy (qi). So the art of herbal medicine is to help maintain this balance. Herbs are, first and foremost, plants that nourish the body in precise and well-defined ways.

To become a Chinese doctor, it helped to be born into a family in which there was already a Chinese doctor, because the knowledge and skill were traditionally passed on within the family. However, if you showed an aptitude for this, and found favour with the local Chinese doctor, you may have been fortunate to have him take you on as an apprentice. There were many things to learn, such as which herbs combined were more effective than by themselves; which are the eighteen herbs that must never be combined. After many years of studying the *Nei-Jing*, becoming familiar with the herbs, and preparing the formulas, you would then be taught how to take the three levels of pulses, and the importance of observation of the eyes, tongue and face, much like the internship that Western doctors now go through. But in those days, a doctor's role was to keep a client healthy.

It is interesting to note that traditional Chinese medicine almost died out near the end of the Qing Dynasty (1644-1911), because of the perception that all things western were better than Chinese ways. The Qings were Manchus and never fully accepted the native Han ways, so in the 1850's when the Portuguese, British, French, Germans, and Americans came to occupy China, the Qings eagerly accepted their ways and started to discard traditional Chinese ways, medicine included.

The ravages brought on by the Opium War and the Taiping Rebellion led to a further decline in medical institutions in China. By 1912, acupuncture and moxibustion were almost forgotten by the population. Traditional Chinese Medicine (TCM) suffered further setbacks during the War with Japan, WWI, and the Civil War between the CCP (Chinese Communist Party) and the Nationalist Government.

During this period, China's 800 million citizens had no access to medical treatment. It took the event of China becoming a socialist country, under the leadership of Mao Tse Tung, to introduce the 'barefoot doctors' who provided medical care in the rural areas of China. These barefoot doctors were trained at medical facilities for 6-12 months, then were sent out into the countryside. But after Mao died in 1976, capitalism was reintroduced and many of the gains achieved under socialism – including a health care system devoted to 'serving the people' – were reversed.

Barefoot doctors, created during the Cultural Revolution, were chosen to receive medical training, not because of their grades or their family's wealth, but because of their dedication to serving the people. They were usually middle school graduates trained in first aid, and they hiked through hamlets offering prenatal examinations and setting broken limbs. Some lived and worked among the people. Many of these doctors were young women who distributed birth control, performed simple and safe abortions, provided pre-natal care, and assisted in the delivery of babies. The service helped to almost eradicate sexually transmitted diseases in China. This service was stopped with the return of health clinics which charged a fee.

It took the interest in acupuncture by the West (after Nixon's visit to China in 1972), and the movement of 'back to the earth' by hippies, to revive the Traditional Chinese Medicine. Today in China, there are medical schools that teach western techniques, and the number of students enrolled for these courses is double those enrolled in TCM. An anomaly in the enrollment for TCM/acupuncture has arisen: half the students registered for TCM are foreign students (from the West)! There are 24 medical colleges in China today, where one can receive six years of training in western style medical treatments, acupuncture and herbal medicine.

Today the Barefoot Doctors are back and, in the late 1980's, over 1,000,000 Barefoot Doctors had been trained in six month to two-year programmes. Today, they are paramedics who learned and practice both Western and TCM.

When we moved to Molynes / Four Roads, in the shop just to the west of us was an elderly man whom everybody called 'Doctor'. His name was Chong Min Yin. Together with his wife they ran the grocery and bar. Sometimes their grandsons, Charlie and Winston, would occasionally, singly or together, visit them. We soon learned that Chong Min Yin had been a Chinese doctor in China but did not practise in Jamaica. But he did have the respect of the Chinese Community and especially that of my parents, because he was consulted for every ailment that befell any of us children.

One Christmas Holiday Ray had his first allergic reaction to eating ham made from Jamaican pork. His face began to swell, covering an area from his neck to above his right eye. That was the end of his plans for the Christmas Dance at the Chinese Athletic Club.

It was this Doctor who gave our dad the remedy. Dad purchased a root

from the herbalist in Chinatown, where he was provided with a special toothed saucer, much like the ginger graters available now in the kitchen utensils section of William Sonoma. Alcohol was added to make a paste. Ray was told to move the root in a counter-clockwise direction and the paste had to be applied with a feather from a duck's wing stroked upwards. The swelling from Ray's jowls disappeared the following day. Why a counter clockwise motion and the upward stroke? I was later told that it was the Chinese custom, and that the upward stroke pushed the swelling towards the top of the head where 'the bad vibes' have a shorter distance to travel out of the body. The downward movement would push these 'bad vibes' towards the inside of the body, which is not recommended.

It was very similar to one of my mother's teachings as I watched her peel an orange with a knife. Most of us will hold the orange with the left hand and the knife in the other. In the process of peeling it, the motion is of pulling the blade towards you. My mom would explain that it is better to push the blade away from the body, as the motion of pulling it towards you creates 'bad vibes'.

Doctor practised Traditional Chinese Medicine (TCM). Unlike western medicine, which seeks to treat the *symptoms* manifested in a patient, TCM addresses the *causes* of the symptoms. In old China the doctor was paid to keep you healthy and if illness befell you, then the doctor's reputation was severely damaged. If the patient was an influential person, that doctor might have been run out of town or killed.

Chinese have been using codified TCM for over 2,500 years. The *Nei-Jing* has potions for hundreds of maladies. The Chinese believe that illness is brought about when the energy, or Qi*, flowing through your body is either out of balance or blocked. TCM uses herbs, acupuncture, manipulative therapy, and food cures as well as exercise, to correct the balance of Qi in the body.

If you ate too much fried chicken, mom would say that you had too much 'nyet hee'* or heat (yang); and you should correct this imbalance by having something 'leung'* or cool (yin), like some watercress soup. Sometimes herbs are necessary to detoxify or rid the body of parasites.

The Chinese have identified and mapped the energy paths throughout the body. If the diagnosis is that energy is not reaching an organ, they would use accupuncture, moxibustion* and cupping* to open the path for the energy. Sometimes they would use massaging of the feet (reflexology), or whole body massage (Qi Gong* massage) to stimulate a sluggish organ. Tai Chi and Qi Gong breathing exercises are daily rituals to maintain flexibility and proper functioning of the body's organs.

Above: Mapping the energy path.

Right; Drawers used for storing herbs, with the balance scales in front

I remember Doctor coming over some nights to attend to dad's numerous ailments. They would sit at the table in the common room with dad's hands outstretched on the table and resting on a folded towel to neutralize the pressure in the reading. Doctor would look at dad's face for several minutes, checking his eyes carefully, before asking him to open his mouth to note the colour and condition of his extended tongue. He would then take dad's wrist between his fingers, and close his eyes to concentrate on assessing the intensity and speed of the four levels of pulses. From these observations he could make a good diagnosis of the malady affecting dad, and the corrections he needed to make.

A trip to the herbalist in China Town on Barry Street was always an experience. The store's name was Lee Tung Kee, and it was dark although it faced south. The north and west walls were lined with 6" x 6" drawers from top to bottom, one side to the other. These small wooden boxes contained fruit, bark, roots, leaves, dried insects, frogs, and even scorpions. In the glass cases were displays of gecko lizards stretched out on a bamboo frame, dried deer penises and tails, reindeer antlers, trays of dried seahorses of all sizes, boxes of ginseng – sliced and whole – licorice root, and brown piles of flaky cicada shells.

Below left; Herbs used in remedies.
Below right; Preparing the prescription

From the prescription Doctor wrote, the herbalist (left) would prepare the 'wraps' of the mixture of herbs, plants, seeds, barks etc. (below right) on the counter. Using a simple balance made of ivory with a brass plate attached at one end, and the counterweight swinging on a red thread at the other end, he would weigh the ingredients on to a large sheet of paper on which he had set out smaller sheets for the individual portions. When not in use this balance was kept in its case,

which was two guitar shaped pieces of wood, pinned at the narrow end and rotated over each other. A cavity to accommodate the plate and ivory beam was carved out between them. So was a pocket for the counterweight. The large barks and horns would be reduced to slivers or thin medallions by a huge

cutter looking like an oversized 'dow mah'* hinged on a cutting board. All nuts and shells, like dried cicadas, were pounded to a powder in a brass mortar with a matching pestle and a leather cover attached to the handle. The portions were wrapped individually and then everything was wrapped in a single parcel.

At home mom would prepare the decoction*. The individual portion would be placed in a special ceramic double boiler, the prescribed amount of water added, and the double boiler was covered and tied with a red string. Then it was left on the stove to simmer for what seemed like eternity, or until the water was reduced by the appropriate volume. Ginseng was a common 'herb' consumed. Its distinctive aroma permeated the home at least once a month.

Yuk-choi* soup was prepared as often as deemed necessary, each batch different from the next to correct a particular condition. Some of the common ingredients include the red grains (gui gee)* that were good for your eyes, lotus nuts, red plum, an elongated inedible bark, and the black bark that is reputed to correct ringing in the ears.

The herbalist also carried a variety of teas and other non-medicinal products that we kids loved. There were large sacks of peanuts and watermelon seeds – red and black varieties – containers of preserved plums (chim-pee moi* and wah moi*), olives (both lam* and ham-lam*), and li jai* and ham saa-li* (pickled Chinese apricots and sour plums).

My cousin, whose father was a Herbal Doctor in China, said that he only knows of two other men, apart from his dad and Chang Min Yin, who were of the same profession. One practised at the herbal shop, Lee Tung Kee, and the other was at a company named Nam Keung.

There are a series of everyday drugs that were staples in every Chinese family, and were used to treat ailments such as headaches, cuts, stiffness, the runs, toothaches, and sometimes serious injuries. 'Ship yin dan'* (aka Saplingtan) is a white powder in a small vial that was taken when you had a headache or a general pain. It turned out that it is Asprin... common ASA, that the Chinese had been using for many years before ASA was discovered in the west.

'E-e-yu'* aka U-I-oil was used for cuts, insect bites, and as a linament for bruises. Tiger Balm, now a common pharmaceutical item, was used for muscular aches and pain, motion sickness (rub some under your nose), fevers (rubbed onto your chest before going to bed), tooth ache – especially one with a cavity (apply a little to a small cotton swab and tuck it into the cavity). No family would be without Tiger Balm, Proof Rum and 'e-e-yu'.

Another linament was 'pak-fah-yu'*, used for those stubborn sore muscles; and the emperor of them was the 'yu-nan-pak-yuk'*. This white powder was used when you had a serious accident like a fall from a height, or a deep cut. If the cut was to the bone,

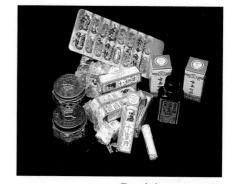

Tiger balm, yu-nan-pak-yuk, e-e-yu, ship-yin-dan

or a finger was severed, the powder was poured into the wound, and the injury securely bound. In a few days the wound would be knitted and healing well on its way. Injuries that may have damaged the internal organs were treated by ingesting the 'yu-nan-pak-yuk'.

One of the more pleasant medications was 'gam-fo-cha'*, a bitter herbal tea that was taken when one had a fever because it promoted sweating. It came in a yellow box (not to be mistaken for the herb tea taken for wash-outs) and the drawn tea was tempered with one or two pieces of preserved lime. Mom would slice fresh limes into two pieces, layer them in a big mason jar and liberally cover them with fine salt. This would stand for weeks as the salt extracted the lime juices and converted the firm green limes into a soft brown preserved lime. The preserved lime would sometimes be used as a condiment.

Alternative Medicine? No, this was Traditional Chinese Medicine.

Written by ©Roger Chen and edited by Sonia Gordon Scott.

* See Glossary

Down Memory Lane

Coconut Trees
Photograph ©Ray Chen

Minnie Chen
SHIP CHIT GOO

HER NAME IS really Shirley Chau So Chan. She was given the name 'Ship Chit' in nursing school (which means number 17), and later was called Ship Chit Goo by her patients and friends. 'Ship Chit Goo' is really Aunt Ship Chit. She married my dad, Wilfred Chin, who was born in Jamaica and attended University in Hong Kong where he met Ship Chit, my mom.

Ship Chit Goo left Hong Kong with her husband and two daughters to establish a home in Wilfred's birthplace of Jamaica in 1948. Wilfred's family was large, and her inclusion in the family allowed her to quickly establish relationships with a great many Jamaican Chinese families. Once she got registered and obtained her licence to practice, her reputation as a qualified nurse and midwife was rapidly established and, as the only Chinese midwife on the island, she was able to create a business for herself.

In the early years after her arrival, she would conduct deliveries at the patients' homes. In 1953 she eventually opened The So Chan's Nursing Home, at 50 Molynes Road, where she practised for 22 years until her departure to Canada in 1975. During her 22 years of practice she delivered many Chinese babies whose parents were shopkeepers. The patients would be delivered and stay in the home for 7-10 days. As per Chinese custom, the mothers were given chicken and wine soup daily, as this helps to increase lactation. By the time mother and baby were discharged, breast feeding was well established, and the mother was well enough to return home and resume assisting her husband in the shop.

Many patients were referred to her by Dr. Lee, a family doctor who did not do deliveries. She also had a good friend in Dr. Arthur Chin

Above: Midwife certificate issued to Chau So Chan in 1946.

Left: Chau So Chan as a midwife in China.

Shirley Chau So Chan as a midwife in Jamaica.

Loy who assisted her in emergency situations, and would do caesarean sections when necessary. She was a good midwife in that she was able to accept cases within her areas of expertise. She was well admired, respected and loved by her patients, and was not only a nurse to her patients, but she became their friend and confidante. She was indeed a very caring, helpful, and kind individual to all those with whom she came in contact, and truly made a difference to the lives of many people.

Ship Chit Goo led an active professional and social life, filling in the time between delivering babies and patient care with generous portions of entertainment, particularly at the mahjong table. She found great joy in the fact that, while in Canada, she was frequently asked to attend the weddings of many of 'her babies', the Jamaican Chinese children she had delivered. To this day many of these same young men and women refer to her as Ship Chit Goo (Aunt Ship Chit).

Written by Minnie Chen and edited by Sonia Gordon Scott.

Down Memory Lane

Devon House in St. Andrew
Photograph ©Ray Chen

Donna Lee
REFLECTIONS OF KINDNESS

IT WAS ONLY ten more days until Christmas. BB guns, dolls, board games, just the best array of toys and books, a dream for any child as Christmas was just around the corner!

My younger sister and I knew that none of these toys, which were in large  bags and boxes, would be for us. There they were, all in the living room, some wrapped in bright red paper, some already tagged waiting for delivery, and some half wrapped. We circled around and around, touching and picking out the ones we hoped would be ours, even as mom kept telling us not to play with the toys as they were for their godchildren. We often wondered who were these kids that were so special to my parents.

It wasn't until many years later, while living in Toronto, that I met one of the godchildren. He was a young man, close to my age who, when he found out that my dad was Donald Chung, exclaimed, "Do you know that the only Christmas presents my sister and I ever received for many years while growing up, was from your mom and dad. They are my godparents you know". When asked about their many godchildren, my parents just smiled. They had close to a hundred.

My dad was an insurance salesman, and he met many persons in his travels across Jamaica's countryside who became friends and clients. For many, he was their advisor, he assisted with legal matters and he acted as their spokesperson, since English was not their first language. As expected, the cultural differences as they settled into Jamaican life and business, brought with it conflict and problems, and dad was asked to intervene and assist. He felt an incredible bond with all Chinese persons – they were his extended family and, as a result, my parents became godparents to many.

It was a way of life and thinking at that time. Small things to others, but things that I remember, such as, never visiting a family with children without taking a small gift, perhaps just

Donna Lee's parents - Donald and Cynthia.

Donna Lee and her sister, Theresa, on their way to school.

some fruit, one of mom's cakes, and/or a bunch of cut flowers from mom's garden. This was the Chinese way, my parents would say.

We also were the recipients of kindness. My family remembers a surprise bag of oranges or Chinese sweets being dropped at our home, in return for assistance with a problem or support during a crisis. It was a gentler time, and a wonderful way to grow up, learning the gift of sharing.

Written by Donna Lee and edited by Sonia Gordon Scott
Photograph to the left and the gifts packages ©Ray Chen

Down Memory Lane

1.

2.

3.

4.

5.

1, 2, 3, Paper planes, paper zeppelins, paper boats were the order of the day. There were others that were made to 'blow air' by holding a pair of 'ears' and squeezing with an inward and outward motion, and another one was folded in such a way that when flopped in a forward and downward motion, it opened with a bang'.

4. Jamaican 'yo-yo' made from the bean pod of the Cacoon plant. A bamboo rod was placed in the holes that were bored through the three top pods. The bottom one was cut on one side and a small hole on the opposite side, as indicated in the photograph. The cord of about 8 inches was attached and wrapped to the bamboo rod inside the pod, and the other end was pushed through the small hole on the opposite side. It was then attached to a small piece of stick. You hold the bottom pod with one hand and by pulling on the cord (stick) with the other hand, the pole turns with the other pods in a similar way as a yo-yo.

5. Wooden toy 'police man' that moves with every squeeze of the handles. These were like toy acrobats and they came in all shapes and colours.

Joy Simpson
"UNCLE KEN" CHONG

I RECALL THE DAY I met Uncle Ken, back in 1966. I had expressed to my father my desire to learn hairdressing and cosmetology. Knowing that I was only 15 years old, my chances for acceptance into Ken's Beauty Salon and Cosmetology School were slim. Following his shift, and while still dressed in his police uniform, my father went to meet Uncle Ken to discuss my chances of becoming a student at his school. As expected, due to my age, Uncle Ken refused. My father did not give up so easily; he took me along with him to again meet Uncle Ken. I recall Uncle Ken saying, 'Mr. Simpson, she is too young, she is so small, she looks like 12 years old'. Maybe it was because I was so cute! (laugh). After further discussion, Uncle Ken agreed to give me a chance. From that day forward Uncle Ken became a second father to me.

My first day at Ken's Beauty Salon and Cosmetology School was very comfortable. Uncle Ken maintained a pleasant family-like environment. I studied and worked with Valerie, Chic, Doreen, Lily, Marlene, Joan, Pauline, Sue, Olive, Yvonne and so many other wonderful people. We found Uncle Ken to be kind and considerate. I remember the time when he allowed me to join another group of students for the evening classes even though my classes had ended for the day. The group included both men and women, many of whom went on to be successful in the trade. If there was ever a need to address any concerns, Uncle Ken would approach the individual privately and confidentially.

Uncle Ken was known for never turning away anyone who wanted to learn, even if they could not afford it. He provided the individuals with a uniform, bus fare and pocket money. The uniform, consisting of a white top, black pants or skirt, and black shoes, was mandatory. Each student was also provided with a badge with *Ken's Beauty Salon* printed on it. We were taught how to be professionals, how to sit, stand, and look our best at all times. His clients were extremely important to him. Uncle Ken preferred that all students and workers remain on the premises during working hours. There was no excuse we could come up with to go outside. He even hired a cook by the name of Inez (a.k.a. Cookie) to prepare hot lunches for us. If we weren't feeling well Uncle Ken would provide any kind of medication we could need. He always had a briefcase with many Chinese remedies to cure any illness.

Through conversation with the other workers, I learned of Uncle Ken's, prestigious clients. Impressively, his clients consisted of Government Ministers' wives (including Mrs. Shearer and her daughter), Mrs. Billings, of Billings Mattress Company, Mrs. Panel, Mother Facey, Meco Blanko (limbo dancer from Ocho Rios), and the wives of the English soldiers who were stationed at Up Park Camp prior to Independence, plus many more. Uncle Ken provided the best treatment and care for all his clients. After Independence, he went to Canada on a three-week study course, then returned to Jamaica to provide his services to Blacks, Chinese and Indians. Under his professional care even those with badly damaged hair would soon be getting styles like flips and upsweeps.

Hairdressing at that time was looked down on as a profession, and it was Uncle Ken who, through his personality and his approach, brought much respectability to the profession. Many of us would have been lost without him.

Uncle Ken is one of a kind; there will never be another like him. He will always be blessed and will never be forgotten. I think I can speak for all of us who had the privilege of knowing him. Up to this day, some of us, like myself, can still phone him for advice about anything. I admire the lifetime friendships he has maintained with many of his former clients. I especially appreciate his concern regarding the well being of my dad.

It was a great loss to Jamaica when Uncle Ken migrated to Canada. Thank you Uncle Ken. God bless always.

Uncle Ken is seated second from the left, with the graduating class of 1967-1968.

Written by Joy Simpson and edited by Sonia Gordon Scott.

Paul Chen-Young
THE CHEN-YOUNG FAMILY

ALBERT (Papa) CHEN-YOUNG was born in the province of Shenzhen in southern China, an only child of parents who were people of some means, being landowners. A picture of his father formally dressed and sitting upright in a straight-backed chair suggests that he was a man of stature.

Papa's real Chinese name was Chen Sen Fah but, over the years, it evolved into Chen-Young. Although 'Albert' and 'Young' were his given Christian names, he was referred to as Chen-Young, which was eventually hyphenated. We are most likely the only Chen-Young family in the world and it has now become the family name on the marriage and birth certificates of his descendants.

Papa's father left him in charge of rice fields and went to Hawaii in search of better business opportunities. From tapes made by Papa, he was a mere teenager when he demonstrated audacity by going to a moneylender and asking to borrow funds for his planned travel to Jamaica. According to him, the moneylender asked about security and, even before consulting his family, he gave the assurance that he would get their permission to mortgage the family lands, which he did. He was then able to finance his journey to Jamaica via Panama in 1918, along with many other adventurous Chinese migrants.

On arriving in Jamaica, he went to live and work with his uncle (Chen Sang) at his shop in Summerfield, Clarendon. He stayed there a few years, sleeping on a straw mat at the back of the shop before moving on to Catadupa, St. James with Winnifred Dawkins, mother of Joyce and Lascelles. He moved again, to rural Smithville in the hills of Clarendon, to start his own shop in zinc premises owned by the Daley's. There he lived with his wife, Iris, and children Joyce, Lascelles (Sonny), Ken, Paul, Neville (Sinna), Monica (Posie) and Lynne.

Albert and Iris Chen-Young's wedding.

Like most Chinese families, we children had to help around the house and the shop even before our faces could clear the top of the counter. We had to cut wrapping paper and learn how to wrap flour, rice, sugar and salt on a Friday evening in preparation for market day on Saturday. Being located in an agricultural community, we had additional chores such as drying and curing pimento, coffee, cocoa and peeling ginger, then spreading it out on the piazza in the morning and collecting it at the end of the day.

Working in the shop from an early age was the genesis of a business culture which is typical of Jamaican Chinese and, indeed, of the race worldwide. We learned the simple facts that you can only make a profit by selling at a higher price than you paid. We also learned how to get credit from the merchants in Kingston and extend credit to the community; how to handle money by receiving payments and giving change; how to win over customers by giving good service with a pleasant attitude; that you can succeed only by devoting long hours to the job, and that honesty is the best policy.

Papa was a quiet man who was not too interested in long conversations, was even more abrupt on the telephone, and hated confusion around him. But what a cook he was!! In the early days he did not allow the helper to cook for him and was stubborn enough not to eat Jamaican food. But all that changed over time and he came to like Jamaican food, especially roast yam and salt fish, and red pea soup. His Chinese meals, however, were special treats, and you would salivate as you awaited his food. Some of his specialties were boiled chicken with ginger sauce, foo gah*, pork and muknee*, pork and ham choy* (which he made from the fresh pak choy), pork and yam, pork and bamboo root (which he would go searching for in the woods), roast chicken, chicken with green peas, beef with ginger, mutton with lime leaves, etc.

About once per month he would go to Kingston on the early morning bus, which left at 5a.m. He would return about nine at night some days later, after staying with his friends at Barry Street, visiting merchants, reminiscing about China, eating and drinking gallons of tea (cha)* and, of course, playing mahjong* – sometimes throughout the nights. We always looked forward to his return when he would awaken us and give us goodies like sow-bow*, chim pee moi*, red popcorn and bean cakes.

There was really not much of a social life in Smithville with its small population, unpaved roads, and neither electricity nor running water. Telephones were a rarity in Jamaica during that period and any urgent matter was dispatched by telegrams at the post office. The only other Chinese doing business in Smithville were the Changs with whom we visited frequently. For social interaction with other Chinese, we looked forward with great anticipation to going, once per year, to the Chinese New Year celebrations in the town of Frankfield, some seven miles away, where the Frankfield Changs would have a large and lively party for Chinese from the surrounding areas.

Papa tried to teach us Chinese but without much success, partly because we were probably too dumb, but also because there was no one to talk with other than our friends at elementary school most of whom were, like us, poor country folks. In fact there was the feeling that if we spoke Chinese we would be 'different' and there was a self-consciousness about being Chinese, when it was not unknown to hear derogatory chidings. Only a very few students wore shoes to school and there were times when we, too, walked barefoot to school to show that we were not 'different'.

So as not to lose touch completely with our culture, it was common practice for Jamaican-born boys to be sent to China to learn the language and familiarize themselves with their cultural heritage. Plans were made for us to go and tall straw baskets were packed, but it was not to be, as at about that time, the Chinese communists were waging war against the Nationalists and plans were abruptly aborted.

Papa was a strong supporter of Chiang Kai-shek and the Chinese Nationalist Party, like most of the Chinese immigrants who came to Jamaica and adored the father of modern China-Sun Yat-sen. He hated the Chinese communists, who had executed his parents, and had no interest in visiting China, even after it became very popular for expatriate Chinese to do so, including his own children, who enjoyed being there to enjoy its rich cultural heritage and to meet the people.

Like many of his fellow Chinese immigrants, Papa supported local Chinese causes like the Chinese Benevolent Association and the Chinese Public School on North Street in Kingston. The School was famous for teaching both Chinese descendants and other Jamaicans the Chinese culture and to read and speak Chinese, also for its annual Chinese New Year festival. However, Papa was not active in any local groups.

In the early 1950s, the family moved from Smithville to a 2-storey build-

Members of the Chen-Young family. *Left to right: Ken Chen-Young, Monica Chen Weaver, Paul Chen-Young, Neville Chen-Young (in circle), Hazel (Lynne) Chen Tafares, Joyce Chen Williams and Lascelles (Sony)Chen-Young*

ing in Spaldings, Clarendon, in front of the market. The shop was downstairs while upstairs were the living quarters. It was quite a step-up from the zinc shop at Smithville. Spaldings was a very quiet and delightful town with paved streets and electricity. For most of the year, the climate was quite cool and comfortable but at Christmas time it became very cold. Spaldings and its environs were known to be among the coldest places in Jamaica.

Business at Spaldings was good, but the family finally decided to own their own place and purchased a corner shop at Four Paths in Clarendon where the climate was very hot all year round. All the children had by then left home to pursue further education, careers and start their own families, all except Neville who died tragically in a road accident in 1969. A similar sad fate followed his wife, Lola, who died shortly after in 1970, leaving three orphans who were legally adopted by our sister, Monica, and her husband, Leon, in Washington D.C.

Papa and Miss Iris left Four Paths and moved to Kingston where they retired. Miss Iris died in June 1987 at the age of sixty six. After visiting Miami, Florida in 1998, for a family reunion where children, grand and great-grandchildren came to pay their respects and to show their love to one who had given so much, Papa Chen-Young died in September, 1999 at the age of ninety six. Present (75 descendants) and future generations will be eternally indebted for the rich legacy of values he left us.

Written by Dr. Paul Chen-Young in consultation with members of the Chen-Young family and edited by Sonia Gordon Scott.

* See Glossary

Down Memory Lane

The town of Black River in St. Elizabeth Photograph ©Ray Chen

Ray Chang
*FAMILY PROGRESSING – MR. JOSEPH
(CHANG GIN SANG'S) FAMILY*

GROWING UP ON Roselle Avenue in Barbican, St. Andrew held some of the best memories for me, my siblings and my cousins. In a sense, we 'ruled' Roselle Avenue. Who were we? We were the Changs. My grandfather, 'Agung'* Joseph (Chang Gin Sang), his wife Lily (Phang Shee) and daughter Vera, lived at number 5 Roselle. His sons and daughter and their families also lived on Roselle Avenue or nearby. Gladstone Vernon – GV – (my father) was at number 3, Rufus at number 7, Leonard in the house behind Agung's and daughter Hazel (Chen), in the house behind GV.

Ray's grandparents - Joseph and Lily Chang

We did many things together. My cousins and I were transported to our various schools – Immaculate Conception, St. George's College and Campion Prep. in the 'Purity bus', which was really a van, but so many of us alighted from it that onlookers termed it a bus. At one time or the other there were over thirty children running around the five houses. Going on family picnics was always organized chaos; we never lost anyone going to and from Prospect Beach in St. Thomas but once, in 1958 when the Yallahs River flooded, the caravan of Changs was forced to detour via Port Antonio on the way home.

But how did Chang Gin Sang and his family get to Roselle Avenue?

Gladstone Chang

Like many Chinese immigrants to Jamaica, Joseph was born in Southern China – more precisely in Guangdong province, Dong Guan, Feng Gang , Ling Pai.

Traditionally, Hakka Chinese keep moving on, mostly to find a better life. Agung was no exception. He moved with two brothers to Bao On, Long Hua, then to Jamaica in 1908, leaving behind a pregnant wife, Lily, and their oldest son, Edward (Zhao Ji). After the birth of daughter Jin Jian, Lily immigrated to Jamaica, leaving Edward and Jin Jian in the care of relatives.

Although well educated by the Chinese standards then, Joseph spoke no English and struggled for at least two and a half decades to support his

Joseph and Lily's children, l-r:Gladstone, Violet, Vincent, Vera, Rufus, (cousin), Leonard.

growing family – Edward, Jin Jian, Vincent, Gladstone, Violet, Vera, Leonard, Rufus and Hazel.

At one stage, to make ends meet, he worked in Falmouth whilst his family remained in Kingston. One imagines the cross island commute was no fun back then. Joseph believed the key to a better life was education and it was the one thing he wished for all his children; however, he could not afford to send his older sons to high school.

With much perseverance and determination at Alpha Boys' School, Gladstone excelled. In 1929, Fr. Leo Butler, S.J., then headmaster of St. George's College (STGC), heard about this young student's struggles and offered to take him, based on deferral of fees ('pay the fees when you can'). Gladstone started at 13 years old and by 16 he graduated, achieving the prize for first and second form in the same year; he achieved distinctions in Math, Bookkeeping, English and even Latin. 'Mr. Chaps', who taught Math to three generations of Changs, maintained GV was the best of the lot (much to my chagrin).

Post STGC was also the post depression years; there were mouths to feed. Gladstone spent some years working at Commodity Store and as a land surveyor to help support his younger siblings, who also had to get an education.

The start of the road to financial success began when Agung started Ideal Bakery, creating the Butterkist brand. When his older brother Vincent died, it forced Gladstone to the forefront. Blessed with great business acumen (according to Agung), Gladstone went about purchasing Valentine's Bakery on Princess Street. My mother Maisie (Moo Young), a strong, independent woman, also purchased shares using her own money. Stories of her pastry recipes are renowned; together with Hazel she was the foundation of the pastry department at Consolidated Bakeries in later years.

Maisie and GV were married in 1942. As the story goes, they met at a St. John's Ambulance meeting; or was it when she deliberately smashed a tennis ball at him? They shared a common love of service and humanitarianism. In Maisie, GV found 'the lady'. A true 'patrician', Maisie was given to few words, and had a sense of style and occasion.

Gladstone and Maisie on their honeymoon.

The bakery took off and was to prosper beyond our imaginings. Agung's dream of tertiary education for his other children was fulfilled when Leonard graduated from Holy Cross and CalTech. Over the course of the next years, and well into the 1990s, the Chang name became synonymous with outstanding Chinese businesses and the best bread. The empire was being formed, with Gladstone at the helm, ably assisted by members of the family.

Agung was respected and admired within the Chinese community and was an active participant at the Chinese Benevolent Association and the Chinese Public School. His strong belief in all forms and types of education and tradition led him to arrange for a Chinese teacher to tutor us in Hakka at home while we attended traditional schools in Kingston.

The 1950s were the moving years. Valentine's Bakery moved to Red Hills Road and the Changs moved further uptown, to Barbican. There was now a dream team at Valentine Bakery; Gladstone 'GV', Rufus, Hazel and nephew Richard 'Dacca' (son of Edward, the eldest brother who was born in China) and of course their respective spouses. GV took the business to another level; Valentine's Bakery was merged with Powell's Bakery, then owned by Canadian expatriates, and Huntington Bakery, then owned by the William Seivright family, to become Consolidated Bakeries – a precursor to our Jamaican motto, 'Out of many, one people'. However, knowing my father, this was not even a consideration – he just had a good eye for business.

GV and Maisie raised 12 children, including five first cousins, the children of Maisie's oldest brother, Jocelyn. We are: Ian, Karen, Carole, Thalia, Hilda, Ray, Denise, Gay, Mary-Joy, Lily, Jo-Anne and Joseph. You would have thought it would be cheaper by the dozen.

Gladstone and Maisie and their 12 children, standing l-r: Ian, Carole, Hilda, Ray, Thalia, Gladstone, Karen. Sitting: Maryjoy, Gay, Maisie, Lily, Denise. In arms: Joseph, Jo-anne.

I remember my father saying it did not matter how big his empire got, he wouldn't be rich enough to leave us each a huge legacy…but what he could and did offer was education for all, in the field of our choice and to whatever level we aspired. What he probably knew then, as I know now, is that education was the best legacy.

Amongst the 12 of us, there are 17 tertiary diplomas, degrees and professional designations. More importantly, we learnt to be independent of thought.

GV and Maisie would have been as proud of us and our families as we are of them. We are all scattered throughout the world now, living considerably different lives, but coming together for significant and defining occasions. Roselle remains full of the best memories, of a time gone by where strong family roots were laid and where a sense of security remains.

That's only a small piece of my story.

Written by Ray Chang and edited by Sonia Gordon Scott.

* See Glossary

Albert

Crafton

Edward

Arthur

Charles

men who fought

Jamaican-Chinese in the Royal Air Force World War II

At the outbreak of World War II, many Jamaicans answered the call to join the armed forces of Great Britain. Over 100 young men from the local Chinese community enlisted in the Royal Air Force. This was quite a remarkable number considering the relatively small Chinese community in Jamaica at that time.

They served as officers, pilots, navigators, wireless operators, air gunners, and ground crews in mechanics and electronics. Some of these brave young men were Hector Chong, Francis HoOnn, Arthur Chin, Noel Chin, Noel Pinchong, Lloyd ChinLoy, Tony Chong, Easton Chong, Eric Williams, Keble Williams, Clifton YeeKee, Arthur MooYoung, Gervase Lee, Alvin Chin, and the Wong brothers - Arthur, Albert, Crafton, and Edward.

The following account of the six Wong brothers during World War II is described by Edward Wong.

Wilfred Lai

My father Charles Wong left his home in Toi San, China, and ended up in Jamaica. He married our mother in 1917 and soon had their first three sons: Charles, Arthur and Albert. Charles was four years old when my father took him to China and left him there with his family. On my father's return the others were born: Crafton Dudley, Edward Carlton, Kenneth Joseph, and Daphne Mildred a total of six boys and one girl.

Shortly after the start of World War II Arthur and Crafton enlisted in the RAF for air training in Guelph,

Canada. It was not long before Albert also did the same.

In 1942 they were enlisting RAF ground staff for training in England. I was not yet 18 years old but they accepted me, and I was trained as a wireless mechanic, servicing aircraft radio systems. Arthur did not make air crew and was sent to England to be an administrator dispatching replacements to various RAF stations where needed. Albert and Crafton finished training and were sent to England. Albert was an officer and was sent to Abingdon, Berkshire, a Wellington Bomber Station. On January 4, 1945 the plane on which he was navigator with six other crew members, was returning from a raid. They lost an engine and were forced to crash land. All aboard died. They all were interred at Regional Cemetery, Blacon Chester.

Kenneth enlisted in the local Jamaican Home Guard. In China, Charles enlisted in the Army and became driver for a senior officer during the war of resistance against the Japanese invaders. He came through the war and worked as a driver of transport trucks to support his wife, son and daughter. When my wife and I visited his home in Xian, China, we were told that he died of natural causes.

During the 1950s the Wong brothers established the electronics company of Wonards.

Edward Wong

104 more Jamaican Chinese who enlisted in the RAF.

Chance C.L.	Chin D.	Ching Hing C.N.	Ho Hing J.	Lue Sang W.P.	Phang U.A.	Wong E.C.
Chance D.E.	Chin D.	Chin Sue R.I.	Ho Lung A.G.	Lyew B.H.	Sun Ken	Yee Kee C.
Chance L.M.	Chin D.S.	Chong A.G.	Ho Lung B.	Lyn C.E.	Williams D.	Yee Sing V.
Chang A.G.	Chin G.F.	Chong H.E.	Hoo J.J.	Lyn C.G.	Williams D.A.	Yin C.E.
Chang B.	Chin H.G.	Chong K.C.	Hoo Fat V. A.	Lyn C.R.	Williams Eric	Young A.M.
Chang O.	Chin I.A.	Chuck A.G.G.	Ho On F. A.	Lyn F.F.	Williams Keble	Young A.S.
Chen D.E.M.	Chin L.	Chung A.	Hosang C.	Lyn R.	Wing D.A.	Young A.T.
Chen E.	Chin La	Chung A.G.	Hosang NVL.	Lyn M.L.	Wing R.A.	Young C.D.
Chen L.V.	Chin L.B.	Chung B.E.	Hosang V.	Lyn V.Y.	Wong A.F.	Young E.
Chen O.C.	Chin N.J.	Chung E.A.	Hosang Z.U.	Ming E.U.	Wong A.I.	Young E.
Chen V.A.	Chin P.C.L.	Chung M.L.	Lowe A.C.	Moo E.G.	Wong A.R.C.	Young K.
Chen V.H.	Chin P.G.	Chung R.	Lowe L.J.	Moo Young E.A.	Wong B.O.	Young V.E.
Chen W.T.	Chin V.	Chung S.	Lowe S.A.	Moo Young L.A.	Wong C.D.	Young V.P.
Chin Arthur	Ching H.A.	Chung S.A.	Lowe S.S.	Pin Chong N.	Wong C.I.	
Chin C.	Chin Loy L.A.	Fung L.	Lue H.L.	Phang C.B.	Wong E.C.	

The Chinese Platoon of the Jamaica Home Guard

(as appeared in **The Daily Gleaner**© *newspaper 10/3/44)*

JAMAICA WROTE ANOTHER page of military history when, in March 1943, the Chinese Platoon of the Jamaica Home Guard came into being. It was the first unit and is up to now the only unit of its kind in any of His Majesty's Forces in all the British Empire.

As soon as news of its proposed formation was received, eager and fit Chinese youths from all sections of the Corporate Area answered the 'Call to Arms'. The enthusiasm they showed was most encouraging. The standard of fitness can be estimated when it is revealed that only one failure was recorded from the whole platoon.

Few ethnological groups in this island are as keen on athletics as the Chinese. And the Chinese student of today usually boasts a fine physique which has been built up on the football, the basketball and the cricket fields. It was no great surprise then that the Chinese platoon which attracted the pick of the families and the pick of the schools stood out in the Home Guards as a physically fit unit.

Their training was regular and thorough and they improved rapidly. On the very first manoeuvre in which they took part they acquitted themselves creditably and in other subsequent exercises they have been better. On one occasion in particular they were singled out by the chief umpire as being exceptionally brilliant.

Their showing is attributable not only to their fitness but also to their capacity for hard work and to their willingness to tackle hard work.

Apart from their ability in the field, they have been spoken of highly on the parade square for their smartness. They have made several public appearances - the most memorable, when they formed a Guard of Honour for His Excellency the Governor on the occasion of China Sunday, December 5 last year. On this occasion, His Excellency himself complimented them on their smart showing. On the recent march through the city, this platoon took part and was given a big ovation.

The platoon consists of men of varying ages, taken from practically every walk of life - merchants, clerks, salesmen, accountants and students. Their numbers have been greatly reduced by departures for the R.A.F., the North Caribbean Force Overseas and other local units of His Majesty's Forces. Those left in the platoon are now busily engaged in instructing recruits.

LT. HEADLEY HO SANG

Most of the boys attend parades under the greatest difficulty and inconvenience, but it is hoped that in spite of this the platoon will again be brought to full strength.

The man who has the distinction of commanding this unique platoon is Lt. Headley Ho Sang, brother of Mr. Dudley Ho Sang, president of the Chinese Wholesalers' Association.

This Chinese officer enlisted in the ranks in March 1943, was promoted a Lance Corporal in August and Corporal in November. After a successful training course at the Command School, Up Park Camp, in January of this year he was commissioned and in July he was promoted to Lieutenant.

Dignified yet unassuming, wearing his uniform well, scrupulously attentive to duty, this officer promises to be a credit not only to the Home Guards but to the Chinese in Jamaica.

Lieutenant Colonel Reginald George Chin, J.P.

A CAREER IN THE MILITARY

THE EARLY YEARS

REGGIE CHIN (Chin Cheu Sang) was born at Chepstowe, Portland, the first son and the second of thirteen children born to Chin Shue and Alice Chin (née Williams (Ngui)), who came from the villages of Sack Mah Gann and Low Wei, New Foo, Tung Gunn, Kwangtung, China.

Home of Reginald Chin in Chepstowe, Portland.

He attended Skibo Elementary School where he developed a reputation as a fearless fighter. "I used to remove the wooden frame around my slate and break the slate into two triangles and use them as weapons. Well my father soon got wise to this and he nailed all the joints of the frame together – they just used to be glued – and that was the end of that." Eventually his father decided to send him to Chinese Public School, in Kingston. With 13 children to feed and clothe it was not easy for his parents. "Most of us either went barefoot or used to wear what was called 'God-blind-me' shoes to school. These were crepe sole canvas shoes, and I had two pairs. You'd wear one and wash the other. I believe they got the name God-blind-me from the fact that when they were washed, we used a thing called 'whitening' to make them look even cleaner. Well the shoes were so white when they dried that just looking at them, especially in the sun, could make you go blind!" he said, laughing. He has a great appreciation for life and laughs easily as he reminisces about his life. "Looking back, life was hard, you know, because many families were very poor, but we had a lot of fun because we didn't know anything different then."

From Chinese Public School he went on to St. George's College. It was in 1945, on first seeing Lieutenant Headley Ho Sang in the uniform of an officer of the Jamaica Home Guard, that first stirred his interest in the military. At St. George's he joined the school's unit of the Army and Air Cadet Force (AACF). As was common with first generation Jamaican Chinese of that era, he was sent back to China to live with his grandparents to get to know the country and culture of his parents. The year was 1946 and he was 15 years old. "It was very interesting but I would say that the most important lesson I learned during this period was respect for elders. You didn't talk back, you didn't argue with your elders. Respect for them was ingrained," he said. Although there was constant political foment, life went on as usual until the Communist Party's defeat of the ruling Nationalist Government in 1949. He remembers morbid scenes of executions and gruesome beheadings and joined millions of other Chinese in a mass exodus.

He escaped to Hong Kong where, as a British subject, he became a resident in 1950. Among other things, he learned to speak Cantonese during his stay and also studied accounting at St. Joseph's College. He then went on to earn the Honour Diploma in bookkeeping and accounts from the London School of Accountancy in 1953.

During his time in Hong Kong he joined the Hong Kong Auxiliary Air Force, a sub-unit of the Royal Hong Kong Defence Force, as a Radar Operator. He was also part of a contingent which represented his unit on parade at the Coronation of Her Majesty, Queen Elizabeth II in 1953, and he returned to Jamaica in 1954, having served in the Hong Kong Auxiliary Air Force for four and a half years.

MARRIAGE, FAMILY & BUSINESS

On arrival, he went directly from the ship to a small restaurant on Luke Lane with friends. It was here that he met his future bride, Dorothy Theresa Lee, daughter of the owner of the restaurant. They were married in 1957 and eventually had four sons, three of whom have become engineers while the fourth became an Optical Technologist. He worked for the Shell Company (W.I.) Limited as an accounting clerk and held a number of posts including Depot Manager (Montego Bay), and Retail Marketing Representative, before going out on his own in 1962, as owner/operator of the 'Reggie's Shell Service Stations'. During this period, he organized the first street dance as part of Jamaica's Independence celebrations. It subsequently became a much anticipated and very popular part of the celebration programme. He also opened a boutique in Lane Plaza (Reggie's of Liguanea), which was run by his wife and sisters-in-law.

A CALL TO ARMS

But the call to military service remained strong. He sold his service stations and, with the blessing of his wife and children, he joined the Third Battalion, the Jamaica Regiment (National Reserve) on 14th November, 1966, and commenced training as part of a special group of sixteen Officer cadets. Training exercises took him to many different countries including England, Scotland, Canada, Puerto Rico, and the British Virgin Islands.

RISING THROUGH THE RANKS

The Battalion was formed in 1961 by then Premier, the Hon. Norman Washington Manley, during the period of the West Indies Federation, to provide internal security and to defend Jamaica. They are a military group that act as a back-up to the regular army while functioning as a unit in its own right.

Commissioned on 26th April 1967, Second Lieutenant Chin was the only Chinese in the Battalion, not an easy position to be in, especially when many of his fellow officers had the benefit of a higher standard of education. This in no way deterred him but made him determined to be the best at whatever assignment he was given. Through dedicated service, personal sacrifice and hard work, he rose steadily up the ladder in the ensuing years. From Motor

Lt. Colonel Reginald George Chin being introduced to General Colin Powell U S Army, Chairman of the Joint Chiefs of Staff, U S Armed Forces.

Transport Officer (1967), Platoon Commander (1968), Second-in-Command of 'B' Company (1969), Officer Commanding 'A' Company, 'HQ' Company, 'E' Company then back to 'HQ' Company (1971-1982).

He served as Battalion Second-in-Command from January 1983 until his appointment as Commanding Officer on 4th July, 1985. He has the double distinction of being the longest serving Commanding Officer (over eight years), and the only Jamaican of Chinese descent to command a battalion in this island.

ACTION

Since Independence, the Battalion's main function has been to perform ceremonial and internal security duties, but on Colonel Chin's watch they have seen quite a bit of action.

They have been assigned, on several occasions, to help contain violence – e.g. the West Kingston riots ('66), the Rodney affair ('68), the State of Emergency ('76), and the violent 1980 general elections. Of that time Colonel Chin says: 'Those were some bad times when we were out on the streets many nights.' The tension in the air was thick enough to be cut with a knife. However, he continued, 'we didn't have any opposition when we went out to keep the peace. We didn't harass people and they respected us for that.' The flood relief operations in western Jamaica ('79) and Clarendon ('86) were other occasions when the Battalion was called into service. 'We helped to rehabilitate many people in those parishes. We assisted the Red Cross with our medical officers; they set up clinics and examined and treated hundreds of people.' Again, on the occasion of the general strike, when even the Police and the Fire Brigade came out, the Battalion had to man the essential services, e.g. hospitals, water resources, police and fire brigade stations. In 1983 members of the Battalion were part of the Caribbean peace-keeping force to Grenada.

AND KUDOS

In 1968 and 1983 the Regiment took part in the Military Tattoo held in Jamaica and, on the occasion of Her Majesty's visit in 1975, they trooped the

Colours for her. They were the first Reserve Battalion, outside of the United Kingdom, ever to have trooped Colours for the reigning Monarch. On their 10th anniversary, in 1972, the Battalion was presented with the Key to the City of Kingston, and in May, 1987, they received the Key to the City of Montego Bay. In 1980, the Government presented the Battalion with a Certificate of Honour for Meritorious Service, based on their work in flood relief duties in western Jamaica in 1979. They also provided the guard of honour at Independence celebrations, the opening of Parliament, the installation of Custodes, and for overseas digni-

Above left: His Excellency The Governor General The Most Honourable Florizel Glasspole ON, CD. presenting the medal of Honour for Meritorious Service on the 17th Oct. 1977 at Kings House to Colonel Reginald Chin.
Above right: Colonel Chin (at right) providing guard of honour on the arrival and departure of His Holiness, Pope John Paul II.

taries. Colonel Chin's Battalion's last public duty, two weeks before his retirement, was to provide a guard of honour on the arrival and departure of His Holiness, Pope John Paul II, on the 9th and 11th August, 1993.

Colonel Chin is remembered by many of the men who served under him with gratitude and deep respect. Gratitude because, during his tenure, he established a savings scheme for the men with the Victoria Mutual Building Society, which enabled many of them to realize their dream of owning their own homes, completing their education or educating their children. It was just one of many ways in which he assisted them to rise above their circumstances and they have never forgotten him or what he did for them.

FAREWELL

On 28th August, 1993, Lieutenant Colonel Reginald George Chin took his leave from the Third Battalion, the Jamaica Regiment (National Reserve) which he had served faithfully for 27 years, with these words of advice 'which have served me well over the years:

> *Always be ready to give of your best*
> *Always be ready to co-operate with others*
> *Always be ready to accept success with humility*
> *Always be ready to confront your personal flaws*
> *Always be ready to attempt the most difficult task.'*

Among his awards have been the Queen's Coronation Medal (1953); the Medal of Honour for Meritorious Service (1977); the Medal of Honour for Efficient Service (1978); First Bar to the Efficient Service Medal (1985 – in lieu of a 2nd medal); Second Bar to the Efficient Service Medal (1989 – in lieu of a 3rd medal); First Bar to the Medal of Honour for Meritorious Service (1989 – in lieu of a 2nd medal). He was also appointed a Justice of the Peace for the Parish of St. Andrew in May, 1979.

Written by Sonia Gordon Scott as told by Lt. Col. Reginald George Chin, J.P.

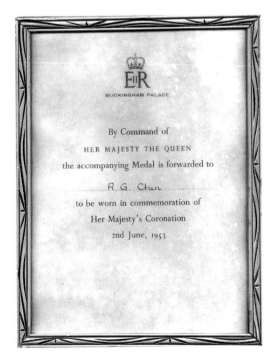

EIIR

BUCKINGHAM PALACE

By Command of

HER MAJESTY THE QUEEN

the accompanying Medal is forwarded to

R. G. Chin

to be worn in commemoration of

Her Majesty's Coronation

2nd June, 1953

Osbert Chung
THE GOVERNOR GENERAL AS A FRIEND

OSBERT CHUNG was born in Port Antonio on June 27th, 1941. The second of four children, he had an older sister, Nerissa, and two younger brothers.

Osbert was born to live a life in the military; it was his love for the military and a career as a soldier that placed him among the few who have accomplished so much in a military career in Jamaica. However, his early beginnings did not, at first, seem promising.

He was expelled from Titchfield High School for smoking Four Aces cigarettes. His mother was a Roman Catholic and, as a member of the choir, she was able to get him into St. George's College through the Church. It was while a student at St. George's that he joined the Cadet Force. He was attracted to the principles and ideals of being a soldier, and he knew that the cadet force could give him the foundation that he needed to be a professional military man. There were the uniforms, drills, discipline, physical fitness competitions, esprit de corps, adventure, but, most importantly, there was the opportunity to commit to the supreme sacrifice of giving his life, if necessary, for the protection and preservation of Jamaica and its people.

He was 17 years old when he graduated from St. George's, and in 1958 he returned to Port Antonio where he rejoined the Cadet Force at Titchfield High School. In 1959, he won an island-wide competition sponsored by Esso, and received the Cup for the best Guard Commander. Winning this event confirmed his love for the military as a career.

In 1961, he was selected by the Jamaican Government to represent the island at the Cadet Centennial Celebrations in London, England, where he was presented to the Queen at Buckingham Palace.

On his return, and before Independence, he was selected by the then West India Regiment to go to the Royal Military Academy, Sandhurst, for two years. By then, Osbert was convinced that he had made the right decision regarding a career in the military. A major turning point was when the Jamaican High Commissioner, Sir Lawrence Lindo, paid him a visit at Sandhurst. He asked Osbert to return to Jamaica, to serve his country by joining the new Jamaica Defence Force. This was quite an honour and he felt humbled at the same time, as he was the first Chinese-Jamaican to have achieved this level of recognition by the Government of Jamaica. In some way unknown to him, he was being groomed for bigger roles back home.

He graduated from Sandhurst in 1963 and, on his return to Jamaica in 1964, Brigadier David Smith sent him to Newcastle to be the Training Officer for all new recruits in the JDF. He returned to Up Park Camp in 1965. Then in 1966, Brigadier Smith appointed Osbert to the position of aide-de-camp (A.D.C.) to Princess Alice, sister of King George the sixth, during her sojourn in Jamaica as Chancellor of the University of the West Indies. This posting was new and the duties were quite different from all previous postings.

Princess Alice returned to Buckingham Palace in 1966, and Jamaica appointed its first native-born son, Sir Clifford Campbell, as Governor General. There was a sense of pride among the people and there was much to celebrate as a nation, in this historic and bold step. The Chinese community also had much to celebrate as one of their sons, Osbert Chung, was appointed to serve as A.D.C. to Sir Clifford. They were very proud of his achievements.

Above l-r: Lucien Chen, Eddie Lai, Neville Smith, Sir Clifford Campbell, Hugh Levy,Sugar Ray Robinson and Osbert Chung.

As the A.D.C., he had to reside on the grounds of Kings House and a certain friendship or bond was formed out of his working relationship with the Governor General. Coincidentally, Osbert and Sir Clifford were both born on the 27th of June and they celebrated their birthdays together for three years. Osbert remembers the occasions when he found on his desk bundles of sugarcane tied up by 'wis' (a flexible vine or root used for tying). On other days, it was St. Julian or Bombay mangos. At first he was puzzled as to who the sender could be. It turned out to be none other than the G. G. himself. This was his way of showing his appreciation and saying 'thank you' for Osbert performed above and beyond the call of duty. The mangoes and sugarcane were from the grounds of King's House which was laden with many fruit trees. It was a period he enjoyed and remembers with fondness. In 1967, Osbert accompanied Sir Clifford and Lady Campbell on a three month world tour which included visits to Canada, the U.S.A., Scotland, England, Germany, France, Switzerland, Italy, Belgium, Holland and Africa. He served Sir Clifford from 1966 to 1969.

Above l-r: Neville Smith, The Most Honourable Sir Donald B. Sangster O.N., K.C.V.O. and Osbert Chung

He arranged the swearing-in ceremonies for Sir Donald Sangster, the Honourable Hugh Shearer and Edward Seaga as Prime Ministers, and had frequent meetings with Sir Alexander Bustamante at Jamaica House and the Honourable Norman Manley at Drumblair, during his tenure as Sir Clifford's A.D.C.

A brief list of famous people with whom he was associated reads like a Who's Who of royalty, presidents and super stars in the entertainment field: All members of the British Royal Family; Her Serene Highness, Princess

Grace of Monaco (the former movie star, Grace Kelly) and her husband, Prince Rainier; Her Majesty, Queen Juliana of the Netherlands; General Charles De Gaulle; Presidents Richard Nixon, and Ronald Reagan; British Prime Minister, Sir Harold Wilson; Pope Paul VI; Secretary-General of the United Nations, U. Thant; super stars of film, Elizabeth Taylor, Sean Connery, and Bing Crosby, and five times middleweight boxing great, 'Sugar Ray' Robinson.

In 1963, he did peace-keeping duties as a soldier in Cyprus and also had military assignments in Iceland, Greece, Yugoslavia, Turkey and Wales.

In 1969, he was appointed A.D.C. to the Governor-General of Canada, the Honorable Roland Michner, for the duration of his visit to the island.

Prior to his retirement from the JDF in 1970, Osbert was appointed Senior Staff Officer for Administration and Logistics in the JDF.

In 1971, he was appointed marketing manager for Rothmans and the House of Dunhill at Carreras.

Between 1972 and 1973 he was appointed Vice-President of National Packaging Corp. (with Carl Hendrickson)

From 1974-1975 he was Marketing Manager of Tropical Battery Company; 1977-1978 - General Manager, National Cash Register.

He migrated to Canada in 1979, but he will always cherish the memories of this island which he has re-visited every year, and will always call home.

Written on behalf of Osbert Chung and edited by Sonia Gordon Scott.

Down Memory Lane

A Sunday afternoon musical concert with the Jamaica Military Band at the 'Band Stand' in Hope Gardens, St. Andrew
Photograph ©Ray Chen

Donette Chin-Loy
LLOYD ASHTON PAUL CHIN-LOY

SERVICE TO FELLOWMAN AND
COUNTRY – NUMBER ONE

I wish my father was here to tell our story. He was such a great storyteller – engaging, knowledgeable, enthusiastic and energetic. He was a kind of 'Chinese leprechaun' – small and spirited. He could tell of the family's roots and history as if he had actually been there. His was a brilliant mind, full of adventure, dreams and an insatiable quest for knowledge.

He passed away in 1998. But who was he?

Lloyd Ashton Paul Chin-Loy (Woon Sen) a.k.a. 'Japs', 'Tojo', was born in Meares, Clarendon, of a Chinese father, Ernest Chin-Loy from Niu Fu, China, and a Jamaican mother of Creole and French background, Daisy Watts. Ernest was one of thousands of Chinese who emigrated to Jamaica for a better life. Daisy, on the other hand, was from a genteel, well appointed Jamaican family, whose roots spanned France, Britain and Cuba. As the story goes, Daisy's parents married in order to unite two estates in Clarendon. Her father was a Jamaican and her mother, Miss Delahay, was of French descent.

Lloyd Ashton spent the better half of his younger life leading two lives after his parents divorced. As a small child he lived with the Watts in Tranquility, Portland, where his uncle, James Montague Watts, was the headmaster of the school. His first cousin, Joyce Watts, tells the story of a "talkative little boy with a very cheerful, attractive little face."

At about 13, Lloyd left his mother's relatives and moved to Kingston to live with his father's relatives, the Kongs, at Kong Brothers in Cross Roads. Mrs. Alice Kong (nee Chin-Loy) 'Ah-goo', was his father's sister. I remember my father telling us about the adventures of living at Kong Brothers where the doors closed at a certain time and after that, only Chinese was spoken. It was, as you can imagine, a completely different life for him, a totally Chinese way of life. Dad embraced all facets of his culture, on both sides, and was very proud to be Jamaican and Chinese. In fact, his knowledge of China was phenomenal. It was as if he had been born and lived there for years. He had never been to China, but his dream of visiting remained until a few years before his death.

His brother-in-law, the Reverend Easton Lee, often tells how Lloyd was a main source of information on China for his radio show, 'Children of the Dragon'. "Lloyd was able to get into details, sometimes sharing little known trivia which, when researched further, was of historical significance," says Easton.

Lloyd attended St. George's College, that bastion of Jesuit learning, where boys were turned into men and where men were thought to think. The STGC days were some of the best for dad. Never a dull moment, he recounted stories of the priests, boxing in the tower, higglers at the North Street gate, and some of his oldest and dearest friends, like John Hanna.

Dad's yearning for adventure and a desire to serve his country led him, at 16, to leave (run away is more like it) St. George's College. He lied about his age and enlisted in the Royal Air Force in Britain. World War II was on, and as my father boarded the ship bound for Britain, he probably did not know then that he was about to encounter a whole new world in the quest for a 'free' world.

The Royal Air Force was dad's life. He served as a wireless operator, based in different parts of Europe. Life in the RAF taught him true patriotism and equality. He told us the story of meeting with a group of soldiers from the United States once, when his ship docked in the U.S. The Jamaican troops wanted to go into town for some R&R, but the black American troops warned them that there were only certain parts of town where 'coloureds' were allowed. Undaunted, the Jamaicans saw this as a challenge. So with great gusto and confidence, the 'Queen's men' defied the 'coloured only' rule and had themselves a jolly old time in the prohibited areas.

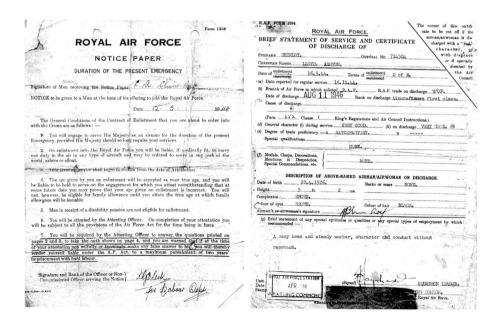

The RAF reinforced dad's spirituality, sense of camaraderie and caring for his fellow soldiers. For many years, and only after his passing, did we realize that dad carried a Catholic prayer book, photos of the saints and a rosary, in his wallet.

In the RAF, dad made lasting relationships which were to continue long after the war. My brother and I recall being children of an RAF man. Curphey Place in Swallowfield, Kingston, was where we first met Santa Claus; where many childhood memories were created with Keeble Williams, Barry Beckford and their families. Where Buzzy Williams, Oliver Marshall, Flight Lt. John Ebanks (a real war hero, who was gunned down at least six times), Keith Levy, Dudley Thompson and many, many others, became familiar names in our household.

1. The Defence Medal 1939-45.
2. WWII Medal

The medals earned in the Royal Air Force were a source of pride for my father although we were never quite sure what they represented. I know he must have told us but we never paid much attention, taking it for granted that one day we would *really* pay attention to the stories of those medals. No doubt they were well earned.

Years later, dad would hold many positions on the Executive of Curphey Place. One great memory for me was being chosen by the Wings Day Committee, to place a wing on the Governor General, Sir Florizel Glasspole. My father was proud. Along with my mother, I attended many functions at Curphey Place. It seemed that the members of my family had now become honorary members of the RAF.

Somewhat of an intellectual, dad's opportunity to pursue higher learning also came from the Royal Air Force, when he was offered a place at the London School of Economics to study for a law degree. He never took up the offer for, after returning to Jamaica, he married mom (Daphne Lee), and I was born soon after.

My father had a number of business ventures over the years including insurance underwriting for Confederation Life. He and mom ran a football pools agency on East Queen's Street. In those days my brother Jonathan and I would help at the office. Then there was the Printing and Allied Services company, where the best exercise books were made. Finally, in the 1970s, my parents bought a building on Half Way Tree Road, which became the birth place of Aquarius Records and recording studio. Those were the halcyon days. In true perfectionist style dad had Mr. Rosser, from Scotland, build a state of the art recording studio, one of the first in Jamaica. The recording industry boomed and so did Aquarius. Aquarius Records was the most sought after store, with an unmatched reputation for service and products.

Many stories abound of recording artistes who passed through Aquarius. Dad gained a reputation on Half Way Tree Road as 'Missa Chin-Loy, de Chiney man with de bes' studio and de record shop'. The downturn in the economy, coupled with other factors, made it difficult to keep up with the new technology and the necessary re-tooling of Aquarius' Studio. In the late 1980s, dad made a wise business decision to lease the studio to the Fab 5 band where it remains today.

More business opportunities abounded and, in the late 1980s, mom and dad opened Fire Side Fast Food, the talk of Half Way Tree. But in the early 1990s, with the introduction of major fast food chains and the expansion of local food businesses, they decided to close Fire Side. Today, the Aquarius building is home to a major fast food chain and other small businesses.

Above the Chin-Loy family. Seated l-r: Daphne, grand-daughter Amanda. Standing l-r: Karen (wife of Jonathan), Donette, Suzette and Jonathan

My father and I shared hundreds of special moments, as he did also with my sister Suzette and brother Jonathan. What I cherish deeply, however, was his passion and intensity when undertaking a project or business venture. He and mom became directors of my public relations company in the early 1990s. Dad was the voice of reason. We had many disagreements over his practicality and sober approach, but it did not dampen his enthusiasm, or stifle his creativity.

His family and friends remember his great zeal and passion for golf. He was a little pro, never daunted by a bad game, or a bad day, even having the temerity to give a lesson or two to a real pro. Dad would press on, keeping focus, seldom breaking 100, but achieving a hole-in-one at Constant Spring Golf Club.

In retrospect, I realize that dad was a philosopher and teacher; after all, he came from a long line of teachers and academics. He had a burning passion for service to fellowman and country. He believed all men and women should have the opportunity to serve.

According to his cousin, Joyce Watts, "the most precious gift to him was a book. I can still remember *The Adventures of Tom Sawyer, Huckleberry Finn,* the *Tarzan* series, *Zane Grey* series, *Oliver Twist.* He read the entire school library including the classics and Greek mythology. He even read the Bible right through more than once." Further, according to Joyce, "he wanted to right all the wrongs in the world."

Lloyd Chin-Loy's life was not marked by national accolades or public recognition, but that did not matter; he was, after all, the 'guy who stayed in the back office'. What was important to him was that he understood his responsibility to others and to country.

My sister Suzette summarized dad this way: "Dad you walked many, many miles before you slept, and I am so proud to say that for part of that journey you were not only my father, but you were my friend. To me you are, and forever will be, truly amazing."

That was the essence of Lloyd Ashton Paul Chin-Loy, as we knew it.

Written by Donette Chin-Loy and edited by Sonia Gordon Scott.
Photograph of medals ©Ray Chen

Stanford Williams
THE ELDERS

IT WAS ABOUT 1916 when the first elder in my life, my father, Ngui Chun Fen arrived in Jamaica from China. Once landed he became James Williams. My mother followed a few years later, and the two settled in Green Island, Hanover.

My father was a friendly, sociable man. I grew up watching him happily interact with people from all walks of life. While building a successful whole-sale, retail, dry goods business, he frequently took time out to help the villagers, and became Green Island's favourite son. He did little and big things. like in 1935, when he helped with the slavery abolishment anniversary celebrations. At his expense, he prepared generous packages of rice, flour, sugar and codfish and handed them out to the large crowd gathered outside his building on the morning of August 1st. He was very open-minded that way.

At Cornwall College, my high school, I'd be reminded about tolerance and appreciation from another authority figure. It happened one day in geography class while reading about different countries and their culture or *habits*. When it came to China, the book read that since meat was scarce, dog was eaten. Now of course in those days in Jamaica, that whole notion was a big thing. That night, after supper, one of my class mates yelled at me in the yard, *"Hey, Chiney! You miss the dog meat?"* and I retaliated with some equally negative racial remark. Well of course he and his friend, two big guys – *huge* – took exception and lunged at me. But at the time I was lifting weights and was ready, and we instantly became a mess of rolling punches. But as it was two to one, I had to do something. So I darted to a window, broke the pane with my hand – I was so angry – and ripped out a piece of glass. *"Come on now, you cowards!"* I was shouting at the top of my voice in an otherwise quiet yard.

And that's when the teacher on duty came out and marched us up to the English headmaster, Mr. Jackson. It was 7:00 p.m. First Mr. Jackson took in the other two boys while I waited outside. Then he summoned me in. *"Now, tell me exactly what happened,"* he said. So I did, and eventually the two confirmed my story. Mr. Jackson turned to them. *"If I hear this repeated by anyone, I will hold you both responsible. You do not let this happen again. It ends here now. Shake hands and forget it."* But when they left, he told me to stay. And then we talked.

"You know, young Williams," he said, *"I've eaten horse meat. I've even had snake."*

"Mr. Jackson," I replied, *"I really don't see anything wrong with eating that or eating dog."*

"Well I don't see anything wrong with eating dog either. It's just part of the culture. But you must remember that some people just can't understand that."

We sat there until midnight and I learned a lot from his time with me that night. As for the incident, the two boys were true to their word. The comment was never repeated.

I was coming into my own at 16 or 17, when we moved to a new home and wholesale provision business at 76 Princess Street, Kingston. The timing couldn't have been worse. It was 1944, and WWII was in full force. Pretty much everything was on quota. Ours was one cask of fish per release, one release per month. We could have sold that in a day. Other stores had better quotas. We were new and at a disadvantage but I soon figured my way around that.

As soon as the releases came out, I wasted no time in rushing to get the wharf order. And then I applied lessons learned from my father – I talked. Each time I'd stop by the Food Control Distribution and drop word that I needed a bigger quota. Each time they'd say how much they'd like to help me, but that they couldn't. One day, on my usual visit, I walked in to see only one person in the office, having his lunch.

"Oh boy," I joked. *"You're the better man. You're having lunch at lunch time. I have all the time but no lunch!"* With that he signalled me to sit and a casual conversation ensued. Eventually I heard the magic words.

"Would you like an increased quota?" he asked.

"You're asking me that?" I said. *"Are you kidding me?"*

"Alright," he answered. *"I'll come up and talk with you after my lunch."* And so he did. And we talked some more. *"Okay,"* he said after awhile. *"You can get any amount of flour and fish, anything you want. But you know I have to get something."*

"Okay," I said. *"What's the deal?"*

"For every cask of fish you get, I have to get ten shillings."

There it was. Now at the time the gross profit on a cask of fish was 25 shillings. But that didn't deter me. The thing was, once you had the right merchandise, you could sell anything. We also agreed on five shillings to him for every barrel of pickled mackerel or pigs tail, and four pence per bag for rice, flour and cornmeal. I went back to the shop and announced the good news. Business went gung ho after that.

At 19 I was ready to go off on my own. At first I got a job selling potatoes and onions with *Chin Yee & Co.* on Princess Street. It was hard work. I had to walk all over Kingston for £7.00 per week. After a month or two, I went to my boss.

"Fook shook,*" I said. *"I'd like you to put me on commission."*

"You sure you want that?" he asked.

"Positive."

My first commission cheque was £75.00. Soon I began selling for other people. It was all work at this point. On Saturdays I earned in one day what I earned in one week. Like my father, I just talked with people. And that's how I got into the quota business. I began strolling down King Street taking note of what was going on. There was a men's store, *John Dor's,* which I'd occasionally stop by. Eventually I befriended the owner, a Mr. Barrow, and began stopping by for more frequent chats. One day he was standing at the door.

"Things are quiet today, I see."

"Shoes," he said. *"I need shoes to sell and I can't get them. Listen, if you know of anyone with quotas they can't use, tell me and I'll buy the quota."*

"How much would you pay?"

"Two pounds a pair."

Again I wasted no time. I went to all the Chinese haberdasheries and found a few with quotas that weren't being used to the fullest. They were bringing in slippers. For those that didn't have a quota, I made a deal. I'd apply for one for them. When they got it, they'd give it to me for a pound a pair.

I did something similar with Atlas thread. At the time it was the best quality cotton thread you could get from England. One day this fellow walked by me, and I just asked,

"How are you with Atlas thread?"

"You want? I have a lot."

"Give me a good price." And he did right on the spot.

"I'll be back," I said. And off I went scouting around Chinatown for takers. I didn't have a car, so I bummed rides, but I also needed something else. Money to buy the thread.

Now I had spent time establishing a close relationship with a particular elder in the community whom I met during my sales runs. Our conversations were at first truncated and stiff. *"Hello, Mr. Wong, I am Stanford Williams."* At best I'd get an *"Uh? Um,"* and barely a glance. That would progress to one question – usually who your parents were – and then maybe a sentence or two.

Young Stanford Williams.

I'd drop in as often as I could. Eventually he became like a godfather. If I got a job offer, I'd bounce the idea off him. If I had an idea, I'd go to him.

On this occasion, I headed straight for him. *"I need to borrow £200,"* I announced. He muttered something as if fussing, but it was not refusal. He moved towards a tall chest in the room and opened it. The thing was crammed with notes. *Crammed.* He pulled out two bundles and tossed it to me. I didn't tell him what it was for, nor did he ask. I then borrowed a friend's car, delivered the thread, and collected the money on the spot. Three, four hours later, I went back to my godfather. *"How much interest you want?"*

He swore at me in Chinese, asking why I talked to him about interest. He took back the £200, returned it to the chest and waved me off. I left with my huge profit intact.

Stanford and Ivy Williams
wedding photo.

And that was my philosophy from an early age. If you want to get ahead, seek advice from those who have already walked your path. Listen to your elders. They have the experience. That's how I survived, and believe me, I went out there as green as could be. It was *their* input that made the world of difference.

Written and edited by Alex Lee as told by Stanford Williams

Down Memory Lane

Dunn's River Falls near Ocho Rios, St. Ann
Photograph ©Ray Chen

Patrick Lee

LESSONS I LEARNED FROM LEE TOM YIN

Lee Tom Yin & Theresa (Dolly) Li were married in 1937 in Kingston, Jamaica and had seven children. He was also a former teacher at Dung Fong Middle School in China.

MY FATHER LEE TOM YIN arrived in Jamaica in 1930, preceded by a brother, Lee Chew, and a sister, Lily, who was married to David Kong. My mother, Theresa (Dolly), was born in Jamaica and she and my father had five daughters and two sons. Here are some fond memories of my father and some lessons that I learned.

THE PEN IS MIGHTIER THAN THE SWORD

My first cousin, Vernon Lee (Lee Ju Kyung), told me this story, years before he suffered a stroke. My father was young and very enthusiastic about joining the Chinese Air Force. As he was about to be commissioned, my father received a letter: *'Come home right away, your mother is dying!'* it read. He dropped everything and rushed home. When he got back to the village in Haa Kung Tam, Fung Gong, he found his mother quite healthy and happy. Her plan to stop her son, whom she loved very much, had worked. She didn't want him to be a soldier, let alone a pilot. She had cried every time he mentioned it.

My father eventually became a teacher and a writer. It was some time after that incident that he migrated to Jamaica and eventually became Editor of the Chinese Commercial News. He also authored and published two books, *Chinese in Jamaica 1957 & 1963*.

LISTEN TO YOUR ELDERS

In 1945, the Chinese community participated in a victory march in Kingston, celebrating the defeat of Japan and the end of World War II *(see photo, Canadian Jamaican Chinese 2000, page 189).* At that time, our family operated Park Lodge Grocery & Ice Cream Soda Fountain at 26b Victoria Avenue, opposite the Palace Theatre. From the sidewalk, some distance from the shop, we watched the jubilation. I remember seeing my father, dressed in a full white uniform, standing on the other side of the road waiting for a car to pass in order to cross. In the excitement of the moment, I started to run towards him. Seeing the danger, he sternly shouted to me with his hands out like a policeman, 'STOP!' Long after that incident I would remember being saved from imminent death because I had 'tang wah'* (listened to my father), and for many years after, I was encouraged always to do so, especially with the end of a gai mow sao* (feather stick).

A LITTLE HAKKA GOES A LONG WAY

When I was 6 years old, my parents had a birthday party for me. I spent many days before the party memorizing a short speech in Chinese to recite for the occasion. It was very short and to this day, over 50 years later, it still stands out in my memory.

At my party, in front of all my parents' friends, I stood on a chair to give my maiden speech. I proudly recited, '*An chae peng yu, lau ngai jo sang ngit, ngai shiffun doe cha nghee.*' The literal translation is: '*So many friends with me celebrating my birthday. I thank you very much.*' Without doubt, I was the hit of the party and received great applause. The guests all agreed that I was 'len tai'* (smart). Those words have stuck in my memory, and I was able to include them in my speech at the launch (or birthday) of my book, *Canadian Jamaican Chinese 2000.*

THERE ARE MANY WAYS TO SKIN A CAT

In the 1960s, one very exuberant reporter with the nom de plume, '*The Saint*', reported quite dramatically in the *STAR* newspaper, '*Picka Peow tickets printed at Chung San News!*' (Picka Peow was the Chinese lottery, illegal at that time). *Chung San News*, published by my father, was the name of one of two bi-weekly Chinese newspapers in Jamaica. When the news hit the streets, I was angry that such a lie could be printed, and I told my father quite vociferously, '*Let us sue the bastard*! *How dare he tell such lies*?' When my father saw that I was not to be easily calmed, he told me this story of the two fools in China:

"*There was a Mr. Wong, who had to go on a distant journey, but was worried about leaving behind the great sum of money he had buried under his house. 'If I leave my home, bandits will come and steal my fortune.' He worried about it day and night. Finally, his solution was to put a sign on the door saying: 'There is definitely no money buried here!' So that's what he did, and he went away on his long journey feeling safe. His neighbour, Mr. Chin, who lived in front, saw the sign and decided to steal the money one dark and moonless night. After a few nights he began to worry to himself, 'What if Mr. Wong thinks it was I who stole the money?' After several sleepless nights of worrying, he came to this solution: He decided to put up a sign indicating: 'I definitely did not steal any money'.*

My father did not want to be like Mr. Chin, declaring his 'innocence'. What he did do was to ask his good friend, Senator Rupert Chin See, who was also Chairman of the Board of Chung San News, to inform Mr. Theodore Sealy, then Editor of the *Gleaner* and Publisher of the *Star,* and also the Police Chief, that they were welcome to inspect our premises at any time. We never heard any more about the incident. The story and "The Saint" also fell into obscurity.

RICHES COME IN MANY FORMS

We lived upstairs at 130 Barry Street, which was almost directly in front of The Chinese Benevolent Society. On the third storey of that building was a temple, which is still there today. In it was the Chinese God, Guang Gung. He overlooked our building and Kingston Harbour. With Guang Gung one storey higher, and facing us, my father came to the conclusion that we would never become rich. After some time, I noticed a painted sign of the Pa Kua* (the symbol of Yin and Yang) on our roof, directly in front of Guang Gung. My father placed it there to counteract Guang Gung's overwhelming power. Well, we never did get rich, money-wise, but I would say our lives have been enriched in many other ways. And, come to think of it, the roof survived Hurricane Hazel, without losing a single sheet of zinc.

STOP AND SMELL THE ROSES

I always saw my father wearing a white shirt, except for the times when, as a little boy, I had to fan him with a large fan (bat sen)* for what seemed to me hours on end. Even when I drove him around the island to collect subscription money for the *Chung San News,* he would be neatly attired in a long-sleeved white shirt and tie. He was always respectable-looking. On one trip, driving from Black River towards Mandeville at break neck, teenage speed, he said, '*A Tung, stop and rest a while.*'

I stopped the car alongside a cane field, and as there was no place to really sit, he sat on a low stone by the roadside. It was cool in the shade, but the picture was not right. I said to him, '*papa, you look so respectable and you a sit 'pon the ground, it no look so good.*' He was really tired because he persisted. '*If any of my friends see me sitting here, they will surely stop, if they don't know me then it won't matter.*' A short time after our return to Kingston, he suffered a stroke, from which he never recovered.

Today, I wish I had spent more time and had had more conversations with him. I was too young and impatient to find the time but I am eternally grateful to my father for everything he gave me – tangible and intangible.

Written by Patrick Lee and edited by Sonia Gordon Scott.

* See Glossary

Down Memory Lane

'Waiting for the train' Bog Walk Train Station in St Catherine
Photographs ©Ray Chen

Karis Chin-Quee
HAKKA COMMUNITY BUSINESSMEN:
LLOYD CHIN-QUEE (ROY)

MY FATHER WAS born a left-hander. His parents, acting according to the dictates of their culture, forced him to use his right hand. We wondered later if that contributed to the incredible precision with which he used his hands. Although he was trained by a school of photography in New York, the skill that he brought to his profession was largely his own. From the taking of the photograph to retouching the negative, to developing the photo from scratch in his own darkroom, he treated each piece of work as his art. Many years after he had given up the studio, people I met felt compelled to express to me, his daughter, how much the wedding photos, or portraits he had taken meant to them; unabashedly exaggerating that he was the best photographer ever. He once used his magical pencil perhaps too well, as a disappointed penpal called off an engagement when the woman in the flesh did not match up to the beauty shining from the retouched photograph.

As a young man spending his adolescence in China, his stunning movie star looks drew young women to him like a Chinese Elvis, as his younger brother Leslie described it. However, I was never sure how much of that beauty staring from the photo was due to his retouching talents; he often admitted that some of his best work was done on his own photos. The commitment to enhancing beauty in a lasting representation providing him with his introduction to the Mandeville business

Above: Karis's dad (left) with her uncle Reggie (Colonel Chin). Feima was the basketball team they use to play for (in Chinese it means flying horse).

community. Like so many Hakka in small towns across the country, his quiet respect for his immediate society resulted in a mutual assimilation. He was even given that Jamaican village title normally reserved for those with old roots in the community; they called him Mas' Roy. My confused little cousin was later heard calling him uncle Mas' Roy. With his acceptance into the Mandeville community established, complete with a wife from Junction, St. Elizabeth, he was ready for the business he would run until he died in 1994.

In the 1960s there were four dry cleaning establishments offering a full range of services to the Mandeville Community. These included Mandeville Dry Cleaning, located in a cream-coloured building with large blue letters. A prime business location, it stood on a slight elevation almost half way between the Parish Council and the Courthouse. Its stone steps also led to a cool passage, which many people used as a short cut on their way up the hill to the market and town centre. The large double doors seemed to welcome people to rest after the brief but intense climb.

Despite this, when the owners decided to sell, the people who were interested were intimidated by the whole operation. Enter a determined and confident twenty-something with her reserved husband who needed to be won over to take on such a daunting challenge. The owners instinctively took to them; this, coupled with his wife's conviction that he could maintain the equipment and get advice from his friend in the same business, eventually convinced Roy to adopt a dry cleaning business as his new shop.

It was funny that, years later, my Kittitian friend, on learning that my parents owned a dry cleaners, laughed in absolute glee to have a stereotype confirmed. He informed me that in his experience, both in the UK and the Caribbean, this kind of business was very popular among the Chinese. He then reminded me of the calypso band called "Chinese Laundry".

In the booming Jamaican economy of the late 1960s and early '70s, their business thrived. Their enthusiasm for and enjoyment of the service industry helped them to easily overcome the initial hurdles. When the country's economic challenges emerged, they survived by reducing their staff and employing some of the same strategies that had helped make the Hakka such a strong business force in the early days. They employed thrift, efficient hard work, exquisite patience with every customer, and extreme self-sacrifice carried out with good humour in indulging the customer's whims. Once a customer asked my mother to hem his pants because his wife did not do it properly and she did! They would also, on occasion, deliver the clothes free, open the shop after hours or on Sunday to deliver one item, and of course, inevitably advance credit. It is a peculiar business this handling of such personal items. To a certain extent this was a luxury service; they were always cognizant of the fact that in an economic bind their customers had the option of doing their clothes themselves. Customers were therefore precious, especially in such a small community. With all these factors it is small wonder that, over the years, one of their contemporary establishments closed down while the other changed owners several times. New establishments also came and went. Another factor in their longevity was of course that Roy did indeed masterfully maintain the equipment, including a huge ancient boiler, at a minimum cost by his raw talent and his amazing hands.

They are now housed in a modern two-story white building and the business name is announced in red letters in a bustling new plaza far from the town centre. Roy's widow carries on with the same spirit that had initially earned them the business and kept it alive. Her moral support still comes from her husband through the memories and his legacy, and the dancers still come at Chinese New Year to bestow continuous good luck on an old Chinese business.

Written by Karis Chin Quee and edited by Sonia Gordon Scott.

D. Tony Wong
ONE LIFE - MANY INFLUENCES

I WILL ALWAYS be grateful to my grandmother for saving my reputation. Without her I would have been forever branded a cry-cry baby, for since the day I was born, I would cry from morning until night, and no amount of teething powder nor infants preservative could alleviate the situation.

At the time, I lived with my parents and paternal grandparents in a two-room home at the top of King Street, and none of them could get any rest because of my constant wailing. One day when I was nine months old, Grandma came home and suddenly announced that we had to move immediately. *'The house is full a duppy,*' she said. *'And that is what's bothering the baby.'*

So we moved to Albert Street, and since then I have been the nicest guy in town. Just ask my wife.

David Wong

I come from a large family. My father (left) had three brothers, and between the four of them, they had 20 children. We were all very close and the families shared nearly everything, including large appliances, like a washing machine which was carried from house to house for each family's washday. This was a chore for us younger ones, but we figured it was for the best. When the family business could afford the luxury, each family got a stereo set. It was this share-and-share-alike philosophy that forged a bond between the families and ensured that not one child would go wanting without help from the others.

None of the children ever had more than the other, and each of us had the opportunity for higher education. Education was of paramount importance in our family. I remember my father instructing a cousin that if he didn't go back to school, he'd always remain a clerk. His grandnephew gave him his word that he would return to school, and a few days later, my father passed away.

The most memorable period of my life is undoubtedly my high school years at St. George's College. The Jesuits were our counsellors and confidantes, guiding us in our spiritual lives and motivating us to make good use of our time after high school. In those five years at St. George's, I learned that I could accomplish anything if I worked hard. Most of all, I formed the bonds of friendship that have lasted until today, almost 50 years later.

One priest stands out in my memory - Father Joseph Riel, S.J., who personally guided me through Cambridge exams so that I could graduate. My only regret is that it has taken me so many years to recognize the importance of this great man's dedication and influence, and that I did not say *thank you* enough.

One most memorable sporting occasion was the day my father invited his friend, the legendary George Headly to our home to play cricket. Every kid in the neighbourhood came to watch. He coached us, bowled at us and batted against us. There could not have been a more delighted set of guys. That was a day in a million, and I was inspired to try more sports. At St. George's my love grew for football and swimming, and I made the school team in 1957 and 1958.

Looking back, I acknowledge that I have been fortunate in life because of all those who influenced me, particularly my father, and as I look eagerly to the future, I hope that my children and grandchildren will likewise take kindly the counsel of the years.

Written by D. Tony Wong; edited by Sonia Gordon Scott.

Down Memory Lane

Negril Beach in Hanover
Photograph ©Ray Chen

Karlene Young (née Chung)
A DIFFERENT KIND OF FAMILY

MY FATHER WAS BORN Chung Men Fah in Hong Kong. In Jamaica he became William Chung. My mother was Edna Cooke. She was half Scottish, half Cuban. I was their third and last child. My parents never married, nor did they ever live together. The first wife papa had in China was not the reason they didn't marry. He would explain it to me one day when I finally mustered the courage to ask him.

'*Kahlin,*' he said. That's how he pronounced my name. '*Kahlin yuh mammy was pretty. Pretty, but stupid.*'

My older sister, Daisy, and I grew up with our mother in Chestercastle, Westmoreland. Papa lived across the island in Moortown, Portland, where he ran his small grocery shop close to the beef shop in the square. We knew there was an older sister, Lurline, who lived with papa. But as young children Daisy and I had never met our sister. In fact, we had not even met our father.

Daisy and I were born a year apart. We were sisters and best friends, happily filling our days with the things that little girls did in rural Jamaica in the 1940s. We went to school, played in the yard under the sun – and sometimes in the rain – and generally helped mama around the house. Our lives were simple, but we went to sleep each night knowing that we had each other.

That all changed one morning when I was six years old. That was the day Daisy left. I had time only to stumble out of bed and run outside to see her climbing into a truck parked outside our gate, its engine humming impatiently. Daybreak had not yet come, but I could see that my sister was wearing one of her fancy dresses, that her hair was very neatly combed, and that she was carrying a suitcase. We did not exchange words, wave, or cry. And just like that, my sister was gone. Mama would explain that papa had sent for Daisy. I would not see her for another six years. And we would not know for as many that he had secretly arranged for Daisy to live with a Chinese couple in Chinatown, Kingston.

Sometime after Daisy left, I fell ill with typhoid fever. I had always been a sickly child, but this time I needed more care than mama could give. She decided to send me to an aunt and uncle in Montego Bay. They were not relatives, but close friends of my father's. Over the next few months, the kind couple carefully nursed me back to health. Auntie was a talented dressmaker, and in that short time, would sew me several pretty dresses.

One morning, I awoke to find my aunt standing by my bed. In her hands was one of my nicest dresses. It was a smart red and white outfit with roses, puff sleeves and red sash. At the foot of my bed sat my only pair of black shoes. We exchanged no words as she slowly combed my long hair, her fingers gently pressing against my head to correct the errant strands. When she was finished, she reached behind the door for the suitcase that lay waiting, placed it in front of me, walked into the bathroom, and shut the door behind her.

My uncle appeared at the bedroom door and motioned for me to follow. He, too, said nothing. Not while riding in the truck that took us to the train station, and not while sitting on the train en route to a destination that would remain nameless. Instead, he continually fed me cakes and soda. I spent much of the time eating and picking up the crumbs that fell onto my lap. It helped to pass the time away. Finally the train screeched past a sign that read "Moortown". I understood then that I was about to meet papa and Lurline. And see Daisy once again.

I knew my father was my father because he told me so.

'I'm your papa,' he said. And that was *all* he said. There were no hugs, no tears, not even a smile of approval. Just a quick sweeping of the eyes that made you pull your shoulders back. Standing behind him was Lurline. She met my shy eyes with a kind smile that helped to loosen the lock that had gripped my knees. Within seconds I was glancing around for Daisy. Tired, homesick and confused, I was anxious to see a familiar face. But Lurline was ready for that moment. As my tears of disappointment began to trickle, she immediately offered me *Ovaltine* and biscuits, and took me into our bedroom to show me all the clothes she had waiting for me.

With Lurline around, I quickly settled into my new life. She and I opened up shop each morning while papa cooked us breakfast and treats to sell in the shop. We also had to leave school during lunch time to help sell. But I didn't mind. Every Saturday papa gave me three pence, and my sister six. We saved that for Chinese New Year. He matched every penny.

Papa was a magician in the kitchen. He whipped up bullas*, cakes, puddings, made his own fah-chung*, corned pork, beef and fish. I used to steal into the kitchen and crouch in a corner to watch him work, but the moment he found me he'd always shoo me outside. But I kept on sneaking in and he continued evicting me. One afternoon, while he was off buying goods in Port Antonio, I baked him a cake from memory and waited for his return that evening. The cake, while clearly a commendable attempt, would not be my best career effort.

'Kahlin cake tough! Tase gud but tough like rock! Wha' you put in it? Nes time you do betta, okay?' I believe that was the first time I saw papa hint at a smile.

Life with papa was not easy. He rarely spoke to us, breaking his silence only to bark out orders about work. I couldn't keep up with Lurline's escapades in treetops and deep rivers, so I made the most of my life there with my books and only doll. I disappeared into those books. A favourite was

Knights of the Round Table. At seven I was reading the *Gleaner* from cover to cover. When Lurline left for Titchfield High, I struggled with my loneliness as the shop became the four walls of my spare time. Freedom came only through papa's permission. At school, my teachers, Mrs. Ranny Williams and Mrs. Lucille Morrison would sometimes pull me aside and ask me why I looked so sad. I never had an answer.

But papa had an even darker side. He was the kind of disciplinarian who would snap into blind rage without warning. Belts and feather dusters were his weapons of choice. Naturally, I feared him. One day, when I was eight years old, our helper asked me to borrow some money – two shillings and sixpence to be exact. Without hesitating, I took it out of the till. This time papa beat me so hard, that his friend from Port Maria, papa Chin, had to intervene.

But afterward papa took me aside and tended to my wounds with the touch of a skilled surgeon. He washed my wounds with Chinese healing oil and medicines he used to keep under lock and key, all the while speaking softly to me about trying to be a good daughter. I would soon learn that it was during my most vulnerable moments that I could see papa's heart. I was lucky for it. My own rheumatic heart, the reason behind most of my illnesses, would remain undiagnosed for years. Until then, it was my father who would reach into his locked cabinet for his strange little bottles, carefully preparing concoctions of Chinese medicines and oils. Comfort often came when he steamed me in one of his potions. Papa also spoke through food. He was forever urging us to '*eat up!*' or '*eat more!*' One day he even sent the helper to school to give me a piece of cake he had just baked and a bottle of cream soda. Cream soda was my favourite.

When I was nine or ten, he married a young Chinese girl. His bride was just a few years older than Lurline, who would leave for school shortly thereafter. My stepmother almost always quarrelled with Lurline, and was marginally fair to me. But her treatment of us always worsened whenever her little brother came by. Papa sent him to school, and quickly looked upon him as his son, leaving little time for his own daughters. An uncle in Port Antonio would explain to us that boy children were simply favoured in the Chinese culture. So we accepted it.

Karlene at an early age.

One day, my stepmother put a suitcase in my room and waited. When a truck pulled up, she told me not to be sad, and then left. It was a Friday, and papa was at the beef shop. They had been married two years. No children came from the brief union.

Years later, when I was 12, I received a letter from my mother who was now living in Kingston on North Street. Addressed to me and Lurline, she told us that she had found Daisy and the Barry Street family that had adopted her. Elated, I begged my father to send me to see my mother and Daisy. At first he refused because mama had by then married another man. Then he softened and sent me to her.

During that precious visit, mama took me to see Daisy for a weekend. We hugged, and remained inseparable in her adopted parents' shop. I remember Daisy smiling a lot, speaking constantly about her new mother. By Monday mama and I were back at her North Street home. But before morning's end, a couple arrived at the gate, claiming that they had come to take me. Another one of papa's arrangements. This time I ran and hid. After not seeing my mother for six years, I refused to be taken away again. That day marked a change in my living arrangements. I'd remain with my mother in Kingston, and see papa only on holidays.

I got married when I was 16. Papa didn't approve, and so didn't come to the wedding. He said I was too young. A few years later I took my first two children to see their grandfather in the country. He told me not to come back. And I didn't. Not for 10 years. Then one day my sister called to say that papa was sick. His stinging words still fresh in my mind, I refused at first to go see him. I finally gave in, but only at her urging.

As soon as I saw papa, the years of hurt vanished. '*Kahlin,*' he whispered from his bed, '*why you stay so long to come?*' First time ever, he offered tenderness in his voice. That was the moment I fell in love with my father.

Before long, papa ended up in the hospital. One morning, my husband and I went to see him, taking with us, among other things, a clean set of sheets. Once there, we changed his soiled sheets and did our best to make him comfortable. On another day, I took him dinner – beef cutlets with vegetables and chicken soup broth. This time papa showed his approval.

'*Kahlin cook this?*' he turned to my husband. '*That Kahlin! As lickle gehl ahways want to be in kitchen! Good cook!*'

The last time I spoke with papa was on a Monday. Having shown some improvement, he was back at home where I telephoned him.

'*Papa,*' I said, '*how you feeling?*'

'*Not too bad today,*' he replied. '*Kahlin,*' he said after a pause, '*I sen you a cheque today.*'

'*What for, papa?*'

'*I jus feel to sen you sometin.*'

Papa's cheque arrived on Wednesday, the day before he passed away. When I went to see him, his hand lay across his head, as if he had spent his final moments in thought. As for his body, it was wrapped in the same sheets I had taken for him.

It would be many years later before an older cousin of mine revealed that my father used to boast, '*that Kahlin, she good gehl. She good gehl*'.

Written and edited by Alex Lee as told by the late Karlene Young.
* See Glossary

Melanie Weston Jakob
CHAN PI MOI, LAWD IT NICE

IT MUS' BE Sunday mornin' wid church music on di radio an' no traffic
pan di road outside
We goin' roun' to Flemin'ton Drive, to see Zsa Gung*
Don' really wan' to go, wi wan' stay home an' play
Don' understan' a word him seh (is only long afta' wi fin' out him was
talking broad country patois wid a tick Chiney accent)
An' wi haffi stan' up at him side and ansa all sort ah question
'bout school work an how wi growin' big-big

Nuh really wan' go, but Lawd, di Chan Pi Moi*
sweet caan' dun!
Him always seem to have some in him pocket,
slip it inna wi han' while him talking to us
An' while him askin' 'bout school an' saying how
wi grow, wi mout'
watering, tinking 'bout how it goin' taste nice Chan
Pi Moi deh 'bout all over di place nowadays, but den
it was big ting fi get one fi eat an' him did always
seem to have dem.

Firs' yuh unwrap di pretty-pretty blue paper, an den di
cellophane one unda'neat, 'crinky! crinky!' as yuh untwis' it
At las' yuh cyan see di Chan Pi Moi, shiny, juicy and sweet
Lawd, mi mout' waterin' jus' tinkin bout it now!

Zsa Gung siddown on di verandah in him silva aluminum chair wid di plas-
tic web strap dem, lookin' out on di street
An' Zsa Po* she walk roun', or lean up gens' de wall, watchin' wi play.
She always have a ol' hat on har head, a blue claat one wid a white ban' go
roun'
An she fol' down di brim, to cover har eye fram di sun.
Har cat-eye glasses tape up wid maskin' tape in di middle, between de two
eye dem
She always wearin' a wash-out flowaz dress wid a apran over it, an' she
push har han' in de apran pockit an' tek out icy mint fi yuh

When yuh tek it, har han' shake but it hol' fiyuh far a likkle while, an' yuh feel har skin, sof' an' papery
Ah neva figget di time she seh "min' di mosquito! It bite hat-hat like a tigah!!"

De boy cousin dem wid dem marble, dem unda de mango tree where it dark an cool an' de groun' damp
De girls dem roun' de back, on di concrete behin' de kitchen near de wash line, playin' dolly an' jacks
De mongrel dawg runnin' roun' sniffin' fah food
Tangerine peel dryin' in de sun in a blue plastic basin pon top of carton box dat dem trow down
Sersee bush growin' on di fence wid di big foo gah* dem hangin' off, green an' hard 'cause dem don't ripe yet
Food cookin' inside, so dish pan knockin', dirty wata trow out in di yaad by di fence, an' di neighbour dem nex' door shoutin' inna fi dem kitchen

But all dat done an' gone by 1979 when everybody gaan an' migrate wan bi wan
Chan Pi Moi can buy in any store nowadays but none so nice as di likkle few we used to get roun' by Flemin'ton Drive....

Written by Melanie Weston Jakob

* See Glossary

Photograph ©Ray Chen

Down Memory Lane

*Treasure Beach
in St. Elizabeth
Photograph ©Ray Chen*

Everard Hoo
BE LIKE THE BAMBOO

MY PARENTS WERE the typical Hakka Chinese couple. They endured much and held it together.

When I was born in 1934, we were living in Cross Roads, Chapelton, Clarendon. My father, George Hoo Ling Kong, was the younger brother of Henry Hoo (Hoo Shao Lin). They were brothers from Guangdong, China. Together they ran a retail and wholesale grocery, hardware and haberdashery business. After a long week of hard work, the two would usually head to May Pen or Frankfield for a weekend of mahjong with their friends. My uncle was fairly disciplined when it came to gambling. But my old man was addicted. Hakka men like him often lost everything because of bad gambling habits – from their *shirts* to their *shops*. Literally. That's how life could change on a dime for their wives, who were usually at home with the kids while their ill fated activity took place. That's how it was for my mother at any rate. Typically, she would be alone with us from Saturday night to Sunday night, because papa would leave soon after we locked shop. I was her second-born, Richard her first. But when he was sent to China I became the number one son, at least temporarily. The position came with privileges that my siblings did not enjoy. Come dusk time, I'd sit with mama on the wide verandah that stretched and wrapped around our large house attached behind the store, whilst the others were in bed. All her chores would have been done by then and she could finally relax. I remember the evening air would always be cool and fresh on our skin.

Mama (left) was a short, broad and cuddly person, and I loved our time together. Sometimes she would sing to me in Hakka while rocking in her chair. Sometimes we'd catch fireflies in a bottle and hang them up like Chinese lanterns. Other times she'd let me chat away non-stop.

'*Where's papa?*' I'd complain in English. '*It's late and I'm sleepy.*'

'*Oh he soon come,*' she'd reply in Chinese. '*You know he doesn't drive, so he must wait for his turn to get dropped home.*' And that's how we spent our time while waiting for my father to return. On the occasional Sunday, she would go with him and friends for a day of visiting, which usually included *ghi-pi** and *yim cha**. In those days the car's weak suspension could barely manage the struggle up and down the crude country roads.

Frequent stops became necessary so that those who needed to, could vomit, and the car could cool down.

At some point, my uncle left the business to my father. Papa, bless his heart, gambled it down to little or nothing. I was about seven or eight years old by then. All we had left was family.

So then he made the decision to sell the business and start over in Kingston. Old friends of the family would tell me years later that if he had just held on to the business during the war, he would have ended up a wealthy man. Apparently he carried good stock – items that became scarce during the war.

The only time I ever saw my mom cry was when we had to pay the price for papa's gambling. By then, her older brother, George Lyn Cook, had become a successful retail and wholesale merchant in St Ann. The comparison couldn't have been easy for her.

The family went through some hard times in Kingston, and moved around a lot. At one point we lived in one half of a house on Pound Road, in the Maxfield Avenue and Waltham Park Road area. The other part was occupied by another Chinese family.

Things were tight for us in just about every way. We, the children, slept five across a bed, head to toe. We also ate lean. In the backyard near the fence, the previous tenants had planted callaloo. Lots of it. So we ate callaloo every day except Saturdays. That's when we'd stretch ourselves for a little beef soup. Otherwise it would be callaloo with saltfish, callaloo with salt pork, or callaloo by itself. To this day I love callaloo with salt fish, and rice. There was *always* rice. Sometimes the neighbours would treat us to ice cream and those three-corner curried beef patties. Now that was pure joy!

Eventually we ended up at $4^1/_2$ East Queen Street, right beside Atlantic Club. Our new address was a house converted into a laundry, so that became our new family business. Why we did that I don't know, because west of us at the corner of Gold Street was King's Laundry. And *everyone* knew that Chiney man! But we stuck with our decision and pushed on.

By then papa had renewed focus and took a job with the US Air Force Base at Sandy Gully, Vernamfield back in Clarendon. His absence finally gave my mother a full hand in the business, and she made do with her half English, half Hakka tongue and good business sense. We kids were too young to help, so she employed staff. But in a strange twist of fate, papa's career change helped us tremendously. Each weekend when he came home, he'd bring laun-

dry from the US air force men for *the business,* and chocolate and other goodies for *all of us.*

Soon we managed to build up some savings, and bought a *ham tew poo** from one Mr. Yee – Melbourne Grocery, just below the famous Melbourne Park. In those days, the Chinese support system was very much alive, and we were, once again, buoyed by this system of support and honour. It meant that we could take over the shop, start paying our debts in installments, and still benefit from suppliers' credit. Call it a temporary partnership. Another option was the *fui**, the Chinese equivalent of what was known locally as *partner*.* These were our alternatives to bank loans. But dog nyam yuh supper if you didn't honour your debts! You'd be blackballed in a flash in the Chinese community!

But by now, armed with some steady cash flow, papa's gambling habit began to worsen in both frequency and skill. I remember mama actually hiding the money from our weekly sales so that she'd have it ready for the suppliers.

One day I saw her sobbing angry tears. My father had taken all the money and blown it on Barry Street. I honestly thought she was going to kill him. Poor mama. She was always the one in the shop so she was there the day the creditors showed up. It was she who had to lose face. Sometime later, one of the big bosses came to see what the problem was. He was Mr. Gladstone Chang of Valentine's Bakery. And I remember him very gently saying to my mother, *'Well, you had better get your low goong* to stop gambling.'* And he gave her extended credit. He was a real gentleman. That man became my hero. He would come to my rescue one more time later on in my life, but under different circumstances.

Socially, however, life was always great. We never really had money, but, boy, did we have happiness! I had all sorts of friends, many joining me and my younger brothers and sisters in little income-earning ventures, like raiding the neighbours' tamarind trees to make tamarind balls for sale at school. We always made sure to put a seed in a couple to make them look bigger. We raised rabbits and guinea pigs – selling some, and eating some. And raised and sold fish. As a kid, there was nothing nicer than earning our own pocket-money!

But we weren't without our issues. Like class differences. I learned about that over time. Like when I was at high school and eager to play football and

Young Everard Hoo

cricket like everyone else. That's when I noticed that whereas the children of the wealthy and middle class had time to play, Chinese boys like me had to hurry home to work in our shops. While the children of the Barry Street wholesalers lived in homes north of North Street in St. Andrew, we lived behind our shops. They played tennis and badminton and belonged to the Chinese Athletic Club. We played on the streets with our Jamaican friends and at the Chinese Public School on North Street, where we joined the Scout Troop. They had cars, we had bicycles. The division was clear. Even my own father's tone of voice changed to one of deference when talking about certain well-known Chinese individuals who had helped to build the community.

So sometimes your own kind would snub you because you came from downtown. But you couldn't let that bother you. We were too busy fighting snubs of other kinds as a group. Insults like the one my mother got one day.

'Madam! Yuh fat, ugly Chiney ooman! Why yuh doan go back a Hong Kong!'

Sure, things got tough every now and again. Financially, socially and otherwise. But we stuck together and pulled through. And we owe that to our parents.

Papa had a lot of Chinese sayings, but one I remember well. He used to say, *"Son, if people insult you, if things go wrong and you're hurt, take it, go with the flow, but don't break and give up on your principles or your dreams. Be like the bamboo. Bend, but don't break."*

I thank my parents for teaching me this by example.

Above L-R: Ah Back (my father's older brother) Henry Hoo Shao Lin, Carol Hoo (née Chang) my brother Richard's wife, and my father George Hoo Ling Kong.

Written by Alex Lee as told by Everard Hoo.

* See Glossary

Down Memory Lane

The Chinese tea pot with the basket for keeping the tea warm.

Tea pot courtesy of Hardingham Collections Photograph ©Ray Chen

Robert Lee
OUR SPECIAL BRAND OF GLUE

I'M NOT SURE if it occurred to us while growing up that we were poor. That's all relative, they say. Sure we had to do the two-mile trek to school barefoot to save our shoes, and certainly nothing we ever had was acquired with a snap of the fingers. But the laughter and sibling camaraderie that filled our small Marlie Hill home kept most of the complaints at bay. There were actually eight of us, but the first child and son, Mok Yan, had been left back in Hong Kong to finish high school while our parents made a new home in rural Jamaica. Our mother missed Mok Yan a lot. We knew this because every now and again we would see her clutching the only photo she had of him while rocking slowly in her chair, her eyes closed. Exactly what she was thinking then we never knew, because we never asked. Our brother was fifteen when mom left him to join our old man in Jamaica. She would not set eyes on her son again before dying in Jamaica 25 years later.

The family's income came from the small shop that sat below our sleeping quarters. We sold everything from ketchup to codfish fritters. Our mother's fritters were legendary, so, for that and many other reasons we liked the cozy proximity to the family business. That and the easy access to the till. We still maintain that the Chinese started the work-from-home practice that's now all the rage these days. We were a closely-knit bunch, a function perhaps of the fact that there was not much communication with either mom, who spoke hardly any English, or with dad, who, although he read and spoke English, was a very quiet and easy going person. In fact, he pretty much left all the disciplining – the tongue lashing, the prodding, the occasional feather duster swiping – to mom. We were therefore a very loud bunch, a contrast to our parents who maintained a calm silence for much of their lives.

Together we learned many of life's important survival skills. Skills that have doubtless been put to good use beyond our growing years. Take speed, for instance, something we practiced heartily at the dinner table. Good food was something we always had, with appetites to match. Needless to say, the serving dish would barely go flat on the table before seven sets of forks would fly to stab the two highly-prized drumsticks. This was always an equal opportunity affair at our house, with no preferential treatment being given to the younger siblings. They would learn the lesson that brute force sometimes prevailed. As for chewing, that process was kept to a bare minimum. I still inhale my food to this day, much to my children's amusement.

We also learned the art of negotiating and reasoning. The Esterbrook pen incident was a prime example of this. A fancy instrument in its day, my father had made sure to provide each of us with one for school, the unspoken but firm understanding being that we neither lost nor damaged it. There would be no replacement pen. So when my brother Alfred's Esterbrook ended up outside, in the toilet pit, one hot and breezy Saturday afternoon, we knew a mission awaited us.

Once discovered, we were immediately gathered for an emergency meeting by the outhouse. At the time, the eldest among us, David, was sixteen, while the youngest, Joyce, was about seven. Alfred was second and I fell somewhere in between, and there was a younger brother, Vincent. The decision to be made was not how the pen would be retrieved, but rather who would go down to retrieve it. Now although it was customary in our household for the younger family members to perform certain duties of subservience, such as pouring tea at the dinner table, we felt that this task required some sense of strength and balance, and so spared the young ones. It was also decided that we really couldn't send the girls down. We would never hear the end of it and still had to live with them for a few years yet. That left David, Fred, Vinny and me. Well David pulled rank and announced that as the eldest he shouldn't have to go. At only nine, we agreed that Vinny was too young to make the trip down. As for Fred, he announced that he was too distraught over the pen and so couldn't go. There ended the negotiating and reasoning. Minutes later *I* was being lowered into the putrid darkness by a not-so-thick rope, my feet resting precariously on a wooden plank we had crudely affixed to it. One of my sisters held a flashlight above my head. I remember wondering, as I clung tightly to my lifeline, if this was payback for some wrongdoing I had committed. Had I finally pilfered too much from the cash register? I would eventually retrieve the pen, handing it to Fred amid much cheering.

It's been decades since the Esterbrook incident, and the Lee family has since welcomed two new generations. We live different lives now, and are enjoying all the rewards that hard work can bring. And yet, it never fails. Whether we gather for a massive reunion, or a meal for a mere six, our chatter ultimately takes us back, not to the moments of personal glory or when fortune and the easy life became ours, but rather to the days of our simple struggles at Marlie Hill. Those were the days when we were three or four to a room. When a trip to Kingston was a big deal. When toys were not bought, but pieced together with parts like an old bicycle wheel and a stick. When entertainment meant backyard cricket, marbles, river fishing for cray fish, or raiding our neighbour's mango or plum trees. And those were the days when I could make my sister, Mary climb the trees to pick and toss the fruit down to us, with no guarantee that there would be any left for her once she descended. It's at such times and gatherings that we revel in our memories and relive the moments when we laughed the hardest and enjoyed, what we still consider to be, some of the best and most treasured years of our lives.

1. Robert Lee in his younger days

2. Robert with his brother Vincent at the beach.

3. Robert along with friends - Bev Chin, Kitty Chong and sister Doris Lee.

At right: Stanford Wong, Robert Lee and his dad having a laugh at dinner.

Written by Alex Lee as told by Robert Lee and edited by Mary Lai (née Lee) and Alex Lee.

Down Memory Lane

Jamaica's favourite the Ackee

Photography ©Ray Chen

Stephanie Charlton
A CHINESE-JAMAICAN CHILDHOOD

CHINESE-JAMAICAN – as a small child I never really understood what that really meant. As a child of mixed background I never viewed my parents in colour. Mommy and daddy were just that – mommy and daddy. There was never a time when I had to explain that my father was black and my mother was Chinese. To everyone around me, I was Jamaican.

It wasn't until I was a teenager that I began to see the tapestry that was my life in a closer and more meaningful way. I realized that I was truly living the Jamaican motto, "Out of Many, One People". My life held a duality that most people, unfamiliar with the make-up of Jamaican society, did not understand. This duality became a struggle for me when I moved to Toronto, Canada at the age of 16. It was here that I was labelled Chinese-Jamaican. At first I was opposed to this: after all, until then I always saw myself as just Jamaican. Then I began to look at my life and I realized that I truly was a combination of both cultures. What I had viewed as normal everyday things were in fact a blending of both my parents' backgrounds and it was only as an adult that I began to see the richness that was my life.

In appearance, I am the perfect blend of my mother and father. I have inherited my mother's small eyes and my father's broad nose, my mother's small hands and my father's wide flat feet. Thanks to my father when I go into the sun my skin turns a deep brown and thanks to my mom my hair is thin and long. But these physical traits are just the surface of what it means to be Chinese-Jamaican. The truer meaning, I've found, is in the juxtaposition of the everyday rituals that punctuate my life and the ways in which my parents moulded me to be proud and respectful of both their backgrounds. I was taught not to view one as better than the other, rather that they were equally important. Both cultures have been seamlessly blended and as such have become my reality.

The only way to understand this blending is to look at the contrasting images of my childhood memories growing up in Jamaica. The way my mother would insist that my sisters and I not leave for school without our morning cups of Milo, while my grandmother would invite us to sit with her and have freshly brewed green tea on the weekends. My sisters and I started most Saturdays sitting with my father and eating either cornmeal or oats porridge, while my mother was busy preparing pak jam gai (boiled chicken and soya sauce) for dinner.

There were actually two food cupboards in my house, one for the every-day or Jamaican items and one that we labelled the Chinese cupboard. The Jamaican cupboard held the tins of mackerel and sardines, Vienna sausages and Foska oats. The Chinese cupboard was stocked with cans of baby corn, Chinese plums, hoisin sauce, gallon containers of soya sauce and packets of dried mushrooms.

Birthdays saw the shrimp chips placed beside the banana chips and guests would be given the choice of either rum and raisin or vanilla and lychee ice cream. If you were sick, my mom would prepare either chicken soup or jook (also known as congee). Weekend visits to Jah Po and Jah Gung would mean my sisters and I would get to raid the jimbelin tree or sit and eat fresh lychee, while my father was constantly bringing home star apples, naseberries and jack fruit.

My father made sure we learnt to appreciate the true Jamaica: always tak-ing us on trips to St. Mary, Portland and Mandeville. My first experiences at Sunsplash and Sumfest, for example, were with my father. For my mother, who is one of nine brothers and sisters, it was important that we appreciated and respected our large extended family. We were constantly meeting great aunts and uncles, cousins, and second cousins.

Family dinners were huge affairs, usually requiring upwards of two days of cooking. The largest of these dinners usually, was Chinese New Year. Then the table would be filled with dishes like sweet and sour pork, egg rolls, Chinese roast chicken, pork and muk nee and chop suey. For dessert, the pineapple upside down cake would sit beside the moon cakes. Today I relish the fact that my family will go for dim sum on a Saturday morning and then come home to ackee and saltfish with boiled bananas and fried plantain.

Growing up, Friday nights meant the adults would be playing mah jong all night. My sisters and I would be in charge of sorting the chips for the play-ers and would then spend hours making pyramids out of the tiles. Today, my cousins and I continue where the adults have left off, getting together to play mah jong as often as possible. Not to be outdone, of course, by the many domino games that are usually started on the table beside us. Both games offer a chance for the entire family, my grandfather and great uncles included, to spend time with the younger generations.

This seamless blending of the two distinct cultures of my parents, has made me the person I am today. I am just as proud of the Wongs, the Lees and the Chin Sangs in my family, as I am of the Charltons and the Hamiltons. My family reunions are a hodgepodge of races, traditions and foods, with my rel-atives spanning the gamut of colours from Black to Asian to Caucasian. Despite the differences in our physical appearance, we understand and embrace the fact that we belong to one family – a unique family with a rich family heritage and a deep understanding of our common roots.

Personally, I have come to regard myself as neither Black nor Asian and to classify me as such would be an injustice. I don't fit neatly into society's definition of either race, and as such I consider myself an "other". To understand me is to understand that I am the product of the shared experiences and influences of my parents, both of whom ensured that I was exposed to the best of both worlds, always standing by me as I searched to find a place in a world too eager to fit me into a neat category. Today, I am a proud member of a unique community, one that embraces its differences and respects the duality that weaves its way through our lives. This is the lesson I hope to pass on to the future members of my family.

Written by Stephanie Charlton and edited by Sonia Gordon Scott.

Down Memory Lane

*Exterior menu board on
the wall*

Photograph ©Ray Chen

Leopold Fong Yee
MY TWO CULTURES

THE SON OF A Chinese merchant and a Jamaican woman, Leopold Fong Yee was born on October 3, 1928. There were two other brothers and three sisters in the family at that time.

Although Leo, as he is called, was much younger than most of the boys that were being sent to China, his father decided to send himself and Edmond, who was two years older, to "*learn the culture*". Their mother was not happy with the decision as she felt that Leo was not old enough, being only 6¹/₂ years old at the time. However, she reluctantly agreed and accepted the custom since many other Chinese families were doing the same with their sons and daughters.

Accompanying them on the journey were Enid and Ordelle, sisters of his older cousin Albert who had been sent to China two years before. They stopped in Hong Kong and, after staying a few weeks, continued on their journey to their ancestral village, *Lin Tong,* in the district of *Yan Ping* that is a part of *See Yep*, in Kwangtung Province, Southern China.

Their stay in the village was cut short, however, by an incident that took place shortly after they arrived. It is something that Leo says he will always remember…

"Next to the private school, built by my great, great grandfather to tutor his two sons, was a small park with three very tall trees. In among the trees was a shrine used by the villagers as a place of worship. The park was located at the main entrance that led into the village, and on either side of the gate were two large ponds.

The villagers were in the process of worshipping and bowing to show respect. Laid out before them was a boiled chicken, incense sticks, and three cups of wine. You must remember that here were two boys of the Christian faith, having just arrived from Jamaica and seeing, for the first time, these strange customs.

Edmond, not understanding the culture, shouted "It is not right to worship idols!" and proceeded to kick over the shrine. Now this type of behaviour was considered sacrilegious, and it brought much shame to the immediate family. Our grandmother was so annoyed she immediately shipped Edmond, myself and our cousins, back to Hong Kong."

They first stayed with an uncle in Kowloon who enrolled them in a

Chinese School. This was much to Edmond's dislike, and because of his rebellious nature his uncle sent Edmond and Leo back to their aunt in Hong Kong.

On enrolling them as boarders at the Diocesan Boys School on the Kowloon side, their aunt was disappointed when the school told her that only Edmond was accepted. It was a high school and they felt that Leo was too young to attend. The problem now was what was she to do with Leo?

This was in 1937, and there was much talk about the war with Japan and China. Many mainland parents were concerned about their children's education and, although the children were well educated in Chinese, they knew very little English. A special class was set up at the school to accept those children who wanted to learn the language.

After much discussion between his aunt and the school committee, Leo was placed in this special class with older children of the aristocrats from China. With English (patois) as his first language, Leo was promoted to the same class as his older brother at the beginning of the second term. He was happy as he was the youngest, one and a half years younger than the other students in his class.

Although it was an English school, one Chinese class was compulsory. Aided by the language spoken at home, Edmond and Leo very quickly became fluent in understanding and speaking it.

Leo's father Willie Fong Yee and stepmother Lum Fong Yee

During their stay in China they learned from their grandmother that their father had migrated to Jamaica as a teenager. In late 1939 he married Leo's step-mother by proxy, while she was still living in Hong Kong and he was living in Jamaica. Edmond and Leo were then taken out of boarding school after their step-mother joined their cousins, Albert, Enid, and Ordelle, who were then staying with another cousin, George Fong Yee.

Being part-Chinese did not matter. Their step-mother loved them as though they were her own children and looked after them while they were in school. In December 1941 the Japanese captured Hong Kong, and in February 1942, she took the whole family back to the village in China. She was a really good 'mother' and of the two boys, Leo was her favourite.

In 1945 the Japanese surrendered, and in the spring, after the Chinese New Year of 1946, their stepmother took the two boys back to Hong Kong to wait for the travelling documents for their return to Jamaica. In March 1947, she saw them off as they boarded an American President Line, the *S.S. Marine Lynx,* which used to be a troop carrier. Their first stop after leaving Hong Kong was Shanghai where a hundred Jews on their way to Palestine (Israel was not yet a country), boarded the ship. The next stop was Kobe, Japan, Honolulu, Hawaii and finally San Francisco. From there, they travelled by air to Jamaica. They had been away from the island for 13 years.

A few weeks after returning to Jamaica, Leo missed Hong Kong so much that he mentioned to his father that he wanted to return. His dad would not have anything to do with this request as he had plans of his own. It was his time to travel. During Leo's stay in China, his parents had separated and his father wanted to return to Hong Kong to bring his Chinese wife (Leo's step-mother) to Jamaica. He promised that they would discuss this matter on his return from Hong Kong. In 1948, Leo's younger brother, Granville, accompanied their father to Hong Kong for the sole purpose of returning to Jamaica with his new wife.

Years passed but Leo's plans to return to Hong Kong were not to be. There was no further discussion on the matter with his father, as he grew to enjoy working at the bakery and living in Jamaica. He loved to travel around town for it allowed him to visit the many Chinese and Jamaican customers in the Corporate area. The thing that he liked most of all was the warm and very friendly atmosphere of the Jamaicans. Because of his good nature and his warm smile, in no time he became very popular among the community.

His dad had two businesses – Fletcher's Land Bakery, and a grocery shop with a bar in Papine. It was his mother who looked after the business in Papine while his father managed the bakery. "Kaiser" was his dad's nick name... and home was at the back of the grocery in Papine.

Leo's mom, Edna.

Papine was the end of the line for the tram-cars and the bus service, but there were lots of taxis waiting to carry people to their various destinations. It was a very busy intersection and there was a constant flow of people who lived in the surrounding areas. All the businesses in the area did well. His mother's name was Edna and the grocery shop was a very popular meeting place. She was well known throughout the region which stretched from Newcastle, Irish Town, Maryland, Mavis Bank, Gordon Town and August Town all the way down to Matilda's Corner. Everybody knew *"Ms Edna's"*. She was an institution.

Just as in China, Leo was adventurous by nature and he would often drive around the country parts. Whenever he would stop to enjoy the beauty of the island, folks in the various areas wanted to know his surname. On learning that the name was Fong Yee they would say, *"Lard! ... is Ms Edna pickney dat!"*

Edna McKay was very proud of her boys as they were well schooled in the Chinese customs and culture. She had much to be thankful for as she was well established in the community, and her two boys had returned to Jamaica unharmed by the war with Japan.

Edna's maiden name was McKay and her family owned the estate called Clydeside in St. James. There were three brothers and four sisters and they all lived abroad with the exception of Edna who was the eldest. Every one of the McKay family had a lot of love and respect for Edna and she would eventually join them in the '60s. Leo still keeps in touch with some of his uncles and aunts.

The only remaining family member in the island from the McKay side is Norma Shirley, the owner of "Norma's Restaurant". Their mothers were sisters and Norma calls Leo her '*Chinese cousin.*'

Leo's father worked the morning shift that started at five a.m.. He supervised the preparation and the day's production, and he usually finished working around ten o' clock. It was customary then, as in most Chinese families, to have the first meal at around ten o'clock in the morning and immediately after the meal Leo would drive him into Chinatown ... Well guess what? His dad loves to play '*Mah Jong'*. Need we say more?

His stepmother gave birth to his sister, Adel, in 1949 and his brother Willie, followed in 1955. They all lived and worked at the bakery until 1955 after his dad passed away and the business was sold.

Over the years, most of the family has moved on to other countries, but this does not prevent them from keeping in touch, as they do ever so often.

The last word is Leo's, who says…

"*I am proud of my two cultures; they have made me a much better person.*"

Above: Leo and Edmond. Next: Leo's family - l-r: Leo, daughter Sandra, wife Linda and son Roderick

Written on behalf of Leopold Fong Yee and edited by Sonia Gordon Scott.

Earle Wong
OUTSIDE LOOKING IN

MY EXPERIENCE growing up as a mixed Chinese was not the most pleasant.

I was born in St. Ann in 1933 to Myrtle and Harold Wong, grocery store owners. My great-grandmother on my mother's side had been a slave, so I knew from an early age what I was all about. But while I embraced both races in me, I never really felt accepted by either side.

Growing up, Sundays usually meant Chinese families getting together in nearby Falmouth so that the men could play mahjong, eat and socialize. I remember my old man taking me along once when I was six or seven. I also remember not feeling too comfortable there. He sat at the mahjong table playing, while I sat in a corner making my own entertainment. The kids who lived at the house were speaking Chinese, so I couldn't join them. I looked at them, they looked at me. After a while I realized that their parents were talking about my not being able to speak Chinese. So I left to go walking, and toured the Falmouth market. That night I slept on the verandah chair. I just didn't feel like I belonged. I never went back with him nor did he ask me to.

I really didn't blame the others, though. The Sunday socials were the only opportunities they had to speak their language. In his defence, my dad did try to teach me. But time became a problem when I began school in Kingston. My half-Chinese mother didn't speak the language either. So she never joined dad for the social get-togethers. Women didn't often go anyway. They were too busy working and looking after the kids. And if she *did* go, she never stayed long.

I never thought to ask my mother what it was like for her growing up, a mixed Chinese, an entire generation ahead of me. I just saw her as a regular Chinese wife and mother. She worked hard all the time and questioned nothing. With one exception. This was the era of arranged marriages, and sending children to China. When my time came, I *refused* to go. I pictured myself working in the rice fields, like the ones in the movies they used to show at school. These were Hollywood movies made during WWII. Well dad was angry, but my mother stood behind me. In the end he was out-voted and I stayed in Jamaica. But I remember saying goodbye to a couple guys from the village who *had* to go.

In Kingston I went to Excelsior High School and boarded with several families. Non-Chinese families. But I never felt at ease, so I kept moving

*A Chinese
Scout Troop*

around. That all changed when I was about 13 and in my fourth year of high school. That was the year I met the Chinese Scout Troop. I was living with a family behind the Chinese Public School, when I saw a group of guys one evening in what seemed to be a meeting. I remember noticing that some looked like me. Mixed. So eventually I wandered over there and met them. The group spoke only in English. It wasn't long before we became fast friends. For the first time in my life I felt as if I belonged.

With the Scouts I was able to relax and let my guard dissolve. I even became a regular face in the Lyn household. Skippy was one of my Scout friends. Suddenly I became more open. I was talking more. Even smiling. And that's when I realized that something was wrong with society. Come to think of it, I don't think I ever broached the topic with my Scout friends. I didn't have to. We were too busy just having a good time.

That said, I continued to be wary of putting myself in the position where I could be told, *'you don't belong here.'* So I never went to the Chinese Benevolent Association and many of the other Chinese meeting places. The only exception was the Chinese Athletic Club, where the Scouts went as a group to play table tennis, but only *after* the members had left. The Chinese Athletic Club was still largely Chinese at the time, and we weren't actual members. Looking back now, that's probably why they chased us off the table tennis tables. To be fair, most of the time they *did* let us stay, as long as we didn't use member's privileges. So while the treatment they gave us might have been appropriate, I guess as a young kid I took it to mean something else.

It was only when I left school and worked for three years, that it finally hit me. I said to my mother, where am I going here? And so I set my sights on England and the Royal Armed Forces. Skippy's plans also included England, but not the Forces. So at 23, I left Jamaica with my Scout friend for new adventures across the Atlantic. The year was 1956.

I didn't know a soul in England. All I knew is that we had landed, and that soon after we were all lining up in basic camp - me and a bunch of guys from all over. And then they made me squad leader. The irony didn't escape me. There I was in Jamaica, my own country, not accepted, and here in this foreign country, I was already a leader. Just like that. They were taking me for what I was at face value. No questions, no preconceived notions, no issues.

I would travel more, and quickly understand that it wasn't about being Jamaican or Chinese. In fact, it wasn't about being a label at all. It was about being me. Earle Wong. In Jamaica, someone was always trying to pin a label on you. That is how I learned about boundaries. And about setting boundaries. And that's not good. Because I realize now that the families I boarded with were actually trying to make me comfortable. But I was always on the defensive, looking for the innuendoes.

And that's how I grew up. As for my Scout friends, we still get together to this day and remain diehard friends. Except now we've added our wives and children to the group. And while time and my global perspective ensure that I now know better, every now and again, I catch myself on the outside looking in.

Written and edited by Alex Lee as told by Earle Wong

Photograph of scout troop from the personal album of ©Kathleen (Kay) Chin

Down Memory Lane

At the end of a 'Market Day' in New Market, St. Elizabeth
Photograph ©Ray Chen

Down Memory Lane

1

2

3

4

1. Wrapping was done this way for sugar, flour
   cornmeal,etc.

2.Paper funnels used for packing black pepper.

3." Butter Cutter" made from guitar string.

4. Uncut salted codfish.

5.Filling system used by most shopkeepers.

6 Empty wooden soft drink cases.

7. Diamond Mineral bottle.

5

6

7

Norman Hew-Shue
THE HAM THWE POO (GROCERY SHOP)

THE CHINESE GROCERY SHOP is a landmark institution for our Hakka culture on which, for the majority of us, memories and family fortunes were founded.

The shops were more or less similar, being surrounded by a piazza elevated from the street to various heights. At Rosemary Lane and Barry Steet (my birthplace), the shop was elevated about 2 feet above the sidewalk. This guarded against flooding from seasonal tropical rains and the regularly overflowing sewer system.

Shop doors were usually of metal-clad wood of two, or even three, folding panels or leaves. In response to the law of the time against Sunday shopping, one of these hinged panels could be guarded by a local lad who would usher favoured shoppers briskly in or out, when the coast was clear. Even back then, serious thought was given to security (more out of precaution than out of necessity). My father ('Foreman') was quite security-conscious and our shop reflected this.

At closing, these doors were anchored by bolts that entered holes in the ground and top frame, as well as large side bolts plus latch and staples. Retainers of heavy gauge u-shaped wires were put in the staples, as were alarm bells on the end of flat spring strap-hooks. The whole door was further braced by heavy wooden bars that slid into wall-slots and iron staples. These bars were of different lengths and were stored vertically between the doors. They were necessary to withstand the occasional kicks and body-slams in the night from idlers congregated on the piazza, but sometimes we would be entertained by a hopeful street band under the lamp-post doing the latest do-wop renditions: "So fine… *So fine… So fiiine ye-ah.... m-my baby issodarn fine – whoa hu oh, yeah uh yeah... so fine...* Thrill me…."

It was the sons' duty to help lock up and we soon learned to correctly assign the bars to their proper places. Higglers, who by their presence might attract customers, might be allowed to leave their wares behind the doors overnight. Sometimes the last door was designed to join with the counter end to form a more secure accessway during opening hours.

Inside the shop, the layout was similarly dictated by practicality and security with the staple and necessity items near to the till, and the uncommon or exotic items (4-7-11 or khus-khus perfume) in showcases or at the far reaches of the shop.

One end of the shop often abutted the street. This outside wall would usually have a small barred window secured by a small wooden door where after-hours purchases might be made, as prompted by insistent shoutings of "Mr Chin! de baby wan' teething powder (or gripe water)". The kerosene oil, coconut and sweet oil, mackerel, red herring, saltfish and other odorous commodities were usually at this ventilated end of the shop. It also allowed for the filling of the kerosene drum. Brown soap was also stored here and was cut from long bars. Next to these were the loose chemical items such as fine and coarse salt, baking and drinking soda, straw dye for staining floors, 'blue' cubes for bleaching.

Most of these provisions were sold piecemeal at low profit, and were a testament to the hard work endured by our parents for our sakes. Packaging varied with the commodity – paper funnels for black-pepper whole and ground; flat wrap for vermicelli. Flour was poured onto paper fashioned into a cylinder which was flattened at one end. It would then be filled and banged once or twice to settle the contents before being closed. This was at the height of colonial times with various systems of weights and measures – liquids and grains shared common gill, pint and quart measures, branching off into gallons and bushels respectively for larger volumes. The tinsmith was a busy man supplying us with measures, funnels, and the long kerosene hand-pump with the marble valve. Pounds, shillings and pence held sway, and I used to hate doing the alcohol excise ledger where all beer, ales, and alcoholic beverages had to be logged. This was in keeping with the fondness of the English for bureaucracy (ever seen a cricket scoring sheet?) which they probably got from us in China.

Further down, near to the till, were the cinnamon sticks, senna, cocoa, and other plant barks or products. The till itself was centre stage with the Four Ace and other cigarettes, lighter fluid and flint, and other frequently demanded items. Also here were the various books pertaining to the running of the business, including the book for credit which, indiscriminately used, have been the bane of quite a few businesses. A 'Ready Reckoner' might be there in later years supplanting the son pan* or abacus of the older generations.

Biscuits: Cheese Crunchies and Animal Crackers; Saltine and Cream varieties in square tins sat beside pastas (from macaroni to 'allitrey' vermicelli) along with Excelsior crackers in the long cardboard box, hot from off the truck. Also in this area would be the hand-cranked blackpepper mill.

Next came the fridge with all its associated contents: Anchor butter, soft drinks, Kool-Aid and Suck-Suck. Earlier generations had a literal ice-box supplied with a block of sack-cloth and sawdust-covered ice from the ammonia reeking ice factory on Harbour and Gold Streets. Later came compressor fridges – the Chong's at Tower Street had a type fuelled by kerosene oil, the workings of which I could never figure out. We, too, had a unique electrical Philco model, bought at McDougall's on east Parade. The handle was in the shape of a "V" in front and any side could be opened by pulling on the appropriate arm but yet it wouldn't allow the other side to work and the door to fall off. I have never seen one like that before or after.

The rest of the shelving contained the less requested stuff – stationery (no envelopes to be sold after 6 o'clock), brushes etc. Preparations from Britain or her colonies – Kaufmanns Sulphur Bitters, Phillips Milk of Magnesia, Canadian Healing Oil (good to cure fowls of colds) or Scotts Emulsion, which we enjoyed drinking, were also stored here.

The counter area complemented the wall shelving just described so that the chopping board was opposite the saltfish, along with one of two scales. The other was for the flour and 'dry goods' area. Under the counter were barrels of mackerel, pigs' tail, and salt pork. Flour and cornmeal were poured from their sacks into barrels with lids, possibly to keep out rodents. My dear father, Foreman, would be standing there with one foot on the barrel in his homemade underpants clicking away at the abacus. He was quite comfortable in this attire as were his customers. One Sunday, however, as he was escorting some local girls out through the yard door, I was surprised to see his tall frame suddenly being yanked towards the gate by one of the giggling girls who grabbed a personal part of him. Very mischievous, these Jamaican girls.

The glass case with the bread, ginger-buns and bullas, would be next on the counter, along with the candy jars – Paradise Plums, Bustamante Backbone (an extremely hard confection likened to, and mocking the virility of the previous PM). The rest of the counter would be in the form of glass cases with items such as Jiffy dyes – I used to be fascinated by the different shades - post office red, emerald and leaf green; flashlights; Okapi knives, from the big one with multicoloured handle to the small one shaped like a key; needles, thread and sequins.

The wooden outside front of the counters usually were covered with advertisements stapled there by salesmen. "Sunlight soap powder – bring some light into your wash". There was usually also an access door to pass large goods under the counter. The space above the counter was barred all the way round.

Carrying the various bagged goods built our muscles: flour was 100 lbs, granulated sugar 110 lbs, and dark sugar 210 lbs. These bags were secured by machine stitching which, started the right way, allowed the stitches to be unravelled with one pull. Similarly, the tin of cheddar cheese required know-how to extract the contents.

The country shop was different in that its provisioning went beyond basic foods and staples to include a haberdashery, bar, hardware and the occasional gas pump. Such was the Williams' shop at Green Island, Hanover. My dear aunt would come to town to order for the shop. I remember accompanying her on one such expedition, entering Hanna's and other warehouses on Harbour Street. The day was spent among bolts of fabric. I overheard one particular type being called 'acetate' (the synthetic age was just starting). At another outlet on King Street I saw the same unmistakable, waterproof kitchen table-like fabric. Quick as a flash I piped up, "that is acetate" to the amazement of my aunt and the sales lady, who remarked admiringly, "Hi! yu know yu cloth!"

The Chinese grocery shops is a landmark institution for the Hakka culture. Below are some of the Chinese shops located in the rural areas and towns across the island.   1. East Street, Kingston   2. Constant Spring Road, Kingston   3. Blue Mountains, St. Andrew   4. Newport, Manchester   5. Cross Keys, Manchester   6. Watchwell District, St. Elizabeth   7. Sav-la-mar, St. Elizabeth   8. Clarks Town, Trelawny   9. Charles Town, Portland   10. Tranquility, Portland

11. *Constant Spring Road, Kingston*   12. *Frankfield, Clarendon*   13. *Spanish Town, St. Catherine*   14. *Grange Hill, Westmoreland*   15. *Cross Keys, Manchester,*   16. *Montego Bay, St. James.*

This, then, was the basic format of most of our parents' shops which provided us with an education, not to be gained anywhere else, by forming a window on to the colourful Jamaican society. My shop was facing Harts' Butchery and also, of all places, a 'sport house' run by a big homosexual black man nicknamed Kai Kai.

LIFE BEHIND THE SHOP

In previous articles, I reminisced about life as experienced from behind my Jamaican shop counter. From the happy prancing Christmas revellers, to the slow crutch-assisted gait of a Kendal train crash survivor, there was a never-ending drama. However, most of the shops in those days had backyards with adjoining tenement dwellings. These provided playgrounds as well as another educational and stimulating window on the microcosm of local life.

We had a large backyard of hard packed earth, which I used to explore, with a milk shop at one end and rooms at one side. There were tenants up to about 1951 when Hurricane Charlie blew all the zinc sheets off the shop's upper floor, with one even swinging on a power line up the lane. After this we moved one block away to Maiden Lane by swapping shops with Aston, my father's friend.

We resided beside and above the shop. There was a completely concreted backyard with about 5 rooms occupied by local families. These rooms were about 50' x 30', with wooden flooring which required periodic polishing with the traditional husk-brush fashioned from a coconut. Beds had mosquito netting and windows were operated by hidden sash-cords and weights. The tenements had communal cooking and washing areas. In those simpler days, one's earthly belongings could fit into those rooms. I used to spend most of my shop hours peeping through the dividing wire-mesh or, being an only child, interacting with the tenants or their kids.

Some of those memories imprinted on my mind are: watching the tenants put a raw egg in a glass of water on the housetop on a sunny Easter day. At noon the egg-white was formed into fanciful shapes because of rising air bubbles. Their reaction would range from happy exclamations: "Lawd a gwine travel a foreign!" or hushed, frightened whispers over a perceived plane or coffin respectively.

We had a tenant, Mr. Kelly, a fair-skinned man who was a driver for D&G (Desnoes and Geddes) soft drink company. He would park his truck in the lane and he liked Perry Como. I spent countless hours with him and learned the words of "Hot diggigty... dog diggity... Oh! What you do to me! When you're holding me tight..." or "Papa luvs mambo... Mama luvs mambo" when catchy songs were the craze.

There was a fellow Hakka gentleman, whose name I won't mention, who ran a Peeka Peow bank, and had four fair-skinned, 'outside' daughters – Norma, Dims, Hortense and Beverly. My father rented out a couple of rooms to these ladies. One day, the other girls hid Dims' clothes when she was bathing. After a long while of fruitless entreaties the tearful teenaged Dims walked out of the bathroom *au naturel.* I happened to be in the backyard and directly in her path, providing another spicy and educational Jamaican memory.

I spent time swapping comics or school books with the other kids. (Remember *West Indian Readers* with stories and pictures about the crayfish that everyone was trying to put in the pot? The monkey that told his alligator captor that his liver was up in the tree? Remember Anancy?) Time would be spent also experimenting with firecrackers in milk tins, or listening to Rediffusion.

There was a fellow called Jack who used to show me how to fly kites on the housetop. His mother (Mrs. Edwards) worked at the Institute of Jamaica in the basement. It was not until later years that the name and voice relationship connected together and I realized that he was Jackie Edwards of local signing fame ("Love me Darling with all your might"). I heard that the family was living at the foot of that hill right beside Joon Sang (Chinese beach) right where Windward becomes Rockfort Road.

One day after swimming, I stopped by the house to say hello. I saw him hustle by with an army of hangers-on or sycophants, which I didn't want to be associated with, so I bowed out. But isn't it funny, as I always point out, how things, people and places tend to always be coming around throughout life?

After the death of my dear father, my mother and I rented out the shop and lived in two of the back-rooms. The role of landlord was thrust upon me, which I didn't relish, especially when the services of Mr. Muschette (a famous and feared Kingston rent-collector, nicknamed 'Naked', because that was the state it was rumoured you would be in when he was done with you), was enlisted for delinquent tenants.

One humorous incident (looking back now – then it was a serious matter) was with a tenant who was troublesome to us and the other tenants. We had no choice but to give her notice, but she was refusing to leave. Then an inspiration struck me after remembering that she could be heard almost nightly chanting and doing some mysterious ritual in her room. I happened to have a real human skull at the time that I had borrowed from Wolmer's to compare with an anatomy book, since I was fascinated by all the holes (foramina) in the base for the nerves and vessels. I held the skull in both hands in front of me, covered with a towel. I turned my shirt back to front, and walked with a slow funny pace, mumbling something and doing everything I could that was out of the ordinary (but not too obviously). In this fashion I circled past her door when she was sitting outside. The towel happened to slip in the process. Not too long after, she vacated the premises, but when I got a painter to work on her room he came to me in alarm, "Mass Normy cum look ya!"

The ceiling was completely covered by a brownish granular coating. "She bu'n guinea pepper pan yu, man". Evidently the burning of this substance is the ultimate obeah act against an enemy. I had to convince the workman that

I was feeling fine and was more worried about possible toxic chemical effects. I wonder if that is why 'crosses a fallow me?' Or probably I should take a bucket-pan bath, with one 'Blue' bleaching cube added to the water.

Written by Norman Hew-Shue and edited by Sonia Gordon Scott.

* See Glossary

Photographs ©Ray Chen.
Photographs # 11 - 16. 'The Chinese in Jamaica, First Edition 1957
Courtesy of Lee Tom Yin.

Down Memory Lane

1   2

3

1. Gai mow sow* Feather duster. Mostly used for dusting off the shelves in the shop, but it was often used by our parents whenever we misbehaved.

2. This photograph was taken at Molynes 'four roads' intersection on the eve of our Independence Celebration, August 6, 1962.
It reminds me of the many instances during an election period, where members of a political party would ask the owner of the grocery shop if "they could borrow some light to connect the amplifiers and the microphones" for the meeting to be held later that evening in front of the shop.

3. Kyak*. Slippers made from wood for wearing behind the counter of the shop. The photograph on the left reminds us of the way we used to put them together when not in use.

Maxine Lowe
CONNECTING TO THE SHOP

WHEN I HEAR a certain four-letter word – S-H-O-P – out pops another four-letter word – W-O-R-K – although, at times, other four-letter words do come to mind. Images of the long, gruelling hours my parents spent behind the counter, struggling to raise eight kids on the measly profits they earned in a hostile world of verbal and physical threats and abuse, stand out clearly in my mind.

As a family-run business, we kids were expected to put in our fair share, and so we all had our individual tasks assigned. The older ones would wait on the customers, restock the shelves, clean out the bread and bun showcase, wrap up smaller portions of salt, sugar, and flour and sweep the shop, while the younger ones would take out the empty soft-drink bottles to the backyard, wrap up smaller portions of butter and cheese, and serve the smaller items, if they could see over the counter. Of course, this left little or no time for socializing since we still had our homework to do. Thank God for Uncle Joe who would swing by the shop on Sunday mornings to take us all to Hellshire beach where we gorged on Mary's fish 'n' bammie* 'n' festival.

We lived in the back of the shop so there were always strange sounds coming from the zinc rooftop. I remember the long, sleepless nights when we lay in our beds wondering if it "mus' be a duppy or a gunman". Footsteps and shuffling sounds were the other strange noises we heard at nights, but that could have been any number of things: the four watchdogs in the backyard relieving themselves of boredom, the two 'mawga'* cats having fun with a dead rat or old newspapers lying around, or even the cockroaches scurrying in the corners with the fortunate rats whose time had not yet come. But then there was talk about the previous owner's wife and daughter who had died years ago, so who knows?

Opening a grocery shop is no easy feat. In fact, it is a very risky business because you never knew if this would be the last time you'd be opening the shop doors or closing them. Your life was always on the line and your whole world could change instantly, in a split second, any time of the day or night. There was the constant threat of violation hanging over our heads, not knowing when we would be preyed upon by the 'have-nots' who were always lurking in the shadows, waiting for their chance to strike. To overcome this fear, you learned to be alert and mindful of your surroundings, checking that your windows and doors were securely bolted and no one was hiding under the bed, before retiring for the night. Out of adversity comes vigilance and mindfulness, and that is a good thing.

Looking back over the years, I realize how much my parents sacrificed to provide for us, so we wouldn't have to go through the hardships they endured. Even though we never showed any outward affection or emotion towards our parents, and we never confided in them about any of our teenage issues, and we never dared talk back to them when we were being disciplined, what remained constant was the love and caring which we interpreted as restriction, indifference, and resentment in our young, undeveloped minds. What I still find fascinating is the fact that we'd be speaking two completely different languages – we spoke Patois to our parents and they answered in Hakka – and we'd understand each other as if we were speaking the same language. Maybe they're not that different after all or maybe we had this invisible bond that surpassed all language from living so closely together.

If we can get past the physical hardships and dangers that are inherent in many businesses today, and not only in Jamaica, shop life is not all doom and gloom. Without realizing it, our shop experiences do become a predominant part of our lives, moulding us into the people we are today. Shop life has taught me many of the skills that, I believed, came naturally. But, on further scrutiny and 'donkey years' later, you have a 'light bulb' moment when you realize that, because these skills are developed over time at such an early age, you take them for granted and mistakenly think you're born with them.

I always thought I had this innate talent for adding numbers quickly, but I have the shop to thank for that. Because we didn't have a cash register, calculator, or adding machine, I had to write down all the prices of each item on a strip of paper and add them up. In time, this daily exercise was a 'breeze' and soon I became the fastest 'adder' in town. I was so fast that when I was in first form, I entered this adding competition on sports day where someone would run up to me with a piece of paper with a list of numbers to add. In two-two's, I had the total and ran back to the other end of the row – first place! But don't let age 'fool yu' – today, I can tally up these numbers faster than you can pull out a calculator to punch them in.

My first accounting lesson started in the shop when papa taught me how to write cheques that he would pre-sign to pay the suppliers, and how to fill out lodgement slips that had to match the cash/cheque deposits to our chequing account. Gradually, I learned about the intricacies of operating a retail business on credit terms (*try to get longer than the standard 30 day net and hold out as long as you can*); supply and demand (*when Betty condensed milk is in short supply, save it for your loyal customers and marry it to another product for the occasional customers who show up only when there's a shortage*); percentage markup (*some items generate more profit than others, so do your homework*); income and expense (*if your expenses exceed your* 'ncome, 'yu salt'); and cash flow (*make sure cash is flowing in and not out, especially when you have outside help*).

But my business experience didn't stop there. I learned how to order goods when we were running low and, even though I was nervous and shaking in my rubber slippers, I couldn't let the person on the other end of the line know I was only 12 years old. Then when the goods were delivered at the front of the shop, I learned the art of being accountable by checking off the actual goods that were delivered against what was printed on the delivery slip, and making sure that the goods were quickly escorted to a safer spot, before they could evaporate into thin air with the help of unseen hands.

Of course, I must not forget to mention that my mama taught me the art of compassion. Even though she was dog-tired and finally able to get some shut-eye, there I would be, trying to put the finishing touches on the white, pleated P.E. skirt she had made for me. Being inexperienced at hemming, and this being such a wide skirt with these tiny pleats, mama knew that I would be up all night hemming, so she did what any selfless, caring parent would do for their child: she sent me off to bed and made sure it was all hemmed and ready to wear the next day.

I can confidently say that my shop experience played a large part in enhancing my communication skills by giving me the opportunity to interact with people from all walks of life: from the uneducated, lazy, free-loading troublemakers, who were in a constant state of oppression, infuriation, and revolution; to the uneducated, civilized, hard-working humble people, who were just trying to make a living to feed their children and send them to school; to the educated, respectable, middle/upper class echelon who would stop by the shop for cigarettes, groceries, or condoms. Fortunately, or unfortunately for us (depending on how you look at it, or who's looking at it), our helper, Gloria, who hailed from Rema*, included some life lessons of her own and taught us the art of verbal communication at the lowest level, in particular, a wide range of 'clawt'* previously unknown to us.

One of my biggest achievements – thanks to the shop – was in third form at Holy Childhood High. Sr. Stephanie announced that there would be a prize for the girl who sold the most raffle tickets for the annual May Fair event, and a prize would also go to the class that sold the most tickets. Well, if it wasn't for our little shop on Hagley Park Road and the steady stream of customers and, of course, my salesgirlship in badgering these poor customers to help a worthy cause, I wouldn't have got my prized Timex watch, and our class wouldn't have got a trip to Puerto Seco Beach. And, to top it off, one of my tickets won the first prize of $100, which was a substantial amount back in those days in the '70s.

Above: The Holy Cross Church located on the premises of the Holy Childhood High School

All in all, we have to take the good with the bad no matter where we go, and even though there were good, bad, and ugly times back then, I try to focus on the nice, the positive, and the happy. I don't believe our children can or will ever understand our way of life back then, that we could actually survive under those bizarre conditions, a world removed from the life of luxury and excess in North America that they've grown accustomed to today. When I'm having a hard time dealing with my own children's materialistic desires, I always threaten to exile them to a week of hardship at my cousin's shop, from which they'll come back with a new lease on life, never wanting the latest Nike shoes or the latest cell phone, just because. Of course, they don't take me seriously because they think I'm making up these shop stories but, one of these days, I just might surprise them.

Written by Maxine Lowe and edited by Sonia Gordon Scott.

*See Glossary

Photographs ©Ray Chen

Down Memory Lane

Town of Falmouth Trelawny
Photograph ©Ray Chen

Aston Lue
COUNTER POWER

WHEN IT COMES TO my childhood days, I recall endless summers when friends would go to movies or parties and have fun, while I, the shop apprentice, stayed closer to home, toiling in the family's Kingston grocery and ice cream parlour. Those who had to endure that teenage ritual may well describe it as the closest thing to kung fu school. You did what you had to do, no matter how many times you'd done it before. You simply dug up the discipline to resist the temptation to go out with your friends or lose yourself in a show on the old black and white television set with the rabbit ears. All roads led to serving the customers. Every step I took to fetch ice cream from the freezer, every reach I made for the *Buccaneer* cigarettes, the *Liquid Foods* or *Diamond* sodas, every slice of *hardo bread* or cheese I cut - they all counted towards my degree from the 'University of Hard Knocks'.

Gung-gung*, at 67 years young, was the one who set the pace. After his enamel mug of steaming coffee and accompanying peanut butter sandwich, he'd open the shop promptly at 9:00 a.m., and begin walking to and fro as he systematically fetched every item for his customers behind that grocery counter. I remember lamp shades and kerosene lanterns being the hot seller in those days. He must have walked a thousand miles behind those counters just selling those alone. Walking, reaching, making change. He would do this for the whole day until closing the shutters at 10:00 p.m. *Po-po** at that hour would re-stock the coolers with sodas, so that they'd be cold enough to quench thirsty throats the next day. In Jamaica, just about every day was a hot day.

Gung-gung had done his own shop apprenticeship decades before in a grocery store at Maiden Lane and East Queen Street. Fresh from China, he was starting over in his 40s and earning £2 a week. In the days he wrapped rice, flour and crackers in white newspaper print. At nights he slept on the counter. Eventually he would save enough to send for my grandmother, whom he had married at fifteen. She was two years younger at the time.

Shop at 41 Waltham Park Road

I can't recall the name of the Chinese organization that assisted them in buying their first business, but the loan was paid off in a short time. They would eventually upgrade to a three-shutter wide shop on Waltham Park Road, where a bus terminus fed them with a constant stream of customers for the years to come. By the time I arrived on the scene, my grandparents were working from morning until night.

It can be an odd collection, those childhood memories that stay with you. Like being seven and barely being able to clear the counter to see treats of coffee strips, sugar buns, mattress cake and plantain tarts. Cadbury chocolates were my hands-down favourite, as my fillings today will testify, or memories of the construction men perched on our tall wooden stools come Friday evening, *labrishing** for hours over several rounds of *Red Stripe* or *McEwan's Strong Ale*.

Life was simple then, but good. The *food* made it even better. I still remember tilting my head back to inhale the aroma of my Po-po's roast beef cooking slowly in the Dutch pot, or her famous *muknee** and pork. The patties we made ensured a quick hot snack whenever I felt peckish. The neighbouring yard directly behind the shop was mango heaven – one huge Bombay tree, one Number Eleven, one East Indian and *three* Julie Mango trees. Little did I know then that years of stoning Bombay mangoes 30 feet above would make me a mean softball player decades later.

Our own backyard was just as prolific with generous fruit-bearing trees - ackee, soursop, sweetsop, coconut and breadfruit. Closer to the ground, the callaloo, bokchoy*, lettuce, long peas and *foogah** made for balanced, organic meals at our dinner table. Sometimes during my work breaks, I'd cook my own *Ackee*, dumpling and codfish meals in an old cheese pan. The pan I would place atop three large stones, red hot from the fire I had made using dry sticks. *Po-po** also raised her own chickens. Those plump brown-feathered hens did some serious justice to her famous *Pak-jam-guy** soups. I used to help her prepare the unsuspecting fowls for the delicious family favourite, by holding the wings and legs while she did what she had to do.

And I'd say that was the point to our lives. We did what we had to do. Serve the customers. Make the sacrifices. Forge a life. And while I may have missed out on many a summer fun, not *once* did I go without a new khaki uni-

Aston & Michelle Lue's family. JJ graduation 2002.

form, *Bata* shoes or food. Today that little boy in the shop now runs several successful businesses with the help of a devoted wife, and is father to four amazing children. They are armed with college degrees and their own unique childhood memories, many of which include carefree weekends at the movies. I consider *that* my reward for working the counter, all those countless hours.

Written by Aston Lue and edited by Alex Lee.

* See Glossary

Penny Williams
MEMORIES OF VINEYARD GROCERY

WHERE TO START? I first thought I would have only two or three stories to tell and then I started jotting down ideas and found the list getting longer and longer! Vineyard Grocery was our home; like most of the Chinese, the shop was downstairs with our living space on the second floor, although the second floor wasn't built until I (the fifth child) was born.

Vineyard Grocery! Who lived in Kingston during the middle of the last century and didn't know Vineyard Grocery and Ice Cream Parlour? Even people from the country who came into Kingston on a visit would stop by to pick up their patties before heading back to country! Vineyard Grocery – on Deanery Road, just up the road from St. Joseph's Hospital and just below Merrion Road. Passengers would get off the bus, JOS No. 3, on Merrion Road and turn south, stopping at Vineyard Grocery on their way home and greeting my mother who sat, as usual, at the front of the shop, "Hi, Miss Ruby!"

Penny Williams' dad, Ernest and mom (Miss Ruby).

In the old days, Vineyard Grocery was an old-fashioned grocery on one side with the big wooden counter all around, and an ice cream parlour on the other side. The ice cream parlour would serve wonderful things like 7-Up floats and milkshakes – made with real malted milk – as well as plantain tarts, patties, cakes and pastries, all made on the premises. The bakery was at the back of the yard and every morning we would wake up to the steady "thud, thud..." sound of Keith, the baker, pounding the dough for the patties to be made that day. There was a huge wall-to-wall table in the bakery and Keith used a block of wood that was about 4' long and 6" square in thickness. How he lifted that log and pounded for so long I have never figured out!

Behind the counter of the Vineyard Grocery shop.

It seemed that everyone in Jamaica knew of Miss Ruby's patties! Unlike all other patties, these were shaped like a pyramid, or a Cornish pastie, and filled with wonderful ground, minced beef, and cubes of carrots and cho-cho. No bread crumbs for these patties! They made a great lunch and so every lunchtime, adults and students alike would come in to buy their "patty and cola champagne".

Then there were the special times, like Easter, when the bakery turned out masses of Easter buns. These would be laid out on big tables in the backyard, and we children got the job of marking each one with different pieces of dough to signify the price of the bun, after which they would be baked. Mom's buns were rich with fruit and, oh what a heavenly smell when they were baking!

Many years later, the ice cream parlour would close and the whole shop became a self-serve style supermarket, one of the earliest in Jamaica. In the grocery, we sold everything imaginable – ham from Denmark in the thick, black casing, Anchor butter from New Zealand, Red Delicious apples and grapes from the USA, cigarettes, Martell brandy, South African port wines, French champagne etc. It wasn't until many years later that I began to appreciate how international our stock had been. At that time, Vineyard Town was an upscale neighbourhood with families like the Issas and Brimos living there.

Do you remember Anchor butter? It came as one solid block in a big, wooden crate and it had to be cut up and wrapped, to be ready for sale. This was done on a weeknight, either Monday or Tuesday – I can't quite remember which – and later in the evening before we closed at 11:00 p.m. (yes, we closed at 11:00 p.m. every night except Sunday!), the block of butter would be taken out of the crate and placed on top of the counter. First they would take a big wire cutter (made from guitar string attached to blocks of wood at each end) and each person would take hold of one end and pull the wire through the cold, hard butter to cut it into smaller chunks. Then those would be cut with a sharp knife into 1lb, $^1/_2$ lb, $^1/_4$ lb and even 2oz. portions which we would wrap in grease paper. Of course, the cutter was not always accurate and sometimes the piece would be a little too heavy. Then the cutter would slice off a little to get the weight just right. Ah! Then the lucky one of us would get the slice of cold, hard butter and put it on a crisp, Excelsior water cracker and munch away. Mmm! It was like eating cheese!

We also had to measure brown and white sugar, brown and white rice, flour and cornmeal to be ready for the busy days later in the week. These staples came in cwt. (112 lbs for you metric folks!) crocus (burlap) bags, which were emptied into big barrels under the counter. Then we made up brown paper bags of 2 to 5 lbs each. Smaller amounts up to 1 lb were weighed onto a square of brown paper (cut from large sheets) and we had to carefully fold the paper over and close the two ends to make a neat package. This took some practice at first and if it wasn't folded well, the package would fall apart and out would spill the rice or whatever! However, many days and months of practice with weighing meant that we got pretty good at it, and we would often get the exact amount with one scoop!

Sometimes, after a night of work weighing sugar or butter etc., papa would go upstairs before the shop closed and then, after it closed, we would troop upstairs to the kitchen and there would be the wonderful smell of hot, freshly steamed rice. Not only rice, but also lap hap* (preserved duck) and fah chong* (Chinese sausage)! Mmm…mmh! Then we would all sit and eat seow yah*. Dinner never tasted this good!

One day, one of our regular customers, Felix, came in and asked for two pounds of grapes. I put the grapes in the scale and got the scale needle right on the big 2. At this point, Felix insisted the grapes were two ounces short and I got so incensed at the thought that he was implying I was cheating, that I flounced off upstairs and mom or someone else took over. Of course, they always went by the motto, "The customer is always right."

In those days, many customers raised their own chickens so we also sold chicken feed – layer, grower and so on. These were in open crocus bags just inside the back door of the shop, leading out to the backyard. Our next door neighbours, the Robinson's, who lived on the corner at Merrion Road, raised pigeons and had a stack of pigeon coops which we could see from our upstairs veranda. Well… usually some of the chicken feed would spill from the open bags onto the floor. This was too much temptation for the pigeons, so the little thieves would fly over into our backyard and step inside the door to quickly grab some of the spilled feed off the floor and fly off again. They must have got pretty fat on all this extra food!

Whenever one of us was sick, mama would buy a young pigeon from next door and Edna, our nanny and English style cook, would make pigeon soup with barley for us to drink. It was so delicious and the dark meat was so tender. The pigeons also pitched on our kitchen roof at the back of the house. One day I walked out through the upstairs door from the kitchen to the backyard. "Plop!" I felt something drop on top of my head. I timidly reached up to touch my head to see what it was. Oh, no! Pigeon poop!! Good old Edna quickly washed my hair for me, to my great relief.

Edna cooked for us only on Friday evenings (Jamaican style) and for Sunday dinner (English style) – Friday evenings because that was when papa delivered groceries in the car to our more well-to-do customers and Sunday, I guess, was to give papa a rest. Papa did the cooking for all other evening meals, Hakka style, which was all very delicious. One of us would be given the task of 'picking over' the rice and God help you if you left any dirt in it! Another task was to 'pick' the bean sprouts – break off the roots – which papa would also not tolerate if incorrectly done. He was fussy but he was a very good cook!

In fact, one of my funniest memories is of papa's style of cooking. He would busy himself in the kitchen, all the while singing Chinese songs (they sounded like operas) and he would leave things covered in the pots for a while. Then he would go up the short flight of stairs to the upstairs tiled veranda, where he would get into the old bentwood rocking chair, tilt the chair backwards until he was lying back and the chair was balanced on the tips of its rockers, and go to sleep! Sometimes, he would even snore! However, in about ten or fifteen minutes time he would suddenly get up, go back to the kitchen and carry on with his cooking. Amazingly, I don't remember him ever falling down or burning any of the dishes!

So, what did Papa deliver to the customers on Friday evenings? He delivered the telephone orders. Near the cash register in the shop was a small box with many little pigeonholes, each of which held a little red book, one for each delivery customer. Every week, the customers would telephone us to give their orders for delivery and we children took the orders over the phone. The customers would order things like: 2 lbs granulated (white) sugar, 1 lb brown sugar, 3 lbs white flour, 2 lbs white rice, 2 tins (Nestle's or Betty) condensed milk, 1 lb butter, $1/_2$ bar brown (washing) soap, 1 cake of blue (clothes whitener), 1 lb saltfish (salted codfish), etc. We would write these down quickly, one item per line as the customer dictated, and then read the list back to the customer to confirm that we had everything. After they had hung up, we would price each item and multiply by the quantity before writing the price down on the right hand side. Then we would total the whole page, adding once down and once up to make sure we got the same total, which meant we had added correctly. The order would then be ready to be filled for delivery.

In addition to groceries, we also sold magazines and comics. They were hung on two thick wires strung above the glass counters, on the side with the cash register, near the door. Every Thursday, new ones arrived with that smell of fresh ink and we would hang them up with little metal clips, carefully at one corner, so they hung down diagonally. There were comics like *Archie* and *Little Dot,* the small comics about World War II, and the movie magazines like *Photoplay,* not to mention the 'trash' love stories like *Romance* and *True Confessions*! We had to hide to read the love stories as mama and papa didn't want us to read them.

Of course, as soon as they arrived we were keen to read the latest. To put them up and get them down we used a special stick with a hook on the end and we developed the skill of setting them on the wire above our heads. We had to take them down carefully and read them very carefully so as not to 'dog-ear' them or they wouldn't sell. Papa, however, hated to see us reading them and we would get a cussing or a gah chuk* on the head because we were not kunpoo-ing*. I could never understand what was wrong with reading when the shop was empty – it was so boring otherwise!

For other entertainment, we were not allowed to play in the shop but we did play in the two storerooms – hide-and-seek, what else? The rooms were piled high with cartons with very little space between and there was also a mezzanine with more boxes on top, so we would squeeze behind a stack of boxes or climb up to the mezzanine, if we were brave. Each room had the usual raw light bulb overhead but these were never turned on, except when someone went in to fetch a carton. So the rooms were always dark, all the better to play hide-and-seek, except that I was mortally afraid of the dark! Of course, I dared not tell the others that I was afraid or they would have made fun of me, or so I thought.

Another source of entertainment was sailing boats on a rainy day. The rainy season was in October and November and, during those months, we often had very heavy rains. The rain would run off the roof of the plaza in front of the shop and join the rushing water in the gutter at the side of the street. We children would make boats from old newspapers and then dash out and plonk our boats into the mini-river rushing by, and watch to see whose boat would go the furthest. I don't remember winning very many times.

So we entertained ourselves within the confines of Vineyard Grocery and we were not usually allowed to play with 'outsiders'. The only exception for me was the occasional visit to Purity Bar & Grill, two doors away from us, when I was allowed to go and play with Dimps Chuck, another Alpha girl. When Purity first opened their doors on Deanery Road, our neighbours were up in arms about a bar opening in our midst and 'spoiling' the neighbourhood. However, Purity did open and remained open for many years, with everyone getting to know "Mother Chuck" much as they knew "Miss Ruby."

Perhaps my most unforgettable memory is that of Hurricane Charlie in 1951. It was a Friday evening, one of the busiest times in the shop and a very rare occasion when Papa, Mama and my eldest sister, Yvonne, had gone to the north coast on a weekend vacation. It might even have been my parents' first vacation together! Anyway, the shop had been left in the care of my Uncle William and my second and third eldest sisters, Phyllis and Nicky. In those early days of the Chinese in Jamaica, once they had established a business they often sent for a sibling or relative to come and work in the business. So my young Uncle William (Ashook*), came from China and worked with us until my father later helped him to open his own business on Half-Way-Tree Road, next door to the Simms of Fah Mee Restaurant fame.

Since it was a busy Friday night, most of the family was downstairs working as, I was later told, people had not believed that the hurricane was coming. Upstairs, in one bedroom, were two big beds – the double sized ones that were so high one had to jump up to get on to them. On one bed was my Aunt Lorraine (Shookmay*), Uncle William's wife, with their baby, Herman. The other had my two younger brothers and myself. When the hurricane started and the lights went out, our faithful nanny, Edna, made us get underneath the beds – Edna, the boys and I under one bed, and Shookmay and the baby under the other.

Soon the wind was howling and lashing the trees and buildings everywhere, blowing the zinc sheets off roofs and sending them flying. In no time our living room windows were broken, and the wind plastered the leaves of the Lignum Vitae tree next door on to our walls. The rain also came charging through the broken windows and we ended up crouching under the beds in inches of water. Edna had had one candle in a candlestick and a box of matches. After several attempts at lighting the candle only to have the wind blow it out, she gave up, and we stayed in the dark, wet and shivering as we had been wearing only our light, cotton night-gown and pyjamas. Fortunately, there was a rubber sheet on the other bed so Shookmay and the baby were relatively dry.

It seemed like forever that we lay there, wet and cold in the dark, before we were in the eye of the storm and calm reigned – temporarily – once again. Then the folks downstairs came to our rescue and we were able to spend the rest of the night downstairs, sleeping on the ice cream parlour tables pulled together and covered with old clothes. Apparently, they had tried to come upstairs, several times to get us but each time, they had been repelled by the wind blowing broken pieces of glass and other debris. During that lull, they were also able to pull up the main shutter of the shop and let out the customers who had been trapped there when the storm had unexpectedly started.

The next morning when the storm was over we could see the devastation outside – great, big trees lying across roads, many roofs without zinc sheets, like ours, and broken glass and debris everywhere. Of course, nearly all the telephone and light poles were also down. I don't really remember the exact order of things after that – it was such an extraordinary time and everything was a bit of a blur. What I do remember is that mama and papa came back, I don't know how. The doctor was sent for and we were all given typhus injections because of the fear of contaminated water – there was no bottled water then! I do remember my brothers and I lying on the big double bed afterwards, sick as dogs with a high fever from the effects of the typhus injections!

Our roof had been badly damaged and would need a lot of repairs, so some of us were packed off to stay with other people. I was sent to my god-mother in Barbican, whose home was hardly touched, and my sister, Avery, was sent to stay with our cousins, the Ho Lungs, on Swallowfield Road. Yes, the Ho Lungs as in Fr. Ho Lung, or Dickie as we knew him then, his father being my mother's brother, and his mother, our Aunt Janet. The other siblings were Loretta, Theresa and Michael. Eventually, like the rest of the country, our home was repaired and we gradually returned to a normal life, but that night remains a vivid memory!

I'm not exactly sure just how typical of the Chinese our family was at that time but what was characteristic, I think, was that our parents worked hard to make a living and to raise their family. We children were expected to help in the shop, go to school and study hard to make a better life for ourselves. Over the years Vineyard Grocery survived attempted robberies, a mild earthquake and Hurricane Charlie, while it provided the background for us to grow up and improve our lives. It will remain in our memories, and the memories of thousands of Jamaicans – Chinese and otherwise – forever.

An ad for the Vineyard Grocery.

Written by Penny Williams and edited by Sonia Gordon Scott.

* See Glossary

Franklin Lue
MONA GROCERY

I REMEMBER MY childhood years at Mona Grocery in Jamaica with much emotion. My parents are Horace & Mary Lue, who owned and operated Mona Grocery.

My father had migrated from China to Jamaica in 1929. After only about 6 months of schooling, and the death of both his grandparents and his mother, he was apprenticed as a shopkeeper to my grand-uncle, Lue Mann Fung, at Liguanea Grocery. My mother joined him in 1937. After a few years at Liguanea, my parents were given sole responsibility of 'Top Shop', Diamond Grocery, also owned by my grand-uncle. By then, they had started a family with my eldest brother, Peter. Unlike Liguanea, where the clientele included the more affluent, Diamond Grocery's customers were from the opposite spectrum of Jamaica's economic population. The location abutted both Stand Pipe and Confidence View Lanes where the residents were more transitory. Nevertheless, my parents made a success of it and, after about two years, were asked by my grand-uncle to return to Liguanea. The family had, by then, grown to three children with the addition of Eugene and Joyce. My parents were quite successful at Liguanea Grocery, and added two more children, Carmen and June.

After WWII, when my grandfather became gravely ill, my parents returned to China. They sold whatever they could, but still managed to package thirty 'containers' for the return to their families. They were fortunate to secure visas for entry into the United States. Given the long voyage, they related how happy they were to be able to bring back fresh fruits from the orchards to the boat for their friends, while in San Francisco.

Unfortunately, my grandfather died before my family was able to make it back to China. Being the eldest male, my father assumed responsibility and provided for his younger siblings. After securing his extended family, my father returned with my two eldest bothers, Peter and Eugene, to Jamaica. On returning to Jamaica, my parents started their own business and bought the property at 143 Old Hope Road. The original grocery was an older, wooden structure. After the experience of hurricane Charlie, my parents resolved to build a new Mona Grocery. I recall my childhood days, exploring the Mona

construction site and forming bonds with Mr. Lewellyn, the contractor. Mona Grocery, with its neon lights and the home behind it, had several innovative features for the time (1952). I recall many visitors, and especially comments on the running hot and cold water to the kitchen and bathrooms, features my parents had learnt about on their travel through the United States. However, I think the aspect of Mona Grocery my parents were most proud of, was their ability to attract customers from the full spectrum of Jamaican society.

In many ways my parents' years in Jamaica, up to 1948, had prepared them for this type of Grocery. I recall them talking about the many important people who were customers while at Liguanea. When I was learning about Marcus Garvey in History of Jamaica in first form, my father related to me the type of Cuban cigars Garvey had preferred to purchase at Liguanea.

Mona Grocery was stocked to cater to a wide spectrum of Jamaican clientele. It included not only folks like... Peter Desnoes and their extended family such as Jim Lim, C.B. Wattley, Sir Alexander and Lady Bustamante, Tony Kelly, Mona Hotel, Sir Philip and Lady Sherlock, and much of the UWI faculty such as Ronald Irvin, and institutions such as UWI Research Institute. Regular customers also included many of the folks in the Stand Pipe and Confidence View Lanes. On my recent visit I was happy to see an old friend with whom I had played soccer, Hilton Cobran.

I would often ride on the grocery bike with 'Jung-Gu-Luong' to make the deliveries. His name was actually Leonard Morris and it seems that he was given the name partly because of his love for gungu-peas with rice. The name originated from my mom's adaptation of English and he worked for my family at both the Liguanea and Mona Groceries and was cherished by us all.

In later years, in the car with my father, I visited many of the most affluent homes in the areas of Mona and Barbican. At the same time, I made lasting friendships with many of the less privileged folks in the area. It is with much fondness that I recall these early experiences and cherish the lessons which provide balance in life.

Written by Franklin Lue and edited by Sonia Gordon Scott.

Mavis I. Young
DEEP RURAL SHOPKEEPING

'SET FAH' IS my Chinese name; Fondly called 'Set' as a child.

For fifteen years I was an only child until my brother Tyrone was born.
Yes, our family was small in terms of Chinese families.
My mother had one sister who died as a young woman leaving four
children, my cousins.

I remember well those years of living and growing up in the country;
"bush" as folks often referred jokingly to deep rural areas.
Hundreds of persons can tell you about life in the era of peenie
wallies* and dark nights.
No radio, no telephone, no piped water, gravel roads, no bus service.
Electricity?
What is that? "Elastic Light" *(electric light)*.
Everyone was deprived but they did not know anything better, except
that one had to make a living and be honest.

So as life became modern, all benefitted from infrastructure
development.
Country folks had their own unique way of describing some of the
modern improvements.
"A bus will be passing here" *(indicating that this is where the bus
stops);*
"Light pon stick" *(street light on a pole).*
They spoke a living language and persons instilled with English
traditions lived side by side with them.

Other changes took place.
Parochial roads lead to the deeper countryside in any direction.
Grey stone walls defined property boundaries in the parish of
Manchester.
Back then, one could walk for miles and not see a human being,
perhaps an animal or two grazing.
All was quietude, stillness.

On some nights the stillness was broken by the sound of singing, drumbeats, trumping (stamping) that floated on the air with clarity until three a.m.
They could be city mission people, or 'wrap head' people *(people at a poco-mania* revival meeting)*.
People had freedom of expression.

On this hill, a stony dry place called May Day, in Manchester, my father built his home and shop and, afterwards, a bakery. This was after he had served many years as an apprentice with very limited knowledge of writing English. Like many others, he matured and gained experience.

Sunday afternoon was time for relaxation in the town of Mandeville. Father listened to the BBC news on radio and he read Chinese newspapers. Then it was time to go to the movies to see American musicals or whatever.

At May Day I spent many hours in the shop, moving about from here to there fetching items, cutting hard barsoap*, measuring this or that oil, weighing, wrapping, dipping into kegs, barrels, boxes; serving in the shop can be tiring.
Friday and Saturday nights seemed endless.

When I retired to bed the helper stayed with me, and some of those hours were spent listening to Anansi* stories, guessing at riddles, laughing at the nasal speech of trickster Anansi, looking at shadows formed by fingers in front of a light; rabbit ears, a dog barking, and many others.

The Home-Sweet-Home lamp shade would darken as the wind tossed the flame, but outside there were many peenie wallies giving out their pale greenish light.

Written by Mavis Young and edited by Sonia Gordon Scott. Photograph ©Ray Chen

E. Muriel Chen (née Hue)
FEMALE AND HAKKA

I WAS RAISED in your typical Hakka family. In other words, I grew up in a world where the only time a woman came first was when there was work to be done.

My place of birth and home was a small seaside town in eastern Jamaica. Judging from the ages of my older siblings, I'd guess that my parents settled there from China in the 1920s. My parents had eight of us, but raised seven after the first died in infancy. Three daughters came first and then four sons. I was the last daughter. I think I understood from way back then that the difference between boys and girls went far beyond the physical.

Our parents couldn't conceal it. They were just following tradition. As a little girl, I remember my

Above: Family portrait - Enid Chen along with parents and five of her siblings.

mother always insisting how she would return to China for a visit as soon as she had a son or sons to show the old people. Well she never made it back. Her boys came too long after when she could no longer afford the money to travel. And she could never have gone sooner with *only* daughters. They would have frowned upon her for certain.

As for my order of birth and gender, it meant being the one to stay at home to help with the house and shop, while my two older sisters went to Chinese Public School in Kingston. So the only real highlight of my childhood came at age seven, when for the first time I knew what it was like to sit in a classroom in our neighbourhood elementary school, or any school for that matter. I would end up in commercial college for one year in Kingston later on, but I had always dreamed of going on to some form of higher education. While that sounds so basic now, the most our parents ever hoped for us girls was that we married young, be good wives, good mothers and business partners to our husbands. In other words, follow tradition. An education was not something many Hakka parents wasted on their daughters back then.

My parents were of the old school. That meant you were to show humility, appreciation, respect, manners, be quiet and learn to make change as soon as you could count. It also meant that my Hakka mother was a great mother, a good wife and, above all things, a hard worker. I could almost always find her either behind the counter or in the kitchen. Mama did just about everything.

She was an excellent cook, made her own *ham-choy*, planted her own *foo-gah*, and reared her own chickens and ducks. While she mostly cooked Chinese, she also made the famous salt-fish fritters, and would fry up a big batch every morning to help sell the bread.

As for papa, he seldom even cooked. The only time he did was when mama had just had a new baby. Then he would make her a special chicken soup with wine and ginger. Just for her. That was the only time I'd ever see her lying down. Or not working. She just never stopped moving, and she had all of us at home with the help of a midwife. For her last baby, she sent me to find the midwife. I always marvelled at how she always seemed to know just when to call for them. So apart from the times when she was having a baby, I don't ever recall her complaining of feeling sick. Actually, I don't even recall her complaining. There was never really any time for that.

In addition to running the shop, mama was also in charge of raising the seven of us. And she was quite the disciplinarian. I remember once going next door to visit my godmother, and taking one of my brothers along. Well like a stroke of bad luck, he fell on his face, which caused his nose to start bleeding. I immediately rushed him back home. When mama saw the blood, she hit the roof and gave me a good *switching*. *'Who tell you to go anywhere!'* she yelled in sharp Hakka. On another occasion, I can't remember what I had done, but all I know is that she began shouting out my name in the house. Well I thought I was going to get another switching, so I hid under the bed. Mama tore the place apart until she finally found me, and then tried to sweep me out with a broom. But I guess by then she felt sorry for me and just left it at that. So I can say I got away at least once!

Needless to say, life in a sleepy seaside town in 1930s rural Jamaica was *slow.* Moonlight walks with my godmother, while beautiful, counted as a big pastime. So did trying to catch *janga** in the river while our helper did the washing. The fireworks show at the occasional Chinese wedding was also big on our list of things to do. And every now and again we cranked up the old gramophone to listen to one of maybe five English records we had by lamp light. But once a year, our uneventful existence in the quiet countryside would be spiced up with a trip to the big city. That's when mama would take a break from the shop, leave papa to run things, and pack us all up for the bumpy bus ride to Kingston. There we'd spend one glorious week with my father's relatives somewhere uptown, and visit with other family and friends in Chinatown. That was our chance to inhale all the sights, sounds, smells and experiences that Barry Street offered to us country cousins. Like my first tram ride.

But that wasn't the only time I got glimpses of what I was missing by being tucked away in the country. Whenever my sisters returned home from school, I'd see how much sharper they looked – so glamorous with their new dresses, new shoes, even lipstick. I remember the first time they came home with this red colour on their fingernails. *'What's that!?'* I blurted out. To which they replied, *'Oh, that's Cutex'*. But that's how it was for me as the youngest girl. I didn't wait for the new dresses or shoes. I waited for the hand-me-downs. But, like my mother, I never really complained. It made no sense to.

I think the only time I really put my foot down and broke with tradition was when my parents tried to set me up in an arranged marriage. They tried a few times, the first being when I was 16. I remember their last attempt fairly well. Mama and I were visiting with family in Kingston. I was at one house, she was at another. Well I was in the house, when one of my friends told me that there was someone here to see me. The 'someone' turned out to be the fellow mama wanted me to marry. He was there at the door with instructions from mama that I was to follow him to the house where she was waiting. Then he towed me on his bicycle, and took me to the house where *both* our mothers were waiting. Afterwards I just told my parents that I couldn't marry that way. I'd eventually meet my husband 'the normal way'.

All that is in the past now, and much has changed since the days when girl babies were nothing to write home about. I thank the Jamaican Hakka women who came before us – the burdens they bore and the sacrifices they made are an inspiration to me. As for their daughters and granddaughters of today, they took that foundation, applied the energy of the Hakka woman, and achieved so much. And I couldn't be more proud of them. Mama used to tell us girls all the time never to envy others and to be satisfied with our lot.

I can honestly say that I am satisfied with our lot today.

Written by E. Muriel Chen and edited by Alex Lee.

* *See Glossary*

Down Memory Lane

Town of Port Maria,
St. Mary

Photograph ©Ray Chen

Sister Josette M. Lee Sang O.S.F.
MEMORIES OF MY GROWING UP YEARS
IN JAMAICA

MY PARENTS WERE shopkeepers, hard-working and very caring that we all received good food, clothing, shelter, and an education – more than they ever had.

Holy Trinity
Cathedral
in Kingston

From as far back as the early 1940s, Sister Lucy, O.S.F., a Franciscan Sister, and Father Raymond Fox, S.J., a Jesuit Priest, took a special interest in the Chinese Community, teaching them the doctrines of the Catholic Faith, and they were able to convert many, both children and adults, to the Church.

During the 1950s and '60s the three outstanding Catholic high schools, namely, Immaculate Conception High School, St. George's College, and Alpha Academy, had a high enrolment of Chinese students. Catholic education was very greatly treasured by Chinese parents because of the high academic standards, good discipline, and religious and moral values inculcated. As a consequence, many Catholic Chinese graduates were inspired to embrace the religious life and the priesthood, chiefly the Franciscan Sisters of Allegany, the Sisters of Mercy, and the Society of Jesus known as the Jesuits. I attended Catholic elementary and high schools and was so influenced and inspired by the Sisters and Priests with whom I came in contact that, on my own accord, I asked to become a Catholic and later to enter religious life as a Franciscan Sister.

Immediately after coming home from school, we would change our clothes to go and work behind the counter in the shop. I remember standing up there to do my homework in between times after hearing: "Serve ya, Mr. Chin!" After shop closed, there were the preparations for the next day's sales: wrapping up and stacking piles of flour, sugar, rice, corn meal, salt, black pepper in paper funnels, cutting up the brown soap, pumping up the kerosene oil from the big drum into smaller containers, brushing down the counter, sweeping up the floor, counting the sales for the day and recording in the book.

The family all ate dinner together, usually after shop closed in the evening and especially on Sundays. Our parents slept on one double bed, the boys slept on another big bed until they grew up, or some had cots, and, since I was the only girl, I had a single bed to sleep in. We shared the few toys, games, comics we had and anything special our father brought home from Barry Street, such as chun pee muy*, gow jew*, sow bow*, watermelon. I remember also, instances of our parents' initiative, thriftiness, making do with what they had. My mother used to pull out the threads from flour bags and wash and bleach the cloth in the sun on zinc sheets until they were white like linen. She would stay up before the sewing machine many a night to make for the family bed sheets, pillowcases, tablecloths, and hand towels as well as under-shirts, underwear, and pajamas. We also used to wear board slippers at home. Clothes, shoes, books were passed on from the older to the younger children as we were growing up.

Chinese New Year was a special event in our home. My father would cook all the special Chinese dinners: pak jam gai*, chicken soup with gin choy*, loy sue*, go pee*, as well as chop suey, chow mein*, chow choy*, pork and yam, ham choy* and jiu nyuk*, Chinese roast pork, duck, fish – you name it! We had it all, as poor as we were, even if not all on the same occasion. We also had lots of sweet oranges, watermelon, lychee, longan, gaw tsiu* and Chinese tea always piping hot. Chinese incense was burnt to remember our loved ones who had passed away. I used to wear a simple chung sam, saw fire-crackers bursting, and I entered into all of this celebration with excitement and fun. This was also one day when we were allowed to stay away from school and the teachers understood.

Our parents took us to the Chinese Temple on Barry Street on certain occasions and we were always amazed, and even afraid of the big fat Buddha statue, and intrigued by the incense and various rituals.

The Chinese Catholic Action Association came into existence, and was very vibrant and active during the 1950s, through the enthusiasm, guidance and dedication of Fr. Tom Glavin, S.J. Many of the graduates of the Catholic high schools joined the Association and became actively involved, even from sixth form. One memorable activity was our annual visit to the various hospitals in the corporate area on Christmas Eve, the young men and ladies wearing red cummerbunds over white shirts or blouses, going around singing Christmas Carols to the patients, bringing cheer to their hearts. We would then make our way to Holy Trinity Cathedral for midnight mass, after which we meandered down to Grand Market at King Street and South Parade in downtown Kingston, buying Christmas Hats and blowing fee-fees* and horns, and having a great time before getting home exhausted and exhilarated on Christmas morning.

Unfortunately the Association dwindled and eventually became defunct due to the vast migrations from Jamaica during the 1970s. Nevertheless, many of the past members still keep in touch and are actively involved in their parish churches in Toronto, Miami and elsewhere. Those who did not enter religious life or the priesthood are yet very devoted Catholic parents and grandparents today, passing on their faith and relationship with God to the next generation.

We went to Chee Gung Tong for the wedding reception of our oldest brother in the mid-1950s, as well as the wedding receptions of several other relatives and friends. I always thought it was a beautiful place, especially when decorated for special occasions.

Our parents took us to the Chinese Cemetery for Gah San* every year, as it was an event which seemed to always draw the Chinese community together, to remember and to show respect and honour for relatives and friends who had passed away.

It was at the Chinese Garden Parties on North Street that we saw and heard Chinese musicians and opera singers. Our family went to these faithfully as our parents liked the social event of meeting with relatives and friends, so they could 'gong tong wah'* with each other, exchanging their daily life experiences and advising, encouraging and amusing one another. I was always astonished and amused at the strange cadence and sounds of the Chinese music and opera singing, especially as I did not understand the language. We always had a lot of fun at the garden parties watching the dragon and lion dances, playing all the various games such as hoopla, pin the tail on the donkey, raffles and rides, and gorging ourselves with Chinese and other goodies such as gow jew,* chow bow,* snow cone, ice cream, popcorn, and sugar candy floss. There were also stage shows – children dancing and prancing, singing, acrobatic displays, plays and recitals. It is too bad that as the community became fearful of going down to North Street, due to the increasing crime and violence of the past few decades, that these entertaining activities phased out of existence. It is good that things are being revived as we have our new Chinese Benevolent Association Centre at Old Hope Road in Upper St. Andrew where, so far, it seems a safer locale.

Our parents used to take us to Barry and Princess Streets by buggy, especially on Sundays when they would go to order goods for the coming week. These weekly visits were also social events for the Chinese community. Goods would be brought to our shop during the week on dray carts drawn by mules.

We had lots of house parties and 'weenie roast' parties with camp fires on the beach – 'basket parties' during our teen years when everybody would prepare and bring food and drinks to be shared. We did not have loud sound systems, but record players with 78 and $33\frac{1}{3}$ rpm LPs, soothing us with such favourites as Pat Boone, Perry Como, Eddie Fisher, Nat King Cole, Elvis Presley, and Rock 'n Roll. Around the campfires on the beach we had lots of fun chatting, telling stories, laughing, singing, clowning around, roasting weenies, rolls and cashews till the wee hours of the night, not being afraid of going home on the roads which were quite safe then in the 1950s.

Swimming at Jung San* beach, Sunday movies at Carib, Regal, Palace, Odeon, and Ward theatres, Airport drive-in restaurant ('Liner Diner'), were all much enjoyed with family and friends.

As we did not have our own private motor car then, we travelled all around Kingston by horse and buggy, tram cars, later on the 'chi-chi bus' and, of course, on foot.

Powell's Bakery used to supply our shop, and their products always smelled fresh and enticing as did the bread, buns and bullas supplied by Hannah Town and other bakeries.

There is much else we could record as we reminisce on the past history of our ancestors from one hundred and fifty years ago, and especially our own parents, recognizing their courage, initiative, steadfastness, determination, honesty, hard-working natures, readiness to make sacrifices in the face of the difficulties of settling and making a living, in a foreign land whose language, customs, race of people were so strange from what they knew in China – the vast country they left behind and its history over the millennia of a different culture and civilization. I still remember my father starting business all over again, with determination, after the disastrous hurricane of 1951, Hurricane Charlie, when most of the goods in his shop were lost to the flood waters.

From tolerating such derogatory taunts as "Chiney nyam dawg!", and being considered second-class citizens in their little grocery shops, the Chinese community has played its part over this century and a half in every sphere of activity and production, for the building up, growth and development of the nation of Jamaica – their island home.

Written by Sister Josette M. Lee Sang, O.S.F. and edited by Sonia Gordon Scott.

* See Glossary

Photograph ©Ray Chen

Down Memory Lane

Kingston Parish Church in Kingston

Photograph ©Ray Chen

Carol Wong
AMONG THE CANE FIELDS OF WESTMORELAND

MANY JAMAICANS have often wondered why the Williams clan (Chinese name 'Ngui') in the parish of Westmoreland is so closely knit. We were even criticized for being 'cliquish', but I believe circumstances, destiny, and culture played a part in shaping this cohesiveness and interdependence. In addition, our elders from our Hakka village, Nu Foo in the Guangdong province of China, practised for generations the beliefs of Confucianism: "Respect elders, take care of the young, and help each other."

Our elders settled in Westmoreland, Jamaica, because our uncle, Jackson Williams, invited his many nephews to join him in his business. As a young man, my father Nathan Williams (Ngui, Back Tseung) and his cousins, arrived in the 1930s to work in their uncle's general store in Petersfield, Westmoreland.

They had never seen Negro people or heard their language before, but pretty soon they learnt their patois dialect, which is a language of broken English mixed with Spanish and Creole. They learnt to do business with them, and tricks of the trade as well.

The cousins also learnt to get along with the local people, although my father related that they were constantly teased and made fun of. This made him so angry that, on many occasions, he wanted to jump over the shop counter, chase them with the 'salt-fish machete' and chop them up! As my father matured, he controlled his temper with the young hoodlums as he grew to realize that the majority of the local people were warm-hearted, friendly, accepting of the Chinese, and would, over time, become his valued customers.

The cousins eventually branched out into their own businesses in the neighbouring districts within close proximity to Petersfield. On Sundays, when the shops were closed, the Williams families would come together in Petersfield for the men to discuss business, the women to gossip or share experiences, and the children to play together. You could say these were their 'support group' meetings, where they could socialize, using their own Chinese language, eat familiar Chinese cuisine, and keep the culture and their families together in this strange land.

My father, with the assistance of a mild-mannered and trustworthy young local man named Ronald, opened his business in Williamsfield District, a few miles from Petersfield. He sold essential goods and basic food items like unbleached flour, unrefined sugar, corn meal, cooking oil, kerosene oil, soap and matches, etc. It was no simple task for my father to cope with the English words for these items, plus dealing in British sterling pounds, shillings and pence.

Williamsfield was mainly surrounded by farms and cane fields. The labourers, mostly Negroes, bought breakfast and lunch items at the crack of dawn, en route to work, usually with a machete under their arm and a crocus bag over their shoulder. On their way home they purchased dinner ingredients, and after supper, some returned to loiter and socialize in the village square. The local people of East Indian descent did the same, but they worked in rice paddy-fields. I remember playing in the mounds of un-husked rice in the rice room, where my father stored their harvested rice for trading. After many tries to climb to the top of the pile, the adults chased my brother and myself out, because they had to scrape the rice grains back into the corner of the room.

Our single level shop with adjoining dwelling was made of wood, as were all the other buildings in the district. The roads were unpaved, and there was no electricity or running water. The modes of transport were on foot, riding a donkey, or using horse drawn buggies. The latter was our choice for travelling to Petersfield on Sundays.

After my father married my mother, Gladys Louise Young, a first generation Chinese from Trout Hall, Clarendon, who spoke English fluently, our shop's piazza became the 'village square' where everyone congregated. As a result, business was brisk, and my parents became totally integrated into the Jamaican way of life.

Another important building close by was the Glenislay Post Office. When my brothers, Keith and Patrick, and I were born, the postmistress, a spinster named Miss Dawes, registered our births and helped my parents choose our English first names. She also taught my father English and became a close friend of the family.

Above: Carol's father - Nathan Williams with wife Gladys and one of her brothers.

The family was also friendly with local farmers and landowners of British ancestry. An elderly English lady, whom we called 'Grannie Becky', taught us English etiquette and exposed us to the fine arts. She owned many paintings, bone china, silver and glassware. She treasured her 'His Master's Voice' gramophone plus many 78 rpm vinyl records. Grannie Becky was widowed and lived in a great house on a hill. Her property was vast, with a river running through it, and we children have many happy memories of running freely all over, and visiting the livestock in their pens or in the cow pasture. Grannie Becky had planted every kind of fruit tree indigenous to the tropics.

Sometimes on Sundays, there were picnics on Grannie Becky's property. While we ate, we watched cricket matches played on the permanent cricket pitch on the levelled area below the house. The children played around the house, and vied for a chance to wind up the gramophone to play music throughout the day. Different people of all races and status came together to enjoy this outing, each other's company and having a wonderful, fun time.

In the 1940s, our family moved to Savanna-la-mar, a port town on the south coast, where ships sailed into dock to be loaded with crocus bags of unrefined cane sugar from the West Indies Sugar Company (WISCo), at the Frome Sugar Estate a few miles away.

The main street, Great George's Street, was then the widest street in Jamaica. It went through the town, ending up at the seashore where the wharf was situated. A narrow, unpaved road led to an old English fort with a lighthouse, where we loved to walk around and explore.

Along the sea coast was a long wall to protect a local market where fish, produce and meat were brought in by local and neighbouring farmers. The market women were themselves interesting and colourful characters. I can remember walking carefully, to maintain my balance all along the sea-wall, watching the waves lash against the double walls. Joyful fishermen brought in their catch in dug-out canoes laden with a variety of seafood. From the same vantage point, it was also interesting to watch the sugar transport trucks travelling to and from the wharf, plus the constant activity of strong, able-bodied men loading sugar onto the ship.

Our stone and concrete two-storey store/building was on the main street, close to the Town Hall, Court House, Police Station and Jailhouse. Opposite were the Imperial movie theatre, a drugstore, and the Anglican Parish Church with a cemetery. Our store added dry goods to the usual stock of general provisions. It was now necessary to hire more local maids, a yard boy, and help in the store. Single Chinese men were also hired to work in the store and provide Chinese meals for the family.

Our immediate neighbours were East Indian and owned a rum bar, which was noisy, especially at nights. We frequently shared their Indian meals, to the dismay of our parents, whenever we went next door to play with their children. It was fun playing among the beds of their vegetable garden, and picking the caterpillars off the callaloo plants. All the neighbourhood children, regardless of race or creed, played together as we walked to Miss Chapman's Basic School.

During the week, the Chinese adults from nearby districts coming into Savanna-la-mar on business came to our home above the store to play mah-jong after closing hours. On Sundays, the Williams families continued the tradition of meeting together. By now, the ladies would give each other home hair permanents and share culinary skills. We as cousins were old enough to go off to the movie theatre together, after the evening meal, while the men played mah-jong.

Similar to the racial harmony in Williamsfield, in Savanna-la-mar people of all races and status came together at church functions, garden parties at Manning's High School grounds, a variety of events on the library premises, and major dance events at the Town Hall. The latter was the first venue where

Byron Lee and the Dragonaires band made their debut in the west end of the island; as well, in later years, it was at the Town Hall that my girlfriends and I made our debuts as amateur models for a community tea party.

Some of the prominent members of the community who were friendly with our family were Drs. Harvey and Carnegie, lawyers Hamaty and McPherson, land surveyor Forrest, Anglican minister Rev. McMillan, Catholic priest Father Knight, Baptist minister Rev. Whylie, the managers of Barclays Bank and the Bank of Nova Scotia, etc. My father's favourite drinking buddies were the Wharfinger, Mr. Nash, and the Honourable Judge Gayle. All these personalities were of mixed races and ancestry like British, Jewish, Syrian, American, Negro and Indian.

There were also our fellow Chinese business families like the Chongs, Lyns, Chin-Fooks, Lees, Chins, Lowes, Lims, Moo-Youngs etc. Many Chinese married local folks as in those days it was difficult to send for mates overseas. My uncle married an Indian woman and had many children. 'Auntie' proved to be an excellent businesswoman and managed the entire household. She always welcomed us warmly and, as kids, we relished the change of food at her house. As teenagers, we looked forward to the dance parties held at their house when we would rock 'n roll and smooch with our cousins and friends.

When my father's Uncle Jackson decided to move to Savanna-la-mar as well, his wife Amy convinced him to hand over the original business in Petersfield to my father, who was her favourite nephew. So my father made a full circle, returning to take over the business where he first started on his arrival in Jamaica from China.

This move proved to be a great decision for the family. The business thrived, being surrounded by cane fields and the nearby WISCo Weigh Station in the Shrewsbury district. Another factor was that Petersfield is situated on the main thoroughfare from Savanna-la-mar on the southern coast, to Montego Bay in the parish of St. James, another port on the north coast of the island. All modes of transportation, including the "Morning Star" buses, plied daily through the town and past our store, which, for a very long time remained the only business place, and the piazza of our store became the designated bus stop. In the centre of the crossroads was a prominent wooden finger sign post. Many drivers did not manoeuvre safely around this, which created much excitement and amusement in those days.

In addition, I believe that we children were fortunate to have moved from Savanna-la-mar, which was fast becoming too developed as the town capital of the parish of Westmoreland. It was wonderful growing up in this new and lovely environment, and being able to walk freely among caring country folk who would not hesitate to scold us if necessary, and even apply a poultice to our wounds.

Petersfield district was a beautiful, lush, fertile and bountiful area, surrounded by acres and acres of sugar cane fields. A variety of trees native to the island were dotted all over the landscape. Fruit trees were found in virtually every yard. There were rivers and streams winding their way all over the various properties. Water tubers, like baddoe* and lily plants, lined the bank-sides. Watercress grew wild among fish and crayfish. Tropical flora and fauna thrived unattended.

Below, the Roaring river in Westmoreland.

The underground spring at the head of the Roaring River is now a tourist site, but in my day it was a tranquil place of refuge for everyone to enjoy. I first discovered this peaceful place on a school outing organized by the teachers of the Petersfield Elementary School; lunch was sweet bun with slices of cheese and an enamel mug of 'wash'* (a beverage of water with lime juice, sweetened with unrefined brown sugar).

After the river roared down below and under a bridge, the water was calm enough for women to wash clothes, children to swim, cattle to be watered, cars to be washed and water to be collected for household use, before it wound its way through the verdant cane fields.

As teenagers, we would tie a long rope from our vehicle parked on the bridge to be suspended into the river. Then, we would climb further up the river bank to jump fearlessly into the torrents and, as we swam down, we would grab on to the overhanging rope to ensure our stopping further on as we gleefully floated down river – oh, what fun! Dangerous fun!

At calmer areas of the river, alongside rows of cane fields, we floated on inflated rubber tyre tubes among the huge baddoe leaves growing on both sides of the channel… such calm and tranquility. The water was clear and pure – it sparkled and glistened on the baddoe leaves we used to collect water for drinking… sheer joy and peace.

This peace and tranquility only lasted during the planting and growing cane season. The quiet countryside was shattered come cane harvest time, when there were flurries of activity all around. Then, there would be cane-reapers chopping feverishly, loading the tractor-driven carts which plied up and down the unpaved road, leaving clouds of blowing dust on the way to Shrewsbury Weigh Station (much to the chagrin of pedestrians, who scurried to the safety of the road-banks with hands covering their noses and mouths). Women bringing food and water to their men-folk would share this dusty fate as well.

After the cane was weighed, huge trucks took it to the Frome Estate sugar factory. As they passed through the district and passed our store, the workers would throw off a few stalks for eating. Young boys delighted in hauling out stalks as slower tractors drove by, or stopped for gasoline at our Texaco Gas Station. Some of the Williams families became cane-farmers, owning acres of their own cane fields and hiring local workers. It was tempting to clamber aboard and take a practice drive on their tractors.

To yield a higher sugar content and get rid of insects, rodents and reptiles infesting the rows of mature cane with long green leaves waving in the breeze, cane fires were deliberately lit in the vast fields, away from the residential area. We watched the inferno in safety from Galloway Lane, as the workers kept vigil to ensure the roaring flames were contained when the winds changed direction.

I have vivid memories of the night sky being lit up with a beautiful scarlet and orange glow. The illumination and the crackling sound of the burning leaves were somewhat eerie, but fascinating to watch and hear. The sickly sweet smell of the burnt cane lingered for days. When the fire burned itself out, one could see the devastation of blackened cane still standing majestically in the aftermath. The cane-cutters emerged likewise blackened after the day's work of cutting, but they were undaunted because the incentive was pay day.

Fashion back in the day.

Over the years my parents expanded their business to include general merchandise, hardware supplies, dry goods, ready-made goods, wholesale and retail grocery provisions, and a 'rum' bar. They also had a gas service station which carried vehicle parts and accessories; plus, a movie theatre, aptly named 'Venus' by my youngest brother, Donny.

On pay day, families came out buying new clothes, shoes, hats and home improvement items. The food and 'rum' bar, with a single Wurlitzer juke-box was the busiest. People milled around in the streets talking and laughing – there was much happiness and jollification all around! Our movie theatre, Venus, was jam-packed and we were sure to show action-packed, 16mm films which were rented from the Palace Amusement Company in Kingston. Every week, reels were shipped via rail to Montpelier train station and, if we could not pick them up, the Royal Mail van brought them. (This was the same route and mode of transportation taken when my siblings and I grew old enough to attend high school in the city of Kingston.)

Venus Theatre was a source of entertainment, not only for the patrons, but also for us as we were highly amused by the reactions of the local people. Some of them got so aroused during the movie that they would jump up, shout at the screen and, sometimes in their excitement, even thump the person next to them as they imitated the actions of the hero, or 'star boy', of the movie.

The Saturday night dances held at the market next door were entertaining as well, and as grown-ups we now realize that it was during this era that my siblings and I developed our love of Jamaican music. The sound of music was welcome, as strains wafted across the district until the wee hours, while we lay in bed, exhausted after helping out in the business, and listened to the latest released records from the U.S.A.

Calypso and Mento music are my favourite and, for me, more than the British maypole dancing event, the 3-5 piece band playing was the highlight of the frequent garden parties held at Petersfield's Elementary School yard. Usually, the band consisted of a guitar, a banjo, a saxophone and a 'rhumba box'. People not attending the fair danced in the street or anywhere they stood... such delightful freedom of expression and movement!

The celebration during the rice harvest was on a smaller scale and the East Indians were less boisterous. The interesting sounds were the rice threshing parties where liquor flowed freely to keep the spirits up, and the workers refuelled as they threshed to songs mixed with grunts. The unhusked rice grains were then left out in the sun for days to dry before being bagged for sale.

Other pay days, which certainly increased our business, were those of the Westmoreland Parish Council's and Parochial Board's fortnightly pay days. Less able-bodied men, and mostly women, would break stones into smaller pieces, which were piled up by the side of the road where they sat and chatted. The Public Works trucks would come by to collect, measure and record the 'guesstimated' (or approximate) square footage. The civil servants and staff of the Public Health Clinic beside the theatre, and the Public Works & Communication Department in front of the rum bar, were our reliable customers who paid their bills and any account credited to them by my benevolent parents.

As I grew older, one of my tasks was to chase down the elusive and errant creditors, and to send out 'dunning letters', which were totally ignored, as were the threats of lawsuits. Our business ended up with a constant stream of numerous bad debts, especially those of fathers with too many children by various mothers... but my parents could not bring themselves to be hardhearted when they came around again begging for credit "until pay day". The East Indian families were better at money management and usually kept their word to pay off their account before opening another line of credit.

Despite the bad debtors, Petersfield was a district of warm, friendly, caring, good and lovely people of a mixture of many different races. Living and doing business in Petersfield gave us the great opportunity of interacting with all the other residents, and a wide spectrum of fellow Jamaicans. There were English landowners and cattle-ranchers like the Custos of Westmoreland, the Hon. Eric Clarke, lawyer Tomlinson, the Smith and Jones families, etc. They would patronize our store and we would visit their homes. As children, we were in awe of the furnishings in their houses, plus the landscaped gardens and grounds, especially the magnificent royal palm trees lining the long curved driveway, and the huge spreading banyan trees.

There were Jamaican 'whites', obviously of British ancestry, like the bank managers, tax collectors etc. A lovely lady comes to mind; she was short, chubby and wore rimless spectacles to suit her nice motherly face. Nurse Campbell was the local midwife and she could be seen riding her bicycle all over the neighbouring districts. She had delivered so many babies, including my younger siblings, Dick (Richard), Elaine and Donny (Donald) that her left arm developed a permanent cradling position.

The East Indians, including the Burgess, Atkinson and Jaggan families, were hard-working, either in the rice paddy-fields or in the tailoring trade. They, like the Chinese, tried to keep their Asian culture. They had good-looking and educated children. Their beautiful daughters were an attraction for the young men in the area, especially the Chinese boys with raging hormones.

The majority of the locals were of the Negro race and my family integrated with all the different personalities and levels of status. My mother usually hired 2 or 3 maids to take care of the house, laundry, cooking and us children. They worked tirelessly for bare minimum wage, and often returned after dinner with their families to do extra chores of their own free will, or just to hang about. They loved us and we loved them. From them we learned a lot of local culture, customs and folklore, including 'Brer Anancy' and 'duppy' (ghost) stories. They delighted us with folk songs, and dancing with hand-clapping. When we were babies, it was so natural for them to constantly rock and sing us to sleep.

I will not forget the devotion of Louise who used to massage my mother's legs, which were often inflamed with varicose veins; in later years Cissy, who nursed my stepmother, whom we called Ah Neung, during her final days dying of lymphatic cancer; also 'Miss B' for her care of my twice-widowed father. I will always remember her traditional beef soup on Saturdays at lunchtime, and her persistent calls for us to take time out from the customers in the store to have her soup. There were so many others over the years of growing up, but their names do not readily come to mind – I only remember their loving care and their children as our playmates, who became our 'partners in crime' as we roamed the neighbourhood, lighting fire crackers and throwing them in yards to scare the dogs and annoy the late sleepers.

Our male servants were the yard-boy, the hired hand in the store, the gas station attendants and anyone wanting to do odd jobs. All the servants, male and female, worked well together helping each other and sharing odd jobs like sitting around and chatting in a circle while cleaning all our shoes en masse.

When cooking their typical Jamaican fare, it was a joint affair peeling yams and other ground provisions, making humongous plain flour and cornmeal dumplings, roasting breadfruits and cooking salted codfish with fresh ackees, or pickled mackerel with callaloo (spinach). They liked to eat tinned corned beef ('bully beef', coined from the picture of the cow on the red label of each can imported from Argentina), and tinned herring and sardines from the Maritimes, Canada.

We children loved to share their food, eating and drinking out of their humble enamel plates and mugs. The food tasted exceptionally nice, and it felt good to be sitting and listening in on their conversation in the patois dialect. It is during these times that I picked up most of the Jamaican idioms, amusing sayings and numerous off-colour jokes.

It was so much fun sitting anywhere near their outdoor fire, with cooking utensils fashioned out of empty coconut oil tins and cheese pans from the store. They were so innovative, making do with whatever they had at the moment, very relaxed, jovial and leisurely, taking everything in stride. They would never hurt us and were quite protective – they all cared about us and became a part of our family.

Other locals who were an influence on me growing up were the post-mistress, Miss Icy, and her staff, the Misses Richards and Gascoigne, working at the Petersfield Post Office adjacent to our store. They allowed me to learn the routine of stamping letters and parcels, sending off telegrams, attending to mail collectors, plus assisting with mailbags in readiness for the arrival of the Royal Mail van. In slow periods, they taught me the crafts of crocheting, tatting and embroidery. They were happy to make many items for my 'hope chest' when I got engaged and was leaving to get married in Montreal, Canada.

Across the street opposite our store was the Anglican Church where I received much of my early religious training. Reverend Haughton, organist Miss Gunning and the church wardens made sure to come to the store to inform my mother about weekly programmes at the church. I have indelible memories of making Easter baskets decorated with colourful tissue paper and filled with food and fruits for the poor. Christmas plays and other Christian pageants were as enjoyable as the sweets we would take along, plus the bun and cheese eaten secretly during the lengthy 3-hour Good Friday services.

Most fun was swinging on the rope to assist the ringing of the church bell, putting up numbers on the board for the hymn guide during service and, of course, playing and scaring each other in the cemetery surrounding the church. Flat tombs were ideal for playing games of jacks, and the tall tomb-stones made perfect hiding places.

The many dedicated teachers, Dunn, Brown, Pennycook, Thompson, etc., made a great impression on me. They earned the respect of the community, and no parent questioned how their method of discipline was applied. If punished, students would not dare complain to or inform their parents for fear of additional spanking. Sometimes, we would mischievously hide the teachers' leather straps.

Within the Petersfield community, many colourful and influential characters evolved and found a place in our village life. There were the higglers who, very early, laid claim to spaces on our store's piazza. Miss Georgie, a mulatto woman, sold homemade cakes of all descriptions. Miss Brownie educated all her children to college level by selling coconut drops, grater cakes and shaved ice with homemade syrup; Miss Wilhel sold salt-fish fritters and 'archie bombo'* (a type of fried dumpling), which were kept warm in a rectangular tin, fashioned with a drawer of live fire coals. Her food-warmer was created by Man Hawk, the village tinsmith. Miss James offered fruit and vegetables for sale; an elderly and miserable woman called 'Ole Fowl' sold ground provisions; Creamo was the ice-cream man who made his product from scratch, and parked his bicycle at his usual spot every day.

The self-appointed ombudsman was Benjie, who settled numerous arguments, and stopped clothes-ripping cat-fights and fist-fights in the town square. With other men, Benjie was also instrumental in chasing, stoning, and capturing robbers who tried to break into our store. He made a citizen's arrest after giving them a thrashing and tongue-lashing. Our parents were loved and respected so it was only natural that the 'chiney shop' would be protected.

Jiggs was the village clown and mischief-maker. The village drunks were 'Scarce-a-leg' Phillips and 'Lachmin', an old Indian woman adorned with silver necklaces and bangles. Somehow they were never left in danger, and at night, someone would see them safely home to their families.

For a long while, Jackie Muschette owned the only vehicle in Petersfield, so he became the person everyone turned to in an emergency when anyone needed to be rushed to Savanna-la-mar hospital. A Mr. Bardowell felt the need to blare music in the entire cross-roads area, which created a happy mood for everyone, including the donkeys tied up near his place beside the Post Office. The braying of the donkeys and their toilet ablutions did not seem to affect 'Missa Bardi'.

Everyone tolerated and cared for each other. We – and especially my mother – helped in many different ways. During the mass exodus of immigrants to England and farm workers to the U.S.A., she took care of the applications for birth certificates and passports, then completed all necessary documents and made flight arrangements for their departure. Following up, we would write letters for the families left behind, read the letters in response and exchange the enclosed money orders. As well, my mother was involved with the Federation of Women rendering assistance to women and girls of the parish of Westmoreland. One of her projects was the local orphanage which was located nearby in Water Works district, above the Dean's Valley Ice Factory.

My father was very hospitable to the travelling salesmen, many of whom welcomed a home-cooked meal and some company during their islandwide business trips. When our fruit trees, especially our famous jew plum tree, was laden, almost all of them returned to Kingston with bags full of plums or whatever fruit was in season.

Below: Carol with siblings. L-R Elaine, Carol, Donald, Patrick and Dick.

On Sundays when the store was closed, we would hurriedly clean and prepare it in readiness for Monday's opening. Then the Williams families, relatives and friends, would head for the beach either at Bluefields or Negril. The most enjoyable and memorable times were the frequent picnics and cricket matches played on the beach. Later on, some of us liked to go water-skiing, spear-fishing, snorkeling and scuba-diving in the warm, clear water under blue skies… Ah, it was the life of luxury and carefree living during this era!

Our home upstairs and behind the store became something of a community centre after my cousin Ronald, and I, with the help of local labourers, built a badminton court beside the theatre, between the banana and papaya trees. As a result,

Petersfield gradually became the meeting place for the Williams families. We now met with numerous visitors and friends to socialize, playing badminton, table tennis, dominoes and card games. Many celebrations were held, one of which was our infamous crab-feasts.

Under the aforementioned jew plum tree was a large, shallow concrete pit, to house the collection of land crabs caught in various areas around the parish. At night-time, each crab hunt with our cousins and friends was an exciting outing in itself. On arrival at our destination we would disperse, armed with machetes, sticks, torches of all descriptions, and carrying crocus bags. When we got back together, everyone had a story about the exaggerated size of 'the one that got away'! My brother, Dick would feed the crabs rice, bread and mango skins to purge them. He made sure to hose down the collection of crabs kept in the concrete pit frequently, and saw to it that the mesh wire covers were kept in place…you could call him the 'crab-keeper'! Ultimately, there were frequent finger-licking crab-feasts, and visiting badminton teams from Montego Bay were treated to this memorable and well-talked-about hospitality.

Likewise, our store's piazza had become the centre of town. Our family had the vantage point and best views from the verandah overhead. It is here that we, as children, expanded our education in living as part of a community, and experienced the Jamaican way of life. We witnessed many life-shaping incidents, including the problems and celebrations of our village people. The most educational was our exposure to politics and religion.

Before the luxury of electricity, we attended Salvation Army meetings illuminated by Tilley gas lamps. The sound of their brass band was most uplifting, and their impressive uniforms commanded our attention. Kerosene glass lamps and 'kitchen bitches' were used for Pocomania meetings. These were entertaining but somewhat frightening when 'Brothers' and 'Sisters' got the spirit, and started getting into convulsive spasms. Their dress was white gowns with blue bands, and head turbans stuck with lead pencils. Other fundamentalist meetings were equally engaging, with the singing of revival songs we had already learnt from our maids.

When we got electricity our parents were generous and, without bias, freely dropped an electrical extension cord from our verandah for use at all political meetings and local campaigns. We witnessed a wide variety of government leaders speaking at the microphone – from the Most Hon. Alexander Bustamante and the Most Hon. Norman Manley, to the Hon. Michael Manley and the Hon. Edward Seaga.

After listening to the propaganda and promises made by these politicians, it was best to respond like my father did. When questioned, my father without hesitation declared that he was a 'Comrade-Labourite', covering himself as a supporter of both the JLP and PNP political parties.

It was simply delightful to grow up in the parish of Westmoreland and to be exposed to country living and friendly, trustworthy country folks. To share, accept and learn the different cultures of the Negroes, East Indians, British, etc., yet maintain the Chinese customs and traditions of our parents and extended family. I am grateful for this experience as part of my father's fortune, setting out to seek a better life in the New World from his village in southern China during the 1930's.

It is said that it takes a village to raise a child, and I can attest to that statement. My rounded-out education was the result of each and every 'Westmorelite', who influenced and enriched the lives of my family and myself, while growing up among the cane fields of Westmoreland.

Written by Carol Wong (née Williams) and edited by Sonia Gordon Scott.

* See Glossary

Carol being mischievous.

Down Memory Lane

1

2

Scenes of downtown Kingston.

1. Looking north on King and Barry Street.

2. Corner of Church and Harbour Street.

Photographs ©Ray Chen

Down Memory Lane

1

2

3

4

*Scenes of
downtown Kingston*

*1. Looking north on
    Princess Street.*

*2. . Looking north on
    Duke Street.*

3. Dray cart.

*4 Traffic jam on Harbour
    and King Street*

Photographs ©Ray Chen

Stanford Wong
*LIVING IN CHINATOWN, KINGSTON, JAMAICA
IN THE 1940s AND 1950s*

I WAS BORN IN 1940 just north-west of the boundary that marked the beginning of Chinatown in downtown Kingston. Chinatown was considered to be the area within West Street to the west, Beckford Street to the north, Orange Street to the east, and Tower Street to the south. My parents and family moved to Barry Street, west of Matthews Lane in the heart of Chinatown, in 1945, and I lived there 'till 1961. I did business in Chinatown until 1976, and continued to take an interest until 2001 when the premises were sold. I have many recollections of living there as it relates to commerce, social life and life in general.

The Chinese Benevolent Association (CBA) was located on Barry Street, east of Matthews Lane. I remember when my parents took me there as a small boy, I was always scared of the huge statues at the entrance as well as the altar on the upper floor. I remember the many statues and colourful decorations around the altar. Most residents of Chinatown did not own cars so the CBA arranged a bus to take us to and from the cemetery on Waltham Park Road for Gah San,* the blessing of the graves. I remember that was twice a year, I believe in April and October.

The *Chung San Newspaper* was located on the south side of Barry Street at the corner of Matthew's Lane. It provided the Chinese community throughout Jamaica with news in Chinese. The editor was the late Mr. Lee Tom Yin, father of Patrick Lee, who has produced the books entitled *Canadian Jamaican Chinese* and *Jamaican Chinese Worldwide.*

Chinatown was the main centre of commerce in Jamaica. The majority of the Chinese were wholesalers; they also had bakeries, bottling and manufacturing companies, and others.

Wholesalers would buy their provisions from the large importers like Grace Kennedy, Bryden and Evelyn, T. Geddes Grant and others, as well as the Government warehouses. They would sell to the shops all around Jamaica. A common sight was the dray carts drawn by horses, which would pick up merchandise from the wharves and deliver to the various wholesalers. The drays also delivered merchandise from the wholesalers to shopkeepers around the city of Kingston and its outskirts.

During the mid to late 1950s, large distributors/importers of grocery provisions started to sell directly to the retail shopkeepers, bypassing the traditional wholesalers, and eventually putting them out of business. Haberdashery was substituted for grocery provisions in the Chinatown area and, lately, grocery provisions have been included by the haberdasheries.

During the late 1950s and early 1960s, as business prospered, Chinatown lost most if not all its residents to the suburbs as the merchants could now afford cars. Today, Chinatown is strictly commercial.

Some prominent businesses in Chinatown in the '40s & '50s, included:

Wholesalers:

a.   Hen Shim Min Tia at Barry Street and Luke Lane (Sidney Chang).
b.   Yeung En Fah Sang at Princess Street south of Barry Street (the Chins – Lane Supermarket).
c.   Man Chun Tong (the Shims)
d.   Daniel Lee at West Street south of Beckford Street (the Lees). (I am not sure here).
e.   Chin Yee at Princess Street north of Barry Street (the Chin Yees).
f.   Wong Chew Onn at Princess Street south of Beckford Street (Wong Chew Onns).
g.   Central Trading at Princess Street south of Barry Street (the Hugh Sams).
h.   Milton Wong at West Street south of Beckford Street (the Wongs).
i.   Lenn Happ at Orange Street north of Barry Street (the Changs).

Manufacturers:

a.   Caribbean Products at West Street north of Barry Street.
     Edible oils, margarine, butterine (Jamaican made butter), soaps, detergents etc. (the Tie Ten Quees).
b.   Diamond Mineral Water Co., Ltd. at Orange Street south of Beckford Street.
     Diamond bottled drinks, syrup, wines etc. (the Yap Sams).
c.   Crescent Waters at Princess Street north of Barry Street.
     Bottled drinks including 'O So Grape'. (the Chin Yees).
d.   Royal Cremo at Princess Street north of Barry Street.
     dairy milk, ice cream and frozen treats, icicles and fudges (the Chin Loys).

Bakeries:

a.   Valentine Bakery at Princess Street south of Barry Street.
     Baked products, bread, buns etc.(the Changs' Valentine Bakery is now Consolidated Bakery).

The following bakeries were located just beyond the Chinatown area, within walking distance.

b. Diamond Bakery at West and Heywood Streets (the Chins).
c. Lion Bakery at West Street south of Heywood Street (the Phang Lyns).
d. Three Star Bakery at Princess Street south of Heywood Street (the Chins).
e. Foot Sang Bakery at Heywood Street and Princess Street (the Chin Foot Sangs).

Restaurants:

a. Cathay Restaurant at Princess Street south of Beckford Street (the Chens).
b. Wing Shing at Barry Sreet and Luke Lane (the Hoo Fatts).
c. Fook Chong at Princess Street south of Barry Street (several operators).
d. Golden Bowl at Luke Lane south of Barry Street (the Changs).
e. International Restaurant at Barry Street west of Luke Lane (the Chong Fahs).

Hardware:

a. Fong Tom at Orange Street north of Barry Street (the Fong Toms).

Chinese Groceries, medicines and general items:

a. Tack Sing at Barry Street west of Luke Lake (the Chins).
b. Shing Ah at Barry Street west of Luke Lane (Chin Choong Yee).
c. Lee Tung Kee at Barry Street west of Luke Lane (Chin Fo Yin).
d. Nam Keung at Princess Street north of Barry Street (the Chung Fahs).

Gas Station:
a. Esso Service Station at Princess Street south of Barry Street (Norman Yee).

Musical instruments and sheet music:
a. Music Mart at Orange Street north of Barry Street (the Ho Sangs).

Furniture:

    a.   Caribbean Association, at West Street north of Barry Street (the Chins, the Chos and the Yees).

SOCIAL LIFE AND ENTERTAINMENT

Many of the Chinese who migrated to Jamaica in the early 20th century lived in and around Chinatown, and most business owners lived above or behind their place of business. Family life was quite traditional. The husbands tended to the business and the wives looked after the welfare of the children. Husbands played mah jong*, bow gye* and pie quee* and wives played the small Chinese cards, gee pye*.

Most who lived in Chinatown did not own cars; the few wealthy merchants who did lived in the suburbs. The mode of transport was walking, trams, buses ('chi-chi' bus), taxis and buggies. The buggies were horse drawn carriages that seated three passengers and the driver. There was a small kerosene lamp attached to the front of the carriage so you could see the buggies at night. Between the mule-drawn dray carts and the horse-drawn buggies, dung all over the streets was a common sight then. I remember taking a buggy ride from Barry Street to my Uncle, who had a shop at Mannings Hill Road, Constant Spring, a distance of about 5+ miles. The ride seemed to take forever, how long I don't know. Sometimes I would go by tram with my parents. I was always afraid when the tram crossed Sandy Gully Bridge as the rail lines seemed to run in mid air with a long drop to the gully bed. I also remember going to Chinese School on Saturdays, and taking the tram on Sundays to Alvernia School in Cross Roads. The tram would go along Harbour Street, up East Street, then up East Race Course (now Heroes Park) to Cross Roads and I would walk from Cross Roads to the school.

Chinese New Year was the biggest holiday of the year. The family business would close at noon and the feasting would start shortly after. After the feasting, my parents would get down to real business, the gambling. At midnight, all hell would break loose. Large business places would set off ten/twelve foot firecrackers. Smaller places would set off six to eight foot ones. At the end of the firecrackers, the huge thunderbolts would explode. I, among many other children, would chase from explosion to explosion to retrieve the unexploded thunderbolts and firecrackers. Double Ten was the next biggest celebration after Chinese New Year. It was celebrated very similar to the Chinese New Year, just a little less elaborate.

A number of places on the upper floors of businesses were gambling dens. Mostly, the men played among men and the women played among women. I remember a few 'ballsy women' who used to play with the men. Mah Jong and to a lesser extent gee pye were played.

A serious gambling den was located at the corner of Barry Street and Luke

Lane. The high rollers would play, in addition to mah jong, pie quee and bow gye. I have often heard the story of a gambler betting and losing his wife at a game... serious stuff. Gambling also took place at our home, sometimes up to five or six tables. A treat was the so foot* given by the winners. I would wake up early the next morning, after the usual gambling session, to search the drawers of the mah jong tables for the small coins, a three penny or six penny piece stuck in the crevices of the drawers.

I remember the pick-a-peow* and drop pan* shops in Chinatown. One was located at the back of where I lived. This form of gambling was illegal and the police raided the shops often. Pick-a-peow was operated mainly by the Chinese, and the buyers were often the lower class, the labourers, the maids etc.

THE CHINS, CHOS AND YEES

One large operator was directly behind where I lived, with the entrance on Matthews Lane. I used to climb on to the roof of my house and peer down through the large opening in the roof next to my home, of the pick-a-peow den. The openings in the roofs of buildings were used for ventilation. There was a small structure approximately 4' wide x4' long x4' high, built above the opening. A large paddle sat in the centre of this structure, with the flat sides facing north and south to capture the wind during the day or night. This forced the wind down to the living quarters on the ground floor.

I watched many times when the pick-a-peow shop was raided by the police. The first thing the police would encounter would be a strong metal door. When the banging started, the operators would start burning the betting forms and everything pertaining to the 'peow'. When the police broke through the first door, there was a second door facing them. By the time they got in, everything was burned, and most of the main operators would have escaped through the opening in the roof. They would scamper down to where I lived and escape out on to Barry Street.

The residents of Chinatown bought their fresh vegetables, fish etc. from vendors on the sidewalk at Barry Street and Luke Lane. These vendors were mainly Indians who sold pak choy*, quin choy*, woon choy*, mustard, lopet*, bean sprouts and more, along with fresh fish and shrimps, a practice that continues until today. There was an oyster cart at Luke Lane, north of Barry Street, and the operator – a man I remember – dressed all in white. Oysters then were three pence a dozen. A second oyster cart was at Barry Street and Matthews Lane. A quite large and heavy fruit vendor, named Edna, also had her stall at this corner.

There was a short Chinese man with double-jointed elbows from Matthews Lane south of Barry Street, who made and sold the best lopet ban*, show bow*, won ban*, wonton* and noodle soup, shrimp fritters (haw gung ban)*, and blue crabs fried in batter. He had a tall brown man who assisted him with the selling, and they would both go around to the many business places and homes to sell their delicious food.

Growing up during that period, there were no concerns about thieves or hold-up men. Many nights I had to walk home in the dark from the bus terminal, located in Parade, all the way down to Barry Street and Matthews Lane. Some nights I walked much further if I missed the last bus after visiting some girls. The only fears I had were from an occasional barking dog and the fear of 'duppyman and ghosts'.

Written by Stanford Wong and edited by Sonia Gordon Scott.

* See Glossary

Down Memory Lane

Mah Jong tiles

Gee Pai
Chinese playing cards

Photographs ©Ray Chen

Norman Hew-Shue
MEMORIES OF DOWNTOWN KINGSTON -
THE INSTITUTE / MUSEUM OF JAMAICA

THE INSTITUTE OF JAMAICA, Museum & Library complex, holds fond memories for me and others who lived in the downtown Kingston core in simpler times past.

Situated in the southern block of Tower Street and bounded by George's Lane and East Street, it is a venerable two storied solid masonry structure. With huge carved pan-elled wooden front doors and thick glass, metal-framed windows, the looming edifice looked more like a fortress than a place in which lie the fond memories of me and my contemporaries. The Institute served as a museum, zoo, library and art gallery, and was our introduction to the Sciences, Arts, Literature and Culture.

The Institute of Jamaica, Kingston.

Apart from being a bastion of academia, the wide smooth front steps served as a gathering place for us downtown Kingston residents in those idyl-lic times. On weekdays the area might get a trifle busy even in the '50s. Tower Street was one way east, and some vehicles came along to turn up Hanover Street. Saturdays were quieter but on Sundays, if we were not listening to Pat Boone ("Ohh Bernadine – Ohh, Ohh, Ohh Ber-na-dine"), we had the down-town area to ourselves, and the Museum would sit brooding over the antics of our carefree youth. We played games such as 'police an' tief', when we would run like the wind on those empty streets – a legacy which made Jamaicans natural sprinters. Street soccer or games of cricket were played in the large concrete parking lot of the nearby Randall's Glass Company. After these stren-uous games or activities, we would relax on the cool red stone steps, and rest in the shadows of the Museum. The sidewalks were wide and sloped gently on the East Street side, ideal for riding homemade bike-skates. We would talk on the steps while waiting for the fudge-man*, or get into spicy banter with the passing ladies of ill-repute from the nearby sport-houses like the Red Apple. "Wha 'appen Chiney bwoy?"

Alternatively, put us there – slim with T.C. (Tony Curtis) hairstyles and tight dacron pants, congregated on the steps, planning our next moves. These might include going to or coming from crashing house parties; going to Joong San*, Gunboat, or other beaches; taking in a movie after mass, while we were all dressed up.

The main entrance to the Institute was on Tower Street and, during working hours, those wide steps would lead past the huge doors up a short flight of stairs to the lobby where a small, pleasant, bald-headed (when not wearing his hat) black gentleman sat in a wooden chair. He was the welcoming committee and general information centre all in one, and to us seemed to be always there almost appearing to be part of the fixtures.

One side of the lobby led past a large bronze bust of Marcus Garvey and a glass case with a large papier mâché model of Jamaica to the back where the Library and Zoo were located.

A flight of steps led down to a basement, a rare level to be found in Jamaica, even in non-residential buildings. This level was visible from inside through long windows at ankle height, and promoted an air of mystique. We used to speculate on dead bodies being dissected there, especially when coming fresh from a Frankenstein double-bill at Gaiety Theatre up the road.

This lower level had a large stuffed sawfish, with long narrow snout and sharp teeth on either side of the snout, as well as armaments and historical artifacts on display, particularly from the days of slavery. I remember seeing a seven barrelled revolver-like rifle, hideous bear-type steel traps for runaway slaves, a metal full body cage and other hideous instruments of punishment and torture. In later years, for reasons nobody could or would tell me, this area was closed to the public and the stairway was barred with ropes.

The west side of the lobby led directly into the Natural History displays: rows of glass cases exhibiting skeletons, stuffed animals, insects etc. systematically catalogued and neatly arranged and labelled with regular and scientific names. I used to spend countless hours admiring the butterflies mounted on a mirror with a huge, metallic blue, South American specimen as the centrepiece. Also the different coloured algae or seaweed floating gracefully in their jars. I tried to recreate this at home by collecting water and specimens, from the seaside down the road, in a large cookie bottle from the shop. But next morning the whole thing was a stinking mass. It took years and working at University of the West Indies (UWI) as Zoology curator, to appreciate how delicate the eco-balance is.

After leaving Wolmer's, I had applied to work at the Institute and actually had an appointment for an interview which I didn't keep, opting to work at Nuttall Medical Centre's lab instead. But, as I showed in previous articles, everything that goes around comes around for me. Years later, I found myself at UWI working closely with a surprisingly young Miss Fisher, the very lady who had set up all the beautiful exhibits in the glass cases that I used to admire.

The lobby itself had a high ceiling and flights of steep stone stairs going up to the Art Gallery. The stairs were flanked by large oil paintings of historical dignitaries. I remember one being of the Hon. Nuttall, after whom the

Medical Centre where I first worked was probably named (going around… coming around). Upstairs was another lobby area with a two-foot model of Columbus' flagship, said to be made by prisoners of the Santa Maria, with a big red Maltese cross on the front sail. The adjoining Art Gallery was where I once exhibited some oil-paintings in an exhibition for self-taught artists.

The iron-grilled side entrance on East Street led up concrete steps directly to the Public Library and Reference Archives, and to a Zoo on the right. I used to browse through books on varied topics, from the *History of Cartoons* with illustrations from the *New Yorker*, including the Addams Family, to the *Life of Ants*. I was fascinated by *Gray's Anatomy* and read about blood, its composition and properties, which probably pointed me toward a career in lab work. The library had wooden flooring which became heavily pock-marked when ladies stiletto heels came into fashion. The top floor of the library housed the historical reference and archival section. There was a large model of a steamship, about 5 feet long in a glass case and I used to go up and study the minute details like the anchor chains. Once I was joined by Victor Wong (Joe's brother – not the singer) who used to be an avid photographer and who came to photograph the model. I watched him checking the lighting with an exposure meter.

The Zoo was invariably the high-point of a visit to the Institute. Making a circuit of it counterclockwise, as far as memory serves me, would bring one past cages with conies, flamingos, Guinea fowls, peacocks and hens, agoutis, crocodiles and alligators, turtles in a large concrete pond, mongoose beside their reputed enemy - the indigenous and now rare yellow snake. The centre of the compound was occupied by a fenced area with iguanas.

Near the southwestern end was a bronze sundial mounted on a stone pedestal with instructions on how to tell time by calculating the direction of the sun's shadow falling on inscribed black and red numbers according to the season. On the eastern side was the back of the library, and a block of buildings which I think housed the botanical pressed flower collection. On this wall was a dried alligator skin, left there probably as a conversation piece as it was reputed to be from one that was shot after it escaped during a hurricane.

Opposite, and beside the iguanas was a large tree, bearing fruit locally called 'jimbilin', which were translucent yellow and shaped like a gooseberry or raspberry. We collected these to pickle and eat as a delicacy. I remember stoning the tree and froze in mid-action when I saw a member of the museum staff looking at me through the library window.

Across the street was the Children's Library where, it was said, the fashion artist Sammy Watson, whose fine sketches of elegant ladies-about-town graced the *Sunday Gleaner,* would find inspiration for his work.

The Zoo and its environs were kept up for years by the caretaker, Mr. Davis. In later years, the Zoo was relocated to its present Hope Gardens locale and expanded. Its place was taken by a heritage centre exhibiting historical artifacts.

The Institute is fondly imprinted on the minds of those of us who were born and grew up in downtown Kingston, within hearing of the bells of the Parish Church. We were defined by the latter just as an English cockney is defined by being born within hearing of the bells of St. Mary-le-Bow church, or simply 'Bow Bells'. It is aptly named the 'Institute of Jamaica' since it reflects an institution that we grew up in and which we cherished. Then was a safer time when the streets of Kingston were our kingdom. It is also concrete evidence of our bond to this Caribbean island that our forefathers made their home.

In popular literature, it is said that going back to a childhood haunt makes one surprised about how small it really is. But the Museum is an exception. May it stand in its majestic grandeur for many years to come.

Written by Norman Hew-Shue and edited by Alex Lee & Sonia Gordon Scott.

* See Glossary

Photograph ©Ray Chen

Down Memory Lane

Colourfully named country buses laden with goods and produce

Photographs ©Ray Chen

Grace-Marie Chin (née Yap Chung)
LAZY DAYS AND SUNDAYS

SOMETIMES BLESSINGS come in disguise. Growing up in Kingston in the late 1950s to the early 1970s was very different from today. Back then, my little Third World island had enough nuances about it to make North America seem like an entire planet away.

In those days, a good majority of the people weren't affluent, and so had to make the best of what was available. My family was no different. We happily immersed ourselves in the simple things that Jamaica had to offer. Like on those hot summer days in the early 1960s, when we'd revel in golden afternoons at the Rockfort Mineral Bath.

Fortunately, my parents had their business at home, so my mother was able to take us to the Kingston spa after she had completed her work and we had finished our chores.

Once at Rockfort, we'd rent one of the two private pools. Each had two changing rooms at the entrance which had a decorative iron gate. Both rooms flanked a common area. On the floor were wooden pallets for patrons to stand on, as the floor always had pools of water. The water had a smell of its own. Of course, I was young then and didn't realize that this was because it was mineral water from high up in the Blue Mountain range.

Rockfort was the kind of place that let you relax in the languor of the tropics. At one end of the pool the water constantly flowed in. At the opposite end it flowed out into the ocean. We even had little fishes swimming in and out of the pool. I guess those were the stronger ones that could swim against the out flowing current.

My siblings and I had our first accidental swimming lesson at Mineral Bath. After a few weeks of just playing in the water, we got bored and started trying to float. By the end of summer we were able to swim the whole length. The feat was one that childhood stories of accomplishment and triumph are made of. A visit to the same pool later on in 1991 would shift my perspective. What I had once considered a near-Olympic size pool as a child, was really nothing more than a five-stroke wading pool.

The Yap Chung family enjoying a day at the Rockfort Mineral Spa.

As we became teenagers, we out grew the small private pools in favour of the bigger and more exciting public one. The latter had water coming through a spout like a fire hydrant, and better satisfied our growing demand for entertainment. Nothing gave a massage like that force of water. By this time we were old enough to spend the day there without adult supervision. Mummy would leave all seven of us along with some cousins to spend the day. But the same 1991 trip home would also re-categorize the public pool from massive to mediocre. By then I had got used to North American sizes.

When we weren't soaking up the minerals at Rockfort, my family and several of our aunts' families and friends would spend lazy Sunday afternoons at Hope Gardens.

The Yap Chung family at Hope Gardens.

We were quite content to play on the grassy lawn and amuse ourselves admiring the colourful flowers. In the background, the Jamaica Military Band would play tunes from the circular band shell. The musicians always looked smart in their red, white and black uniform with cords and brass buttons. So well polished were their instruments that they glistened when the sun caught them. I enjoyed every part of the band – from just watching them set up, to their performance, to watching them pack up and leave in their bus.

Since we didn't live far from Hope Gardens, we'd sometimes take a drive there after attending 6:00 a.m. mass at St. Peter and Paul. The atmosphere was usually different at that time of the morning – more peaceful and quiet. Most of the times we'd be the only ones there, so it was much like wandering in our own private garden. Back then the peacocks and peahens lived near the nursery. I remember feeling honoured if the peacocks displayed and strutted their colourful feathers for us.

Sometimes my cousins and I would spend entire summer days at Hope Gardens, making sure to fill our metal lunch pans with food and drinks to last us. These were the same kinds of lunch boxes that are back in style after 25 years, with an aluminium flask on one side with space for food. Mine had two metal latches and a carrying handle on top. In those days that was the extent of our fast food outlets.

Feeding the ducks at the Zoo.

There is one particular Hope Gardens visit that I will always remember. After looking around the mini zoo at the back of the gardens, we stopped by the iguana lizard pen. The pen was made of concrete and had a ledge about eight inches wide that went over the inside at an angle. This time some of us decided to rest a bit on that same ledge. As we shifted around to get more comfortable, we turned our heads to see one of the larger, uglier lizards sitting right next to us. I was terrified of lizards (and still am). I took off for the zoo exit without concern for anyone. It was every man for himself. Quarrie would have been impressed that day.

As we became teenagers, we'd be allowed to spend time with our cousins in MoBay. The trip by diesel was always eventful as something always happened. Once we were delayed thanks to some boulders that had rolled down the mountain.

In the summer of 1969, over 20 young people stayed at my aunt's and her brother-in-law's house in MoBay*, which were side by side on the same property. Every morning for about two weeks, we'd find ourselves at the Samuel Chin Hardware building in the upstairs living quarters. And each time there awaited us a full breakfast of porridge, juice, toast, meat and the whole works. After breakfast we'd head for Doctor's Cave Beach where we'd spend the rest of the day under the sun playing chess, chatting or working on our tans. In the evenings it was off to a big dinner and then back to the house. I remember struggling to sleep each night after being in the sun all day. Our skin wouldn't stop burning and itching from the heat of the sun. In those days we didn't have air conditioning to help relieve the after effects. To make matters worse, we were using baby oil instead of sunscreen. We were essentially cooking ourselves.

Those were dreamy days in paradise. We never imagined that one day we would leave a life where summers are endless for one where summers are measured in weeks. But that's life. The memories keep me warm.

Written by Grace-Marie Chin (Yap Chung) and edited by Alex Lee.

Down Memory Lane

The Giddy House in Port Royal
Photograph ©Ray Chen

Down Memory Lane

1

Scenes of Kingston.

1. Aerial view of Kingston

2. Cross Roads early 1960's See the Yellow and the Checker taxi cabs, the Four Aces cigarette billboard.

3. Barclays Bank, corner of King and Barry Street, Kingston.

2

3

4. Victoria Crafts Market
   at the bottom of King Street,
   late 1950's.

5. Interior view of the
   vendor's stall in
   the Craft Market.

6. Half-Way-Tree
   Square, in the late
   1950's

Photographs on pages 252-255
©Ray Chen

Down Memory Lane

6

Facing page:

1. & 2. Old Shilling coin which dates back to 1834 that was used during the period of the S.S Prinz Alexander arrival in Jamaica in 1854.

3. Featured here are Shillings, Willie Penny, Half-a-penny and a Farthing which is a quarter of a penny.

4. Coin bags that were used by the banks for deposits.

5. Paper money.

6. Music of our youth that we listened and danced to, LP, 78 rpm and 45 rpm.

Down Memory Lane

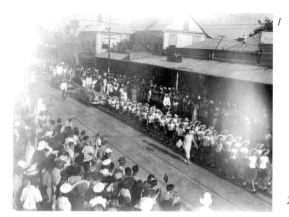

1. & 2.Parades Celebrating the Peace Conference after World War II.
As part of the victory celebration in Jamaica, portraits of the
World leaders were displayed at the back of cars. They were: U.S.
President Roosevelt, England's Prime Minister, Churchhill, China's
President Chiang Kai Shek. Russian's leader, Stalin , above, was
carried by the Chinese community.

3. Front entrance to the Chinese Public School, decorated for the
celebrations.

4. & 5. Participants of the celebrations.
Photo Credits, 1. Clive Chen, 2. Ivy (Lyew) Williams,
4. 5. & 6. Everard Hoo

Gloria Lyn
MEMORIES FROM A JAMAICAN VILLAGE

I WAS BORN IN A small village called Springfield, in St Elizabeth, Jamaica in 1930. My most inspiring and greatest influence was my parents who taught my siblings and me the utmost importance of a strict morality, a strong sense of duty, honour, a conscience to do what is right and, significantly, a disciplined work ethic.

I will try to put this story of my parents in the context of village life. My father owned a country store, a petrol station and a bakery placed in what was called the village square. The shop was on one side of the square and opposite, on the other side of the road, were two buildings for storing goods. Upstairs in one of these buildings was the post office where the postmistress also lived. There was also a meeting hall for the Salvation Army which was given to them by my father for what I believe is called a 'peppercorn' rental.

I mention this description of the square as every building has disappeared over time, except for a very small part of the main building of the shop which was falling apart when I saw it, and part of a store room attached to it and a water tank. Nothing is left, not even a stone step or a corner stone of the smaller buildings – the storerooms, the post office, the building for the Salvation Army, the house for the delco (a generator), the bakery and the larger part of the shop. It is as if the bush had reclaimed its own, as Jean Rhys wrote of another place in *Wide Sargasso Sea*. When I returned many years later and saw this wide expanse of trees and grass, it is as if the village square never existed. My parents' friends and customers have all died and it is only in my memory that the village and the villagers live on. Many of their descendants have left, and most have emigrated to North America and England. I recall small picturesque rural homes, and gardens full of roses, ferns, crotons and

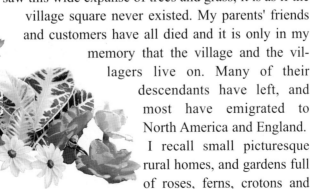

lilies, and a background of startling deep colours of climbing plants and fruit bearing trees – mangoes, oranges, grapefruits, lemons, limes, mandarins – also coffee and annatto* by the roadsides. I must mention the breadfruit and ackee trees, the two-coloured leaves on the star apple trees and smaller trees bearing the rose apple, which was such a favourite. There were also, among so many varieties of fruit, sweetsop and sour sop and guavas and red apples. This is the setting I remember.

My father also had properties with unusual names such as Bonny, Woodlands, Shakes, and Red Dirt. Some of these properties had Jamaican hard woods such as mahogany and blue mahoe, and I am fortunate enough to have furniture made from these scarce and valuable Jamaican woods. Here in Canada, where I now live in retirement, the sight of these woods reminds me of my childhood in Springfield.

Many years later when I became familiar with the characteristics of literary gardens I recognized these elements in the 'garden' of my memory. There was the gentle breeze, the birdsong, the abundance and the scent of beautiful flowers and, unlike the other gardens (only in Eden were fruit trees present), this garden had many fruit trees. The water of a running stream flowing nearby was also missing. But I need to mention the plentiful fruit, hanging low enough for the grasp of a child's hands. This small area of the parish was lush and green all the year round because of the daily rainfall and a very cool temperature. The fields were always covered with grass, the ponds full to brimming, and the scenery was a child's paradise for walking, in full view of the varying colours of the hillsides covered with the deep mauve of the 'wandering Jew' and the other colours of wild flowers. It was perfectly safe for me to wander far and near as my mother was sure that the villagers would take care that I came to no harm.

Springfield was very high in the hills, free of the risks and dangers of malaria carried by mosquitoes. The freedom from mosquitoes accounted for the largest Moravian congregation in Jamaica (at that time), as the missionaries chose Springfield instead of Black River to build their first significant mission. Too many died from malaria from their first attempt in Black River.

These are some of my memories – the joy of long walks as a small child and, when I had to attend the one room elementary school, the mile long walks to school in the early mornings and the return trip home in the late afternoons.

My memories of childhood help me to see how I was shaped into the person I am. My parents set the example of hard work. Working in a shop means work is never done. When in later years I saw the way other children lived, I realized that we never had any school holidays as we had to work in the shop at the busy seasons of Christmas, Easter and the Emancipation holiday in August. So our lives, my siblings and mine, consisted of school, studies, and working in the shop. It was not until many, many years later that I had a 'vacation'.

There were no industries in or near our village, no sugar plantations or rum distilleries, no banana estates which would employ large numbers of people, so the village escaped the obvious negative consequences of the old plantation system. The villagers did not have the experience of living in barracks or being ordered about by overseers. They did not have to suffer the hierarchy of the plantation. The villagers owned their own plots of land and their own homes. They were proud, dignified, and independent, and were strict about propriety and manners. Their main values were honesty, good manners and hard work. There were rituals to be observed, so much so that when customers came to the shop the greeting with my mother could take quite some time with inquiries about relatives and about the health of the whole family. The business of buying and selling was not the main event.

The time came when my mother's friends spanned three generations or more of a family. The villagers became my mother's nearest and dearest friends. There were no Chinese families living nearby and unlike the city of Kingston, Springfield had no Chinese school or club or shops with Chinese groceries. The seaports of Black River and Savanna-la-mar, the nearest towns

to Springfield, would have a few Chinese families but they were too far away for regular social gatherings. Ethnic groups in Jamaica would tend to gather socially with their own. My parents adopted the villagers and they in turn adopted my parents. My mother was 'Miss Ada' and they named my father 'Teacher', a name signifying respect. In a true neighbourly way we were all responsible for each other, and there was an authentic sense of caring and involvement in each other's lives. I saw how my parents gave credit to people who had no money, and they would pay back the loan in small amounts when they could.

My parents' relationship with the villagers could be said to be both complex and simple. On one level Springfield was just one of many Jamaican villages but, on another level, it seemed that my father thought he had transplanted a Chinese village to the hills of Jamaica. He assumed the role of 'the village elder', settling disputes, helping those in need, and providing transport for the sick as we had a car and a truck for transporting goods for the store. I do not have any clear recollection of the role of the police, but I think there was what was called a district constable. I do not recall the presence or need of the constable or the police. My parents learnt the use of Jamaican home remedies such as the use of fever grass and other plants for a 'bush bath' to reduce fever, and my mother never hesitated to provide Chinese medicines to people who were ill and who were only too willing to take whatever she offered. This is just an example of the many ways in which a Chinese family and a whole village exchanged ideas and customs. My mother saw no contradiction in being a Buddhist and a Moravian at the same time. She became a benefactor of this local church and I recall ministers from England living at the Mission house. There was also some connection between the church and the school but I was never sure what it was.

Springfield was not a large village. A few miles in any direction and one would be in other districts such as Woodlands, Cheviot Hills, Four Paths, Donegal, Compton, Pisgah, Berkshire, and others which I have forgotten.

Another aspect of village life that is worth mentioning is the matter of language. My parents spoke Chinese to each other and sometimes to us as small children. They learnt the creole of Jamaicans and conversed easily within the village. When we started school, my mother mistakenly thought that learning Chinese would hinder our progress in standard english and stopped speaking Chinese to us. In spite of what she thought, if we had learnt her Chinese dialect we would just have been bilingual to our decided advantage in later life.

I am the eighth of the nine surviving children my parents raised, and the first girl after six boys. Two of my brothers did not go on to further studies after they finished high school. One became involved in politics and the other was employed as a car salesman in a firm in Kingston. My parents thought education to be of the utmost importance and early on decided that we should all be sent to Kingston to attend the best schools in the city. From this small village in Jamaica the other boys spread across the world: one became an electrical engineer in the Fu Dan University in Shanghai, China, another became a doctor from Jefferson University in Philadelphia, U.S.A. Another went to Georgia Tech in Atlanta, Georgia, U.S.A., and graduated in Industrial Management, and one went to St Louis University and graduated as a dentist. My younger sister got an advanced degree in Biological Science from Fordham University, New York, U.S.A. From my one room elementary school I left home to attend a prep school in Kingston and then St Hugh's High School. Of course it is evident that I am being selective in my recollections for the purpose of summarizing my offering in this collection of memoirs.

I graduated from the University of the West Indies (UWI) with a Special Honours degree in English, and then I got an M.A. in English from the University of Toronto, Canada, on a CIDA scholarship. Thereafter I did research in England and the U.S.A. I was employed as a lecturer at UWI and, a few years later, I was awarded a Commonwealth Scholarship and did research in England for two years. Later in my career I was awarded a Fulbright Scholarship and became a Fellow of the Bunting Institute and a Harvard Officer in Cambridge Massachusetts, U.S.A. I should explain that the Bunting Institute was connected to Harvard/Radcliffe and the Fellows became part of the Harvard community. I did not have any administrative duties there. I retired from my post as lecturer at UWI in 1992 and emigrated to live in Canada. I mention the above just to show how my studies started in the one room schoolhouse in Springfield and extended to many institutions overseas. I would expect that many other Jamaicans have had this experience. I wish to show that my experiences in the village shaped my life, both personal and professional. I never forgot my beginnings in Springfield and always made sure people knew of my Jamaican heritage. My best friend and I grew up together at St Hugh's High School in the forties. She has worked professionally in Montreal for many years while I lived and worked in Jamaica. In spite of the geographical distance and separation she is still my best friend.

My life in the village and the influence of the people there taught me to respect Jamaicans and to take pride in my beginnings in this small place in St. Elizabeth. I have met Jamaicans all over, in the U.K., in the U.S.A. and in Canada, and being Jamaican has been the distinguishing feature of our relations. Jamaicans have been high achievers all over the world and have won the respect of persons in all professions. I owe my professional success, or what degree of success there is, to my upbringing in a Jamaican village, my education in Jamaican schools, and the University of the West Indies. I am also indebted to my parents who showed by example the absolute necessity for morals and ethics in leading a good and useful life.

At this time, many years have passed and my parents, now deceased, have children, grandchildren and great-grandchildren in Jamaica, Canada, England, and the U.S.A. I can see the distance there is between their lives and these children, both culturally and socially. One does not need a great imagination to see the differences between growing up in a country store in the hills of Jamaica, and working as successful professional men and women all over the world. One could say the change was from simple country folk to well educated professionals. But in spite of this cultural and educational distance, if I were to say what is my greatest hope, it would be that they follow in the tradition of my parents, of service to the community, good manners, kindness and respect to all, and a strong sense of honour and duty. Above all, my parents believed in raising a family of good and useful persons. To my mother "goodness" was the constant measure of the worth of a person.

My parents settled in Springfield, Jamaica, far from Guangdong province in South China, and now their descendants are scattered over two continents and the island of Jamaica. Of all the achievements I may recount, the triumph of my parents - over poverty, drought and floods, over wars and persecution, - is the greatest. I was very fortunate to have such loving, kind and selfless parents. They earned the respect and regard of all the people who mattered.

I did not mention the nature of politics in the village. I recall mention of a few of the Governors and their wives, Governor Richards, Governor and Lady Foot, several Colonial Secretaries, and many officials of Government such as members of the Legislature and persons who ran in local elections. But my recollection is that the villagers were not very interested in politics and were very humorous in their comments. In the tradition of many West Indian communities I do recall that they created satirical songs of the several politicians whose weaknesses they derided, and that was about the degree of their involvement. I remember also that Lady Foot was unduly anxious about common law marriages and had dozens of couples married in what was called 'mass weddings'. I do not know how seriously these ceremonies affected the accepted mores of rural communities. Of course, over the years, there had been many changes in Jamaica both socially and economically, and one of them would be the violent and near savagery of political conflict. Village life could never be the same as I remember it. Those country folk with their peculiar character and personality died a long time ago.

Finally I need to say that I consider myself very fortunate to have had my childhood in rural Jamaica. From my reading of West Indian novels I would say that my experiences are not unique to me. My sojourn in Kingston to attend prep school, high school and the university, was typical of many other Jamaicans who made this journey to further studies. My frequent trips back home to Springfield in the school holidays, however, reinforced my rural upbringing and made my memory of people and events even more indelible and accurate.

I must thank Ray Chen for inviting me to write this essay as it encouraged me in a way to try and recall details of my past and to put them in writing. This essay is the story of a people, a time and a place that no longer exist.

Written by Gloria Lyn and edited by Sonia Gordon Scott.

* See Glossary

Photographs ©Ray Chen

Joyce Chung
GROWING UP IN OLD HARBOUR BAY

OLD HARBOUR BAY is a small village in St. Catherine whose only means of livelihood when I lived there as a child was fishing. Despite always being infested with mosquitoes and sand flies, it is famous for the best quality fish in the island, and several canoes are owned and operated by the families in this district. When you pass through the town of Old Harbour you will see people selling tasty fried fish and bammies.

I remember that there were two main churches, an Anglican and a Baptist Church beside which was a bakery. There was an elementary school in the heart of the village with a graveyard surrounding it, where we used to play the game of 'Jacks' on the tombs. Attending elementary school was not pleasant in the 40's and 50's. The headmasters were stern, very strict about schoolwork, so much so, we were punished with beatings from a cane or leather strap if we made a little mistake in our work. In the mornings we had devotions and we had better be there in time to say prayers and sing a hymn. If anyone was late, he or she would be singled out for strokes from the cane or strap. Although we lived across the street from the school we were late at times, for we had to help in the shop before we left home.

I lived my days in fear of going to elementary school. I remember to this day a geography class in which I received a flogging with a strap across my back for not knowing the answer to a location. I went home crying to my mother and showed her the ugly red marks and bruises left from the beating on my buttocks, but my complaint went by the wayside. I suppose in those days flogging was accepted as punishment for not knowing your work. I had even mentioned in anger that mom should have taken my case to the police, for that was real brutality. There were worse punishments handed out to rude boys. They were held down on a table and whipped across their backs several times. We had an exercise book called the 'Press Book', which was kept in a closed cupboard and only taken out on Fridays. We were given sentences to write in this book with the use of a common pen dipped in ink. Upper strokes were light and lower strokes were heavy, and you had to be very careful not to make a mess with the ink. This was done with extra care and good practice. Obedience and discipline were emphasized.

My family owned and operated a small grocery shop which sold basic food products…flour, rice, salt, saltfish, sugar, sardines, corned beef and matches on one side. On the other side there was liquor of all sorts. I witnessed fishermen, who smoked and drank a lot to keep them awake when they went to sea at nights to draw in their pots, falling to the ground, drunk from white rum. For people looking on this was fun to watch.

Although our parents spoke very little English, as shopkeepers, they were highly respected in the community. And we children were taught to respect our helpers. We played well with the coloured children and learned to accept them as equal in many ways for we played together, attended the same school and the same churches. We were taught good manners and discipline.

We lived under very poor conditions. Our only source of light was lamps and lanterns fed by kerosene oil, by which we did our schoolwork. Water was scarce and had to be caught in buckets at night when the pressure was low. I cannot forget helping as a child, carrying buckets of water from a short distance to home. But we were taught to help in the home and business. After the shop was closed, we had to help cut up margarine and wrap flour, sugar, and salt.

My brothers were always out bird hunting or sea bathing, while our older sister would be at home in the shop. Most times we went barefoot for each child owned one pair of shoes, usually worn to church or when we 'went to town'. But the simple way of life had its pleasures too. On weekends we would roast cashew nuts in the yard. We would pile up bricks on two sides with a space in between, where we would put firewood and make fire under a piece of zinc pierced with holes from a nail. The cashews were placed on the zinc and it was so nice to smell the aroma from the roasted cashews and to eat them freshly roasted. They tasted so good!!

Fresh, good seafood was our main source of nourishment and we ate freshly caught fish almost every day. On Saturdays and Sundays goats and pigs were butchered, so we had fresh meat too, and there were times when we got freshly cooked shrimps and lobsters. On some weekends we would visit a family friend when guineps were in season. We would spend almost a day there picking guineps, eating a belly full, and would end up sleeping under the tree. Another pastime we enjoyed was bicycling to an orange grove in Old Harbour where we were allowed to pick and eat as many oranges as we wished. Then we would fill a crocus bag and the boys would ride home with it. While at the grove we had coconuts picked, drank the coconut water – which was very refreshing – and then we'd sit in the shade and cool off before paying for the oranges.

Toys were very basic and were made from match boxes and empty reels from cotton thread. It was fun to play in the rain and put used match sticks in the water and watch them float down the gutters. We played 'cock fight' with the flowers from the Poinciana trees, backyard cricket, small table ping-pong, no bat baseball, and we'd catch crabs in traps and put them in drums for the fishermen. We were happy in our own simple pleasures and have remained a close family to this day.

Written by Joyce Chung and edited by Sonia Gordon Scott.
Photograph ©Ray Chen

Down Memory Lane

1. *Fishing boats, Treasure Beach in St. Elizabeth*

2. *Rafting on the Rio Grande River in Portland*

   Photographs ©Ray Chen

Rose Chin
GROWING UP WITH LINNETTE

AS I STOOD on the shuttle bus with Ray Chen one very cold night in February, waiting to be moved from the new terminal in Toronto to the old terminal for customs clearance, I wondered what excited me the most when I was growing up in Kingston. I wondered, too, if there might have been any passion in the life of a poor family, apart from the taste of a piece of chicken or just plain gravy on rice.

But then it suddenly dawned on me that my life was filled with unconditional love from my mother and my big sister Linnette. There were no hugs and kisses (never knew what those were), only their unselfish devotion to us. And now I wonder about their passion. Of course! *We* were their passion!

There were many days of living in one bedroom, with two double beds set up in an "L" shape which would sleep four girls and a mother, and a chinky cot which would be folded down for the one boy in our family. How did our mother manage? She survived by getting up very early in the mornings, parching her peanuts, boiling her sugar and – voila! peanut cakes, which she packed away in a pan and peddled to the ice cream parlours in the city. My younger sister, Bibby, and I would often go with her… pan in one hand, Bibby in the other, and me holding on to her dress tail. Off we would go to take the 'chi chi' bus and anxiously await the treat of an ice cream or a piece of cake from her clients. I often wonder how my mother ever made it. It was her positive way of dealing with life… laughter. Nothing was ever going to prevent her from getting a few dollars to feed her children. There were days of just 'cha'* with rice and she would say its soup and rice. Finally we graduated to saltfish and Batchelors chicken noodle soup, even a roast chicken once a month. Those were fun days growing up, nothing to worry about, not even a hungry belly!

Linnette

My sister Linnette is the eldest of five children. In reminiscing with my brother we look back at the days when she wanted us to believe in Santa Claus. She was about 12, he was about 10 and I was about 5. She got a branch of the lignum vitae* tree, stripped the leaves, wrapped some cotton around the baby branches here and there, then told us to hide in the bathroom as Santa Claus would not come if we did not hide. Of course all four of us hid in the bathroom and then she said 'come out now'. Santa had come and left. We were disappointed not to see him but, lo and behold!

He had left our gifts hanging off the branches like fish on poles. There was so much excitement, so much awe – as we pulled at the gift packages, red crepe paper tied with nylon string with our own names, that Santa had left for each of us – the best pair of socks! How happy we were. In later years I began to wonder, why did he not leave Linnette a gift?? …he did, the greatest gift of all… her siblings' excitement. That's Linnette and that's how she has always been.

It is funny how Linnette comes to mind each time I think of the happier times in my life. We laugh a lot when Bibby and I get together with her. We often talk of her time as a teenager who began to work at sixteen just to help our mom to support us.

We also discussed how she ended up with Francis whom we just hated!! Hated because he was not a Jamaican, he came from Hong Kong and he had the weirdest friends…When we used to walk home from church, he and his friends would drive up to us and ask her if she wanted a ride home. She refused as she pulled us to cross the street. Francis would then make a "U" turn to ask why we preferred to walk home. We would cross the street again and he would "U" turn again and this went on for weeks. Linnette would often just look ahead and ignore him. Somewhere along the line she must have felt something as they started seeing each other, with all of us as the chaperones. If he took her to the movies, he surely had to have six fares, as well as feed all of us at Rainbow's or Dairy Farmers with ice cream and roast beef sandwiches after the movies. Looking back, I think Francis not only courted Linnette, but ended up buying a family. Linnette often told me that whenever anyone got serious about her, she first let them know that they would be marrying her family as well as her. My brother said to me the other day, that it was she who gave him respectability. She bought him his first pair of long khaki pants so he could keep up with his peers at St. George's College. I envy her very being… if each of us could have even one percent of her goodwill to mankind, we would be so blessed….

Written by Rose Chin and edited by Sonia Gordon Scott

* See Glossary

Joe Pinchin
FOR THE LOVE OF COMMUNITY

I WAS BORN in May Pen, Clarendon on March 8, 1919 as one of three children to William and Earlinth Pinchin. The original family name was *Chin Pinchin*. But over the years it evolved to become simply *Pinchin*.

Even though my mother was Canadian, I was nevertheless accepted by those who were full-Chinese because I spoke the language. She also spoke beautiful Mandarin, having learned it in China where my parents and I lived for three short years. I will never forget the day we were leaving China to return to Jamaica. I was six years old at the time and Chiang Kai-shek was fighting Mao Zedong's communist forces. We were making our way through one town under the watchful eyes of the soldiers positioned all around, when we came across a general. He was wearing a handsome silk suit, and was sitting stoically on a big stone. As we slowed to a halt in front of him, he looked at us with a pause and said, '*let them pass*'. Then he patted me on the head. '*You're going away, young man. Never forget your country.*' And I never did.

My great-grandfather was John Pinchin, the founding owner of Sing-Wong-Wah, the first Chinese wholesale business on Barry Street. It was a relatively large enterprise that stretched for an entire block from Matthews Lane to Princess Street. He was also the respected President of Chee Gung Tong, the Chinese community's association which was also located on Barry Street. As his grandson, I have to admit that I was treated like royalty. During Chinese New Year, for instance, I would go to Chinatown like everyone else did. But by the end of the day I would have collected so much *fung-bow**, I'd have to take a *mah-cha** home. I still remember the driver complaining to my father one year in particular. He said, '*I know your son have money, you know! And yet still he telling me six pence for big man, and trupence for little man!*' And that's exactly what I paid him.

Back in those early days, I was one of only a handful of Chinese children born in Jamaica, fluent in both English and a Chinese dialect. It was an advantage that would result in a close relationship between myself and the community's elders. From those early days they would beckon me to come and speak with them. That special bond grew even stronger over time. In fact, it may well have influenced my appointment years later as the Secretary of the then very powerful Chinese Retailers' Association, a community volunteer association that had its roots in the 1800's. A man by the name of Lee-Fat was the

President at the time. He was like a father to me. I still remember the Association's address – 45 Luke Lane. It would eventually close its door in the 1950's.

I still remember my first meeting at the Association. I was barely a young man, and easily outnumbered by the older businessmen. They were all speaking in Hakka, all talking about business, and sometimes all at once. I took my seat and focused on the notes I was responsible for documenting. That difficult task would become easier with time. The meeting room itself was huge. Old Chinese paintings and large black and white portraits of prominent Chinese businessmen and community leaders stared down at us from the walls. My own grandfather's picture was among them. In his portrait he very much exuded the aura of the stately 6'2" scholar that he was.

I would soon learn that our busy group had its share of political spice. In those days, most members were devout Chiang Kai-shek followers. One day, a pro-communist member took down the national flag at the Retailer's Association, and flew the red flag in its place. Well the phone calls began coming at me one after the other. The incident even made it to the newspapers. If I recall correctly, the whole thing ended when I threatened to chop down the flagpole if that flag was not removed immediately.

My relationship with the Association's members grew stronger as the years went by. I was 29 when I married. When my wife, Maria and I had our first child, a daughter, they all insisted on having a dinner for me. It surprised us because in those days such grand celebrations were still reserved for boy babies. '*We don't care,*' they insisted. '*It's your child.*' And they took care of everything. It was unbelievable. There were 30 or 40 tables at this dinner, with a collection of money and gifts of 22 or 24 K gold jewellery. *Every* table had a bottle of wine and whiskey. I remember sitting there speechless. Simply speechless.

But the good deeds were always reciprocated. At one point I was emcee for just about every Chinese wedding. One Sunday I had three to attend. Three! The first was in Kingston, the second in Old Harbour and the third all the way west in Falmouth. To make matters worse, I was battling a – shall we say – less than settled stomach.

I consider my work with the Chinese Retailers Association a great reward. It really was the doorway to all members of the community – from the poor shopkeeper to the wealthy merchant. At one point I was like the village lawyer, with many coming to me with troubles large and small. One day I was the translator in a tax dispute. The next day I was helping someone in court. Even matchmaking appeared on my résumé. Some days I'd arrive home in the evenings to find five or six men sitting on my veranda, waiting for me. I would do then what my grandfather did before me, and counsel those who asked for help.

I remember one particular incident which always stayed with me. It involved a young boy who was not showing respect to his parents.

'*Why is it,*' I asked, '*that you have no respect for your father?*'

'He's not educated,' he said.

'True, he may not be educated,' I replied, *'but without an education he still managed to send you to university. You should drop on your knees and thank him.'*

And that is how I feel about my past. Thankful.

Above: *1962 - Picture featuring (L-R) visitor from Scotland, Edward Seaga, Joe Pinchin, Sir Alexander Bustamante, Norman Manley, Ivan Levy (Chairman, Jamaica Broadcasting Corporation - JBC), Mickey Hendricks (Manager - JBC), and visitor from Scotland.*

Right: *1968 - Picture featuring (L-R) Madam Peng Yu, Joe Pinchin, Mrs Pinchin and the Chinese Ambassador Peng Yu.*

Written and edited by Alex Lee as told by Joe Pinchin.

Down Memory Lane

Shop in Spanish Town St. Catherine

Photograph ©Ray Chen

Peggi Russell
MY CHINESE CONNECTIONS

I CAN'T REMEMBER just when I discovered that my Chinese friends were in fact "Chinese"! I just know that over the years I have had many, many friends of Chinese origin and, in fact, in my own family, there are now quite a few family members.

It started when my younger sister and I, at maybe ages 6 years and 8 years respectively, became friends with two little girls, Carmen and Lorraine Hugh Yeun, who were the same ages as we were. Their parents had a grocery shop in Williamsfield, Manchester, about 2 miles from our home and we used to see them in the shop – the top of their heads and their eyes almost covered by a fringe – just barely visible above the counter. Their mother was always calling to them to behave but they didn't seem to us to be doing anything wrong. Pretty soon, we were spending alternative Saturdays with each other's family – a big thing in those days for our mothers were equally stern and did not allow their children to venture from home.

There were little details of that family that fascinated me – their daddy did the cooking, and we looked forward to the delicious, varied Chinese dishes. He did a lot of the food preparation too; for instance, I can remember the long strings of sausages hanging from the ceiling in the kitchen while they were being cured. He spoke very little English so there was a lot of gesticulating going on from him to us. My sister and I just nodded for we were very shy but had to remember that we were told by our mom to be polite and behave ourselves. He wore slippers which seemed to be made with rubber-soles but they had about 2 strips of something looking like leather across the front. Their mother worked in the shop and she spoke quite a bit of English (or something like English, because we understood her more). Her hair was most of the time curled up in these little bumps which are now known as 'Chinee (Chinese) Bumps' and we later learned that she did this in order for her hair to look curly when she combed it out. (Of course now in the year 2004, we hear these bumps being labelled as belonging to another nationality)…. The girls wore their hair long, but clipped back on either side with long, silver-looking clips which I really liked but could find nowhere to buy for myself. Their mom's eyes sparkled and she had a quick, witty answer to anyone who came into the shop and was cheeky to her – I guess that was why she was able to communicate so well with all and sundry. On the days that the girls spent with us, my mother seldom let us out of her sight – she was paranoid about *"not letting anything happen to the children"*. We were only allowed to visit our family farm (two pigs, many chickens, some pigeons, five goats, four or five cows, about a dozen rabbits, two guinea pigs, two dogs and a cat) and have picnics on the lawn at our home. We managed to amuse ourselves quite well, however, with storybooks and dolls' tea parties, etc. Somehow when we were at their house there seemed to be many more exciting things to see and do!!

There were five children in that family – three boys who teased us quite a bit, and the two girls who were the youngest. Their big brothers helped in the shop. Then one day the girls told us quite excitedly that their two elder brothers, Arthur and Bunny, were going to China – *"to learn manners"*, they told us. Of course, at that age, we had no idea where China was or why these boys had to *"learn manners"*. They seemed OK to us – even if they did tease us a bit. Off they went and we grew up but we were separated when we got to high school age – our friends went to one high school in Mandeville, I went to another and my sister (apparently the smart one in the group) got a scholarship to a well-known Kingston girls' school. What seemed like many years later, there was big excitement in our friends' household – their brothers were coming back home. To our surprise, when the boys arrived, they seemed all grown up and could no longer speak a word of English! Pretty soon the elder son got married – the entire family was ecstatic – I believe that marriage was arranged. We still keep in touch with our little friends, even though they too married and moved away to the United States.

I went to a high school in Mandeville and from the very first day at school I met many more Chinese friends – there were two girls in particular, Iris Fong and Paulette Lyn, and about four or five boys – Edwin Lyn, Douglas Lyn (not brothers), Richard Chung, and others. My friend – a non-Chinese girl, Yvonne – took one look at Edwin from day 1, and they became friends and remained great friends throughout school until they eventually got married! We had a wonderful time growing up, and again we have all remained great friends although many of them now live abroad.

My Chinese friends at school were brilliant although they did not seem to study while I had to plod along. They seemed to have a formula which made learning easier. One friend in particular, Iris, won a scholarship to university to study languages but later gave it up to get married. My other friend, Paulette, met and fell in love with a Trinidadian Chinese young man – Peter Ewing Chung. My dad was honoured and very pleased when she asked him to give the toast to her parents at her wedding. Her parents seemed very pleased also, although they did not speak too much English. My father always claimed my Chinese friends as his *'daughters'* - he loved their *'almond eyes'*, he used to say.

He was pleased when one of his two sons chose a part-Chinese girl, Tonette Lyn, to be his wife. They have two children – with almond eyes, of course. His other son chose a Lebanese girl, Jennifer (Mattar) as his wife, and they had three sons, John, Jason and Jeremy. Had my father lived longer, he would have seen two of these three grandsons marry Chinese girls also, John married Jackie Chin and Jason married Simone Chung. His cup would surely have run over!! It seems my father's family is slowly becoming more and more 'Chinese'. But then, isn't that Jamaica? Like it or not, we're truly *"Out of Many, One people"*.

When we were growing up in Mandeville, Chinese families pretty well dominated most if not all of the businesses. They owned the grocery shops and later the Supermarkets, as well as the restaurants. A treat for being good was to be taken, on Saturday morning, to the *Coronation Grocery/ Restaurant and Ice Cream Parlour* (which was just that) and to be given ice cream and Jello with pineapple topping. It tasted so delicious – completely different from what our mom prepared for us at home – but then, maybe that was because it was a reward for something. This establishment, owned by the Chungs, was also famous for its patties, milk shakes and *lady fingers*... mmmm. It was rumoured that the mother in this family was from 'a Royal family line in China'. She was very gracious and always made time to have a little chat with our mom. Her children also were very polite and somewhat shy and there were great meetings of the families when her elder daughter decided to marry a man from Scotland!! The families had to give their permission. When the town of Mandeville started to expand, and this building was demolished to make way for a more modern structure, the owners, who were by this time the son of the original owners and his wife, opened a well-known restaurant – the Mandarin – in the same area, but downstairs below road level. To date, there has been nothing in Mandeville to rival this restaurant in ambience or food.

The feasting and celebrating at my friends' weddings were something else. One was in Kingston. I recall the sumptuous meal, the decorations, the red and gold from the invitations to the reception, the champagne and other drinks (especially the very special *rice wine* for very special persons), the merry-making and the fact that it took place on a Sunday at the very early hour of 1:00 p.m. because of course almost everyone was in business and no other day would be convenient. The fireworks went on and on forever, it seemed. The entire place was enveloped in love and family.

I remember the Chinese holidays in Mandeville when pretty much the entire town closed down because they operated most of the businesses. The rest of us felt so left out. Going into the town of Mandeville via Main Street, there was Lyn's Grocery at the corner of Villa Road and Main Street. At the top of the hill was the Yee's Grocery. After passing the Police Station, there was Compton House (which was unoccupied when I was growing up but which I'm told was once owned and operated by the Lyn Sue's), then S.F. Lyn & Company beside that. Miss Mary Lyn (widow of Maurice Lyn) operated a business beside that, and beside her the Lyn Kee Chows, then the Moo Penn's. Rounding the corner you would come to the Chung's Coronation Grocery and Restaurant, then further on the Fongs Queen's Store. At the next little *square* there were: Chung's Emporium, Arthur Chung & Company, the Chung Sangs and more. With the exception of Arthur Chung who sold car parts, all the rest were grocery stores. Going to Ward Avenue, there were some more Lyns (owners of Lyn's Bakery – famous for their hard-dough bread), and in the town itself there was Walter Lee's Supermarket and 'Put-together' owned by the Hughs. There were a lot of Lyns in Mandeville – come to think about it, I'm not sure they were related.

As I said, there were some very serious meetings of the *"Chinese Clan"* when there was a big decision to be made regarding someone's daughter wanting to marry 'outside' to a foreigner. Of course I heard most of what went on as three of the brides to be were sisters of my friends. One actually eloped, as she could not take the pressure. Her husband was American and they went there to live. All this did not faze us in anyway – we never thought of the actions of the older Chinese as being prejudicial – but everything seemed most romantic to us – after all we were youngsters at the time!! We went to parties together, to the movies, to Bluefields or Gallion Beach (not too far away from Mandeville) and on picnics or exploring the caves (ugh!!) which run underneath the town of Mandeville, etc.

After I left school and I went to my very first job, a very tall Chinese young man worked at the bank opposite to where I worked. He seemed mesmerized by me but I was very, very shy. So he used to just come to my office and sit and look at me! I think he got transferred and I got the measles or vice versa so that fizzled out. I worked for about six months at that job and then joined a big multinational company. On my very first day I met a part-Chinese young man – Ken Phang Sang. He and his wife Monica kind of became my *guardians* and we have remained firm friends since. Then a young Chinese national, Hon Wo Lee, joined the staff for a short time. I think he kind of liked me and found it difficult to understand why I did not seem to want to accept his overtures. He complained a lot about what he perceived as my *'likes'*. But I found him a little domineering where women were concerned, not like my male (Jamaican) Chinese friends – I guess it was his culture. He went back to China after about a year.

Another Chinese couple I met at work became my firm friends – Dalton and Maureen Chen Sue. Maureen is godmother to my first born. We met for the first time when her husband literally crashed into me on the road – he used to be a very fast driver. Our husbands used to play dominoes together every Friday evening – it was quite funny as my husband was very tall and Dalton was very short. Again, we went everywhere together. They migrated and, after they left, another Chinese friend – Terry Chin Hing (née Lim Sue) - had all us 'girls' to lunch. There we sat and cried – not eating very much but lamenting that our friends had gone to live in Florida. I am afraid our 'lunch-hour' went on for a very long time that day – it was a wonder we were not fired from our jobs as all of us worked at the same place.

I still have many Chinese friends in Mandeville and indeed in other parts of Jamaica. I enjoy their hospitality, and I love their food, their graciousness and kindness and their sense of humour. I still marvel at their ability to present things, however small, however simple, in very creative ways. After I became an adult I added many more Chinese friends to my circle, in particular Terry's three sisters Katy, Angie and Jenny – who I see quite often. Although their father was first-generation Chinese, their mother was a real mixture of Jamaican heritage – from St Elizabeth. Their family is really very interesting as they (only girls), in appearance, look quite different, even though their features have much in common. They were brought up in the Chinese way and have all married Chinese men. So it seems we are right back to Square One!!

I have remained friends with many of these childhood friends, even though a lot of them migrated to Canada and the US. Just recently I met up with two of them – Iris Williams (née Fong) and Paulette Ewing Chung (née Lyn) and their husbands in Florida and the reunion was something else. I had not seen them for many years but it was just as if there had been no time of separation at all – we talked and joked well into midnight!

Written by Peggi Russell and edited by Sonia Gordon Scott.

Down Memory Lane

The distinct sound of the 'peanut vendor' whistle created by the steam from the boiling water.

The panut cart is built in three sections. The bottom one holds the burning coal and water fills in the mid-section.
The heat from the burning coal brings the water to a boil and the outlet for the steam creates the sound of the whistle. The heat from the boiling water also helps to keep the peanuts on the upper section warm.

Photograph ©Ray Chen

Kennedy Tai
LILY AND CLARICE

LIFE IS COMPLEX, beautiful, ugly and wonderful. We have no control over the circumstances of our birth. But after that, to a large extent, we determine what our life will become, tempered by God and the special people who enter our lives. To be born and raised in Jamaica at a time when it was a young, beautiful and colourful place, was a blessing like no other.

One of the greatest influences on my life was the genuine relationship

Kennedy standing at right with parents, brother and sisters.

between my parents and our *guimahs**, Clarice and Lily. The two were with our family from as far back as I can remember. In fact, they were more like surrogate mothers. Our parents were simply too busy making ends meet. There were five of us to mind – three girls (Fay, Colleen and Agnes) and two boys (Michael and me). Clarice and Lily took care of us literally from the day we were born. They cooked for us, gave us our baths, washed our clothes, treated us to many an outing, wiped our tears when we fell down and cut our knees. And they helped my Chinese parents raise us in a Jamaican world. In our formative years, all things Jamaican came from them. They were the perfect bridge.

I remember them so well. Clarice was brown-skinned and a staunch Norman Manley/PNP supporter. Lily was darker and a die-hard Busta/JLP supporter. Needless to say they had an ongoing tradition of colourful bantering, with each spouting taunts like, '*Gweh! My paaty betta than feyu!*' The Tai household was guaranteed to be privy to such passionate dialogue especially after one or both had attended a political meeting the night before. But they didn't fool us. They *thoroughly* enjoyed the verbal jousting. And so did we. Because of them, the Tai children knew *all* the latest PNP and JLP political songs and ditties.

Lily, the more vocal and animated of the two, lived close by on George's Lane. She'd often take us there to buy salt-fish fritters. Sometimes we played with her children, with her two oldest, Vi and Millicent, doing many things with and for us. Lily was the *ultimate* storyteller, often entertaining us with *Anancy** and *duppy** stories while she ironed. First she'd start the story in a normal tone. Then as it progressed, she'd breathe life into it by varying her tone and volume, and dancing, gesturing and prancing about the ironing board. When the climax was approaching, she'd lower her voice to a whisper and then simultaneously leap at us while shouting, just like a duppy. We were both delighted and scared out of our minds, and *totally* addicted to story-time with Lily. It was pretty much like living with our own Miss Lou.

I'd venture to say that of the lot of us, *I* was Clarice's favourite. She spoiled me silly. I mean she did *everything* for me. I vividly remember being five and accidentally knocking over a frying pan of hot oil onto my right foot. It was Clarice who flew through the streets crying, with me in her arms, my foot already bubbling and black from the stinging oil. I screamed all the way to the doctor's office two blocks away on Hanover Street. At that time we were living on Barry Street and George's Lane. I honestly think she cried as much as I did. The burn mark on my foot is a constant reminder of that day.

Clarice was also the one who would go to Chinatown to buy soya sauce, *wah mui*, dung goo** and other Chinese stuff for my mom. On those days she'd disappear from the house at about 9:00 a.m. and return much later at about 2:00 or 3:00 in the afternoon. Of course, the whole trip should have taken her about an hour at the most. I don't know what she told mama when she came back so late on those days, but here's the truth. Since Clarice *had* to pass the courthouse at King and Barry Streets on her way back, she could *not* resist slipping in to listen to the big cases going on at that time. She was a big Dudley Thompson fan from back then, long before he entered politics.

These two women were responsible for many of our childhood memories. Whenever the huge U.S. airplane carriers came into Kingston harbour and offered a free tour, off we'd go to the bottom of King Street. We'd have to board small launches that took us out to the carriers because they were too big to dock. That was such a thrill for us because we'd never been on a boat before, big *or* small. Once on board we were allowed to look at and even touch the guns and airplanes. Other times we'd go to the King Street dock to see the American gun ships there.

Kennedy (on the right) with sisters and brother, (l-r) Fay, Colleen, Michael and Agnes

It was Clarice and Lily who marched us all to the Jamaica Institute, so that we could borrow books and bury ourselves in the exciting world of pirate and mystery stories. And when the Institute had free movies – by advanced first come, first served tickets – Clarice and Lily never failed to secure tickets for us. They even organized several trips to the small zoo by the museum on East and Tower Streets. That's where we went to see alligators, iguanas and snakes. It's also where we went to eat some very sour gimbelin* that grew on a tree right by the alligator cage. I'd often sneak up to the second floor to see the ship in a huge glass bottle and marvel at how they got such a big sailboat into it. At Christmas time, we headed for King Street and the Christmas market to look at all the toys displayed on the sidewalk around Parade and in store windows. *Times Store* and *Justin McCarthy* were two such stores that tempted us with the hundreds of toys that we could only own in our imagination. And whenever we tired of our cramped shop space, the two took us to the Cenotaph of Jamaica at Church and Barry Streets so that we could play a bit.

Lily eventually left for the United States, where her family could look after her as she approached her golden years. As for Clarice, poor and with no family of her own, her final years were difficult ones. She pretty much depended on the money I sent for food and simple things like a coal stove. And this wonderful woman, this generous human being who had taken the time to expose me and my siblings to as much learning as she could, had to rely on another lady in her yard to correspond with me. Clarice had remained illiterate until the day she died. When that time came, I arranged for a proper burial for her. Her friends would later write to say that the priest had read aloud my last letter to her before she died. In it I had thanked her and Lily for all that they had done for us, one last time. They were, without a doubt, our earthly guardian angels.

Clarice on her way home

Written by Kennedy Tai and edited by Alex Lee.

* See Glossary.

Above photograph ©Ray Chen

The last time Kennedy saw Clarice was on a visit to the island in 1989. He took several pictures as a keepsake. Sadly, the film was damaged and he never got his pictures. Soon after, his sister came across a perfect picture of Clarice. She found it in Ray Chen's book called...
Jamaica- The Beauty and the Soul of the Land we Love.

Maurice Tenn
KNOLLIS DAYS

IN THE 1940s, Knollis was a small district in St. Thomas-Ye-Vale, two miles from Bog Walk in the parish of St. Catherine. It stood at the crossing of two important roads: the road from Bog Walk to Riversdale and the hills of St. Mary, and the road leading from Lucky Valley and the hills of St. Catherine to the important market town of Linstead. Along both roads – marled, not asphalted – produce moved from the hinterland to railway stations at Bog Walk and Linstead, in mule carts or on donkeys. Knollis became a rest stop for farmers and travellers. Adjoining the railway line was a race track where racing took place on Wednesdays, and gymkhanas* with horses and donkeys on special local festivals.

My parents settled here, circa 1940, having previously lived and moved all over St. Catherine. A shop with living quarters had become available for rental. It was wartime, and there was a shortage of fuel – petrol and kerosene oil – as well as other staples such as rice, which was imported pre-war from Siam and Burma in South-East Asia. But it was in the middle of a sugar area, surrounded by the great sugar estates of Tulloch and United Estates. Later, a building site became available and my parents bought it and built an 'upstairs' building, with the shop premises on the ground floor and living quarters upstairs. This style became typical, as it afforded greater security from thieves and saved on rental.

I attended the local primary school a mile away, known as Tulloch School and named after the estate that had made the land available to government for the building of a school. We all walked to school barefooted. Few could afford shoes (imported from England), or even crepe soles as the canvas shoes were called. These were worn only on special occasions such as going to church, or to the annual fair organized at Bybrook.

We had some great teachers, who imposed discipline by the switch (cut from a nearby tamarind or guava tree). The guava broke easily but the tamarind, because of its flexibility, had a special sting. We also had a great headmaster, one Mr. G. B. McLeod, especially feared because he had taught generations of our collective parents. Even the parents were afraid of him. He did not spare his own son (the future Dr. Glen McLeod) or his daughter. G. B. as he was called, lived in Linstead and rode to school on his horse. Motor cars were a rarity in those days and had to be parked for lack of petrol.

School began at 9:00 a.m., and woe betide those who came late! The teacher's hand never seemed to tire, and I always felt sorry for those who had to walk three miles to school in the mornings. There were seven of us siblings, and as we advanced from babyhood to childhood, we got to know the corresponding generations in the neighbouring families. Everyone knew everyone else for miles around, unlike Kingston where one did not even know one's neighbour. Friday was a special day in country schools. Very few students went to school as they had to assist their parents in the field to prepare the 'load' for market on Saturday, selecting the best produce and bagging it carefully.

We assisted our parents in the shop business, which included serving behind the counter or in the inevitable bar. My father had a produce licence which enabled him to buy cherry coffee, cocoa in the pods, bissy* or kola nuts. The cherry coffee was processed in a mechanical pulper, fermented, and then dried or sunned on the concrete barbecue. We had to keep an eye on the weather because, at the sight of rain clouds over the Sligoville hills, we had to race to sweep up the coffee into crocus bags before the rains came. This was also true for cocoa beans. Whenever we accumulated twenty blue seam crocus* bags of dried and cured produce, they were shipped by truckers to the produce dealers in Kingston for sale overseas. Produce was in great demand for the war effort, and this aspect of the Chinese grocery business in the rural areas was different from Chinese businesses in Kingston.

Whereas our cousins in Kingston went to the beach on Sundays, in the country we flew kites. To the astonishment of Jamaicans, my father made some Chinese kites in shapes which the villagers swore could not fly. But fly they did, to the amazement of all the surrounding villagers. One of the happy memories I have is of flying these strange Chinese kites with my father on the race track or common on Sundays, or after school.

One of the pleasures of country living was going down to the local river and catching fish or shrimps. As the shrimp invariably had sharp claws, the art was to catch them without being bitten or clawed. In those days, the countryside was not as deforested as it is today, so that the rivers had much more water than now. It is sad to see how the rivers and streams of Jamaica have declined.

Sundays were special days for us. We would bicycle to Linstead for the eight o'clock Mass at St. Helen's Catholic Church where I would meet other Tenns from Bog Walk. After Mass we went to the premises of Tenn's Bakery in Linstead, an establishment owned by a cousin, Mr. Ernest Tenn that specialized in 'duck' bread, buns, and 'bulla'*. The bakery was the regular meeting place for the Chinese in north St. Catherine on Sundays. There they played mah-jong,* pie-que*, and other games. All the children would gather round and watch, and whenever someone won a good hand, 'sore foot'* would be distributed to the children. Some professed to understand the games but, as they were played in Chinese, I never picked up any understanding.

The highlight of the day came in the early afternoon, at about three, when the games were put away and out came chop sticks and other utensils. The tables were then packed with goodies such as boiled chicken, duck, Chinese mushrooms of all kinds, Chinese vegetables, rice, and many traditional ingredients such as lopet*, fah-chong*, impeow*, and so on. Children sat at special tables, while the men ate and gossiped about the war in China against the Japanese, and about their relatives back in Tung-Sang or China. As dusk came, we would say goodbye to cousins and friends, and mount our bicycles to ride home.

Chinese were very patriotic to their fatherland. There were frequent fairs at the Chinese Public School on North Street to raise funds for buying aeroplanes for the war effort led by General Chiang Kai-Shek, the Chinese war lord. We would be taken by our father to these fairs, where we had a great time meeting with other family members from all over the island.

Primary school days seemed all too short. Before I knew it, through the intervention of Father Harney, the Jesuit priest at St. Helen's, arrangements were made for me to enter St. George's in Kingston. I discovered that quite a few students took the train every day to Spanish Town and Kingston. I rode my bicycle the mile and a half to the Bog Walk station in the morning. There was the special excitement of going through the four tunnels between Bog Walk and Spanish Town, and hearing shrieks and gasps from the girls as the entire train went through a blackout for a few minutes in the tunnels.

The train journey ended at the Barry Street station and in those days the trains ran on time. You could set your clocks by them. The train departed from Linstead each morning, stopped briefly at Bog Walk, and left at precisely 6:45 a.m., made more stops in Spanish Town, Grange Lane, and Gregory Park, arriving at precisely 8:50 a.m. in Kingston. St. George's school bell rang for morning assembly at 8:00 a.m, and classes began at 8:20 a.m. As the buses were overcrowded, most students walked from the railway to school, including a contingent to Kingston Technical on Hanover Street, Excelsior, then on North Street and, of course, St. George's. There were two afternoon trains to Linstead daily; the first one left the Barry Street station at 2:15 p.m., the other at 4:30 p.m.

In my first year at St. George's, there was a long railway strike during which the trains did not run. Arrangements were made for me (and later my brothers) to board in Kingston with my grandmother. But I always returned home on Friday evenings to help in the shop for the weekend. Indeed, this was the way of life for my friends whose parents invariably were shopkeepers. Working in the shop taught us the value of money and sharpened our minds, especially in mental arithmetic, as we collected money, made change, or added up the bills of various customers. As the currency was then in pounds, shillings, and pence, with a complicated system of converting one into the other, one had to know one's multiplication tables inside out, and backwards and forwards. Consequently, Chinese students always excelled in mathematics, as they do to this day. As maths provided the base for the sciences, Chinese students also did very well in these subjects.

The Chinese were largely Roman Catholic, therefore it is not surprising that they dominated St. George's College. I recall that on the occasion of the Lunar New Year, (called locally 'Chinese New Year') it was not uncommon for the school to be virtually deserted. It was a three day holiday. My father always had a feast of Chinese dishes to which prominent local customers were invited. Many, many years later, when I worked in London at the Jamaica High Commission, I met a young Jamaican mechanic, Wilson, from Knollis, who reminded me that one of the highlights of his youth was coming to my home on a Sunday and also partaking there each year of the Chinese New Year's dinner!

Written by Maurice Tenn and edited by Sonia Gordon Scott.

* See Glossary

Down Memory Lane

Main Street in Browns Town, St. Ann
Photograph ©Ray Chen

Sister Theresa Lowe Ching, R.S.M., Ph.D
CHINESE CONTRIBUTION TO THE CHURCH
IN JAMAICA

THE STORY OF the Chinese migration to Jamaica, beginning with the arrival of 472 Chinese from the harsh labour conditions of Panama in 1854, is well known and documented.[1] What is not so well known but nonetheless is of vast import, is the story of the early beginnings of the Chinese involvement in the church in Jamaica and the significant contribution that they have made in forwarding its mission. The focus here will be limited to the Roman Catholic Church although it is certainly not the only denomination in which Chinese have been active members.

A most important aspect of this part of the story relates directly to the involvement of the Chinese in the grocery business from the first migration in 1854. It became even more so in the subsequent migrations between 1856 and '70 and again, in 1884, when 680 Hakka came to the island at the invitation and expense of relatives and friends, in order to fill the labour gap that existed at that time. It was in the small shops that many second and third generation Chinese learnt that "hard work and long hours were the key to their success."[2] From 'behind the counter' they also learnt to develop meaningful, though sometimes ambiguous, relationships with the majority Black population as they gradually became assimilated into the Jamaican society.[3]

Thus it was out of that environment of the shop that Father Francis Osborne traces the beginnings of the conversion to the Roman Catholic faith in the person of a young girl, Blanche Acquee, born to Mr. And Mrs. Daniel Acquee in Glengoffe on August 25, 1904. Although both parents were non-Christians at that time, the assurance that the child would be brought up as a Roman Catholic, and the presence and commitment of a Roman Catholic godfather made it possible for the child to be received into the Church. The subsequent move of the family from Glengoffe to North Street, Kingston, in the vicinity of St. Anne's school in 1904, brought the child under the influence of the Allegheny Franciscan Sisters who owned and administered the school. After being confirmed by Bishop Collins, Blanche Acquee became an 'enthusiastic apostle' and set in motion a rapid increase of Chinese converts to the Roman Catholic Church.[4] Father Leo Butler, then pastor of St. Anne's Church, initiated what was to become a significant apostolate in the Church community upon the reception into the Church of Doris Lee Young who joined the Acquee family, a later addition to the family with the birth of another daughter, Blossom, and an older sister, Eva. Subsequently, dozens of Chinese children would be baptized and, for the next forty years, that apostolate among the Chinese would flourish.

Father Butler's influence increased after he became headmaster of St. George's College and with the assistance of Sister Sylvia, O.S.F., his apostolate extended to a community of Chinese entertainers who entered the Church en masse, following the instant conversion of twenty-five of its members.[5]

Conversion among the Chinese was to expand significantly into the rural areas and among adult Chinese beginning in 1925, through a mission that was conducted by Father Simon Tang, a Jesuit Priest from Canton, China, who was ministering in New York at that time. A centre for the instruction of adults was subsequently established at Gordon Hall and was later moved to St. Anthony's School, 80-84 Orange Street, nearer to Barry Street where the Chinese community concentrated much of its activities.[6]

The focus of the Chinese on the education of their children made the Catholic Schools another significant avenue to conversion to the Catholic faith. It was thus that Catholic elementary education began to play an important role in laying a solid foundation for the faith in many. Subsequent to that, when the option of sending children to be further educated in the homeland was virtually cut off by the events of World War II and the communist occupation of China, St. George's College, Immaculate Conception High School and Alpha Academy were to become the favourite high schools for taking students beyond the elementary level. As Father Osborne puts it:

Ambitious, studious, and industrious, these pupils used their native ability to the utmost, and what their fathers accomplished in the business world, their sons and daughters achieved in the intellectual. From high school to university was the logical step some matriculating in English, others in Canadian and American universities. These higher studies broadened their horizons and opened the professions to them. The result has been doctors, lawyers, architects, engineers, and seminarians and priests.[7]

It is with this historical background and out of this milieu that a few Chinese young men, and a greater number of Chinese young women, opted to dedicate their lives totally to the service of the church and become Priests and Religious Sisters. The story of the entire contribution that these Priests and Sisters have made, particularly in the fields of education and social work, is impossible to tell in this brief overview of their contribution. However, highlighting only a few of them might give an indication of the quality and extent of the service they have rendered towards the development of the Jamaican church and society.

The outstanding contribution of the former Jesuit Priest and Founder of the Community of the Brothers of the Poor, Father Richard Ho Lung, is widely known and appreciated and needs no further elaboration here. Not as widely known or acclaimed is the work of the numerous Chinese Sisters who, at one time or another, have been and many still are, members of the Allegheny Franciscan Sisters and the Sisters of Mercy, to name only two communities who owned and administered respectively Immaculate Conception High School and Alpha Academy, the two high schools that many Chinese Catholics preferred to attend from the beginning, as indicated above.

Sister Maria Goretti Lowe

From among the Allegheny Franciscans, Sister Maria Goretti Lowe has emerged as an outstanding educator, leader and spiritual guide. She taught at various elementary schools before moving on to become Vice-Principal of St. Joseph's Teachers College and Area Coordinator of her community for eight years, during which time she served one term as President of the Conference of Major Superiors of the Antilles. Currently, she directs the Franciscan Spirituality Centre in Kingston. "My life story," she claims, "should give young people the assurance that the religious life is a life fully lived, embracing everyone and all of creation." Her greatest desire for the church in Jamaica is that there should be "a continued commitment to education which has fostered so much growth of the church."

Sister Avril Chin Fatt

Avril Chin Fatt, daughter of Alfred and Eva Marie Chin Fatt attended Immaculate Conception High School and subsequently, as an Allegheny Franciscan Sister, graduated from St. Bonaventure University and, later, from Boston College where she obtained an M.A. in Mathematics Education. A life long educator, Sister Avril ministered at St. Joseph's Teachers' College for thirty-two years beginning as a lecturer in Mathematics, then becoming Vice-Principal and later, Principal of the institution. Sister Avril also served her religious community as Regional Minister of Jamaica for eight years, and is currently completing four years as a member of the General Leadership of her congregation. She recalls fond memories of a nurturing family environment and a similarly caring church community, where common values were communicated and reinforced, i.e., the values of love of God and love of neighbour, of service and of working together and not in competition with one another.

Sister Grace Yap

Sister Grace Yap grew up in the 'country village' of Papine where, at that time, Revivalist religious meetings and other aspects of the Jamaican culture could be experienced first hand. From those early years, Sister Grace became very much aware of belonging to two cultures, drawing life and nurture from both. At home in both cultures she reflects, however, on how her Chinese heritage "prepared me well", as she says, "for religious life as it reinforces the Gospel values. My faith in God strengthened, and I try to walk in the shoes of others and see life through their eyes." Sister Grace currently brings the Franciscan spirit of joyful service and love of all creation, and offers hope to the disadvantaged poor in Trench Town and other inner city communities.

From among the Sisters of Mercy, Sister Marie Chin, daughter of Hubert and Etheline Chin, hails from Christiana, Manchester. From an early age, she came under the influence of the Passionist priests in Christiana and the Sisters

Sister Marie Chin

of Mercy at Alpha Academy. Her experience of the values that she learnt at home and in the church, such as responsibility for those less fortunate and in need of shelter from suffering, and compassion and reverence were "made of the same fabric, a seamless garment". It is not surprising then that Sister Marie's life of service as teacher, as director of young community recruits, as Administrator of the Sisters of Mercy in Jamaica and now, President of the Sisters of Mercy of the Americas, has been marked by a passion for justice and the empowerment of the less fortunate. Sister Marie's hope for the church in Jamaica is that "it be a church for the people of Jamaica, always grounded in the Gospel values of love, justice and peace."

Sister Mary Benedict Chung, another prominent member of the Sisters of Mercy, likewise grew up in rural Jamaica and was educated by the Sisters of Mercy. Strongly influenced by her parents, Frank and Beryl Chung, she experienced a strong family bond. She learnt to respect the old, to value hard work

Sister Mary Benedict Chung

and to be loyal to family members and friends. These values and others were to become her mainstay when she entered the Community of the Sisters of Mercy and began a career of lifelong service to the disadvantaged poor, first as teacher and school principal, and now as Administrator of the Laws Street Trade Training Centre, where numerous persons from the inner city of Kingston and its environs find opportunities for training in music, computer technology, home economics, catering and sewing, and become employable there or elsewhere. Most important of all is the experience of care, respect for their dignity and concern for their growth and welfare, that many acclaim as the hallmark of Sister Mary Benedict's 'holistic' service.

Love of the poor and passion for justice underlie Sister's hope for more priestly and religious vocations, and greater participation of the laity in the church, for the needs of the disadvantaged are manifold and the labourers few.

Working along with Sister Mary Benedict at the Laws Street Trade Training Centre is another outstanding member of the Sisters of Mercy, Sister Irene Chen See, eldest daughter of Arthur and Ina Chen See from Pisgah, St. Elizabeth. Sister Irene's experience of the value of the sacredness of life from

Sister Irene Chen SeeT†

childhood was to make an indelible mark upon her. It enhanced the quality of service that she would give as a Sister of Mercy in later years to the orphans and other disadvantaged children whom she would serve at Alpha Boys' School, Alpha Girls' School, and later, to the sick at Kingston Public Hospital. Sister's dedication to bringing life to those most in need of a more humane standard of living continues in her work at the Laws Street Trade Training Centre, where she administers a bakery to provide skills training and employment for the underprivileged in the surrounding inner city communities. Like Sister Mary Benedict, Sister Irene also hopes to see more labourers in God's vineyard and, above all, a growth in faith among Christians.

As these Sisters tell of their early experiences in their families, the influences on their formation and the values that were learnt, a common thread emerges. The presence and examples of caring parents, a sense of pride in being Chinese, fond memories of the celebration of Chinese festivities, particularly the Chinese New Year celebration and the delicious food that was lavishly shared with friends and neighbours, the inculcation of the values of loyalty, honesty, hospitality, discipline, hard work, respect for elders and compassion for the less fortunate, stand as significant influences in the formative experiences of all. Interwoven in all of that was also an experience and appreciation of a contemplative stance towards life and nature thus giving evidence, it is to be noted, of a certain integration of Confucian ethics, Buddhist compassion and Taoist contemplation that are deemed by some to mark Chinese religious experience.

In the environment of school and church, the experience of caring Priests and Sisters provided the safe space that parents provided at home, and mitigated the more threatening aspects of Western culture that the society as a whole presented. Values that were stressed at home were reinforced at school and in the church. Hence, it was relatively easy for individuals with more than an ordinary gift of idealism and generosity, and the desire to be of service, to make the transition from home to religious life. Several vocations to the religious life were thus nurtured and came to significant fruition in the past sixty years.

But time moves on and the situation, in families and the church, has changed significantly. No longer are there any vocations to the priesthood and religious life coming from among the Chinese population. The more recent Chinese migrants from Hong Kong and the mainland of China are neither being converted to the Roman Catholic Church nor to the other mainline churches, but rather to the more fundamentalist Church of God. Only time will tell what form their eventual contribution to the church in Jamaica will take, but significant it doubtless will be.

Written by Sister Theresa Lowe Ching, R.S.M., Ph.D. and edited by
Sonia Gordon Scott.

1   Walton Look Lai, The Chinese in the West Indies 1806-1995 (Jamaica/Barbados/Trinidad: The Press University of the West Indies, 1998).
2   Francis J. Osborne, S.J., History of the Catholic Church in Jamaica (Chicago: Loyola University Press, 1988), p. 336.
3   Cf. Easton Lee, From Behind the Counter (Kingston: Ian Randle Publishers, 1998).
4   Osborne, p. 335.
5   Ibid., p. 339.
6   Ibid., 340.
7   Ibid., p. 341.

Sister Benedict Chung
INTERVIEW

Interview conducted by Easton Lee and Vincent J. Chang

Published in the Chinese Benevolent Association
Chinese New Year – Year of the Tiger booklet
February 1, 1998

INTRODUCTION

For over 30 years she has worked among the people as teacher, counsel-
lor, mother, sister. The sound of children playing in the schoolyard next door
floats up to the second floor, as we sit down to talk with Sister Benedict at the
Laws Street Trade Training Centre. The school next door is Holy Family
where her work in the area began. We are sitting outside her door as she lives
there, directly above one of the several workrooms. This is not strange for her.
She grew up living either behind or above her parents' shop. As a child she
knew no luxury. We asked her…

EL: *What was your early life like?*
SrB: I was born in Troy, Trelawny. My parents were Frank and Beryl
Chung. They came directly from China, therefore we are first generation
Chinese. My father came to Jamaica after his father had come to Jamaica, and
had started a business in Troy. My grandfather returned to China and sent his
two sons, Edward and Frank, to run the business. There are five of us who

were born in Jamaica. I had one sister who died recently, who was a nurse in Canada. Alvin lives in New York, Albert is a professor of Biochemistry at the University of Pittsburgh, Jean – her married name is Williams – lives in Atlanta, and my eldest sister who was born in China was married to a Lee and lived in Port Antonio.

EL: *What year did your parents come to Jamaica?*
SrB: I'm not sure…my father came about 6 to 7 years before he sent for my mother and a year later I was born. I was born in 1931, so I would presume my father came around 1924. At age 11, I was sent to boarding school in Mandeville at Mount St. Joseph, run by the Sisters of Mercy. Cynthia and Jean went to Alpha Convent, Albert went to Cornwall College, and Alvin being the first boy after three girls, had the privilege of going to China. When I graduated from Mount St. Joseph after taking the Senior Cambridge exam, I entered the Sisters of Mercy Convent at Alpha at age 16.

EL: *When did you know that you would enter the religious life?*
SrB: Well…one of the sisters had a lot to do with it. Living with the sisters in those days, you really got a lot of religious influence in your life. We, the boarders, had daily Mass, evening rosary, and the sisters used to speak frequently about their work at Alpha. Sr. Marie Theresa really was the one who inspired me to enter the Convent at Alpha. I originally wanted to be a nurse, and thought seriously about the Dominican Sisters who were at St. Joseph's Hospital, but Sr. Marie Theresa came to Mt. St. Joseph from the Boy's School – and she was so enthusiastic; her whole vocation was helping the poor and that very much appealed to me.

EL: *Part of the Chinese tradition was that the Taoist nuns and monks in Buddhist tradition would care for the poor. Did you have any influence from that part of your life?*
SrB: Yes, my mother used to speak about the Buddhists. We used to call them 'Li Woo Ma' and – if there was a disaster – how well they helped, so I was influenced by that also.

EL: *What was your parents' reaction to your entering religious life?*
SrB: My mother was very much with me. My father was a bit hesitant, didn't think I would last; that within six months I would run back home. He didn't think I would like the life of confinement because I was very tomboyish (*laughs*), the good time girl. Actually, we grew up with my uncle's children who lived across the street from us, and they were mostly all boys. So we girls didn't play with dolls and such; we played catapult, cricket and football – that type of thing.

EL: *And in all this time, you never thought of marriage and having your own family?*

SrB: That was not a big attraction at the time, considering my age, and I was not really exposed to any of that. I was exposed to boys but it was more like friendly rivalry – more friendly (than anything else).

EL: *There are others who have chosen religious life, who work in schools and hospitals, etc., but you have chosen to work with the poor and in one of the most volatile areas in the city. Tell me how that came about.*
SrB: Well, when I first entered the convent, I was sent to the Alpha Boys' School – you had no choice really, you were just appointed. I very much liked the boys. Then after a year, I was sent to the Alpha Girls' School where I stayed for five and one-half years.

EL: *This was the orphanage?*
SrB: The Alpha girls orphanage. I felt very much called – I really wanted to do this type of work. When we were novices and young sisters, we used to go to the almshouse. We used to go to the TB place every Saturday with one of our veteran sisters – Sr. Mary Barnard who really loved the poor so much – and I think everything just stuck on to you (*laughs*). Then I was appointed to go to Alpha Primary School in January 1961 and, all of a sudden, the appointment was changed overnight and I was sent to Holy Family School – right in the heart and beginning of the Rasta movement, and the area has really been a volatile one from the very beginning. But I feel that you can make a contribution, and it is among the poor that you are to make it – that's where you should.

EL: *What has your life been like working in this area? You've earned a certain reputation as being a tough person – but just. Have you ever felt exposed to all the dangers that are around you?*
SrB: You DO feel exposed to all the dangers that are around you – unless you have no feelings – but I have never felt threatened. I think everybody kind of owns me and I own them in a sense that, if there is a conflict and I step in and try to do something about it, they always listen. And that is a very gratifying thing and maybe you have to be careful not to lord it over them, but (remember) that you really act as an intermediary and a friend in all situations. It has taken years to gain the people's confidence. They'll tell you about their guns, they'll tell you about a murder, tell you about their private lives, they'll come and ask your opinion and that sort of thing. It has been a very fulfilling time down here for me.

EL: *Would you change anything – I mean, about your own life and what you've done so far?*
SrB: No, I think if I had to live it over again, I would come back here to work. I think if there's anything to change, it would be to try to make an even greater effort to change the people, to kind of uplift those who have been really down, and especially to make the women more independent of the men, and

make them employable in such a way that they don't have to take abuse from anybody.

EL: *So much has happened at Holy Family since you first came. What exactly happens on the compound now?*
SrB: When I came, there were 600 children in the school, now there are over 1,200. What we did was we expanded the school – bought the property next door and built six classrooms, a hall, a remedial classroom, staff room and a caretaker's cottage. Then we bought another property next to us and built a library and three other classrooms, plus other facilities for the staff. We then acquired the Barbara Manley Centre for the infant school.

EL: *Isn't there a bakery attached now?*
SrB: We thought, what could we do for the people in the area? We had some women, parents who had (sewing) machines, and we asked if we could get work for them. So we had them in the multi-purpose hall. They brought their (sewing) machines and we begged more machines and got work for them to do. That led to the idea of a training centre, which was built 11 years ago by the Rotary Club of Kingston. So then we built a bakery. Then we have the Home Economics class, which trains girls in childcare, meal planning and that sort of thing. There is also garment making, crafts (embroidery, crochet), weaving mats and so on, plus a little catering to earn some funds to help with commercial projects, and to help feed the hundreds who come to beg food everyday.

EL: *The bakery is also commercial, right?*
SrB: The bakery is the only income-generating project that we have. From the bakery we pay all our utility bills, tutors, staff and food for Highholborn Old Age home that we have taken over.

EL: *Are you the only religious one on the staff?*
SrB: No, Sr. Eileen mans the bakery, Sr. Clotilde – the sewing room.

EL: *And you're at the school still?*
SrB: No, I retired from the school three years ago – thank God.
        (*EL laughs*)
        Make sure you put that in – "Thank God".

EL: *In all this time working down here, have you ever felt any racism?*
SrB: I have NEVER felt anything like racism. Nobody has ever said to me, for example, unless they said it behind my back, 'You're a Chini' or 'You're from China' or anything like that. Wherever I go they say, 'Hi Sister…Howdy-do, Sister… Sister, a come to ask you for something…Sister, beg you something.' It's never any other way. No matter where I walk, all over the place, in the night or in the day, it's always the same.

EL: *What do you consider your greatest success and your greatest failure in all of this?*

SrB: (*Laughs*) Is there any success? How do you measure success? It's not a thing where you have money or say, well, we made money. My greatest success I would say is the tremendous reception you get from the people and whoever comes to us, be it poor or rich, you are welcome in the community once you say you are coming here. And I feel that this has really been a blessing in my life. I also feel that if you talk to the people, they will listen to you. I don't know if we've failed. We've failed in that you can't do all the things you try to do, and I consider that more as a setback than a failure.

EL: *I think I know the answer to the next question, but I want to hear you say it. Through all of this you have had the influence of your mother, your parents. What do you think has been the mainstay in all of the things you tried to do?*

SrB: Well, let's just put it simply – with God and the Holy Spirit that moves each one of us. And I feel that God is that creative spirit that moves us to do what's good and there's this bond between His people and us. I would say that it is really God who is at the centre of all of this.

EL: *What would you like to see happen now?*

SrB: I'd like to see the Centre with more students right now because to get the people – and I don't know if it's my fault – to get the people to come to the Centre from the area, the immediate area, is like pulling out your wisdom tooth. They don't want to come and, if they come, they want to accomplish whatever is to be accomplished immediately. They want money, they want to be paid, even though you are paying for the materials, you are paying the tutor and the whole course is absolutely free – we don't charge one red cent. But you can't get these people to come. Last September we started with 12 girls around the area and concentrated on teaching these 12 girls how to make garments, because the Free Zone and those people are always asking us. They feel that the girls are disciplined. You know. They come to work on time, they take their one-hour lunch break and they are back. Whereas, if they are coming straight from their home, they don't have this kind of discipline – they have no idea of time. Well, they stayed less than a month and they started to drop out one by one. We tried to make it so attractive – we gave them materials, promised them that when they learned to sew, they could sew from home, we would get them machines – but that never helped. The people we have the most success with are the people from outside of the area. We have girls from Bull Bay, Stony Hill, and Edgewater and there are a lot of people who appreciate this more than anything else.

VJC: (*Condensed*) *Do you think that the problem is that life is not hard enough because they can always find something to eat, or that we are making people dependent on handouts?*

SrB: We try to make them self-sufficient but you know what is the problem? The money that comes from foreign (abroad), especially more so now.
At Christmas, foreigners come – one gives out twenty thousand at a corner,
one gives out ten thousand at that corner – and there is always this idea that
they try to get away, you know.

VJC: *It must be disheartening because you are trying to help the people
from this area first.*
SrB: Yes, I have all these hundreds of kids who leave Holy Trinity every
September and you want someone to work in the bakery. It's like searching for
a needle in a haystack. And when you get one, they drive you up a wall. You
have to exercise an enormous amount of patience.

VJC: *One last question: Do you have a Chinese name?*
SrB: Rona Chung – Moy Yin

January 12, 1998

Edited by Sonia Gordon Scott.

Down Memory Lane

Negril, Westmoreland
Photograph ©Ray Chen

Phyllis Kong
CONVERSION OF THE CHINESE TO ROMAN
CATHOLICISM: A BRIEF ACCOUNT

WHEN BABY Blanche Acquee, daughter of Mr. and Mrs. Daniel Acquee formerly of Glengoffe, was baptized on November 13, 1904 in the Roman Catholic Church of the Holy Family, Cassava River, St. Catherine, it set in motion the conversion of the Chinese in Jamaica.

A few years later when the Acquee family moved to North Street in Kingston, Blanche was sent to the nearby St. Anne's Primary School that was run by the Franciscan Sisters of Allegany. Since Blanche was a baptized Roman Catholic, the school principal Sr. Agatha, O.S.F., arranged for her to be prepared for her First Holy Communion and, later, to receive the Sacrament of Confirmation. From then on, Blanche became an enthusiastic apostle, bringing her siblings and friends to Fr. Leo Butler, S.J., pastor of the church, for instructions. Fr. Butler was thus faced with an apostle among the Chinese as, over the next several years, Blanche continued her work of conversion of young Chinese with the assistance of her sister Eva. Fr. Butler soon became headmaster of St. George's College and turned to Sister Sylvia, O.S.F. to assist with instructions, as more Chinese boys and girls continued to join the Roman Catholic faith. Conversion was carried further when Fr. Simon Tang, S.J. of Canton, China, while on a tertianship programme in New York, was assigned to conduct a mission among the Chinese in Jamaica. Fr. Tang's work extended to Chinese adults who knew little English. He was ably assisted by William Pinchin, an influential Chinese businessman in downtown Kingston. By 1925, the number of Chinese Catholics had increased to 3,000 through these efforts.

ROMAN CATHOLIC EDUCATION

The Roman Catholic schools were also instrumental in the process of conversion. Chinese parents learned to entrust their children to the Roman Catholic priests and nuns for the discipline and solid moral training that they instilled in children attending the Catholic Church and schools. Such virtues were the same as those handed down within the Chinese culture. In the beginning, Chinese children of the first generation attended Catholic elementary schools but some did not go beyond that level because they were required to work in the family grocery shops. Yet the Catholic faith was firmly implanted in those children who had received only a few years of Catholic education at the elementary level. As the years went by and Chinese families became more financially secure, it was possible for the children to remain as students, moving to the next level of education in high school.

Many of the boys were sent to St. George's College where Fr. Butler, S.J., was the headmaster and with whom they were already familiar. In 1950, Chinese boys accounted for forty-three percent of the student body at St. George's. The girls were sent to Immaculate Conception High School, which was operated by the Franciscan Sisters, and the Convent of Mercy Academy (Alpha), which was operated by the Sisters of Mercy. The Chinese were known to be an industrious people and so the children pursued their studies with natural talent and ambition. In addition, Chinese parents taught their children that, through education, they would be able to progress in life and be relieved of the hardships that they the parents had to endure.

In 1960, of the ninety-one students at St. George's College who passed the Senior Cambridge (Ordinary level) examinations, forty-seven were Chinese; of the thirteen who passed the Cambridge Advanced level examinations, five were Chinese. Thus the opportunity was created for many Chinese who excelled in high school to go on to higher learning at universities abroad, some through scholarships awarded them, and afterwards to enter the professional fields of medicine, law, engineering, architecture etc., and even religion.

VOCATIONS TO THE PRIESTHOOD

Through close association with the religious orders, a number of Chinese Catholics responded to the call of vocations to the priesthood and other religious orders. Four of those called to the priesthood were the diocesan priests Rev. Fr. Kenneth Kong, Rev. Fr. Alfred Lee Sang, Monsignor Kenneth Mock Yen, and Rev. Fr. Richard Ho Lung, founder of the Missionaries of the Poor (M.O.P.).

Rev. Fr. Kenneth Kong: Three years after graduating from St. George's College in 1954, Rev. Fr. Kenneth Kong entered St. Michael's Seminary in Kingston to commence studies towards the priesthood. Nine years later, having also studied at St. John's Seminary in Brighton, Massachusetts, Fr. Kong was ordained in the priesthood on June 16, 1966. At his first solemn Mass offered at Holy Trinity Cathedral in Kingston, four Chinese took part in the offertory procession: Dudley Chai Onn, William Look Hong, and Carmen and Marlene Kong.

What inspired Fr. Kong to enter the priesthood? The lifestyle of the religious orders and their dedication to God, he says. In particular, Franciscan

Sisters Martinella and Terrence Marie at St. Anthony's Elementary School and, later, Jesuit priests Fr. Leo Quinlan and William Rafferty at St. George's College had inspired and encouraged him. It has been 47 years since Fr. Kong entered the seminary and 38 years since his ordination. He continues to serve as Assistant Pastor at Stella Maris Church on Shortwood Road in Kingston, having previously served at various parishes in Kingston and Montego Bay. The years have been fulfilling, he says, and he's happy.

REV. FR. ALFRED LEE SANG: The Rev. Fr. Alfred Lee Sang was born in Kingston on March 24, 1935, the third of ten children of George Lee Yim Sang and his wife Lily Liu Swee Len. Following graduation at St. George's College in 1954, he entered the teaching profession at Campion Hall Preparatory and afterwards at Chinese Public School, where he taught English and Mathematics. He then moved to the private sector and worked in the airline industry for 20 years, starting with BOAC/BWIA in 1960 and ending with Air Jamaica, to which he had been sec-onded when that company commenced operations in 1962.

In 1981, Fr. Lee entered St. Michael's Seminary, finally giving in to a call to the religious vocation which he'd had since high school and with which he had been struggling over the years. After studying at St. Michael's, the University of the West Indies, Mona, and at Loyola University Chicago in the U.S.A., Fr. Lee was ordained a Diocesan Priest on September 29, 1985, along with Rev. Paul Collier and Rev. Kenneth Richards. There was a grand turnout of the Roman Catholic laity at the Holy Trinity Cathedral that day, for it had been many years since there had been an ordination of native Jamaicans. It brought hope for the continued spiritual care of the people of Jamaica.

Fr. Lee has since been assigned pastoral duties in several parishes in Kingston and in the deep rural areas of St. Mary. He currently serves as Associate Pastor at the Church of Reconciliation in Portmore, St. Catherine. Although Fr. Lee did not enter the priesthood early in his life, he has always been closely involved with the Church and in social services. He has been happy being a priest for the past 19 years and has experienced deep peace with the Lord. "I thank God for this vocation," he says.

MONSIGNOR KENNETH J. MOCK YEN: Monsignor Kenneth J. Mock Yen was baptized at Holy Trinity Cathedral, Kingston, in 1939, the year he was born to Joseph and Hilda May (McGhie) Mock Yen. He grew up in that parish and later taught Sunday school until Sr. M. Ignatio, O.S.F., sent him to assist at St. Anne's Church. At St. Anne's, he got close to Jesuit Fathers Charles Eberle, Harry Mallette, Leslie Russell and John Alexander, and was fascinated to learn that Frs. Russell and Alexander were Jamaicans. When Fr.

Russell died, he offered to become a priest but that was not to be at the time. As time went by, he also met Jamaican Diocesan priests Monsignors Richard Watson, Joseph Vidal and the then Fr. Edgerton Clarke, who later became Archbishop of Kingston.

Monsignor Mock Yen's early years were influenced by the Franciscans: Sister M. Daniel Sullivan, O.S.F., and Fr. Mathias Manly, O.F.M. Through them, he became a member of the Third Order of St. Francis. The years in the Third Order inspired him once again to offer himself to the priesthood and the then Bishop of Kingston, the Most Rev. John J. McEleney, S.J., D.D., encouraged and then accepted him at St. Michael's Seminary in September 1963. Monsignor Mock Yen studied also at St. Joseph's Seminary in Liverpool, following which he was ordained a Diocesan priest in August 1970. A few years later, in 1974, he did further study overseas and obtained the Master of Sacred Theology (1975) and Doctor of Ministry (1977) degrees. In 1991 he was invested as Monsignor and from 2002-04, he served as Vicar General for the Archdiocese of Kingston.

Monsignor Mock Yen has served on the boards of a number of Church associations and in the public service, and has been assigned to several parishes in Kingston. He continues as Pastor of Sts. Peter and Paul Church where he has been since 1981. He enjoys singing and with his melodious voice has, on occasion, treated his congregation to a solo or a duet performance with Miss. Theresa Menzies during meditation at mass.

Rev. Fr. Richard Ho Lung, MOP, receiving the Poverello Medal, Franciscan University's highest honour, for witnessing in the spirit of St. Francis.

REV. FR. RICHARD HO LUNG, MOP: In 1959, the Rev. Fr. Richard Ho Lung, MOP, entered the novitiate for Jesuits at Boston College in Massachusetts following graduation from St. George's College in 1958, and was ordained a Jesuit priest in 1971. During his years of study, he has obtained M.A. degrees in English (1968), Philosophy and Divinity (both in 1971) and a Ph.D. degree in Humanities (1974). Fr. Ho Lung has also taught English and Theology at the University of the West Indies, at Boston College, and at St. George's College.

In 1981, he made the painful decision to leave the Jesuit Order to establish a new religious community of men – Missionaries of the Poor (MOP) – who would dedicate their lives to the service of the rejected and destitute in Jamaica. However, it was not until October 7, 1997, that the Missionaries of the Poor was officially recognized by the Vatican. By then, he had already established several centres in Kingston, housing retarded, destitute and homeless adults and children, of varying ages with various needs. Fr. Ho Lung has since extended his mission overseas to countries such as India, the Philippines and Haiti, garnering postulants along the way.

Fr. Ho Lung also has an interest in and talent for music and the theatre, and has written over 300 songs and musical plays for live stage performances in Jamaica and for overseas tours, for which he has received awards. In 1991, he received the Pro Ecclesia et Pontifice Papal Award in recognition of his service to the Church, and in 2002 he received the Poverello Award from the Franciscan University of Steubenville. Perhaps his greatest honour has been to receive visits at his missions in Kingston from Mother Teresa in 1986, and His Holiness, Pope John Paul II in 1993. With 33 years in the priesthood of which the last 23 have been with the MOP, Fr. Ho Lung continues his service to the poorest of the poor and to God.

Researched and written by Phyllis Kong and edited by Sonia Gordon Scott.

Sources of information:
History of the Catholic Church in Jamaica, by Francis J. Osborne, S.J., Chicago: Loyola University Press (1988)
Personal interviews and sundry articles.

Down Memory Lane

Meeting point of the Rio Grande and the Back Rivers with the John Crow Mountains in the background, Portland

Photograph ©Ray Chen

Cecil Ho
*THE 'CHINESE CHURCH' - SPREADING THE
WORDS OF THE LORD*

IN THE SIXTIES, Swallowfield church was commonly known as the 'Chinese' Church because, at that time, most of the congregation was made up of the descendants of the Chinese who first came to Jamaica – eighty-five percent Chinese and the remaining fifteen percent, non-Chinese.

Today the numbers are reversed and Chinese make up less than five percent. Swallowfield is a multiracial church with a growing congregation that runs in the hundreds. Under the leadership of Cecil Ho, who is the only surviving Elder and one of the original founding members, the church has continued to grow with a registered membership of over seven hundred. Hundreds more attend services who are not registered members. A true testament to our motto… "Out of many, One People".

You have to wonder how this came about, and, in looking back…

Swallowfield was born from the vision, dedication, and hard work of

Hubert and Helen Gallimore

Hubert and Helen Gallimore. They had been missionaries in China for more than fourteen years, serving the Christian Missionary and the Alliance Missionary Boards before returning to Jamaica, due to the escalation of the war between China and Japan. Between them, they had a vision for starting a mission among the Chinese-Jamaican community.

From humble beginnings, they established evangelistic Mission Services for Sunday School, and a mid-week prayer meeting was also held at homes. Soon a variety of activities were established such as Bible Study, and other teaching and social activities were also planned. To the enjoyment of the members, many Easter and summer camps were held at the home of the Gallimores.

Easter camp 1952.

The Gallimores deliberately encouraged the members of the mission to join up with some local evangelical churches while maintaining their involvement in reaching the Chinese community for Christ. While mid-week services were held at members' homes, Sunday School activities were held initially, at the First Missionary Church, East Street, and then in the early 1940s at the

Moravian Church at Duke and North Streets.

It was largely the teaching of Helen Gallimore that had the greatest impact in the lives of Cecil Ho and other Chinese members, who were to play a greater role in the Mission.

In 1948, when the Gallimores retired and moved to Mandeville, they asked several believers to form a committee to continue the work. This committee included Cecil and Eli Ho, the late David Ho and others. The original founding members numbered thirty in all and were made up of Chinese and non-Chinese Jamaicans.

Young Cecil Ho and Eli Ho.

Cecil's father taught himself English by reading the Bible and he encouraged the boys, Cecil, David and Raymond and their sister, Leneda, to be active members of the Mission. Their parents later became disciples for the Lord.

As the work continued to grow, there was a strong desire to acquire a property to centralize the activities and to develop the ministry more effectively. It was also felt that the work should be consolidated into a local church since a number of the believers, especially the older Chinese, were reluctant to join any other local church.

A decision had to be taken as to which denomination the new church would be associated with. There were three major considerations:

(i)   It was felt that the Jamaican situation would not allow for an independent Bible church;

(ii)   The mixed nature of the society made it unwise to form an ethnic church and;

(iii) There were three denominations with which the work had been closely associated: Associated Gospel Assemblies, the Missionary Church Association, and the Assemblies of Christian Brethren.

The decision was taken to become part of the latter, and a significant percentage of the members of the new church were persons who transferred from other Assemblies, particularly Maranatha.

Boys Quintet

October 1970 saw the completion of the Chapel and the official inauguration or birth of Swallowfield Chapel at a Service of Dedication. On the Oversight Team were Henry Wong, Eli Ho, Harry Leung, Cecil Ho, David Ho, and Leslie LimSang. The dedication coincided with the launching of an intensive two-week crusade.

Shortly afterwards, the first baptism was held. Teams, led by Eli Ho, conducted island-wide gospel meetings. A male quintet and a female quartet ministered in music, and the work continued to grow.

Girls Quartet 1950 and the gospel team of 1951

The major aim of the Assembly was to minister to the Chinese community, primarily to those who did not speak English. Because of the high percentage of Chinese in membership, the church was then called the 'Chinese' Church, and during Sunday morning services, the sermons were translated into Chinese by Brother Eli Ho. Translations were discontinued in the seventies, partly due to events that took place as a result of the socialist policies of the then present Government. Those policies caused many Jamaicans, Chinese included, to migrate overseas and the church lost many of its Chinese members.

For almost thirty four years Cecil Ho has devoted his life to the Mission and he is still very active in its administration. He remembers with fondness the time when he was a young boy, wearing short pants, and going to the same church on Duke and North Streets.

"We give you thanks, O Lord, for your loving kindness, for Your truth and Your Faithfulness to us here at Swallowfield Chapel." Cecil Ho.

Written on behalf of Cecil Ho and edited by Sonia Gordon Scott

All photographs are from the personal album of ©Kathleen (Kay) Chin.

Roger Chen
THE CBA TEMPLE

IN THE HEART of old Chinatown on Barry Street in Kingston is the old Chinese Benevolent Association building which now lies unused. Perched high on the third floor of this building is what's left of the Temple where past generations of Chinese citizens came to pay homage to their ancestors.

Confucius taught that one should honour one's parents and, by extension, one's ancestors. Zeng-tze, a pupil of his (and a CHEN), wrote extensively on the filial duty of a son as taught by Confucius. It is through the practice of these teachings that westerners believe that the Chinese worship their ancestors. If you call extreme devotion and love for your parents worship, then it is so.

Nevertheless, in each home and village in China there was an altar dedicated to the former head of the household, or the founder of the village. In the home, usually in the greater sitting area, there would be a little tablet flanked by two candles and a small offering of a fruit or two, usually an orange or persimmon. Above the tablet would be a charcoal sketch of the former head of the household. The family would 'bai sin'*, or pay respect, to the spirit of the ancestors on all occasions that should be celebrated – the birth of a child, weddings, families visiting (like those coming from overseas to visit for the first time), the day of the 'Ching Ming' festival, families leaving and, sometimes, a death in the family.

In the village, a special ancestral hall or 'chiu tong'* houses the tablet recording the founder of the village. It gives the history of the founder – where he originally came from, when, his full name, birthday, when he died, and the names of all his sons. His wives and daughters all go unrecorded. It is here that most family celebrations are held, and where the new bride performs one of her first duties – paying homage to the ancestors of her new family. Here also is where all the family records are kept – who married whom, when, how many children there were and all their names and birthdays, who left the village and where they went – really the history of the village. Unfortunately, during the Cultural Revolution, Mao wanted to cut the ties of the younger generation with their ancestors and so encouraged the Red Guards to destroy all family records. This way, if you couldn't identify with a 'family' then your loyalties would be to the State or country. Thousands of family records were destroyed and lost forever.

When the Chinese migrated to Jamaica, they brought with them their Buddhist and Confucian beliefs. But they were from different villages and clans and still desired to fulfill their filial duties. So they built a temple to the patron of their region. In the temple hidden on the third floor of the CBA building, is the altar with Tam Gung sitting atop the dais and looking, with an unobstructed view, south-ward over all the surrounding buildings out to sea. This is fitting because Tam Gung is the patron for the Hakka people of Guangdong province as well as for seafarers in South China. Several stories are associated with his name – that he has the power to perform miracles, and that he was one of the organ-izers for the protection of the boy emperor of the Song Dynasty, when the Mongols pursued them into south China. His surname is 'Tam' and they call him 'Gung' out of respect.

The Altar, the place to worship the ancestors.

No matter where you 'bai sin' to pay homage to your ancestors, the ritual is identical. It's as follows:

- It is customary to bring food offerings to the patron and ancestors; it could be simply a cooked chicken and some fruits or, if at the ceme-tery during the Ching Ming celebrations, a whole roasted pig plus fruits and liquor.

- Before the official bai sin starts, several rounds of firecrackers are set off. This is supposed to inform your ancestors that you are here and wish to honour them. Some say that it is to drive away all evil spirits lurking around.

- You light three incense sticks for each receptacle in the temple hall.

- Standing before the altar, you raise the bundle of lit incense sticks in front of you and above your head, while you tell the patron or your ancestors why you are there. For example, to report that there has been a new child added to the family, or that the son of a former res-ident has returned to visit the family village, or that you are the new wife of one of the village resident, among other things.
- You bow three times from the waist while you are doing this.

- Then you place three sticks of the lit incense into each of the recepta-cles.

Top: Symbols of the weapons that were used to protect the spirit of their ancestors.
Above: Wooden tablets that show the records of the founder of the village. his full name, birthday, when he died and the names of all his sons. These are usually kept on the table at the altar.

- If there is a gong or drum installed in the temple, you strike it three times to complete the ceremony.

- Gifts of "ghost money" and other paper offerings are also burnt to send them up to your ancestors for their use. Paper cars, houses and appliances are not unusual these days.

Another reason people come to the Temple is to seek guidance from the patron. Citizens come to the temple to *qiu qian* (to divine by the lot, otherwise known as consulting the fortune sticks) before Tam Gung. The oracular tool is a bamboo tube that holds 103 narrow bamboo sticks, each stick bearing a number. The ritual of divination is:

- Holding the bamboo container, the person kneels down in front of Tam Gung and continuously shakes the bamboo tube holding the sticks while repeating the question he/she wishes answered.
- Eventually one stick gradually rises above the others and falls to the floor.
- The number on the stick is noted, and the slip with the corresponding number is taken from the rack and read.
- The oracular verses on the paper are the responses from Tam Gung.

There are two types of 'fortune sticks'. In the temple is the one using 103 sticks. The verses are from the oracular book called 'Tian Hou Ling Qiann' (the Queen of Heaven's Efficacious Oracular Sticks). Sometimes they are so mysterious that you often need a professional *qian* decipherer to explain the meaning of the verses.

The other bamboo tube has 78 'fortune sticks' and uses the verses from the 'I-Ching' for the answers.

Sometimes a person might come to seek a prescription for their malady. Instead of consulting the fortune sheets, they would get a prescription of Chinese herbs with the same number as that of the stick.

Written by ©Roger Chen and edited by Sonia Gordon Scott

Photograph ©Ray Chen.

* See Glossary

Fay Chang Allen
CHANG'S EMPORIUM (HALF WAY TREE)

MY FATHER, Percy Chang (Chang Wei Bin), was born in the village of Tam Shui, Hui Yang County, Kwantung Province, China. He came to Jamaica in 1921 at the age of 13 to work for his uncle, Albert Chang, at Community Store, King Street, Kingston. On April 12, 1931, he married my mother, Alice Chin Loy, who was born at Sandy Gut, St. Catherine, and together they started their own business in a small rented shop with living quarters at 90 Half Way Tree Road. He later bought 86 Half Way Tree Road and, on August 15, 1947, papa opened Chang's Emporium. Half Way Tree was so named because it was half way between Constant Spring and downtown Kingston. Its defining landmark is the clock tower, which may well have replaced one of Jamaica's storied cotton trees.

Mr & Mrs Percy Chang at their Silver Anniversary in 1956

Chang's Emporium was located between Powell's Bakery (now Clock Tower Plaza) to the north, and the world famous Glass Bucket Club to the south. Dairy Farmers was down the street, and Mr. Lim Shue's shop was up the street at the junction of Half Way Tree, Constant Spring and Hope Roads.

Across the street was a Texaco Gas Station, the Half Way Tree Post Office, Cock O' the Walk Bar, and beside this was the waiting room for the tram car. Yap Chung's grocery was at the corner of Hagley Park Road and the beginning of Constant Spring Road by the clock tower. Holy Cross Church and Holy Childhood School were across the street diagonally south of our shop.

Chang's Emporium in Half Way Tree

Up to 1947, there were two tram cars running from Victoria Pier through Orange Street and Cross Roads to Half Way Tree. One would continue and terminate at Constant Spring, and head back to Victoria Pier using the same route. The other would turn up Hope Road and terminate at Papine. If you lived in Half Way Tree you could take any of these trams. From Victoria Pier a third tram went to East Street and out to Rockfort. Half Way Tree was a suburb and Constant Spring and Papine were considered country.

Mule-drawn dray carts were in common use to deliver groceries, and sometimes my cousins and I would hop on to the back of the dray for a short ride to Half Way Tree Square. The water trough for the mules and donkeys was at Hope Road next to Mr. Lim Shue's shop.

Our playtime activities were simple and great fun. Mimi, Egerton, and I would play jacks on Granny's steps, and our favourite yard games were skipping rope, marbles and hop scotch. We skipped to "Room for rent apply within, when I run out you run in...", and "Mosquito one, mosquito two, mosquito jump into hot callaloo...". Later, Glen, who was a year younger than I, was allowed to join us.

The beds when I was growing up had springs with coir mattresses on top. They had iron frames with legs and small wheels. One night at bedtime, we were all jumping on the beds and having a rowdy time, when the bed Glen was jumping on slipped through the rotten wood of the old flooring and ended up going through the shop ceiling. We were shocked into silence at the sight of the lopsided bed, and afraid that we were going to be in big trouble. We quietly crept downstairs as the shop was still open and, sure enough, there was the leg of the bed sticking out of the ceiling. Surprisingly, papa never said a word. I think he was more relieved that the whole bed did not come crashing through the ceiling, kids and all.

Then, as now, nothing can more quickly spoil a good summer holiday from school than to have chicken pox or measles. When I came down with these illnesses for two consecutive summers, and my two cousins were similarly afflicted, granny, my mama's mother, would kill one or two of her pigeons and make delicious soup for consolation (and healing). Granny had come from China at the young age of sixteen via Vancouver, across the Rocky Mountains by train, and then by sea again from New York to Kingston. Her journey is an odyssey by itself. She lived next door with my Uncle Ernest, Mimosa (Mimi), and Egerton's father, Uncle Butty (Albert), and Uncle Herbert. Although we lived separately we all lived 'together'. It was Uncle Herbert who gave me my first dancing lessons to the tune of "Jealousy".

Mimi, Egerton, my brother Astor and I loved to skull* Sunday school. We would take long walks going in the intended direction towards Holy Cross Church, but we would then continue on to Ruthven Road, Trafalgar Road, and down Hope Road back to Half Way Tree. We were often tempted by the smell of roasting peanuts and the siren sound of the vendor's steam whistle. If we had money we would buy one packet of his mouthwatering peanuts and share it.

Because mama was a first generation Chinese Jamaican, she could be very Chinese, or Jamaican when she was ready. She knew all the Jamaican expressions. As all children, we loved to run around and play hide and seek in the dark. Mama used to say to us, "Mind! chicken merry, hawk dey near". To teach us to save and to have patience, mama would use the Jamaican saying,

"One, one cocoa full basket". Another was "When yu han in lion mout, tek yu time draw it out", and another "If yu want good, yu belly mus' run" and, "De humblest calf suck de mos' milk".

Cheddar cheese and butter, staple products, were delivered in very large, circular blocks which had to be cut by hand. Papa and Tai (papa's trusted employee) would stand at opposite ends and slice the cheese with a fine wire until it was small enough to use a knife to cut it into quarter, half and one pound pieces. We would hang around watching this endeavor hoping for the tasty smaller slivers to come our way.

Broken eggs were never wasted from the shop's refrigerator. We would add salt and black pepper and slurp it down our throats. Boxes of tomatoes stacked high were a treat, especially with salt added. So were American apples, pears and grapes. Living above a shop was convenient as we never ran out of food. If the shop was closed for the night, all we did was lift the trap-door and go downstairs for whatever we needed.

The shop was never completely closed except on Good Friday and Chinese New Year. Even on a Sunday, it opened until lunch was ready and papa would lock up. But even then, our meal was always disturbed by some-one coming to the side gate asking us to sell them something. Sunday was always a short day for papa. He would often sigh and say, "Sunday dun a'ready".

In 1950, papa decided to double the shop and living quarters upstairs. The family was growing larger. There were now 11 children and another on the way. Being a 'hands on' person he supervised the building of every inch of the Supermarket, starting from the foundation of reinforcing steel to the pouring of the concrete. Old Mr. Adams, his foreman, was constantly at his side. It was exciting to see a building start from nothing and progress into a shelter for a family and a business. I can still smell the wonderful aroma of newly cut wood. Mahogany, cedar and pine were sawed and planed by hand to make showcases, gondolas and shelves for stocking out goods .

It was during the building of the second half of the supermarket, in 1951, that Hurricane Charlie decided to vent his fury on Jamaica. The storm hit us after nightfall and the first big gust of wind blew down the fence from Cock O' the Walk Bar across the street. We had to flee from upstairs because some of the zinc was soon blown off the roof, and the rain was pouring in. Egerton was the baby. Lucky for him mama picked him up from her bed as we all ran downstairs to take cover under the concrete area of our front veranda, which nowadays would be called a family area. Her bed was soaked when she went back upstairs. Papa, mama, Tony and G (Alsalita) spent the night sweeping out water which came pouring into the shop. We were all so occupied in deal-ing with the situation, looking after each other and buoyed by the strength of our parents, that fear did not occur to us, which was a blessing since it was such a dangerous time.

The following day, after Charlie had passed, it was bright and sunny. The shop was opened for business as usual. Customers, who had not taken this hurricane seriously were left without food, and the shop did brisk business.

In opening Jamaica's first supermarket in 1951, papa took a daring risk, especially for a man essentially alone as the breadwinner and with so much family responsibility. From his example all of us learned a valuable life lesson about the entrepreneurial spirit, and the rewards and satisfaction of working hard which, hopefully, will be passed on to following generations.

Inside Chang's Emporium.

As Jamaica's first supermarket, it caused quite a stir in the island. Of course, being good Catholics, the place had to be blessed. Fr. Thomas Glavin, S. J. came and as he stepped into the shop and passed the two cash registers, he said 'these have to be blessed first' and this he did with much ceremony. He then continued to wash everywhere with holy water, including the children.

Our customers had to be taught to serve themselves and push their carts around. Those of us children who were old enough were recruited to help in this. With my lack of patience and quick temper, I would often be in trouble for back-talking the customers. As a shopkeeper's child, I had to learn that the customers were always right.

Because we were the only supermarket stocking imported foods, our customers included some famous names, amongst them were Noel Coward, Errol Flynn and Oscar Hammerstein. The Governor of Jamaica was also a customer, although not exactly full self service. His groceries had to be delivered by bicycle. He was not alone, as other customers who would call in orders requested delivery.

Living beside the world famous Glass Bucket Club was like having entertainment in our backyard. Mr. Joe Abner, an American, was the owner. He brought to Jamaica many live celebrity shows, including Xavier Cougat and Abby Lane. Later, Mrs. Abner had floor shows with local songs and dancers which were equally entertaining. I loved the calypso and mento music. "Linstead Market" and "Open the Gate", were two of my favourites and I would sometimes copy their movements, which were not at all ladylike in those days. This would put me in big trouble with mama.

Papa built a platform at the back fence between ourselves and Glass Bucket. It gave us great pleasure to have nightly entertainment (if a little 'pirated', to use today's language), as we all climbed up to watch the shows. In the '40s and early '50s the people who went to the Glass Bucket wore gowns and tuxedos, or suits at least. They were like a show themselves. Christmas Eve and New Year's Eve were gala events. We all stood wide-eyed admiring the guests.

It was on Christmas Eve in 1948, that our little sister, Jennifer, died at five months of age. I remembered we were standing on the platform watching a show when we were called down. Jennifer was a blue baby. The Panamanian

Consul, a doctor, had told my parents that when she was a little older she could be taken to Miami for an operation, but that was not to be. Poor mama, she held on to Jennifer and would not let her go. She cried for her baby all night. Jennifer was buried on Christmas Day, a sad day for all of us. Mama said she was the prettiest of all her children.

As time went by, the Chang family grew to thirteen living children; two died very young. Anthony (Tony) was the eldest, then Alsalita (G), Annette, Astor, Fay (that is me), Glen, Patrick, Gail, Elizabeth, then the four small boys as we keep referring to them. The eldest of the four was Victor, then Egerton (Paulie), Xavier and Nicholas (Nicky). We were the baker's dozen.

The Chang family

As the family grew, the older ones had to care for the babies as mama was busy helping in the shop. They had to be fed and bathed, and made to have their naps in the afternoon. Egerton was my charge, but I also inherited Victor as Annette went off to Nazareth College in the States. Putting them down for naps, I would lie with both of them beside me and pretend that I was asleep. I was the one who would doze off and wake to find that they had slipped quietly off the bed and were running around downstairs in the shop. It was a tug of war to get them back upstairs, holding on to one and running after the other.

We had helpers, but their time was taken up with cleaning, washing and ironing. Being a big family, there was a lot of housework to get through each day. The older girls would also be relied on to help set the table and wash the dishes. We were also given the task of giving the younger ones their vitamins and breakfast in the mornings, then later washing them up for prayers and bed at nights. Papa and G did most of the cooking.

I felt important when papa would call us to help him count money for deposit to the bank. We sat around one of our two dining room tables and stacked 12 pennies, 20 shillings, and half crowns (two shillings & sixpence). Papa would make sure the count was right by the height of each stack. Here I witnessed first hand the value of those long hours of work in the shop.

A regular event for us was the Sunday morning (7:30 a.m.) children's mass at Holy Cross Church. In the church we would see many families, including Mr. and Mrs. Wong Chew Onn and family, the Aston Chen family and us, the Chang family. We were required to be on our best behaviour and if we got fidgety, there would be ominous glares and the suggestion of unspeakable consequences for misbehaviour. As we crossed the road to head home, papa and the four small boys, in their pajamas, would be waiting for us (a sort of dress reality check for us, 'prettied up' for mass), and we would all walk home together to a sumptuous breakfast which papa had prepared.

A favourite pastime on a Sunday was to stand at the open windows of the front veranda and count the cars driving by. In those days not many people had cars. Our 1939 Buick was replaced by the first automatic control Plymouth Station Wagon. It was nicknamed 'The Battleship', and the name was well suited as the chrome luggage rack looked like the railing of a ship. It gave us sterling service.

As a special treat after finishing our Sunday chores, the older children in our family would take the bus to see a movie at either Carib or Tropical Theatres. In the fifties, it was safe to take the bus to go anywhere in Kingston. When we came home we would discuss the movie, and eat again before going to sleep. Papa always told us never to go to bed on an empty stomach, but we ate because as young adults we had very healthy appetites.

Mama wanted the girls to learn the things she did not have the opportunity to learn since her parents could not afford this. So she sent her girls to take piano lessons at the Narcisse School of Music at the corner of Cecelia Avenue and Half Way Tree Road. Miss Lisa Narcisse's home was large, with a wrap around veranda and a beautiful garden. We could sit on the veranda and do our theory lessons, or in the garden. Miss Narcisse was a gentle, pleasant lady who was always smiling. Mrs. Beryl Mair also taught, and she was upstairs. She was a little stern, especially when I did not practise my piano piece to her standard. I preferred to have Miss Narcisse teach me!

Gail, Elizabeth and I were taught ballet at Hazel Doran's Ballet School. This was at Villa Maria on Old Hope Road. We would have a lift going to lessons but, returning from ballet, Tai, who was papa's trusted person at the supermarket, would ride his bicycle to come for us and we would all walk home under his watchful eye. From Villa Maria, we would turn on Oxford Road, where we used to admire the lovely large residential homes and their well manicured lawns. From Oxford Road we turned north on Half Way Tree Road past the Telephone Company and headed home. Miss Doran once had a ballet recital at the Ward Theatre. Both papa and mama were in the audience, and they were proud as we had good reviews in *The Gleaner* the following day.

I enjoyed ballet lessons, and would sometimes play the piano for hours. I had fun just going through our piano books, picking a piece, and if I did not like it I would go on to another until I found one I enjoyed, which I would practise until I knew it. Sometimes, Tony and Annette would sit by the piano and sing 'Martha' from Little Fantasy, or 'Beautiful Dreamer' together while I played. Both Tony and Annette had the best singing voices in our family. Annette also played the piano very well. She was my mentor.

TV had not come to Jamaica as yet so we all made up our own fantasies. Gail, Elizabeth, and I would play a classical record on the gramophone and pretend we were prima ballerinas on stage, as we danced our hearts away. Of course, Glen would invite himself and imitate us, much to our delight. He loved to dance the part of a toreador, stamping his feet in time to the Flamenco music, and I would lift my skirt and dance around him. His favourite record was Tchaikovsky's Nutcracker Suite especially Waltz of the Flowers. He also liked O Holy Night at Christmas.

Even in a large family it was easy to get in trouble with mama or papa. For me, a lapse in controlling my temper was all it took. They contrived to let me get over it as we would say today. I would lock myself in the drawing room for hours. Naturally, I would get hungry and stick my head out to ask Gail for biscuit and cheese. Neither mama nor papa paid any attention, and finally I released myself from my self-imposed punishment.

Papa loved gardening. His first garden was a small plot on Mr. Cargill's land where he planted vegetables. As little girls, he would take us to help him and later, he bought two lots on North Odeon Avenue and two on South Odeon Avenue. He made his garden on the North Odeon lots. He was happiest tending to his plants, and we enjoyed helping him. Having papa to ourselves, and without the worries of the shop, he was very relaxed which was a joy to us.

During the summer holidays, papa would take us over to St. Andrew High School to play cricket. The teams were made up of the older children mixed with the little ones. We did the running around for the ball. Papa preferred to bat and bowl.

I loved when it rained at nights. The sound of rain clattering on the zinc roof, feeling the security of being neatly tucked under the covers in a warm bed, and knowing that my parents were near.

Papa used to make his rounds, covering us. We loved to say he was counting his children. When the girls got older, he would say, "Ma, go cover your daughters". As a child whenever I felt ill I always wanted papa, who would lift me in his arms and it was a comfort. Whenever I had a cold, out came the Vicks Vapour Rub, or the Thermogene, and he would rub my chest and back with his healing hands. He would say, "Dr. Spododum will get you better". Yes, he was our family's own Dr. Spododum.

It was about this time that Tony met Winnette. They were married at Holy Cross and the reception was held at the Glass Bucket Club. Having Winnette was like having another sister. She would make sure I was well groomed when I went to parties. She combed my hair and plucked my eyebrows, and took great care to put on my make-up.

How did I ever get this old? Sixteen, and I did not know any boys to invite to my Sweet Sixteen Birthday Party! Well, lucky for me, I had a bunch of good girlfriends who invited the boys for me. The party was a success, and even to this day, some gentle guy from days gone by would confide that he was at my Sweet Sixteen Party and I did not know.

Suddenly, all my friends were having Sweet Sixteen Birthday Parties and I was invited. It was torture to ask my parents for permission to go to a party. I think they invented the word TORTURE. Mama would say "ask your father"; Papa would say, "go ask yu modder", and this would continue for half an hour before I would get permission, of course, not before answering their questions of whose party it was, who the parents were, and promising to be home by midnight.

As Chinese, we never mixed with non-Chinese children. Some of my friends were Mavis and Barbara Chang, Rosalie Chen, Joyce Wong Chew Onn, Terry Wong Lim, and my cousin Marie Chance. We would gather upstairs 'Changs' and play table tennis on the front veranda. Terry was a favourite with papa. She was so exuberant that papa named her 'Live Wire'.

Every Saturday night was a party night, every public holiday was a 'Day Jump'*, birthday or basket party. We danced through our teenage years. Whether the boys kept the girls constantly turning to the Rock and Roll beat, or 'rent- a- tile' to slow music, it was a wonderful time to be growing up. It was good, clean fun and everyone who grew up during the '40s and '50s would agree 100 percent that it was the very best time of our lives.

The Wong Chew Onns had a big house where Premier Plaza is now located. Joyce, their daughter, and I were good friends. We both attended Immaculate Conception High School. My parents would allow me to visit Joyce since the families knew each other. They had large Alsatian dogs who loved to growl, snarl and bark whenever anyone approached the gate, but I was never afraid of them. Eddie and Sammy used to hang around us girls. Sammy was my first date if you can call it that. We walked to the Odeon Theatre to see a movie, and guess who was sitting behind us? Yes, my brother, Glen, my self-proclaimed protector and my knight in shining armour.

We always looked forward to Christmas as it was an exciting time of the year. We would start shopping from the middle of the year to be finished buying our gifts in time for Christmas. Trimming the Christmas tree took a whole day and all the children in our family were involved. Of course, having the shop downstairs was great. We sold everything for Christmas including all the imported fresh trees and trimmings. We always thought our tree was the best. We would spend the entire day just trimming our tree, and every night until the tree came down, we would just sit and be mesmerized by all the beautiful coloured lights, especially the bubble lights. Presents would be added everyday until the space under the tree was full.

Papa would know exactly what present he wanted to give mama. He would give G the money to buy her gift. Mama must have been the first to own a set of Clairol Heated Curlers, because of the American advertisement "Shame on you" for women going around with curlers in their hair.

Christmas was not only for the family but for the supermarket customers as well. One Sunday before Christmas was set aside for us to help wrap chocolates or liquor for our good customers. It was a chore, but it had to be done to show our appreciation for their business. I remember mama with the list of customers, ticking them off as each present was selected and wrapped.

G and I went to Immaculate Conception High School but, like all good girls, I was always in trouble with Sr. Davidica, our Headmistress. I was always in the most misbehaved classroom in school. Many a time we would be in trouble, not only with Sr. 'D' but with the Prefects for not wearing our jippy jappa* hats. Sr. Anne told us to pray to St. Jude (the Saint for Hopeless Cases) when we took our Senior Cambridge Examination which was in November. I remember going to Anna Wong Lim's Sweet Sixteen Party during our exams, and G keeping me up nearly all night when I came home to study Biology.

One Sunday, around mid-morning, Sr. Emmanuel from Immaculate came into the supermarket. She asked papa, "Where are the girls?" papa, with a lifted eyebrow, told her his Princesses were upstairs sleeping! We were not, but we never lived it down with Sister.

Papa's princesses were vain indeed. Goya powder and perfume permeated the air upstairs Chang's in the afternoons as G and I bathed and dressed ourselves to help in the shop. Tony and G, as the older ones in our family, helped papa and mama in the shop.

Learning to sew my own clothes was a necessity. I could take 1 yard of cloth and make two tops. Making the cloth 'stretch' was my skill. Papa would look at me with feigned disgust when he saw my dress with the back cut out nearly to my waistline. Crinolines* were the fashion and they were starched very stiff. By the time I graduated from Immaculate, the shift* was in fashion. At graduation, we had to wear white under our white gowns. I made my shift dress and was very proud of my design, but Sr. Ambrose was horrified when I took off the gown at the end of the ceremony. She asked one of the girls to quickly put something over me as I was walking around in my slip, but this did not deter me from always trying to be 'in fashion'.

In January we started commercial classes. Sr. Ambrose was a saint to have us in her class. She was in such a hurry to be rid of us that Marie and I were the first to be chosen to be interviewed for a job at Standard Life Assurance Company, at the corner of Barry and Duke Streets. In the office we passed Dickie HoLung and Leighton Hugh, diligently pounding at their typewriters. They were learning to type.

It was natural for Dickie, Leighton, Marie and me to make a foursome. We would go to the movies and later head to the Courtleigh Manor Hotel to dance to Sonny Bradshaw and his Band. Dickie was a good dancer. He was also full of jokes and laughter. Dickie is Fr. Richard HoLung. God called him to His service, but we still have wonderful memories of those special times.

"We wish you a Merry Christmas, we wish you a Merry Christmas, we wish you a Merry Christmas and a Happy New Year......Now bring us some Figgie pudding, now bring us some Figgie pudding, now bring us some Figgie pudding and a cup of good cheer". Our group from the Chinese Catholic Action Association merrily sang our hearts out, and brought Christmas cheer to the Hanson Leper Home in Spanish Town at Christmas.

Since most Chinese were Catholics, the Chinese Catholic Action Association brought our young people together. Our Moderator was Fr. T (Thomas) Darling Glavin, S.J. We went on many picnics together, sitting on planks at the back of a truck, and also going on a Pilgrimage to our Lady of Assumption in Morant Bay. Sometimes there would be wiener roasts at night at Brooks Pen Beach around a driftwood fire. These were memorable times for me as it seemed we were always singing and having a good time wherever we went. Reggie Chin and Albert Lyn were always making us laugh at their jokes. Alfred Lee – now Fr. Alfred Lee – had a good singing voice, so did Marie Chance.

Being crowned Miss Chinese Athletic Club in 1959 was the biggest shock of my life. There were many other lovely girls, but somehow I was chosen. It gave me self-confidence to move on to other chapters in my life, and, for this I am grateful.

On November 25, 1961, I was in New York studying when news came that my beloved brother Glen had died in a car accident at Central Village. He was returning from a Byron Lee dance in Spanish Town, when the car in which he was a passenger went under a parked truck. This was a terrible shock, and I will always believe that whenever someone you love dies, a part of you dies with them. I was left with an emptiness in my heart. He was just 21 years old. Papa and mama never recovered from this loss.

As our family reeled with grief, Fr. Dennis Crutchley, S. J., Pastor of Holy Cross Church arranged the entire funeral. The Chinese Catholic Action Association, priests, nuns and friends were of great comfort and support during this period of despair. Glen had always been an altar boy at Holy Cross, and there were many who have told me that we lost the priest in our family. God had taken him to a higher service.

As you can see, our parents had lots of hungry mouths to feed and educate. This was a feat, and they accomplished it to great admiration from us. My mother insisted that we should have a good education. We all went to private schools and had our High School education. Annette, Astor, Gail, Elizabeth, Victor, Egerton, Xavier and Nicholas all went to Universities overseas to complete their education. I was not into going for higher education, so I went to study my beloved fashion at the Fashion Institute of Technology in New York City. This school was chosen by Annette, who was at Fordham University. She wanted to make sure I had a degree (Associate in Applied Science), and if I wanted I could continue to University. This did not prove to be the case, but my time in New York prepared me for a fulfilling period of my life working in the fashion business. I am forever grateful to the wisdom of my parents and their insistence on the need for good education.

I am most grateful to have been born in Jamaica of Chinese parents. I have had the best of both worlds. I have my Chinese upbringing and traditions, and my Jamaican roots and humour. I especially enjoy the rhythm of a good calypso or a "Tiny Wine-y".

Written by Fay Chang Allen and edited by Sonia Gordon Scott

* See Glossary

Roger Chen
MEMORIES - GROWING UP IN ALLMAN TOWN

WE MOVED TO Allman Town, 9 Prince of Wales Street, when I was about 3 years old. I think I was 3 because I recall my brothers, Washi and Ray, attending the public school beside us while I stayed at home. The school had a zinc fence all around, and the south side of the property was lined with Acacia trees. The caretaker lived beside the school at the top of Lord Elgin Street but I don't recall his name, only that Alvonia Lyn and her mother also lived there. Across the street at the corner where Lord Elgin Street turned south was the little grocery store, run by a black proprietor, where we used to buy snow ball (shaved ice with syrup poured over it).

Kitty-corner to our shop was the shop where the Changs had their business... I can only remember Hermine, Mavis, Joe and Winston living there. Two houses to the west was the home of the Blairs who had many children. They had an open back truck and a contract to haul citrus. I recall they would sometimes return from the farms with the truck overflowing with oranges or grapefruit, and the boys would throw the fruit to the locals from the back of the truck. They were offered free land in Australia's outback and the whole family moved there. Dad kept in touch with them. I can still see Mr. Blair sitting in his rocking chair, holding that contraption he had screwed into the bulb socket, and administering his shock therapy. Sometimes when they didn't have electricity he would come over to our place to do it.

This shop was called 'Peace Conference Grocery' after the event that took place at the end of WWII, and was located at the corner of Prince of Wales Street and Lord Elgin Avenue. Like all 'chiney' shops it had living quarters attached to it. You had to step up, via a wooden step, into the common living room. The only bedroom on this side was also off from the shop. Behind the living room was the kitchen and bath. It was really one large area with a raised concrete dais on top of which 2 or 3 coal-stoves rested. A sink and wash-up area was to the right. In this corner also was the bathroom, complete with a slatted wooden floor and the familiar wooden stool. A single cold-water faucet was attached to the wall.

"Peace Conference Grocery" Allman Town

Three other rooms were across the courtyard from this building. They were rented out

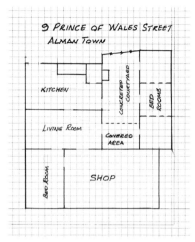

9 PRINCE OF WALES STREET
ALMAN TOWN

KITCHEN

CONCRETED COURTYARD

BED ROOMS

LIVING ROOM

COVERED AREA

BED ROOM

SHOP

separately to three spinsters (I believe they were sisters of the land-lady, Mrs. Gibbs). There was a lady in the room beside the kitchen who would always hail me to thread her needle. Poor lady was far sighted and had a huge growth on her right cheek, but nevertheless did her own sewing. As these tenants died off, dad added the rooms to our living quarters until we had all three rooms. He added a fence from the end of this row of rooms to the back of the kitchen, then concreted the whole area and added a zinc-roofed shed behind the shop.

Before we took over the three rooms, the ducks and chickens used to live under the raised floor of the building. Of course the smell of their nests and droppings permeated up to the rooms, but that was nothing compared to the odour of decaying flesh of ducks that died under the cellar. Dad had to pay the 'gui-jai'* to get rid of the car-casses and he eventually had the openings to the cellar blocked off.

But nothing could beat the outhouses. They were at the back of the prop-erty, and ours, the middle one of three in a row, was the only one with a light. It had a big hole and a small hole... not even a seat over the hole. And before you sat to do your business, it was customary to slam the cover at least three times to drive the roaches away from the hole. But if you lingered too long, as happens when you are reading comics, you would feel the tickling of your bum from the feelers of the roaches. That meant it was time to complete the paper work and leave.

Fruit trees grew vigorously on the property around the outhouses, and the guineps were the biggest and sweetest you ever saw or tasted, the breadfruit tree bore in abundance, and the mangoes, black and Hayden, were the best you could eat.

Easter was a big event. The Gibbs would bake their traditional Easter buns in the big wood stoked oven in the kitchen. They would make huge round buns and the aroma of the buns baking would cause you to drool for the end piece.

My first school was Bognor's Prep., run by Mrs. Boothe. She had a com-mercial school initially, but was persuaded by my dad to start the prep school for the benefit of the numerous Chinese families that were in Allman Town at that time. There were us (the Chens), the Changs (Mavis and family), the Lees (Doris, Mary etc.), the Youngs (Dorothy), and other families.

Bognor's Prep School

The mango trees in and around this property were the centre of attention: bombay, common, number eleven and black mangoes. During mango season we could hardly concentrate on our lessons because, with each rush of wind, we would hear the ripe mangoes rustling as they fell through the leaves, ending with a 'buff' on the ground. We could hardly wait for classes to end to rush out and claim the prize. Stoning the tree was also a seasonal pastime, but not all stones thrown into the tree came down to earth immediately. One day our class was held under the huge lignum vitae* tree, and one of these errant stones decided to come back down. Guess whose head it landed on!

'Chebby chase' or 'it' as they now call the game, was a favourite among us kids, and we ran everywhere, even on top of the roofs of neighbouring houses. One day, to avoid being caught while being pursued on the roof, I jumped onto the branch of the coolie plum tree that was beside the building. They don't teach you that these limbs are brittle, so when I landed on the limb it broke and I came crashing down with the limb. One of the branches almost tore my right arm off, and I am lucky to have only three stitches as a souvenir and reminder of this incident.

Bognor Prep School - circa 1945

My mother's first cousin, Tai Yee, visited us often along with her daughter, Gloria, and their cousin, Pearl Wong. Many nights we used to sit on the bed over in the extension eating roasted corn and telling ghost stories about 'rolling calf'*. We used to bet our kernels on the game paper-hammer-scissors. After a session of ghost stories none of us would venture to cross the courtyard to the main building, even though no more than about twelve feet separated them.

My first 'puppy love' was Juliet Harris who had long blonde hair and lived two houses away from the school. I would spend many afternoons after school at her house with her and her sister, Irene. One of my treasured possessions was my collection of lyrics that I cut out from the newspaper and pasted in an old exercise book. Before Juliet and her family moved to Vancouver, Canada, she borrowed my book. That was the last I saw of both Juliet and my collection of lyrics.

*Race Course now known
as National Heroes Park*

Race Course, that big expanse of 'police macca'*, was not far away. We were forbidden to go there, but nevertheless we would sneak over there on race nights to watch the cycle racing, and to hear the familiar "two, two, two,…" of the announcer warning the cyclists that there were only two laps remaining. This was where Ray lost his front teeth. Taunting and stone throwing would erupt between local gangs, and one day an errant stone caught Ray in the mouth. Many Christian groups from the States would stage meetings here, as would the circus and Coney Island with bumper cars, and they would bilk the locals of their monies also.

In spite of the police macca, the tall grasses and the summer months were a special time for lovers. Hidden by the darkness and the grasses, they would have their trysts in anonymity until one night, under a moonless sky and an onshore evening breeze, some mischievous person lit the dry grass. The gently waving grasses suddenly came alive with couples rising from the ground like ghosts from the grave and scampering away, some with bicycles in tow, others with blankets dragging behind them. What a sight!

Welli, our eldest brother, liked biology and zoology; I remember him spending Sundays dissecting rabbits, and studying cockroaches. I got the one and only scorpion sting because of him. Those of you who recall the living conditions in Jamaica in the 1940's, especially in Allman Town, can relate to this. Welli wanted some cockroaches for his science class, and although he didn't think twice about handling them dead, he didn't like to catch them, so I had to catch them for him. There were always roaches under the wooden step that led from the shop into the living area, but you had to be quick in grabbing them because as soon as they saw light they would scatter. I had caught some already, but there was what looked like a big one in the corner of the step:

> Welli: *"Get that big one!"*
> Me: *"No, dat a scorpion!"*
> To which he commanded: *"No, put it in the bottle."*

Like an obedient younger brother, I grabbed the scorpion. Bare handed. I don't remember what I said when the scorpion stung me, but I'm sure there were some nice Jamaican phrases in there.

Speaking of scorpions, whenever mom or dad saw one they would get the scissors or a pair of tweezers to capture it. It was then placed in the collection bottle... all scorpions with their stings intact, soaking in white overproof rum. They would use this 'liniment' for pains or stiff arthritic joints. My theory is that the venom from the scorpions would permeate the alcohol and, when this is applied to the area of the pain, it would provide some analgesic relief.

And talking about pain... I recall the whipping we used to get from mom if we misbehaved. She would, with one smooth motion, grab the 'gai mow sow'* that was stuck in a hole in the cornice of the doorway, and whack us across the calves. This 'gai mow sow' is a feathered stick duster made out of cane. Sometimes we would run away to hide behind the bedroom door amongst the clothes hung there, or under the bed. But if she caught us, we'd get two whooshes on the calf. And woe betide us if the weals were still there when dad came home. Without question, if he saw weals we would get another licking. Supplementing the feathered stick was the usual 'gat chuk'*, or knock on the head with her knuckles, and the twisting of the ears. But we would always get a hug when we settled down. Mom, wherever you are, we love you.

As was common in Jamaican families of that era, every summer we went through the ritual of 'The Wash Out' to strengthen and cleanse our internal organs, especially the stomach and intestines. We were given this at the start of and end of the summer break. It began with a dose of cod liver oil – a tablespoon full each morning for a week. Then we were given a choice of either Brooklax or herb tea. Brooklax was like Exlax, a laxative in a chocolate base. Don't let that fool you... it was never pleasant to take. Herb tea was a concoction prepared by Benjamin's pharmaceutical company, packed in a rectangular tube in a curry coloured wrapper. It is the vilest beverage a kid could ever take, even when it was sweetened with condensed milk. The effect of either of these was a whole day or two of the runs. You dare not stray far from home.

There was another twist to the end of summer ritual besides The Wash Out. Because we ate all kinds of unsupervised snacks we had to be 'dewormed' before returning to school. I don't recall if this preceded or followed The Wash Out, but it involved taking of an innocent looking Chinese candy, conical in shape, but possessing the necessary pharmaceuticals to rid your intestines of worms accumulated during the summer.

Many itinerant vendors came by the shop. There was the barber who came once a month to cut our hair. We sat on a stool in the yard where he draped us in a cloth and clipped our hair with his hand clipper. For the occasional treat, there was the Chinese man with a broken arm riding his bicycle with the 'shut pan'* strapped on the back cradle, coming to sell sow bow* and won ban*, steamed Chinese buns and puddings. My favourite sow bow was the one filled with crushed peanuts and sugar. And there was 'Bag o' Wire'. He was either a Syrian or Jew who carried a burlap sack and bought scrap metal from everybody. This was a war effort to recycle all metal products.

The bed that I shared with Washi and Ray was of a metal frame with steel slats held in place by coiled tension springs. It was topped with a mattress made of coir (the outer coconut trash) and ticked throughout with bits of cloth. I was given the inside position, against the wall, so that I would not roll off. But there were occasions when I slept alone that I would awake to find myself under the bed. I had rolled off, and then rolled back under the bed.

All of us who grew up in Jamaica at that time know what 'bed bugs' are.

These tiny insects, when they were not controlled, made our sleep miserable and peppered our skins with red blotches from their bites and our scratching. Each month the bed would be purged of these pests. The mattresses would be beaten and the ticking and rolled edges would be separated and inspected for bugs. Occasionally we would get the flit gun* and spray them with DDT. (In these days of environmental concerns and with our knowledge of health issues, these are not actions we would take now). Their favourite hiding place was in the coils of the bedspring. Not only would we poke the coils with kerosene oil soaked rags to drive out the bugs, we would spray the coils to make sure that any that the rags missed would be killed by the DDT. They were quick and not easy to catch, but the most effective and environmentally safe method was to prepare a special soap. You soaked this bar of soap in a dish of water until it became soft. Armed with this you lifted the ticking, prepared to slap the bar of soap on the bugs which would become embedded in the soft soap before they got a chance to run.

There were three kinds of soap available to the general population: sweet soap, like Palmolive; carbolic – generally used as a disinfectant soap – and brown bar soap. The latter was an extruded brown soap that was about a foot long (~30 cm). It was sold by the inch and was the soap of choice by the poorer population. It was rather soft, so it didn't last too long for washing. To overcome this, mom used to set aside several long bars to allow them to age or harden before use. Before the advent of powdered soap, the household helpers would use these bars to wash the clothes. They would scrub them in a tub on a washing board, and all whites would be boiled in a large oil tin, which had been cut open and washed to get rid of the oil. The tin was filled with water, the whites were added, and the tin was set on stones over a wood fire. The washed clothes would be hung on a line or spread on the zinc roof to 'catch the sun'. Those that were yellowed were rinsed in water containing 'laundry blue'.

During the wet, rainy season when the mosquitoes were out, so would be the mosquito net. It hung from a nail in the ceiling above the bed and was tucked in around the mattress. You would enter this 'tent' through an overlapping slit in the netting, making sure that no openings were left. If even one mosquito got in, that night would have been a restless one.

HURRICANE CHARLIE: AUGUST 17, 1951

I was only nine going on ten years old when Hurricane Charlie struck. Looking back on the event, I recall my dad telling us four boys to move from the back rooms, which were separated from the main building by a courtyard, to the bedroom beside the shop.

That night the winds howled and the roof leaked. All four of us huddled in one bed in the same room as our parents. When the winds ceased temporarily, apparently when the eye of the hurricane was passing over us, dad opened the window and looked out. Then following the instructions that were previously issued by the government, he blocked it open so as to equalize the pressure in the room when the winds returned from the other direction.

The next morning I remembered looking out the window into the courtyard only to see that the roof of the building where we, the children, would normally have slept, was completely blown off. You'd be looking up at clear blue sky. And all the Jell-O in the shop was soaking wet. I managed to eat a pack before dad told me not to. I remember also the coconut trees blown down and the street boys having their fill of coconut water and jelly! These are the only memories I have of it.

VISITS WITH THE WONG CHEW ONN'S ESTATE ON CONSTANT SPRING ROAD

While we lived in Allman Town, Mr. & Mrs. Wong Chew Onn occasionally picked me up on their way home on Fridays and I would spend that weekend with them. They were very close to my parents because Mr. Wong came from the same village in China as dad... Tien Sim Wei.

I remember the mango trees in the back lot... and yes the tall grasses that towered over me. They had a big round fishpond filled with goldfish in the middle of the turn around in the front of the house. There was a pump swing in the middle of the front lawn and we would spend hours, or what seemed like hours, in that swing until the mosquitoes ran us in. What stands out in my memory is the low concrete wall that fronted the property. And the huge barn-like garage where so many bicycles and wagons were stored... heaven for a kid that could only dream of having one.

There was a huge kitchen off on another wing of the building with strange contraptions to my child's eyes. I can see now the huge hot water boiler stoked with wood. In those days, hot running water was the ultimate luxury. Only cold showers for us in Allman Town and at Molynes Roads.

The first time I saw guinea chicks and geese was up there, roaming free. And the three big dogs. I recall also that they had a refrigerator that ran off kerosene oil!!

Lots of fond memories.

MOLYNES ROAD

We moved to 50a Molynes Road around 1953-1954. This was Molynes/ Four Roads where the No.13 bus ended its run; the boondocks of greater Kingston. I was just entering my teenage years and we had to take the bus everywhere we went. We could take the

Chen's Enterprise Molynes Road

*St. Andrew Parish Church
at the corner of Hagley
Park and Eastwood Park
Roads - Half Way Tree*

bus in front of the Government Buildings at King and Barry Streets in downtown Kingston, pay a double fare, and travel directly to Four Roads. Or we could take the Constant Spring bus to Half-Way Tree, walk over to the corner of Hagley Park and Eastwood Park Roads, and catch the bus by the church and cemetery. If we were coming home late at night, we would make sure to stand right under the streetlight – to keep away the duppies*. Or we would make sure to join any group that was waiting there. When I started riding a bicycle, on reaching this corner my speed would noticeably pick up and I would be whistling and singing until I reached 21 Molynes Road... the two storey shop where Jumby and his sisters lived.

I remember when we first moved there the bombay mango tree never bore any fruit. Had never borne fruit from what the previous tenants said. Then the carpenter from White Horses, St. Thomas told me that I should "beat the s—t out of it if it no bear fruit." I couldn't see what that would do, but I didn't have anything to lose, so I took a machete to it and chopped the lower trunk all around. That summer the tree bore mangoes for the first time, and for the whole year.

*Molynes 'four roads'
intersection*

We raised chickens and ducks and had a large chicken coop complete with perches for them. Mom bought me 2 pairs of pigeons and soon I had to be building pigeon boxes on a regular basis, they multiplied so rapidly. Occasionally a stray pigeon would join our flock when it mated with one of ours. Any new birds we bought, chicken or pigeons, had their wings clipped to prevent them flying away. By the time their feathers grew back, they called our place home and would always return to roost.

We tried to grow vegetables behind the house but the only thing that grew successfully was gungo peas. The soil was tough and no amount of manure from the chicken coop would make it productive. The only good thing from the gungo peas plants was the leaves that mom used to prepare a footbath for my frequent athlete's foot infections. I suspect I got the athlete's foot from wearing the same infected shoes daily, not realizing that I kept re-infecting my feet. The itching and cracks would go away after one or two treatments of the gungo peas leaf bath.

Welli bought me an air rifle and I became quite good at shooting moving targets which I hung in the mango tree, as well as the numerous rats that the grocery store attracted. One Sunday mom and dad were ready to leave to visit someone when, for some reason I can't recall, I shot one of the drakes. What a chastisement I got that time! Mom had to change back to regular clothes to gut the duck before they left. They took away the gun for a long time.

Our parents also taught us how to kill and clean the chickens and ducks. We would hold them by the wings and head in our left hand, pluck the neck of feathers before slicing their throats and draining their blood into a saucepan that had some salt in it. When the blood coagulated, we would cut it into cubes for soup. The fowl we would put into the cistern and cover with a pan until all the thrashing had stopped. The feathers would be plucked after we poured hot water over the carcass to make plucking the feathers easier. Then the fowl would be gutted. There was one time we were killing a duck and, after the thrashing had stopped, I lifted the pan only to see the duck with its head off to one side standing up looking back at me. We had to cut off the head completely.

One day in the shop there was this kid that made a nuisance of himself. I took it upon myself to hit him with the feather stick. That was a mistake I would never repeat. The boy returned with his uncle who spoke to dad about the incident. Dad apologized for my behaviour, and then called me to stand before the uncle and apologize as well. Then he took down the feather stick and handed it to the uncle and told him to strike me as well. I was never so frightened in all my life. The uncle never struck me. He accepted our apologies and left.

Living at Four Roads shaped my life to this day. I never drink alcoholic beverages because of what I observed there. Doctor had the bar across the street and every Friday and Saturday night the workers would spend a good deal of their pay getting drunk. Some would be so drunk that they would be rolling on the street in front of the bar unaware of what the street boys were doing to them. These scenes made me resolve never to put myself in that situation, and from then I've stayed away from liquor.

But there were humorous sides to helping in the shop. On pay day if a man came into the shop and called one of us over to the side we knew instinctively that he wanted condoms. Some would also order Guinness stout and a can of condensed milk. The opinion was that this would make them virile for the night and give them unbelievable staying power... '50s Viagra. Young working ladies would come in looking for blue corn flakes – our code name for Kotex.

SHOP EXPERIENCES

Life as a child in a 'ham tdiu poo'* is an education in itself. On Mondays and Tuesdays we spent the slack periods wrapping crackers in 6 and 12 units. The water biscuits came in a huge wooden crate (about 2'x2'x3') and they were sold by the dozen. Sometimes lunch would be a few crackers with a slice of herring, or a piece of salt fish. The herring or salt fish would be roasted in the ash of the coal stove that was always burning. During pear season lunch would be a bulla* cake and a slice of avocado pear. Mattress* or spring (mattress with icing) together with a soda, especially Nugrape from Kellys, was also a favourite lunch combination.

Other things we would pre-wrap for the Friday and Saturday rush were butter, peppercorn and salt. We rolled small cones for the peppercorns and wrapped $1/4$ lb packets of salt. The New Zealand butter came in 100 lb blocks and we would spend a whole evening cutting and wrapping it. We would cut the butter with a piano string with wood blocks at the ends. Sometimes the butter would come in pre-wrapped in 1lb units. We were adept at cutting this so that we could get nine '$1/4$ lb' packs from two 1lb packs. The profit to the small grocer was so small and was controlled by the government, which had price control and set the selling prices for all commodities. Dad used to tell us that when we used a can of condensed milk from the case of 48, we already lost money on the case. Another way of increasing their margin was to add water to the dry codfish. These came in huge wooden barrels from Canada and they were usually quite dry. So to increase the weight, the shopkeeper would take out the fish he hoped to sell for the week, and spray water on them. The dry fish would absorb some of the water and the now moist fish would increase his yield from the barrel.

How can you make large sums of money from a 'ham tdiu poo' when the average customer comes in for "half a gill a coconut oil, one Zephyr cigarette, and a quattie* wot a salt pork"? On top of that, preferred customers could come in with their books to 'trus' the food. i.e. take the groceries on credit. The customer or servant would bring in the book into which each transaction would be recorded. In theory the accounts should be settled at the end of the week or month. But some well-to-do persons never paid their bills.

The chances we took as children in the shop! Saltine crackers came in a rectangular tin container, with very sharp edges. Most tinned stuff or paper products we would haul down from the shelf and catch. But we took chances with these tins of biscuits. We hauled them down the same way and caught them, oblivious of the fact that the sharp edges could inflict a severe cut to our hands. Not to mention that if we dropped it the whole tin of biscuits would be useless.

In December the Christmas decorations would go up never to come down until after the Chinese New Year. We would cut strips of crepe paper, twist them and string them from around the perimeter to the centre of the shop where we would have a cluster of balloons or a paper bell. Our shop would always have music being played from the living room. Mantovani, the Troubadors, Nat King Cole, some classical pieces, hits of the day... you name it, we played it. Then there was the earthquake that struck on March 1st 1957. I remember leaning into the shop at the door from the living room when the earthquake struck. Ray was in the shop at the time, and I could see all the groceries on the shelf rocking back and forth. Ray then turned to hold the doors of the glass cases closed because they had all the wines in them. Other than being frightened to death we were okay... and nothing broke that day.

In our family we need only mention 'the grapes...' and it brings back memories of an incident that at the time brought a lot of rage in the family, but now we laugh at it. It began with a grapevine that Welli brought home before he left for his studies in Canada. That would be 1953 just after we moved up to Molynes Road. For six years it grew and never once hinted that it would produce a bunch of grapes. Then in the spring of 1959 it blossomed, and we were so overjoyed that we paid special attention to the vine. A single bunch of grapes grew and each day we watched it mature, longing for the day that it would be ready to be picked and shared amongst the family. We figured that in a few days more we would taste the grapes. Before that day arrived, Washi had a friend come over to visit. He went to the back yard to look for Washi, then a few minutes later returned to the shop with the bunch of grapes in his hands, picking each one off, eating them and commenting on how sour they were. We were all livid, but mom would not allow us to tell that 'friend' that we did not appreciate what he had done. This is the memory 'the grapes' elicits from us.

During the summer of 1962 I returned from Canada for Ray's wedding. I was in the shop one day and thought I would be helpful in ridding the shop of some cockroaches. I had seen some hiding under the tin sheet cover of the counter, and decided that I would kill them with a spray of insecticide. Big, big, mistake. I removed the wrapping papers from the slots under the counter, then proceeded with the flit gun to spray between the sheet and the counter. I had never seen so many cockroaches in all my life. They scampered from every nook and cranny of the counter and ran every which way. Fortunately it was a quiet period during the day. Roy, our helper, and I were mashing and squashing roaches everywhere. I never bothered them again.

REFLECTIONS

The other day I had to reflect on Mom and her learning English. It dawned on me that she was learning to speak English at the same time we as kids were also learning to speak English. She came to Jamaica never having been exposed to English, started a family in a strange country, and had to survive. I can never forget the difficulty she had in pronouncing 'purple'; the best she could do was 'purp', but she always had a good laugh over it.

Family was a priority to our parents. They always made sure we met and got to know our immediate families. That's why Welli and Washington spent summers with the Chen-Sees in Springfield, St. Elizabeth, and Ray spent time with the Williams' in Sav-la-mar, and I spent time with Tat, Carmen, & Maggie at Snowhill, Portland. Each summer I would take the 'Gleaner'* car over to Snowhill for a week or two, and Tat or Carmen would come back to Kingston for holidays. We grew up together like brothers and sisters so that today our bonds are still strong.

The earliest recollection of mom's affection for us is of our visit to Tai-yee on Spanish Town Road. I was maybe about 4 years old. We were on our way home after one of our frequent visits with them. We came downstairs to hail a buggy (maa-cha or horse-drawn carriage) and at the same time some rowdy street-people came by, grabbed mom's purse and ran away with it. She had it under her arm as she helped Ray into the buggy. We were all afraid. But I remember mom hugging me close, and moistening her finger tips with her saliva, gently rubbing my ear lobes and saying "mn kong, ah; mn kong" ... "don't be a fraid, don't be afraid". All fears melted away in her arms.

Speaking of Tai-yee's place on Spanish Town Road, it is the only place I know of that had a trap-door over the stairs that led from the business downstairs to the living quarters upstairs. You had to climb the stairs, knock on the trap door so that anyone near the opening would clear away, before you lifted the trap to access the upstairs.

As teenagers there were always parties to go to, especially basket parties on Saturday nights. For families not tied to a grocery store that was okay, but for the rest of us it meant that we had to lock up shop before we could go anywhere. By 10:00 p.m. we were already cleaning up in anticipation of closing the shop at 11:00 p.m. sharp. Stanny would already be there waiting for us, so we wasted no time sweeping up, washing up the chopping block and machete, covering all the perishables, then barring the doors. We would then rush for a quick cold shower, dress, and be gone off with Stanny to the party of the night.

Some parties dragged on late enough for us to attend 5:30 a.m. mass right away, followed by driving to the beach for the rest of Sunday. But if we had to come home early, I mean 4:00 a.m., one of us had to scale the fence to open the gate that was latched from the inside. Then we had to enter from the side entrance to the bedroom. No matter how quietly we crept in we would always hear mom asking "Hon Wei, is that you? Are you okay?" then she would be quiet after we answered "yes". She would wait for us to be home and be satisfied that we were okay before she could fall asleep. That was how much she loved us. On holiday weekends, we would plan a whole day's outing to the north coast, to Puerto Seco or Dunn's River Falls. We would hire a truck with wooden slat seats, pack picnic baskets or boxes, and a whole truckload of us would be off for the long weekend. Those were really good times.

1959 and 1960 must have been a very sad, proud, and stressful time for mom and dad. Washi left for England in August 1959 to pursue his dream in ballet, and nine months later I emigrated to Canada to study engineering at McGill University. Six years before, their eldest son, Welli, left for Canada, and now we followed. Sad, because we were now leaving only Ray and Lillian behind with them... their children were now leaving home for good. Proud, because we had followed their teachings and urging to be the best that we could be. We knew also that we could not disappoint them, their hopes and dreams rested with us. Stressful, because now we may need to call on them for support while away; because they now had fewer hands to help in the grocery; and because they would miss the children that they had raised and loved so dearly. At that time I never gave it much thought, I was just caught up in the excitement of leaving home. But I have now had the experience of my own children leaving home and I can appreciate the stresses and heartaches we had caused them. But our situation was a little different from theirs. Our children were only a few hours away and they came home during the school breaks. We left for another continent, at a time when communication was expensive and not as convenient as today. And our leaving must have brought back memories of their journey from the village of Tien Sim Wei in China to Jamaica.

Written by Roger Chen and edited by Sonia Gordon Scott.

* See Glossary

Down Memory Lane

Postage Stamps
remind us of the historic events
that took place and of the people
that sometimes made it happen.

* *The Coronations of Kings*
  and Queens
* *Abolition of slavery*
  proclaimed in 1838
* *New Constitution, 1944*
* *The First Caribbean Scout*
  Jamboree, 1952
* *Jamaica at Expo 67 in*
  Montreal, Quebec, Canada
* *University College of the*
  West Indies celebration
* *Winston Leonard Spencer*
  Churchill, 1874-1965

Before and after Jamaica's
Independence in August 1962

Rose Chin
GROWING UP

I ALWAYS THINK back to the times that were impressed most indelibly in my mind in my growing up years, and my thoughts seem to always centre around the period I spent in primary school on the corner of Fleet and Laws Street, East Branch, later to be called Holy Family, which was run by the Mercy Sisters, also known as the 'Sisters of Mercy'.

The classes were co-ed and there were very few Chinese. There are fond memories as this is the place where I got my first 'love letter' thrown through the window at me, by a very good looking, light skinned boy called Robert Smith. I got them daily in variations of the following:

Roses are red, violets are blue, sugar is sweet and so are you !!!

We must have been about six years old…, not only my first love letter but my first 'blush'! Ah, the innocence of youth!!!

Then there was a particular little boy who really hated me (or so I thought). He would call me 'chiney nyam dawg', as well as when I passed his gate on Laws Street to go to school in the mornings, he would run out of his gate and give me a rass lick* in my back. It was stressful to go to school and I would always be in tears. Remember those were the days of pen nibs and Lion ink. Well, I decided that I was not going to take this anymore. One particular Monday morning as I passed his gate, he looked over with his usual 'greeting'. With my ink bottle top unscrewed and well placed in my left hand, I waited for him to pounce on my back with his fist. Was he ever sorry after I flashed my uncovered ink bottle, and laced him with its contents all over his face and his nicely pressed and starched uniform! All he could do was scream for his Mama. I never 'nyam dawg' for him anymore after that.

I also learned from Sister Theresa Rose responsibility. I was in charge of doling out the free crackers, cheese and skim milk to each child although, if I did not like the girl or boy, they got the skimpiest amount. I also learned from this blessed nun that being poor was not an excuse for not reaching for the heights of greatness…she taught me that reaching for the moon but landing on a star is really not so bad.

Ink bottle and pens.

Written by Rose Chin and edited by Sonia Gordon Scott.

* See Glossary

Photographs ©Ray Chen

Monica Chen
GOOD OLE PORTY

AS A CHILD GROWING UP in a rural village about six miles from Port Antonio, life was, to say the least, exciting. At the age of four, you woke every morning in anticipation of what *could* happen today.

First, you were awakened real early to get dressed and have breakfast to be ready for the 'bus' when it came by. This 'bus', which travelled from an unknown place called Kingston, was the one that took you back and forth to school in Port Antonio, but sometimes it never arrived having 'broken down' on the way. Two alternatives were presented then – walk the two miles to the railroad siding to catch the Diesel coach (you would then arrive at school after 10 o'clock), or stay home and re-study your homework.

Of course, we always opted for the latter solution as, behind our shop was a vast pasture-land overflowing with guinep and guava trees. At the first opportunity my siblings and I would sneak through the gate in the fence and run for the trees. But sure as fate – in ten minutes time – there would be calls shouted in Chinese: "Aayaah – where you gawn*? We need you 'cun poo*'", and if you took too long to return you'd most likely get a 'gat chok'* in your head.

To us then, life in a 'ham-teaw poo*' was harsh; at the constant beck and call of customers for "gimme quattie flour", "serve me trupance salt fish and me no waan no tail." But it was even more harsh for the villagers in this rural area. I did not understand what they did to earn a living, and even the very basics were missing. Water was obtained from a spring two miles away, where they also did their washing and took their baths maybe once weekly. While we had two gas-lamps in the shop, and three "Home Sweet Home" lamps in the living area at the back of the shop, what did the villagers do for lighting? We had a Caledonia wood burning stove, complete with oven, but how did they cook?

We had rain gutters installed on half the side of the shop/house that led into three or four huge drums to store the water when it rained, and whenever there was a drought the 'gweema'* had to fill at least one of these drums – zinc-pan by zinc-pan of water carried on her head from the spring.

Every morning before starting breakfast, the Caledonia stove had to be cleared of the previous day's ashes and re-stocked with wood, and on Saturdays the 'gweema' had to blacken and polish the stove. This was done last, *after* a full day spent cleaning the wood floors in the living quarters. The floors were cleaned by first wiping with red ochre, then melted wax was put on a coconut-husk brush and, on her hands and knees with the heel of her right hand hitting the brush, she 'went to town' making a rhythmic drum-like sound as she polished the floor with vigorous back and forth movements of the brush. One sure didn't lack exercise in those days!

Entertainment? We had never heard the word and I am sure neither did the hard-working villagers. I remember we had a Victrola – called a record player these days – that had to be wound by hand and, of course, there was only one brand name: HIS MASTER'S VOICE. It stood about 5 feet tall, far above my head so I could not wind it, and I cannot remember ever hearing it played. In any case, we had only two records which seemed to be church hymns. The logo was fascinating: a bull-mastiff sitting beside a huge loudspeaker. I always used to wonder if this dog really heard his master's voice when this thing was being played.

As children, the only life we knew was at school or in the shop as we were not allowed to visit or mix with the villagers. Caught talking or laughing too long with a 'gweesi'* child, you might just get another 'gat chok'. So any little thing that broke the monotony of a day would be considered exciting and would be talked about for weeks after. Even the arrest of a young boy by the village constable for the theft of one dry coconut. One great excitement that lasted for weeks was the hold-up of the mule-drawn delivery dray in a remote corner of the winding road. In those far-off days, delivery of our goods ordered from the wholesaler in Port Antonio was done by a dray every Thursday. On this particular Thursday, I remember the old man wondering why, by six o'clock, the dray had not come. Lo and behold, next thing we heard the dray cart man had been found, tied up in a clump of bushes where the mule was standing idly by with an empty dray. But more excitement! The village constable, on riding his bicycle close to the bank and peering everywhere, discovered the bag of sugar and the bag of flour hidden under a dense tree.

Another exciting event had to do with 'Christianity converts' and the first hurricane I ever experienced. These *'pacquee'** missionaries had come in to the village to convert souls and had built a 'church', made solely from bamboo, on the pasture-land right behind our shop. Even the very seats were made from bamboo and the roof was thatched with branches of the trees on the pasture. Their hand-clapping services on a Sunday, when the church would be overflowing would intrigue me, and I would stand and peep through the fence and enjoy the singing. Alas! It was not meant to last.

One morning we woke up to the rain pounding the zinc-roof. It rained and rained and never let up, and about mid-day there was a great crash. The church had been blown down and completely wrecked by a severe wind never to be built again. Little did I know then that this was a hurricane. We had no radios to warn us and the first inkling we had was when an old-timer came by and said to my father, "Mr. Eddie – look like we a get 'breeze-blow'". I, in my child-like state, found it all wonderful and exciting, especially when that night all the villagers whose houses had been blown away, crammed the shop premises to sleep on the floor. This meant, of course, that we also had to sleep in the shop in chairs brought from the living quarters, and had to watch that no one 'teaw dungsee.'* While the old man doled out the remaining bread and buns, the villagers sang 'deliverance' sankeys the entire night. But the rain just would not stop.

When morning came the weather was clear, but the premises had leaks everywhere. I can still remember the old man trying to get the wet stove going and the wet wood burning so that we could have some breakfast. In the end, we had hot rice and canned salmon cooked with hamchoy*. Such lasting impressions! To this day, salmon/hamchoy remains one of my favourite meals.

From stories told by the old man, he had come to Jamaica with his father at fourteen years of age, and although he had only two years of schooling, he spoke and read English clearly, and could write a mean hand. He was very vocal and spoke loudly (some would say he shouted), especially against injustices like being arrested for one dry coconut found under a laden tree, in a grove of a hundred laden coconut trees. He somehow came to be called Chairman.

Eventually, life took me to live and work in Port Antonio among the Chinese who had put down roots there, and there are many happy memories of 'good ol' Porty' at this time.

What we considered a great day was going to Sunday mass, then swimming over at Navy Island, returning for lunch, going to basketball at four o'clock, then ending up at the Sunday-night movie.

Wonderful friendly days, yes. We had a Chinese Athletic Club where we lived and breathed basketball. We dared to challenge Chinese Clubs in other areas, and even the American Servicemen when they came for shore leave. We never ever once thought we would be beaten. We were so confident in our defense guard at the rear who was tall, lanky and so sure to block all throws that he was affectionately called Iron Gate.

We even had a Ladies' Basketball Team. Where, I wonder, are these ladies now? Happy days spent with friends in youthful, simple, innocent past-times. Its good that we can look back with pleasure on the memories and pictures from that past.

Written by Monica Chen and edited by Sonia Gordon Scott.

* See Glossary

Ray Chen
MY STORY

AS I READ THE STORIES submitted for this book, I realized that there were many of us who would have been on board ships bound for China, had it not been for the intervention of wars in China. For Gloria Palomino and Winston Chung Fah, it was the start of China's war with Japan. For me, some years later, it was the start of the internal battle with Chairman Mao and the Communist Army. Luckily for us our journeys were aborted.

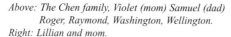

Above: The Chen family, Violet (mom) Samuel (dad)   *1*
*   Roger, Raymond, Washington, Wellington.*
Right: Lillian and mom.   *2*

My journey started when I was about
eight or nine years old. My uncle (my dad's brother) and his wife did not have any children, while among my family there were four boys. Our only sister came at a later date.

I was my uncle's favourite nephew. He would usually yell for me, very loudly, whenever he got drunk at any social function or celebration, which was quite often.

True to Chinese custom, one day my dad asked me if I would like to spend some time with my uncle and aunt. Unknown to me at the time, he was actually handing me over to them for keeps. Really, for keeps… *Can you picture him taking me by the hand and handing me to him saying... "Here, you can have this one."*

My own family was then living and operating a grocery shop in quiet Allman Town. Off to Spanish Town Road I went to live with my aunt and uncle who operated a 'Rum Bar' close to the Coronation Market. It was quite a change from Allman Town.

There was so much noise from the vendors, in and outside the market, shouting at the tops of their voices to draw attention to their goods. Then there were the boys with the pushcarts and the bicycle riders, all hustling for whatever open space remained after the sidewalk vendors finished spreading out their wares. Jubilee Market was at the eastern corner of Spanish Town Road and West Parade, and the distance between the two markets was about $1^1/_2$ miles of total chaos.

We had to be careful whenever we walked among the colourful country buses with names like *National Queen, Blue Rose, and King Mavrick.* The buses that just arrived were busy unloading passengers and their produce –

yams, breadfruit, cassava, sweet potatoes, sugar canes and all their ground provisions – all tied up in burlap sacks, which was carried on the top of the bus, while the other buses were loading bags of sugar, flour, cornmeal, salted cod fish, cases of Betty brand condensed milk, cooking oil, Lannaman's sweets like paradise plums, mint balls and 'ju jubes'(a soft jelly-like candy) for the shops in the country. I can remember the sweet taste of the 'white peppermint candies with a little red one on top' and the grated coconut sugar cakes (grater-cake and cut-cake) that the vendors themselves made, displayed and sold from a wood and glass case.

I remember well the day a lady, who had just arrived, was getting off the bus when someone grabbed her handbag with all her money and other valuables. *"Tief! Tief! stop him! Lard him tief me bag!"* she yelled, then she started to cry. The purpose of her journey was to pay the supplier and make purchases on behalf of her father who owned a small farm in the country. The police, who arrived minutes later, warned the other passengers to be careful as it was a daily occurrence. Young men preyed on unsuspecting women and small boys by stealing their handbags or wallets.

My adopted sister, Ena, shared many a morning breakfast (served by my aunt) which consisted of chocolate Ovaltine mixed in *cha** (Chinese tea, and the only available source of hot water) with Nestles brand condensed milk as the sweetener. Can you imagine the taste?!

After selling the 'Rum Bar', we (uncle, aunt and I) prepared for our journey to China by boat. We boarded the ship at Victoria Pier, which was located at the bottom of King Street in Kingston, and it was here that my mother and dad came on board to see us off.

There were a lot of people all around, as other relatives and families also came to see their sons and daughters off. The activity reminded me of Spanish Town Road, with suitcases and boxes instead of baskets being shuffled around. The noise and the atmosphere of so many Chinese reminded me of a garden party at the Chinese Public School on North Street, except that we were on board a ship preparing to leave.

The news from China in the local Chinese newspaper was that the Communist Army invasion of China was in full force. They spoke of fierce fighting and the cruelty with which the army treated the population. Memories of the recent war with Japan drove fear into my mom's mind for my own safety. Now that I am older and wiser, I suspect that at the thought of not seeing her son again, my mother reacted like any other mother would have. As she bade goodbye to my uncle and aunt, she took me by the hand and decided then and there, that it was time for me to 'come home' with her. Ena returned to her parents' house too.

I sometimes wonder what would have been the outcome if the wars had started at a later date and we had all ended up in China as planned. I guess that we, Gloria, Winston and I, have much to be thankful for, that both wars started when they did. Who knows? Maybe we would have ended up being the first members of the 'Jamaican-Chinese Posse'* over there. Wan Luv mon!

MY CURIOUS ADVENTURE

My brothers and I were brought up at a time when we could walk, ride or drive on the roads at any hour of the day or night without fear.

I have always had a curious mind and sometimes it would take me into areas where I should not venture. Take for instance the time I decided to follow the route of a gully that was close to home. This gully was close to where Tyrone Chen lived, on Arnold Road, and our shop was on Prince of Wales Street in Allman Town.

Climbing down the wall was not as easy as I had thought, for in the process I scraped the skin off my elbows and the toes of my Bata buggas (sneakers). The pain in my elbows was far from my mind for I was just relieved to reach the bottom in one piece. My troubles could have been much worse.

As I journeyed south alone, I could hear the horns of the passing vehicles, the ringing of the bells by the riders on bicycles, and the loud chatter of people walking by on the roadway above the gully. From a distance I could see the shops that were familiar to me. I passed under all the streets in Allman Town – Regent, Prince Albert, Hitchins, Wild, John, Sarah, Stephen and Hanna Streets.

I was not afraid because I was close to surroundings I knew. If I yelled out loudly enough, the folks above would have rescued me and taken me to the police at the Allman Town Station, who would then have taken me home. Luckily for me, too, it was a sunny day.

As I explored the gully, I met other children from the area playing cricket on the smooth concrete surface of the gully, using three stones at one end as a wicket, a piece of wood for a homemade bat, and a worn out tennis ball for a cricket ball. A single stone was at the other end to mark the spot for the bowler.

There were girls playing 'jacks' with a rubber ball, and others just skipping to the tune of 'room for rent, apply within, when I run out, you run in'. Another group of boys were just running around for fun, while an older set practised to improve their game with an old soccer ball. There were also several groups of men sitting on stools or wooden crates by the edge of the gully wall, playing some sort of a game such as dominoes or ludo. Others were just standing and looking on at the outcome of the game. Occasionally, I would see a dead animal lying on its back, all four feet up in the air and the 'john crows' (vultures) circling above.

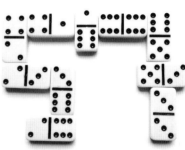

Jacks, ludo board and dominoes

Somewhere in Kingston Garden another gully joined up with 'my' gully and so I had to remember which one to take on my return journey. The space was quite wide and open with a lot of bush all around. This 'bush' was really Pink Coralilla, a wild plant known locally as 'Bridal Bouquet' which grew in profusion with no attention or watering needed. There were the odd mango trees hanging over the adjoining zinc fence by the gully and coconut trees swaying in the breeze.

I was now into 'foreign territory'. Close by was St. George's College, while a little further on North Street was the Holy Trinity Cathedral. It was a Saturday and there were no classes or church that day. I walked past North Street and travelled southward passing Charles, Beeston and Hollywood Streets. East Queen Street was the next cross street and I was close to High Holborn Street.

I was really venturing into 'foreign - foreign - territory'. The sounds were different. It was also much noisier. The buses passed above letting out thick black smoke from their exhausts, while music blared from speakers at maximum volume. The cars were going faster and horns were used more frequently. I was really in the heart of the city.

We used to visit the home of Gloria Lyn's parents when they lived on East Queen Street, which was now very close to where I was in the gully. The sounds from the street above were somewhat familiar, except for the congregation singing from the church on Sunday afternoons. Gloria (Chen See) Lyn's family lived next to the church and we would visit quite often on Sunday afternoons with our mom.

It's funny how distances seem much longer when you are young. I figured that it was another thirty minutes walk from East Queen Street to the end of the gully, where it opens out to the harbour below Harbour and Port Royal Streets. The Rae Town Prison was nearby. At this point, I had seen enough and decided to head home passing Arnold Road. I was also beginning to feel thirsty and hungry and I had no money in my pockets.

Today, I now travel with my cellular phone and credit cards, but all we had in those days by way of childhood long distance phones were two empty and clean condensed milk cans connected by a long cord stretching from one can to the next. *"Hello? Hello? Can you hear me?"* That would be quite a distance from Allman Town to East Queen Street and we would need more that a roll of cord to connect. Right? Right on!!

The folks that I met or who saw me were awed. *"This little Chiney bwoy, him one a walk in-a-de gully! Him brave eh?"* The time it took to reach home seemed shorter because I walked a bit faster as I had been gone for a long time. I told no one in case word got to my parents and I ended up 'getting a licking' with the feather brush for going on such a foolish journey.

What story was I going to tell my parents, to explain how the Bata buggas got damaged? Fortunately, they did not ask.

'BOAT' RACING

Surprisingly, by today's standards, the gully was relatively clean. But there were areas where waste water from the streets emptied into the gully and flowed out to the sea. Most of the time it would evaporate before reaching that destination as the temperature on the concrete was just too high.

It was the practice then for each household or yard in most communities to have a common "stand-pipe" that was used by all. The water from the pipe emptied out into the gutter at the side of the roads or streets. Early in the mornings, the street cleaners with their long handled brooms would sweep the gutters, aided by the water, removing the morass or other litter.

I remember especially the rainy seasons when my brothers and I enjoyed racing our match-sticks or paper boats in the same gutter water. *'Go man go!'* we would urge our match sticks or paper boats using our hands in a whipping motion like jockeys on the back of a race horse. Our mom would order us to come in from the rain just after we became soaking wet.

SIDEWALK VENDORS

Very few grocery shops were without their sidewalk vendors, usually a lady who occupied space on the piazza. There was a special bond between these "higglers" and the owners of the shops that went beyond the space they were allowed to occupy. There are instances when they acted as nannies to the shopkeepers' children, and at the same time they 'kept an eye out' for the stock when it was delivered by the suppliers. They were like our extended families.

They also provided one stop shopping for the customers of the grocery shop, as they could purchase other provisions from the vendors such as yam, scallions, thyme, potatoes, tomatoes, and the various fruits in season – mangoes, oranges, sweet sop, custard and otahiti apples, guineps, jew or june plums, red plums of every description and cherries, to name a few. The owners of the shop would usually grant the vendors space to store their provisions somewhere on the inside of the shop or in the yard until the following day.

I was told of an incident that occurred while I was away from the shop. On this particular day, the shop was quite busy and our son, who was only sixteen months at the time, was spending time with 'Foodie' as the vendor was called. It was noticed that he came in from the piazza all flushed and red in the face and his grandparents immediately thought that something was wrong. Maybe he was coming down with the flu. They were quite relieved to learn that that was not the case. 'Foodie' had shared a Red Stripe with him. She gave him a sip, not much, just a sip.

Roderick with 'Foodie'

CHRISTMAS AND THE JONKONNU

It was Christmas time and the season for festivities was on us. There was no school until after the New Year and we looked forward to lighting the fire crackers especially the B-I-G ones... the *Bow Chung* ... POW!! How many of you remember the tingling feeling in your fingers just after having one explode in your hand?

It was a time for excitement, Santa Claus, a visit to Dixon's Toys Store, fire crackers, lots of Chinese goodies with families and friends.

And Jonkonnu (John Canoe).... Well this Christmas, as I stood outside the shop in Allman Town listening to the '*pudum, pudum, pudum*' of the drum and everyone dancing to its beat, I was fascinated to say the least, for it was the first time that I was seeing these dancers. Standing next to us were children from the neighborhood, for we were all on Christmas holidays.

The dancers were colourful and well dressed and usually in the group there was a man carrying the head of a horse, or another wearing a mask with a set of cow's horns on top of his head. *"Here comes Santa Claus, Here comes the man with the horn, right down Santa Claus Lane".*

Voodum! I was so frightened; one lick on my head. As I ran away crying, I could hear the laughter of the other kids who thought that it was funny. I did not think so, as I ended up with a '*coco*' (a raised bump) on my head. Merry Christmas! From then on, I paid more attention to these particular dancers.

OTHER PHOTOGRAPHERS

Sang Sang Photo Studio was a familiar household name, known to everyone. It was located upstairs in a building on King Street, and most Chinese families would go at least once per year to have the family portrait done, as well as when there was a new addition to the family and they wanted to send the pictures home to China.

It was years later – we were in our late teens then – when the fascination with the camera took hold of me. I had always been interested in photography. It was exciting to take the picture but more important was the process of developing the film and being able to print the images of what had just been taken, especially the girls we liked...ah, puppy love. Roger (the first photographer in the family) had gone to McGill University in Montreal, Canada. I remember the first camera I owned, a Kodak sent by my friend, Tony Buckley's aunt, who lived in New York City. My next camera was a Minolta which I bought from Stanley Motta. After having it for 6 glorious weeks I lost it on a school picnic at Castleton Gardens. I was so upset.

Snap shots, which had been the order of the day, were finished. I never considered it as a profession, as I did not have a camera for quite a while. Then came the day when I borrowed a camera from my friend Lascelles. Well... the rest is history. Today, it is all digital cameras – Nikon and Fuji, Epson and HP.

Other Chinese photographers who documented the state visits of Kings and Queens and the beauty queens of the pageants, weddings, birthday parties, graduation exercises, family gatherings and so many other social events, were Pierre Chung of Ocho Rios, Gil Kong and his brother Phillip, James Chung, Astley Chin, the news photographer for the *Daily Gleaner,* Louis Chin from Cathay Photo Studio, Phillip Chuck, Lloyd and Isaac Tenn and Howard Moo Young, who won several awards for his contribution to advertising and won, on several occasions, the annual National Photography Competition.

9   *James Chong*

To me, photography is a tool with which we record the things that are dear to us. The things that will pass our way only once. Like the growing up years of our children. There are instances where I was a little too slow in pressing the shutter and I lost the opportunity to record a moment in time. That image will never come again.

They say that "a picture is worth a thousand words," but there are memories that cannot be recorded on film. Memories that come from what we hear, touch, feel and taste. It is these memories of my growing up years that are my fondest ones. Here are few:

I was born at the corner of Water Lane and High Holborn Street in Kingston and our landlord was a Cuban named Garcia. My Godmother was one of their daughters, whose pet name was 'Chi-Chi' (not the bus!). Her dad made one of the nicest homemade ice creams which he sold in a 'jack-ass corn'* shaped cup. I will always remember the combined taste of the ice cream and 'jack-ass corn'.

Living in Jamaica during World War II did not mean that we didn't need to take precautionary measures. I remember the sound of the siren (it used to be called the 'korchie') coming from the direction of the Kingston Ice Factory on Harbour Street. Our mom would immediately pull the dark curtains to cover the windows during the nights when the lights were on. She would then stay to comfort us until we fell asleep.

I often saw other boys jumping off the sides of a tramcar while it was still in motion. I decided to give it a try and fell flat on my face the first time. Little did I know that you have to keep running with the tram when you hit the ground, otherwise you can injure yourself. It never happened again as I quickly learnt how to jump off.

10   Gil Kong

We were living in Allman Town when Winston Chang came up from behind me and told me to close my eyes and open my mouth. I foolishly did and he stuffed a handful of bird peppers in my mouth. Lord, it was so hot! I don't remember what happened after that. He ran away. He was much faster than I.

But all this was nothing compared to that first kiss… how sweet it is… memories…

Have you ever wondered how we allow young children to walk or to take the bus by themselves to go to school? Some of them travel for miles. Our visitors to the island must marvel at this practice.

Jamaica is truly an amazing country and one of the most beautiful islands in the Caribbean. As for Jamaicans… what is there to say…. The nicest, most loving and beautiful people to be photographed.

I am honoured, as a Jamaican, to have been given the opportunity and the privilege to document through my photography, the stories and history record-ed in this book. The things that are dear to me. These are the memories and the legacy that we pass on to our present youth and future generations.

'NUFF, 'NUFF IRIE and Wan Luv,

Ray

Written by Ray Chen and edited by Sonia Gordon Scott.

* See Glossary

Photographs 1and 2 - Courtesy of Roger Chen
        All others ©Ray Chen
            9 - Courtesy of Kathleen (Kay) Chin
            10 - Courtesy of Gil Kong

Bev Lue
MEMORIES OF MOORE TOWN

IN NOVEMBER OF 1953 my parents, Edward and Jena Chong (right), and five children including myself, relocated from the cool, hilly township of Darliston, Westmoreland, to the very lush, rainy, mountainous Maroon town called Moore Town, in Portland. My parents went there to operate a general store. I was too young at the time to remember the move, but my mother said when dawn came and she viewed the new environment, she found it traumatic! She had never felt so close to nature and to the interior of Jamaica. Mountain ranges loomed in front of the store. These are the John Crow mountains. Along the northwest direction from the store, hovered the Blue Mountains. Of course, these mountains are really far away, but my mother felt as if she could touch them. There was just dirt all around, no asphalt streets.

The wild Cane River (a tributary of the Negro River) divided the town area. On entering the town the main buildings are the Anglican Church and the town's only school on the left of the river. A footbridge spanned the river to allow access to the right side of the river where our store stood. It is said that slaves built this footbridge. In general, small houses dotted the landscape. I can recall the constant splashing sound of the river as it dashed over the stones and pebbles. During the drier seasons when the river became shallow, delivery trucks that entered the town could drive on a flat area across the river to deliver merchandise. On the very rainy days, and this was often, the river swelled and rushed and rose to a height over the footbridge. In these times, my

At right: On entering the town the main buildings are the Anglican Church in the background and the town's only school in the foreground.

Monument for Nanny of the Maroons, National Hero of Jamaica for whom the town was named.

parents depended on the men and young lads of the town to carry the goods across the bridge. This was a great time for us children who could not cross the footbridge to go to school. The river also afforded many fishing days. We could catch crayfish (janga)* and minnows (tiki tiki)* that we children, with the helper's assistance, would make a fry feast of these tiny creatures to go with our mud pies that we baked in the clay stoves.

I still recall attending the local school where my mother taught and the principal was Mr. C.L.G. Harris, later the lifetime Colonel Harris of the Maroons. My mother told me that the usual date for school admission was seven years. She used to teach me at home, but because I cried constantly to accompany my two older sisters to school, Teacher Harris gave my mother permission for me to attend at age 5. School was fun, and I remember reciting the timetable forwards and backwards, every morning. In addition to the regular curriculum, the girls had sewing lessons while the boys went gardening. Supplements of milk and cheese were given to the school and distributed to all students.

I have memories of putting on my Sunday best, sewn by my mother, and attending the church on Sundays. From the church yard, my siblings and I would look across to our back verandah to see our mother signalling to us that the home-made ice cream was ready. This would be our Sunday treat of papaya, soursop* or grapenut ice cream. The many tombstones in the church yard provided a good level surface on which we played the game of 'jacks'* and jumping games. However, we had to be careful as the helpers warned us about pointing to the graves, with the consequence of losing our fingers. The helpers and the locals who came to the store introduced us to the different kinds of duppies*, including the rolling calves* that hide in the holes of the pasture land. Darkness was a real challenge to me, as I had to "dodge the duppies" to get into my bed at nights. My siblings and I would hold hands tightly to make one rush across any open doors to again dodge the duppies.

I remember the frequent beating of drums in the nights. Now my mother tells me that the sound of the drums would last for the entire night, ending a little before daybreak. It was an eerie sound, especially in the wee early hours of the mornings. She said the only solace that the drums brought her was a safe feeling that outsiders would not dare enter Moore Town to rob or steal on those nights. The Maroons used a horn (the abeng)* to summon and rally the residents for meetings (political or decision-making meetings). Sometimes the drums were used for pocomania* meetings.

While my parents operated the shop in Moore Town, my dad, Edward Chung, also procured another shop that he operated in Mill Bank, a rural town in the interior facing the John Crow Mountains. The front of the building faced the mountains, while the back faced the main street. This was due to the fact that many years ago there was a huge landslide that brought down ridges of the mountains. The landslide caused the river to change its course, hence the change in position of the building. My youngest sister was born in Mill

Bank. The same original building has remained even when Les, my sister, last visited in 1994.

The shop in Moore Town was previously operated by Mr. Chung Men Fah, our cousin. Our family arrived in Moore Town, November, 1953. We left in April, 1959 and moved to Kingston where my parents ran the Chisholm Avenue shop. Since then I have visited Moore Town on two occasions. In 1986, I returned to visit with my husband, Franklin Lue and Tracey, our first daughter. I had the privilege of visiting a vibrant Colonel Harris, who had very fond memories of my family. The footbridge that crossed the river was completely washed away. My childhood memories were shattered as I had remembered the church as a huge cathedral, and sprawling lands on which the school sat. Now everything seemed so small and eerie. I left Moore Town in a hurry, not wanting to be there as dusk drew nigh.

I returned to Moore Town in 2004. This time I was thrilled with the experience. Again, we visited with Colonel Harris, who still has fond memories of the family. The school has been expanded, and the principal is a former student of my mother's at the Moore Town School. The church has been renovated. A new bridge that allows access to cross the river has replaced the washed away footbridge. There were many of the town's people milling around. Many who remembered most of my family by name, and even the address to which we had moved in Kingston. Some also remembered years ago when my grandfather (originally from China), would go boar hunting and bird shooting with them in the hills. It was exhilarating to meet and talk with the locals, and the weather was beautiful. I was left with very pleasant memories to take with me.

Written by Bev Lue and edited by Sonia Gordon Scott.

* See Glossary

Down Memory Lane

Shop in Knollis, St. Catherine Photograph ©Ray Chen

Clive Fung

ANECDOTES OF A HAKKA YOUTH

"Sweet are the uses of adversity, which like a toad, though ugly and venomous, wears yet a precious jewel in its head." – *William Shakespeare.*

READER, IF YOU ARE looking for a success story, this is not one. So stop reading and turn to something else in this excellent book. The bright Alex Lee asked me to provide, for publication, anecdotes of an earlier life. I do so with pride and pleasure.

The nostalgia of anecdotes is my theme. Those periods of the past that are always remembered for the incomparable fun, drama, excitement and challenges that shaped our lives.

Patrick Lee, publisher of books, defined the boundaries of the Chinatown of our youth: North along Heywood Street; south to Water Lane; east to Orange Street; and west to Pechon Street.

Everard Hoo, the exemplary scoutmaster, observed, quite rightly, that far north of this rectangle lived the 'upper crust' who played tennis and badminton on fancy private courts. I am a product of West Street between Tower Street and Water Lane. Like the splendid scoutmaster, my playmates were mostly blacks. We, who lived near the sounding sea, would often '*teef out*'*

Kingston Harbour. A typical native coin diver who welcomes the ships as they dock and who affords an unusual amusement for visitors to the island. Old postcard - ©Duncan Keith Corinaldi.

to join the 'little bad black boys', as our parents used to call them. We would go crabbing with them along the train lines of the Jamaica Railway Corporation; play cricket and football in the public streets and sidewalks which were our playground. We would go fishing and swimming, stark born naked, in the waters of Kingston Harbour, where we often competed with them diving for coins: nickels, dimes and quarters thrown to us by sailors of the great grey battleships of the U.S. navy that frequently docked at the pier and sent their enlisted men on shore leave.

There is a technique to diving for coins. When one is flung to you in the water, it does not sink in a straight vertical line. It zips forward and backward at an angle of about 45 degrees. So when you see it slipping away from you, don't go after it. Just submerge slowly and position yourself for the return.

It was great fun, but in my case there was a sad end to it. I had to give away all that I had won to my competitors, for to be caught with them at home meant instant flogging. Going to sea and playing with the 'little bad black boys' were forbidden. And when Charlie Fung, my dad, started the whipping, it never ended until he got tired or the belt broke.

Crabbing required other skills. When crabs are running wild, usually in rainy seasons, they can be easily subdued with a stick or your feet. But if one is in a hole, you have to use a stick or steel rod, thrust it quickly under its belly and pin it to the roof of the hole. Then you start to dig.

In those days, every Chinese man or boy had a black sidekick who would 'kill' for him. These faithful heroes were often referred to as 'Chinese Standard Equipment'. 'Bruk Kitchen', the great runner, was mine. He was so called because he once broke into someone's kitchen, stole a huge soup spoon and sprinted up West Street with it. Bruk Kitchen was a master crab catcher. He would deftly dip his hand into a hole and pull the crab out by its back, its claws snapping.

The first time I tried it, almost instantly I screamed a Jamaican bad word and pulled my hand out of the hole quicker than I had put it in. There was an oversized crab dangling from my thumb by its little claw, which was the dangerous one, and me trying in vain to flash it off when Bruk Kitchen shouted: "Don't fight 'im Clive. Put 'im on the ground and make your hand play dead and it will let go."

I did just that and, as he predicted, the crab released my finger and ran off, whereupon Bruk Kitchen swiftly picked it up and dropped it into the bag.

SCOUTING

At age 10, I joined the 1st Chinese Scout Troop. Some months after, Jamaica staged a World Scouts Jamboree, a most colourful and electrifying international event with scouts from all over the world participating. Charlie Fung shouted a terrifying "NO!" when I asked for permission to attend. Still, I 'teef out' and went.

Young Clive Fung - "The little rebel".

About noon one day, as I strayed from my tent, I was suddenly and powerfully swung up in the air and landed on strong, broad shoulders. Then he put his wide hat on my head. It was so big it covered my eyes. Graham Charlotte, a brawny Caymanian sea scout paraded with me on his shoulders all around the camp grounds. Then he took me to his tent and fed me hard boiled turtle eggs and turtle steak. Years later, I heard it said that turtle eggs are an aphrodisiac.

Keith Lyn and I formed a harmonica duo and often thrilled other scout troops at camp fires. Then one day, Keith discovered that he could sing better than he could play the harmonica and evolved into a capital crooner, musician and a first class entertainer. I went on to be known as a troublemaker. Said Everard, master of scouts: "If you say 'A', Clive says 'B'."

When the Jamboree ended, I went home and fell asleep. Hours later I was awakened by my dad and asked: "Where were you for the last two weeks?" "Up at Joyce," I lied. Joyce was my half-sister who was living with her husband in Bath, St. Thomas, where they operated a wholesale-retail grocery and dry goods store and bar. It was usual for us to vacation with her during summer holidays.

Then the beating began. And although I was screaming in pain at every blow of the belt, I really didn't mind it. After all, a few moments of punishment was hardly a high price to pay for weeks of pleasure at the Jamboree, where I'd had a ball. It was a bargain. Moreover, all I had to do was bear it until dad got tired, which he eventually did. He pulled out a sheet of paper from a drawer, handed it to me and walked away. It was the front page of the *Daily Express,* an afternoon tabloid of the *Gleaner,* carrying a huge picture of a little Chinese boy riding the shoulders of a tall, muscular black scout. The caption read, "Graham Charlotte of Grand Cayman, giving little Clive Fung a bird's eye view of the camp". How was I to know that a Gleaner photographer was among those taking pictures? Worse still, my eyes were hidden for most of the ride. Then he returned and went through his usual after-beating ritual. "Show me where you got the beating" he said to me. I showed him the weals and the bruises.

"Did it hurt?", he asked.

"Yes."

"Say yes Papa." ….

"Yes Papa."

"Do you know why you got a beating?"

"Yes Papa. I told a lie."

"Will you do it again?"

"No."

"Say no Papa."

NO PAIN NO GAIN

From that moment on, I kept my promise never to lie to him again. This I guaranteed by never again asking for permission to do anything or go anywhere. I would assess the situation or event and if the frolic was worth the flogging, I simply took the risk. That was all. I had become a rebel.

Moreover, I was quite fed up with his flip-flopping. He would tell you yes; and when the time came he would change his mind and say no. But in fairness to him, he dealt this unfairness to all of us. What his motive was I still do not know. Was it to prepare us to accept and tolerate disappointments in life? If that was it, then it worked. At any rate, it worked for me. When confronted with disappointment my first reaction is to laugh, then get down to business.

The worst instance of his about-face was the night of my sister's graduation ball. She had sought and received his permission weeks before. We heard a car drive up and the horn blow. Her fellow graduates had arrived to pick her up. There she was looking so beautiful and radiant, she could easily have been mistaken for that movie star Ann Blythe, the resemblance was that close. And what a gorgeous dress! If my recollection is correct, she had made it herself. Painstakingly. Every cut and stitch was hers. She was now perfectly prepared to become the Belle of the Ball.

But that was not to be. She descended the stairs and when she reached the bottom, dad was waiting. "Where are you going?" he asked. She told him. "Go upstairs and take off your clothes," he shouted, "You are not going anywhere!" This, coming from a father who had always drilled into us: "Don't fool anybody and don't let anybody fool you." Also, "Your word is and must be your bond."

I felt sorry for her but blamed her totally for putting herself in this situation. It is said that experience is the best teacher; but only fools go to the school of experience. In other words, it is best to learn from the experience of others and she had a lot of mine to learn from. The countless beatings I had endured and still remained alive, ready for the next one. What is a little pain to pay for a lot of pleasure?

What she should have done was to slip away during the day when he was not at home, take her graduation stuff with her to a friend or relative, and from there, at nightfall, go and have a ball. It would have been worth a great deal more than any 'backsiding' our father could dish out. If only she had believed in my philosophy and song: No pain, no gain!

SPECIAL SUI MEIN

Dad and I just kept drifting further and further apart. He came home one night about 9:30 with a lot of Special Sui Mein, as was customary when he won substantially at Mah Jung. Mah Jung, that compulsive pastime of many Hakka fathers while Hakka mothers slaved away for up to 16 hours daily in the grocery shops. Mothers walked a very thin line between practising a culture and being played for a sucker.

Then as usual, he began calling us downstairs, each by name, to eat Sui Mein which we all loved with a passion. Only this time my name was not called. While they were feasting, lying on a cot in my bedroom which overhung the dining table, I overheard Mother Fung asking him:

"Why didn't you call Clive. Is he not somebody too?"

"No," he replied, "He is not somebody too."

Hot tears stung my eyes, followed by some giggling as I regained my composure and longed for the day when I could buy my own.

GIVE HIM RICE

Charlie Fung taught me many things. Most lasting and beneficial of all was the art of woodworking. He was a genius at it, a true perfectionist. In all my years I have never met or seen any other craftsman who could even come close to matching his skills. Not even me. Watching him work was far better than watching TV.

To bond wood together he never used nails just glued joints. Mortise and tenon. Where he couldn't use mortise and tenon joints, he used screws, never nails. He must have learnt this technique from his native village in China, for I remember some years ago watching a documentary about one such village where the inhabitants built wooden houses along the same lines. No nails. Only joints and dowels.

For the heavy work of ripping thick planks of lumber into workable pieces, he would call 'Brownman', a tall muscular mulatto, to do it. Chiselling out mortises and cutting tenons were his responsibility and he trusted no one with it. He did it so perfectly that when we were gluing and clamping them together they squeaked loudly, and he would nod his head with pride and approval.

His staunchest admirer was 'General' Barley Gordon, a World War II veteran, so called because he would round up all the little boys in the neighbourhood, dress them in army uniforms, and with wooden guns they would be drilled and marched under his command in the streets and lanes. They were called 'Barley's army'. 'General' Gordon would stand looking over the zinc fence for hours, at dad toiling away.

One day dad had some planks of mahogany to split up and Brownman was nowhere to be found so he said that I should do it. We secured one of the thick pieces of lumber on the worktable. Then he drew a straight line down the centre, gave me the rip saw which was almost as tall as I was, and told me to "saw on the line". I began at a very rapid pace, maybe a hundred miles an hour, while he just sat and stared at me in silence – never uttering a word. Within a minute or two, I collapsed from sheer exhaustion and wobbled to the ground, the huge saw falling on top of me. He laughed a good and hearty laugh. Then when I stopped breathing heavily, he got up, gave me a lightly oiled rag, told me to wipe the sides of the saw and said: "All right, do it like this."

He reduced my haste to about 50 strokes per minute. At that slow movement, I could saw all day, non-stop – only I had to make very frequent visits to the pipe of a concrete cistern for water. After a few hours of this, General Gordon looked over the fence and said: "Mass Charlie, from morning you have the little young boy sawing and sawing and sawing. Look how he is sweating like a river. Poor thing! Mass Charlie, you want to kill the little young boy?"

Charlie Fung laughed: "No man. Nothing is wrong with him. He drinks too much water. All he needs is some rice. I will soon give him rice."

PASS DE HAMMER

One Sunday afternoon, I was giving my little brother a whipping for doing something that I found disgraceful. Without warning, I heard the front door slam shut, I was held from behind with a firm grip, and the strap began to tear into my legs. Charlie Fung in action again. I was stinging his favourite son.

After a few bruising blows, the belt broke. He threw away the piece he had in his hand and shouted to my brother: "Pass de hammer! Pass de hammer!" Until this day, I could not tell you what he intended to do with it. To bash my head in? I did not stick around long enough to find out. God alone knows how I managed to break away from his clutches. I imagine that fear must have given me winged feet. Up the stairs in a flash, up on the roof, jumping and sliding down the electric pole and dashing up West Street at a speed that would make Ernie Smith sing: "Quarrie was a bwoy to I-man." Donald Quarrie, as most of you know was, in his day, Jamaica's greatest Olympic sprinter. I turned right on Barry Street and never stopped running until I reached Rum Lane and my Aunt Ivy, cleaner of ears. She was my favourite aunt. Big, fat, sprawling Aunt Ivy who, in my childhood estimation, must have weighed close to 300 lbs.

"Clive," she would holler, "Come here let me clean out your ears." With my head resting cosily in her broad soft lap, she began the operation with a hair pin. Nobody can clean ears as soft and sweet as Aunt Ivy. What a divine feeling! So thrilling I often wished it would never end.

SEE DEM T'INGS FLYING OUT DERE?

Near 12 years of age, I asked dad, how come he was not sending me to college like everybody else? "You!" he replied, "before I waste money sending you to college, I make a hand cart and give you to push." With that pronouncement, he presented me with the first important turning point of my life. Then and there I realized that if I wanted anything in this world, it wouldn't be coming from him or under his roof.

A few months later, I left St. Aloysius Boys School. My elementary education had come to an end and I was destined never to know what a college classroom looks or feels like. My father had other ideas. I was taken to his rice plantation deep in the woods of Spanish Town. It was reaping season and I was to be watchman for the next two months or so.

When we arrived, he took me to the little wooden farm house, showed me a canvas cot which was to be my bed, pointed to a bag of rice and said: "That is rice. When you are hungry, boil it and eat it."

"Where is the meat?" I asked him.

"Meat? All right. Look behind the door and bring what you see." It was a 12-guage shotgun. He taught me how to load it, press it against the shoulder, bend slightly forward, take aim and squeeze the trigger – BAM!

Next he took me to the door and stared into the wide open fields and sky and said: "See dem t'ings flying out dere? Dat is meat. When you want meat, shoot one of them and cook it."

That was one of the most charged moments of my life. Buzzing with adventure and excitement. Beyond the expectations of any boy my size or age. The opportunity of firing a gun, much less bird-hunting! I felt like kneeling and worshipping Charlie Fung for it. Even now, whenever I see stories in the news of child soldiers in Somalia and other parts of the world, it brings back memories.

Gahlings (egrets) were plentiful. They came in two colours, blue and white. The whites were easier targets for they allowed you to come closer than the blues. But the blues were tastier by far. So too were ground doves which you had to shoot in clusters; and water fowl – coots – which lived in the deep, dark reed-filled ponds. When you hit one, you had to strip naked, dive into the water and swim and struggle against the weeds to get it.

But there was a downside to this kind of hunting. At that age, I could only handle four shots per day after which my shoulders felt as if they were tearing apart from the heavy jerking of the gun. If I had not bagged a bird within those four tries, it would be a meatless day. Fish in the pond and trenches added to the diet.

No electricity, no conventional bathroom or shower. Only water dipped from the trenches and canals for domestic purposes but that was all right. After all, scouting had long prepared me for this and I was 14 plus.

Shamed by one of his friends about not sending me to college, for which I had become too old, Charlie Fung sent me to the Jamaica School of Commerce only to tell me after a few months, that he had no more money to complete my commercial education.

Desperation forced me to accept a job paying three pounds ten shillings per week at the Jamaica Omnibus Services Ltd. I literally had to beg for it as, given a typing test of fourteen words, I made twelve mistakes. "Give me the job Mr. Gert, and don't pay me a penny until I can prove to you that I can type," I offered. Why did I get the work?

"Because," said my boss, an Austrian, *"I have faith in the Chinese."*

Clive Fung at the Jamaica Omnibus Services.

Night after night, for weeks, I went back to the office and practised copy-typing for hours. That is how I became a typist. A year later, my boss said to me: "Young Fung, we are getting some printing machines and are going to do our own printing in the company. I have just convinced the General Manager about it. You will love printing, for it was invented by the Chinese." He was right. At first sight I fell in love with printing, and that was my first step on a long journey to becoming a printer.

THE FINAL SOLUTION

Four years later, I left J.O.S., and with three friends, started a little print shop. When my father heard about this, he saw gold and instantly demanded twenty pounds weekly for boarding, up from five pounds. He must be joking. When I told him that twenty pounds was my new salary for a month, he said I was lying and shouted: "Take your ~!@#$%A&*? out of my house!"

Five pounds weekly was what we, the partners, had agreed on as a sacrifice until the printery took off, so I had to ignore my father's leaving orders. Then one night I came home, late as usual, and there was no dinner. Every night following it was the same, and I was told that he dumped what was left after everyone had eaten.

No problem. It only meant that we had to cook dinner at the factory. Charlie Fung tried again. This time he changed the lock on the door but that was easy to thwart, for I had become very skillful in climbing the light pole, up on to the roof and then slipping through the window of my boxed-up room at the back of the building.

But he never gave up. One Saturday, for lunch, I invited a co-partner for pumpkin soup, that being a regular Saturday special of Mother Fung. When I went upstairs, there on the floor were scattered all my clothes and there were four men playing Mah Jung in my room. The canvas cot I slept on was neatly folded and tied, leaning upright against the wall, and Charlie Fung, cool as a cucumber, was reclining in his folding chair with a toothpick in his mouth. He had found the final solution, and it worked.

My partner, who is a Chartered Accountant, asked: "What happen Clive?"

"What happen? Charlie Fung serious."

"What are you going to do now?"

"I don't know. But just help me gather up my things and keep them for me."

Upon leaving, I looked at my dad and said: "All right papa, you are serious. I am leaving, but as of today, if anybody asks you if Clive Fung is your son, say NO! Because if anybody asks me if Charlie Fung is my father, I am going to say NO! But give me five years, and I will be in a position to run you out of my house." And with that we left West Street.

Of course, that was just big, boastful empty talk. I was so angry I just had to get the last word in. After all, how does one acquire a house on five pounds weekly? I was sorry for the accountant, poor fellow. He didn't get to taste Mother Fung's fabulous pumpkin soup.

What does a young man do when he is kicked out by his father? Bum a night with a friend. The next night with another, then another, then another, and go the rounds again. Then after a few weeks of this, the accountant realized what was happening. For almost two years he shared his home with me, until the little print shop sort of took off, and he didn't charge me a cent.

"How can I repay you for this?" I asked him when I was leaving.

"Only by becoming a success Clive. So go and make a success of yourself."

What a touching moment of my life! And what a friend! As Marc Anthony
in Shakespeare's Julius Caesar would say: "When comes such another?"

One afternoon, about three years later, a nurse from the University
Hospital called. "Your father is a patient here and he wants to see you," she
said. Week after week she called with the same message and week after week
she got the same reply: "Cho, tell Charlie Fung that when I wanted to see him,
he chased me out of his house. So I am not coming."

On an August Wednesday after lunch, my youngest sister came to the
office and asked me to take her up to the hospital. A bus strike was on and she
had no other means of going to see the old man. So I took her. At the hospital
she said: "Clive, since you are here, why not come inside?"

When he saw me, he said: "Oh yu come."

"Yes," I said. "What happen to you now?"

"Clive, I am going to die,"

"What! No man, you can't die yet. You have to live for at least three more
months."

"Why?"

"You remember when I was leaving three years ago? I said that if you give
me five years I will be able to run you out of my house? Well papa, the house
is started and will be finished in three months. So you can't die now."

He calmly said to me: "Come for me on Saturday morning. I want you to
take me somewhere."

"I want to take YOU somewhere too," I told him.

Then he said: "Listen to me. I have some money with which I could do
either of two things. I could take a Far East tour and spend all of it and enjoy
myself, or I could leave it for all of you. What should I do?"

"Take your Far East tour and spend all of it on yourself and have a grand
time. Leave nothing for us. Because if you do, that is exactly what we are
going to do with it," I advised him.

"Don't you want any?"

"No! When I wanted it you threw me out of your house. You can keep it
now." He didn't say a word in reply.

Saturday morning he gave me a 9 x 4 brown envelope and told me to keep
it. I dumped it in the car pocket and took him to the construction site, and then
to his bank. There in the manager's office he said:

"Mr. Jones, this is my son."

Mr. Jones said: "What!"

Charlie repeated: "Yes, this is my son."

"Then Mas' Charlie, what about the other two. Are they not yours too?"

"No. They are away. This is my son."

Mr. Jones said: "I can't believe this. All the while I see those two ledger
cards, Charlie Fung and Clive Fung beside each other and it never struck me

that you two were related. Now tell me something Clive: Charlie Fung is your daddy?"

I had a flashback: "If anybody asks me if Charlie Fung is my father I am going to say NO!" What do I do now? Three times Mr. Jones had to ask that question before, with tear-filled eyes, I said "Yes". The ledger cards were closer together than we were.

When I reached home afterwards, I took out the envelope and noticed three words written at the bottom of it: "Add Clive Fung." It was his will, and 'Clive Fung' was the last name mentioned in it. How strange!

I could not make it around his Special Sui Mein table but I made it into his will. I must be serving a good God. Now I can buy all the Special Sui Mein I want with Daddy Fung's money.

Reader, what do you think? Would I have driven Charlie Fung out of the little house on the hill? He did not stay around long enough to find out. He died in November, three months later. If only Gore's Tile Factory had not had a month-long labour industrial dispute, he would have seen the little house completed.

Alex Lee's final question: "Clive, if you had your life to live over again, what would you change?"

"Nothing! Only that I wish that Charlie Fung had evicted me somewhat earlier than he did. As it is, I have no difficulty finding three meals a day. If he had chased me out a year or so before, I am sure I could have increased that number of meals to at least four or five."

THE SEARCH FOR EAST WIND

When I was offered the Pagoda, the magazine of the Chinese community then owned by the late Senator Rupert Chin See, and which had not been published for many years, I asked for a copy of the subscription list before I accepted. It contained about 2500 names. I ran a poll covering every parish of the island. The question was: "Why did you subscribe to the Pagoda Magazine?" ninety percent of the answers in one paraphrased sentence were: To read 'From the Desk of East Wind'. Of that, 70% added 'the gossip columns'.

That was enough reason for me to conclude that any publication launched from within the Chinese community that did not have a contribution, directly or indirectly, from 'East Wind' was doomed to a bad start. But who was this East Wind? And where was he? Nobody knew. I finally called off the search. Pagoda and I will just have to do without this wind of the east.

I was right. Support for the first four issues was very low and discouraging and it fell lower still as the majority refused to renew their subscriptions. I was convinced that I had made a terrible mistake in acquiring the Pagoda Magazine and planned to give it up. Then, just when all seemed lost, suddenly, into my office strolled a neatly dressed and bespectacled Chinese gentleman with an envelope. "Are you Clive?"

"Yes. And who are you?"

"I am East Wind. Well, Leslie R. Chin writing as East Wind. And I brought an article for the next issue of the Pagoda."

And that was the beginning of a long, trusted, firm and friendly relationship that over the decades grew firmer and friendlier still, and is quite likely to remain so.

I was right. Pagoda Magazine needed East Wind and within a year the magazine took off. East Wind was blowing again. On that updraft, Pagoda soared to new and unparalleled heights, outselling every other locally produced periodical, as subscriptions more than doubled, and advertising revenues – well let's just leave it at that. Leslie Chin and I eventually became partners. Moreover, I became virtually the sole owner of the little print shop and Pagoda, for the first time in its history, was printed in full colour, a far cry from its original black and white presentation.

Then came his finest hour. Under the penname of Ron Marshall, Leslie wrote a brilliant and stinging article which was harshly critical of the Michael Manley administration: 'Michael Manley – the Joshua that Failed'. It was a masterpiece. And for weeks I had to be fending off angry calls from P.N.P. fanatics and activists, especially one of Chinese origin. East Wind had whipped up a storm. The Chinese P.N.P. zealot was furious: "What are Ron Marshall's qualifications for writing about Michael Manley?" he demanded.

"Show me one thing in that article that is not true," I dared him.

"What are his qualifications? I want to know what are his qualifications?"

"Since when does one need qualifications to write the truth?" I asked him.

He hollered even louder: "What are his qualifications?"

Finally, I said to him: "Sir, are you telling me that if I am not a fireman I cannot tell you that your house is on fire?"

On the positive side, we had to go back to press as demand for the edition rose dramatically. Purchases from a few foreign based corporations numbering in the hundreds were sent to their head offices abroad. Leslie R. Chin, a.k.a. Ron Marshall, had gained international fame. It is said "It is an ill wind that blows no good." If that is true then with deeper conviction I can say: "It is an East Wind that blows a lot of good." At any rate, where Pagoda was concerned.

Then came the threatening rhetoric of Michael Manley, that 'five flights a day' pronouncement which began a huge wave of Chinese-Jamaican migration to North America, and Leslie R. Chin was swept along with it. Gone was the cornerstone of the great publication of the Chinese community. Gone too were Pagoda's captive subscribers and readership. The bells had tolled for the proud and flourishing Pagoda, its life snuffed out, never to live again.

IT MADE MEN OF THEM ALL

FOOTNOTE: Being kicked out by one's father at an early age is not unique, nor is it the worst thing that could ever happen to a child. In fact it usually proves a blessing in disguise and I would strongly recommend it to any father of a rebellious juvenile. I have known quite a few who shared this fate. It made men of them all and most are earning plenty more than three meals a day.

Most notable of all is Leslie R. Chin who emerged the finest journalist ever of the Chinese-Jamaican community. His was literature at its best, and in the field of journalism he was perfection personified. A master baker as well, he consistently produced excellent edibles. Clearly, a stern and sterling achievement of an East Wind who was blown out by his father at an early age. Wouldn't you say so dear patient Reader?

And of the accountant, if my being a success is the only payment he will accept for the extraordinary compassion he showered on me, then it seems that I will forever be indebted to him. At best, he is receiving his payments in very small and insignificant amounts.

"Sweet are the uses of adversity, which, like a toad, though ugly and venomous, wears yet a precious jewel in its head."- William Shakespeare.

Written by Clive Fung and edited by Sonia Gordon Scott.

* See Glossary

Down Memory Lane

Hanging tangerines, Photograph ©Ray Chen

Sing Chin
HENS, KITES AND CEMETERIES

I WAS BORN SING SLUN CHIN in 1947 in Canton, China. I left China about four years later with my older brother, Fong, and my mother, Chin Sem Kun Yung. Our vessel was the *Blue Funnel Line*. We were headed for the West Indies, where my Jamaican-born father, Arthur George Chin, waited to meet us. The journey over was horrible. I'm pretty sure Hurricane Charlie had something to do with it, especially since we pulled into Kingston Harbour just one day before it hit the island.

As a young boy, our home and shop were in bustling Kingston, on Waltham Park Road. In fact, we were neighbours to what was then, and still is, the Chinese cemetery. *Our* grocery store was a small one. The rented 500 sq. ft. shop claimed the front of the property, while the two-room living quarters claimed the back. One was our bedroom with two beds. The second was our kitchen, dining and living room all rolled into one. The backyard was our chicken coop. That's where we raised hens for sale and personal consumption.

Our family had little material possessions, but lots of resourcefulness. For instance, Fong and I often sported shirts and shorts that mom stitched from chicken feed and other cotton bags. We took the teasing from the neighbourhood kids in stride. That's what we were given to wear. End of story. In our family there was no time or wherewithal for material or other indulgences. So no birthday parties, no holidays, no social life, no gifts. Nothing. A Lone Star gun from an uncle when I was nine was – well it was the lone exception.

Of course, we had our chores. One I'll never forget is the chicken coop. Each morning before leaving for school, without fail, we would clean the large pen, which was chained to a shady plum tree, and feed the 100 or so hungry birds. That was the easy part. Each night after homework and locking up the shop, we'd have to go into the back again, this time with a smaller cage, catch each bird one by one and bring them into the kitchen for the night. Fowl theft was a real problem those days. Well I still don't know which was worse. The fresh multiple scratches I incurred each time we did this, or the incessant noise of irate hens coming from the kitchen all night long as we tried to sleep. Fong and I did this every day, including Saturdays and Sundays when we helped our parents run the shop.

I'd be lying if I said that we didn't put up some healthy resistance to our chores. *Especially* on weekends. That was when our no-

nonsense father would come up with foolproof ways to keep his two boys close by. I won't elaborate further, except to say that I'm quite certain that today some of his techniques would be considered ahm, *questionable*.

When we *did* manage to steal some time to just be boys, we had good fun. Sometimes we'd walk the hour or so to Greenwich Town Beach and catch *tikki tikki* fish for our aquarium. Or hop over to the cemetery where we had some of our best hide and seek games. Other times we'd slingshot grassquit birds out of the lignum vitae trees and into our dutch-pots.

We also learned early about mixing business with pleasure. We loved making things with our hands. So one year we began making and selling cardboard Christmas hats for 3 pence each. We made those one dozen at a time. Not long after we added paper and bamboo kites to the inventory. Those we sold for a penny each. And we *still* made a profit.

Yes, our childhood was a not an easy one. Those were tough times. But if we are the sum total of our experiences, then I have few regrets. Put it this way. I have nothing against chickens.

Written and edited by Alex Lee as told by Sing Chin.

Photograph of chickens ©Ray Chen

Down Memory Lane

Shop in Philadelphia, St. Ann

Photograph ©Ray Chen

Winston Chung-Fah
ROLLINGTON TOWN DAYS

TRADITION IS WHAT brought me to Kingston from my home in Clarendon. The year was 1948, and as the firstborn son, I was on my way to China to become steeped in the ways and culture of the fatherland.

But then the war between the Communists and Kuomintang escalated, and the war and all its horror stories halted plans for that journey. So my father decided that I would remain in Kingston. My cousins and I would have to settle for the local alternative – Chinese Schools that were subsequently established. At that point home became Jackson Road, in Rollington Town with my *anyong**, my *abak** and seven cousins.

The days were full for us children. In the mornings we attended regular school. In the evenings we trekked down to Rockfort for Chinese School. After completing both, we went about our shop chores – tasks like wiping down the counter, oiling the chopper and machete, wrapping crackers, making funnels for salt and black pepper, wetting the cod fish, wrapping them in $^1/_4$, $^1/_2$ pound packages…. Of course, this is all before the days of the supermarket.

Pictures from Rollington Town.

But shop life had its interesting moments. *Oh yes.* I remember *anyong* instructing me in the ways of profit margins. She'd say, okay, listen now. When you're measuring out the goods into the scale to sell, as soon as you start to pour, the customer will instinctively look up at the scale. So what you do is tip the scale a little with your finger underneath to get an extra ounce or so. Because that is the ounce that is going to send you to school.

Well one day after that I was serving a customer, but didn't know that she had already caught on to our little trick. So I'm there doing my thing, chatting her up, measuring, weighing and wrapping up the flour or whatever it was she was buying. Then when I'm done, she looks me straight in the eye and says, *'Okay, now measure it again and put back in the ounce.'* Oh, man!

My *anyong* was a special woman. She showed me fairness. What her children got, I got. Always, keeping in mind that I was the half-Chinese relative. *Abak* was a barber and a Chinese herbalist. He was always mixing concoctions. In fact, we used to catch frogs for him down by a well on Jackson Road. He'd boil them and mix in all sorts of stuff. And let me tell you – when he did that, the whole neighbourhood wanted to move out! But then people would come in droves to buy his medicines. Especially on a Sunday.

At Jackson Road, we had the experience of life in a commune. We were poor. Really poor. We lived behind the tiny shop in one big room. And we *all* slept there. A single bed sheet divided *anyong* and *abak* from us children. On our side we had two double beds. Girls on one, boys on another. And we slept head to toe *across* the bed. Because shoulder to shoulder couldn't work. There's not enough space for that luxury. And once you're in the bed, you couldn't even shift an inch, or the poor man at the edge will fall off. And you *knew* that if you got up in the middle of the night to use the bathroom, you're not going to be able to squeeze back in. Because the second you left, everyone tek the little ease up! But it worked, you know. We managed. Managed and never complained.

There's a lot I won't ever forget. Like my board slippers or *kyaks*. That was one of three pairs of shoes I owned. I had those, my 'God-blind-me' crepes, and one pair of dress shoes. My cousin Eddie and I were the youngest. So we got all the ill-fitting hand-me-downs. Man! We used to *swim* in some of those pants.

Then there were our rushed hair cuts. My uncle may have been the barber, but it was our auntie who trimmed us. Like on a Sunday *while* she's cooking and doing a couple other things at the same time. A Hakka woman's work was never done. Of course, my uncle would be lying on his bed, fanning the heat off himself.

In those days we had no electric fans or even a fridge. The closest we got to a fridge was a 25 lb piece of ice from the ice truck. We'd take that, cover it in sawdust, and wrap it in newspaper. Believe it or not, it kept the ice the whole day.

As for meals in our household, Sunday dinners were a treat. That was meat day – when we'd have a little pork, beef, and chicken. We reared our own fowls, of course. From the feathers to the blood, we wasted *nothing* from it. So you didn't miss Sunday dinner for anything. Because the rest of the week you'd get pure rice, *seeyu** and salt fish.

At the table you ate with chopsticks, and *never* with your left hand. That was considered bad luck. Another rule was that you had to take the piece of meat directly in front of you on the serving platter. If you went digging for a better piece, you'd get a chopstick lick in the head from *anyong* or *abak.* What can I tell you? We learned some good foundation lessons.

But more than anything else, those Rollington Town days taught us how to share. How to care. And really *appreciate*. Sometimes I wonder if we made it too easy for the next generation. We did it out of love, and they're doing better financially and otherwise. But that appreciation for life, for our heritage. Do they really have it?

Written and edited by Alex Lee as told by Winston Chung-Fah.

* See Glossary   Photographs ©Ray Chen

Rudy Chen
CLEAR FROM LIFE ON A DUSTY ROAD

WHEN I CAME into existence in 1941, my parents lived at 28 Spanish Town Road, western Kingston. I was the youngest of three, which included a sister – also born in Jamaica – and a brother born in China. My sister, however, was taken to China at the age of three or four, to be raised in the Chinese culture, and did not return until her late teens. I was supposed to follow the same path but it did not happen. When the Communists took over mainland China, my sister and brother had to flee to Hong Kong under the cloak of night through barbed wire fences. Any plan of sending me later ended then and there, and I continued along the path of becoming an upright and contributing Jamaican citizen.

Spanish Town Road was, and still is, a main thoroughfare, bustling with heavy traffic. Buses, trucks, cars and carts...carts drawn by donkeys or mules, and carts pushed by humans. Dust and noise reigned throughout the day. Life on this stretch of road was anything but dull, for we had numerous bouts of fisticuffs among sidewalk vendors in a turf war for prime space. Then there were the political demonstrations that ended in riots, the saloon brawls on weekend nights, after much consumption of rum, and the frequent wild shootouts between police and thieves. Dad always warned me to steer clear of any disturbance and, since machetes were often brought into play and bottles thrown, I would watch these action-packed episodes from a bedroom window upstairs. It was always a treat to watch two female higglers fighting because, at some point, the women would graduate from pulling each other's hair to ripping off each other's clothes, resulting in a much anticipated strip show. Sometimes, though, even taking the precaution of securing a safe spot at an upstairs window did not provide protection. One morning, as I stood by the window watching some policemen chasing a thief, the thief turned and fired some shots. A bullet strayed upward, whizzed past my ear, and lodged in the wall of my bedroom!

My father, James Chen Kee-Onn, from the village of Yam-Ten in Guangdong province, came to Jamaica in 1927. My mother, Lily Hugh, from Hong Kong, came soon afterward. The only thing I can recall of my dad's life in China is that he had a job drying small fish by the seaside at Sa-Tau-Kok... the type still sold in packages in Chinese supermarkets. He had heard from friends, and from news circulating in his village, that a better life could be made in the West Indies. Since he had friends in Jamaica, he solicited their sponsorship and, through their lawyer, was successful in emigrating to Jamaica. Once there, he worked for these friends until he saved enough money to establish his own business, and to send for Mom and some relatives to participate in it. Business was booming in downtown Kingston, and the west end of Spanish Town Road was thriving. Although the area was rough and primitive, dad decided to brave the danger and make a start there. He opened a bar and, later, a grocery was added. The hours were long, the work arduous, but the family persevered and, finally, the pounds, shillings and pence slowly added up.

Dad was the eldest member of the family, which meant, in those times, that he was 'lord of the manor'. He made the decisions and expected obedience. He was strict with Mom and me and, when he thought fit, would conduct business in a stern manner. Being totally dependent on him at the time, I did my best to play the obedient son, working hard in my studies and helping him in the bar.

Of course, there was dad's lighter side. He loved to read and kept abreast of world affairs. On weekends he would take me to the beach, to the cinema, or to visit with friends. Mom would often accompany us on these visits and went with us to garden parties. What great outings for the family these parties were! There we ate our fill of steamed buns and dumplings, enjoyed games at various stalls, delighted in stage performances of song and dance, and met up with our friends. In my case, they would be my schoolmates from the Chinese Public School. In the beginning, I socialized with my own kind, as dad wanted it that way. He explained that conversation was easier because of our common heritage, and that this would prepare me for my planned stay in China. When the trip was cancelled, he no longer discouraged me from having other friends when I moved on to high school at St. George's College. In my twenties, I went to dance parties at friends' homes...and dance we did! We would start off with the fast tunes – everything from calypso to reggae to rock 'n roll and the Bee Gees. At midnight we took a break to dig into some heavy food, like curried goat and rice. After that, we would switch to slow dancing. The merriment went on 'till the wee hours of the morning.

When my sister returned home, she was already a young lady of about twenty. Struggling to learn English, she ended up adopting the colourful patois of the street higglers, something she has retained to this day. Being of a friendly and loving nature, she struck up easy friendships with Chinese merchants on both sides of our street and, in a short time, fell in love and got married to the boy next door. I met my brother for the first time in my early twenties, after he emigrated from Hong Kong to Jamaica with plans to take over the business eventually. This was not to be, for an unfortunate event took place that scared the wits out of him, and sent him scrambling off to seek his fortune elsewhere. A riot against the Chinese broke out on our very street, and my poor brother witnessed, first hand, the hatred and destruction. Shortly thereafter he moved to England where he had friends.

The experience of being caught in the centre of a riot was a frightening one. Whatever the true reason was that sparked it off, the screaming throng was out to get our kind. That night we could not eat or sleep well, for we did not know if the rioters would gain entry into the house. They tried breaking down the front door and tried scaling the walls and zinc fences. We kept guard in complete darkness. Thieves seized upon this opportunity and did some heavy looting in various shopping areas and plazas. After it was contained, the political bigwigs met with a representation of shopkeepers and community leaders to formulate a plan for restoring full order. A fragile peace came upon the city but the mood remained tense for a while. Little by little, we resumed the task of making a living, and looked toward the future.

Today, I still rank the experience of living on dusty and frenzied Spanish Town Road among my fondest memories. I don't regret growing up in the thick of it at all. Life in my youth was tough but exciting. I have learned from it, and it has made me appreciate the sweet life all the more.

Written by Rudy Chen and edited by Sonia Gordon Scott.

Down Memory Lane

Main Street in the the town of St. Ann's Bay, St. Ann

Photograph ©Ray Chen

Albert Lim Shue
LIFE CYCLE - AN EXPERIENCE

I'M A PORT ROYAL City kid. My parents, Irene and Charles Lim Shue had two boys. My brother Frank, and me.

We lived in Port Royal for a few years after my birth in 1937. At the time it was a thriving little town, where everyone knew everyone else and got along just fine. I just loved it there. The sea was our playground. I fished, I swam and hung out with my friends. Even our elementary school was right by the sea. There were four or five Chinese families in Port Royal, and we all lived harmoniously with the black Jamaicans. It was only when we ventured into Kingston that we sensed some minor racial problems, such as intimidation in the form of name calling.

Growing up, my parents emphasized our culture. Mom would say, '*Son, no matter what, always remember that you are Chinese.*' When I was still small enough, she'd put me on her knee and repeat ever so patiently in the softest Hakka, '*Son, this is peegung (nose). This is nee-yim (ears). This is joi (mouth).*' Sometimes she'd tell me stories about the China that she missed. I'd go looking for all those stories in our history books, but could never find them. When at the dinner table we ate with bowls and chopsticks. If you spoke in English, you got two chopsticks in the head. This is how we were at home.

The fun and good karma continued on into my young adult years, in spite of the fact that I was always made aware by the majority that I was a *Chiney* man. Now in those days I had two main loves – the Chinese Scout Troops and basketball. The scout troop taught us things western that our Chinese parents could not due to a lack of time or experience. The basketball was just pure fun. At one point we formed two teams with some other young *ship-it-dams** and

First Chinese Boy Scouts Troop at the first Caribbean Jamboree at Up Park Camp, Kingston, Jamaica, 1952. L-R, Back row: Donald Chen, Everard Hoo, Leslie Chin, Robert Chang, Joe Chen, Albert Lim Shue, Alex (Gunn Yen) Lee, Albert Lyn, Eric Hoo, Clinton Woung. Kneeling: Colin Chen, Clive Fung, Leroy, Andrew Hoo, Donald, Gilbert Chen.

ban-tong-fahs*. We were the Eagles and they were the United Aces. At my initiative the United Aces was a mixed team. Together we won the League Knockout Cup in our first year. And when the Central & Pan American games were held for the first time in our newly built National Stadium in 1962, I and many other Chinese Jamaicans proudly participated in basketball games and other activities. It was a good life.

Some of that would change for me three years later with the 1965 disturbances.

I woke up in my Vineyard Town home at 5:30 that morning to begin my day as a self-employed travelling salesman. I remember leaning over as usual to switch on the radio to the news. RJR came to life as I turned up the volume. And that's when I heard the broadcaster's voice. *Riot on Spanish Town Road...gas station on fire...businesses burned down on Princess St...looting ...!*

2 *Above: 1957 Senior League Basketball & Knockout Cup Champions. Standing: Canute Adams, Dacosta Leung, Raoul Grubb. Kneeling: Albert Lim Shue, Nelson Tait & Clifton (Tenny) Hugh.*

Call it denial, call it stubborn youth. I got dressed anyway and headed out the door and into my car to begin my week long journey into the country. It was 7:30 a.m. by the time I hit Central Village. That's when I turned my car around and paused. Do I take Spanish Town Road or Washington Boulevard? I ended up taking a circuitous route that included Half Way Tree, Cross Roads, Torrington Bridge and Orange Street.

At Orange Street I stopped at a light. Across the street on my right was Torrington Pharmacy, which was owned by Tony and Dr. John Chin's parents. Across from that was Dairy Farmers. At the lights sat a fruit vendor. I was in my car, and she was on my left. And then she looked up, glowered and mouthed off something at me.

I sensed some animosity, but didn't take much note of it and continued along East Race Course. I made a right turn at Light and Power, turned back on Orange Street and then to North Street. Again I was stopped at a light next to a vendor. Again another bout of cursing. At that point I headed straight for my office on Princess Street. It was now 8:15 a.m., and everything was pretty much closed. Across the road were Royal Cremo and J.H.G. Mapp and Co. All quiet. When I pulled up, I saw that my office door was still closed. Standing on the sidewalk was Sam, one of my staff members, and Melvin, a customs broker who rented space from me.

'Mel,' I said. *'Whappen, man?'*

'Albert you nuh hear that the man dem coming to Princess and Barry St. to burn down de place?'

'You know what, Sam?' I said. *'Fly the door'.* The door was really shutters. I went up the stairs and into my office where I remained, glued to the radio. Minutes later Sam bolted up the stairs.

'Mr. Albert! Mr. Albert! You betta lock up de office 'cause I hear a gang coming to burn down Chinatown!'

I immediately called my wife who was working at the Bank of London and Montreal on Harbour Street. She assured me that her manager was personally driving home all the Chinese staff members, and that I was not to worry. The bank managers at the time were all foreigners, and mostly Canadians. I told her I was going to go get her brother in St. Thomas before heading home.

And that's exactly what I did. I returned to Kingston that evening with something to defend ourselves with in case the situation worsened. We just didn't know. That night, my brother, brother-in-law and I spent the night at my house awake and waiting. Outside you could hear the indecipherable shouting interspersed with the unmistakable cries of '*Chiney!*' in the mix. Chinatown would remain quiet for the rest of that day and night, with most sitting it out, and only a few opening for business. No one even dared to venture into Spanish Town Road where the riots first sparked.

As for the cause of it all, fingers pointed to a lover's spat between a Jamaican Chinese man and his Jamaican girlfriend, which had been mistaken for an altercation between an employer and employee. At least that was the popular rumour.

Fortunately, nothing happened that night to force us to defend ourselves. But a few days later, I was walking along King Street when this guy came tripping down on his bicycle, stopped in front of me, and threatened violence.

This time I let him know that I'd defend myself if I needed to. He moved on. I think it was at that point that I decided it was time to go. I could not see myself, a young man of 26, living like that. I took some time to consider world events and the fate of the Chinese in other countries that had been granted independence. At that time, Britain was relinquishing her colonial empire in various countries, Jamaica having just been granted hers in 1962. I still considered myself a Jamaican of Chinese parentage, but decided that the future as a minority in Jamaica would be limited. I left Jamaica with my wife in 1967.

And while I consider 1965 as a significant point in my life, I will forever see the Jamaica that I left as a special influence in my life. It gave me the best foundation years a man could ever ask for, and I will always love and have the greatest respect for my island in the sun. How can one ask for more when one has had the best of two worlds.

Written by Alex Lee as told by Albert Lim Shue.

* See Glossary

Photograph 1 - ©Everard Hoo
Photograph 2 - ©Albert Lim Shue

Phil Chen
'MISSA CHIN' MEMORIES OF EARLY JAMAICAN MUSIC

THIS ARTICLE is being written from a Chinese point of view – 'Missa Chin' (Mister or Miss Chin), as we Chinese were called, regardless of correct surname. It was more like a term of endearment in a land where, without a nickname, one was considered low on the popularity or hecklers' list.

I was blessed to be born in the land of mongoose, mangoes, and Marley, in the city of Kingston, Jamaica, the capital of mento, ska, rock steady, reggae, sun splash parties, and endless rum and Coke. Our way of life led us to be totally colour blind, living in harmony among one another. It was a paradise where the association of a black man and a Chinaman was as clear as the sunshine, or the wonderful sound of reggae in one's ear.

CHINESE JAMAICANS

In the early nineteenth century, the central government of China considered all Chinese who migrated to Jamaica and elsewhere criminals, as their exodus was not sanctioned by the government. Upon arrival at their destination they received no welcome and got little protection. Like migrants everywhere who travelled in large numbers for economic reasons, the Chinese left for Jamaica without adequate resources. Their only possessions were their physical ability to toil, honesty, a desire and will to take care of their loved ones, and hope that in the final analysis, they would return to their native land to live their old age in comfort and die in peace.

Phil Chen

In 1884, the Jamaican land barons, hard-pressed for workers because of the liberation of the African slaves in 1838, pressured the government into finding them additional labourers. It was then that the Hong Kong government introduced 700 Chinese workers who were all sent to the plantations in St. Thomas. These workers were from the Taishan area, Fui Yang, Dung Gon, and the Bao On countries. Slowly, the Chinese fled to Kingston and started their own businesses. From these humble beginnings, immense progress in the Chinese community was made. The rate of Chinese immigration was further accelerated by the ease of entry into the colony.

THE CHEN CLAN

I was told that my great-grandfather, John Chin Fook, was among the workers who had fled to start the Hackney Carriage business in Kingston. Out of necessity to feed seven children, my parents went on to open Specialty Grocery (5 Constant Spring Road, Half Way Tree by the Clock Tower, right next door to the Rainbow Club). After closing time, my dad would stay up till 5:00-6:00am, and with brush, ink, and paper pursue his dream and his true calling, the arts of calligraphy and poetry.

While I pretended to sleep, I would peek out from under the blanket to see his smilin' face as he meticulously put the finishing touch to yet another masterpiece. In the meantime I would be mesmerized by the mento sounds of Calypso Joe next door at the Rainbow Club, doing renditions of *"Back to Back, Belly to Belly"*, *"Naughty Little Flea"*, *"Linstead Market"*, *"Wheel an Tun Mi"*, *"Please Mista Don't You Touch Mi Tomato"*, etc. I was hooked, and had found my calling – music – as de banjo man gracefully slid up and down de neck. Being a true artist, my dad's responsibility to his business had started to decline. I remember returning home from school one day at age 13 to discover that we had been kicked out of the shop. I knew then that I had to leave the ghetto to make something of my life, if not for me, for my parents. I had heard enough of the Cultural Revolution.

THE UNCLE AND THE COWBOY

My next step was to acquire a guitar, and I knew opportunity was just around the corner. I would sneak out of my geometry class before lunchtime and, by investing my lunch money, I was able to hop a 'Chi-Chi' white bus downtown to 66 Orange Street. Music Mart was the only music store in Kingston, owned by Mr. and Mrs. Ho Sang. They also sold sewing machines.

After listening to a rendition of Bach concertos by a brown-skinned Einstein-looking organist with frizzy hair, and surveying the latest Singer or Necchi sewing machines, my eyes finally set fire on a graciously showcased, sunburst Fender Jaguar. It was just like the one Rupert Bent played in Jamaica's number-one band, Byron Lee and the Dragonaires. I was in shock – a totally speechless kid in a candy store. Because I lacked funds, I secretly memorized the shape and went around the corner where, in my geometry book I recreated every miniscule detail.

After many weeks of waiting, my uncle, Luther Chen, (who had a furniture shop) finally included the wood for my guitar in one of his customers' large order of furniture. I bless them both. A tall, black guitarist of Arawak descent, who sported a neat Brylcream hairstyle and rode a shiny motorcycle from the Rainbow Club next door, was helpful in the rewiring of magnets from a bicycle generator for the pick-ups. I think his name was Cowboy. I bless and thank him.

CHINESE ROCKS

Chinese involvement in music was varied in the form of producers, musicians, record shop managers, and more. Byron Lee set the precedent in the mid-'50s with Florence Wong on keyboards, Keith Lyn on vocals, 'Father' on congas, and 'Dudge', part-time percussionist and hubcap king. Half-Chinese Ernest Ranglin was the first to be given the Order of Distinction and was a major contributor to the music of artists like Bob Marley, Jimmy Cliff, Jackie Edwards, Coxsone Dodd, and Duke Reid. He invented ska's 'pick and roll' doubling of the bass line style of playing, and arranged Jamaica's first million-seller, *"My Boy Lollipop"* by Millie Small. (For the historian, Rod Stewart played harmonica on that number.) Ranglin would be voted number-one jazz guitarist in London, 1964.

The Vagabonds, led by Colston Chen (rumour has it he was the first electric bassist on a ska record, namely Derrick Morgan's *"The Hop"),* Stanley Yap (drums), Lloyd Chang (vocalist), Herman Chin Sang (early organist), and Errol Hugh (MC), was managed by Cecil Moo Young. I was to join later, on their departure for England, to promote ska with Jimmy James and Count Prince Miller.

Because of Jamaica's proximity to

1. *Colston Chen in front, with Phil Chen.*
2. *The Vagabonds letterhead*
3. *Count Prince along with The Vagabonds*
4. *The Vagabonds*

Cuba, Latin music was prevalent, hence, Club Havana, owned by my friend Tony Chin Sang's family. There, one could enjoy Latin music and see rumba dancers like Margarita Mafood, Caledonia Robinson, fire dances, Cedric, a Chinese singer, a Chinese magician, as well as the many local bands like the Mighty Vikings, the Vagabonds, and Kes Chin & The Souvenirs.

Kes Chin – the hip-shaking, maracas-swinging Chinaman – was our own Jamaican Perez Prado. His musicians included Australians Denis Sindrey on guitar, Lowell Morris on drums, Peter Stoddart on keys, and the great bassist/steel guitar player Audley 'Mr. Wasp Chipmunk' Williams, brother of Granville Williams, Byron Lee's dynamic organist.

Denis Sindry and engineer Graham Goodall married sisters Fay and Cherry Wong from Retirement Road, and would become very instrumental in the development of early Jamaican music.

THE MIGHTY VIKINGS

Above Wong Lim Wholesale and Haberdashery (123 Princess Street, specializing in mackerel, flour, sugar, saltfish, bustamante backbone, patty and

pigs tail), and across from de market square, the Wong family's daily ritual would find them gathering around

The Mighty Vikings.
Back row, l-r, Esmond Jarrett, Chummy Miles, Peter Miles, Bobby Ellis, Winston Manning.
Second row, l-r, Hux Brown, Wallace Cameron, Desmond Miles, Neville Hinds (seated) Tony Wilson, Lester Sterling, Sonny Wong.
Front, Victor Wong

de piano after the closing of the shop, while the elder music teacher, Florence, tickled the ivories. This led to her being the first keyboard player for Byron Lee and the Dragonaires in 1954, the start of The Buccaneers and The Mighty Vikings with Sonny and Victor Wong as lead vocalists, and Margaret as lead singer of Ingrid Chin and the Carnations. This daily treat to passers-by was an important, integral family get-together, as important as ackee was to saltfish or bulla to pear.

The Mighty Vikings would go on to back popular artists like Bob Marley, Wilfred 'Jackie' Edwards, The Blues Busters, Tony Gregory, Roy & Millie, Desmond Dekker, Jackie Opel, Laurel Aitken and Horace Forbes, as well as to make the Higgs & Wilson classic, *"There Is a Reward"*, plus two LPs of their own. One lasting memory of my brief stint as guitarist with the Vikings at Club Havana on Fridays, was on February 28, 1964, when Victor commented just as he was about to commit to *"Sukiyaki":* "Phillip tun de reverb on! Mi sey tell Desi fi tun on di damm ting or mi naw go sing" ("Phillip, turn the reverb on! I say, tell Desi to turn on the damn thing or I won't sing"). Funny how certain things stick in one's mind. This one certainly did. It was history in the making.

The Mighty Vikings went on to be the number one band for RJR (Radio Jamaica and Rediffusion) in 1965, securing 2,411 votes. Carlos Malcolm and his Afro Jamaican Rhythms received 2,367 and Byron Lee and the Dragonaires got 956. Thanks to Winston 'Buggas' Chin Quee and his brother Tony, who ran the Jamaican Commercial Institute on Duke Street. Upstairs of the Institute was the band's rehearsal spot, cum-typewriting-secretarial-and-bookkeeping HQ.

KG's

Neville Cha Fong had taken over this record shop from Kenneth George and didn't bother to change the sign. So he became known as "KG." This one-car garage-sized record store was situated at 84 Slipe Road, across from the popular landmark, Carib Theatre. This tiny shop was a common meeting place, especially on Fridays (pay day) where friends would come to su-su-su-su (tete-a-tete), renew acquaintances, and put their weekly record acquisition in front of the food, telephone, rent, water or gas bills. The shop's mascot, Babi, was a slightly crazy, peace-loving, dreadlocked rasta, who could be seen puttering back and forth in front of the shop all day long.

Upon entering, one would notice the vast number of LPs displayed on both sides of the walls. It was then that you would come face-to-face with Neville's wife, Madge, sitting neatly cross-legged on a high stool in front of two turntables, the latest singles in her hand. Behind the smile she would DJ the hits, giving you exactly 10-15 seconds (if you were lucky) to decide if you liked it or not, then she would quickly shuffle on to the next, blasting through the leaky TL12 tube amp and the homemade 15" speakers.

I remember KG telling me his modus operandi where he would tune his radio to a hip Miami station, hook up an open reel tape, and go to bed. In the morning over breakfast, he would quickly scan the tape like Madge with the 45s (10-15 seconds per song) and with the great knack or genius, make a note of all the hits, hop on a plane for Miami that same day, and have the hits for sale at KG's the next day.

KG & Madge were very instrumental in teaching that artists and melodies know no boundaries. Their musical 'library' included Patsy Cline, Otis Redding, Ella and Louis, Bert Kampfert, Roger Williams, Skeeter Davis,

Louis Jordan, Matt Monroe, Mantovani, Ruby and the Romantics, the Drifters, Sam Cooke, Jimmy Clanton, Nat "King" Cole, Bing Crosby, Bill Haley, Marvin Gaye, Jim Reeves, The Beatles, Hank Williams, Johnny Tillotson, Jackie Wilson, Stan Getz, etc., etc., as well as all the reigning local talents – we bless them.

KING KONG

Lloyd, Cecil, and Leslie Kong, who were into selling real estate, also had Beverly's Ice Cream Parlour at 135A Orange Street (at the corner of North Street). Les would later become one of Jamaica's leading record producers. When Desmond Dacres (Dekker) turned over the Patty showcase in his determination to get noticed, Les was afforded the chance to record his first local hit, Desmond's *"Honor Your Mother and Father"* in 1963. This led to a worldwide smash hit *"Poor Me Israelites,"* Jamaica's second international hit after Millie Small. Les also produced Jimmy Cliff's British Top 40 *"Wonderful World",* and the early Bob Marley hit *"Judge Not",* with the riddim section of Jah Jerri (guitar), Ashlund Parks (drums and drumbago), Lloyd Brevelt (bass), and Theophilus Beckford (piano). Les would sit behind the console with his dark glasses on, irrespective of the time of day. He said nothing, but with a shake of his head, the artist would have to try again. A smile and a nod denoted a hit, everything copasetic (cool, O.K).

The camaraderie between the Chinese and the black population was clearly demonstrated in Les Kong's production of Derrick Morgan's huge hit, *"Blazing Fire,"* part of a celebrated feud directed straight at Prince Buster. Derrick starts with the Chinese sentence "ne tang mung zai" which translates to "you are a damn fool." He even goes on to call himself a "black head Chiney," taking sides with the Chinese.

Mr Derek Chang, the real estate mogul, had a love for the saxophone and music, which led him to form the Derek Chang Orchestra with Hermine 'Dots' Chang on bass and an all-Chinese cast. There were many Chinese producers-cum-record shop owners. One notable was Justin 'Top Deck' Yap, who produced *"Confucius"* for Don Drummond. Randy Chin produced *"Leaving Babylon"* by Bonnie and Skitter and Rico's *"Special"* on the Randy's label, 1959. (During the British ska revival, Rico would play with Jerry Dammers, Terry Hall, and The Specials). JoJo Hokim had Channel 1 Studio and, with The Mighty Diamonds, gave us *"Country Living."* Herman Chin Loy had Aquarius Studios, and Michael Shadeed (a half-Chinese) produced *"Three Blind Mice"* with BaBa Brooks and the Skatalites.

The Vagabonds

JAMAICAN INVASION

On Thursday, April 23, 1964 at 4:00 p.m., I said goodbye to my brother Franco, Keith Lyn, Carl Brady, Noel Seale, and ticks. The Vagabonds were setting sail on *The Ascania* (a banana boat, to be exact), leaving behind Victoria Pier #3 and Kingston Harbour for the 'Mother Country', London, England. Sixteen days later on Friday May 8 at 5:00p.m., via Madeira, Lisbon, and Vigo, we landed at Southampton in the land of the King and Queen, fish and chips, Shakespeare, The Beatles, and The Who. My dream to build a better life for my mom, dad, and family was being realized. Nuff respect to Colston Chen and Uncle Luthor. We were met by Tony Nelson, our manager, and had our first taste of fish and chips and oxtail soup while freezing our butts off.

The Vagabonds - standing from left to right: Wallace Wilson (guitar), Carl Noel (keyboards), Colston Chen (leader/bass guitar), Winston "Sparrow" Martin (drums), Rupert Balgobin (percussion) Phil Chen (guitar). In front is "Count Prince Miller" (entertainer/MC). Missing from the picture is Jimmy James (vocals).

The Vagabonds consisted of Colston Chen (bass), myself (second guitar), Wallace Wilson (lead guitar), Sparrow Martin (drums), Rupert Balgobin (percussion), Carl 'Grog' Griffith (sax), Carl 'Breadback' Noel (organ), Jimmy James and Count Prince Miller (vocals), and Roger Smith (tour manager and Copa Club owner). Our goal was to promote ska, which was limited to the West Indian market but, in order to appeal to the English audience, we were recommended to change our style to R&B by Peter Meaden (former manager of The High Numbers/The Who) who became our new manager. With the departure of Colston, I switched from guitar to bass. Having the same agency as The Who led us to be their support group every Wednesday night at the Marquee Club, until we secured our own Monday night. While The Who played original material, their love for R&B would find them doing their own version of *"Dancing in the Street"* by Martha and the Vandellas, complementing the 'Vags' rendition of *"On Broadway"* by the Drifters, plus numbers by Otis Redding, James Brown, etc. from our R&B repertoire.

MAXIMUM R&B

From 1965 to 1969 the mod scene was in full swing and The Who and The Small Faces were considered two of the top hip English bands as well as the Vags, Gene Washington, Herbie Gains, and Ronnie Jones (who represented the American R&B). As Richard Barnes rightly described the period: "In the early sixties, a lifestyle evolved for young people that was mysterious, exciting, and fast-moving. It was directed from within and needed no justification from without. Kids were clothes-obsessed, cool, dedicated to R&B, and their own dances. They called themselves mods."

It was common to walk down the Shaftesbury Avenue visiting the many music stores and be confronted by John Lennon, Paul McCartney, Jimmy Page, Eric Clapton, or even Jimi Hendrix. I first met Jimi at the Marquee before he went to play before a crowd of 40-50 people. At first I was a bit hesitant, as his attire reminded me of the dreadlock rastas at home. (Even though they were peace-loving religious people, you would get one that sometimes was out of control, swearing as the rum began to dictate. "Don't worry if dem swear an get drunk, mek sure the money is right," mom and dad would tell me.)

This wonderful time of starvation, exposure, and exciting music allowed the Vags to travel over the European continent – Paris, Holland, Belgium, etc. – and as far as Budapest, Hungary to represent British pop.

In 1969-1970, communication in the Vagabonds camp had broken down and, with my £200 departure fee (which I sent home to my parents), I embarked with a bass in hand on a solo session career for real. I was controlling my own destiny.

Playing with Jackie Edwards, Bob Marley, Johnny Nash, Millie Small, Jimmy Cliff, Dandy Livingstone, Laurel Aitken, Desmond Dekker, and the occasional British pop sessions with Mickey Most, etc., led to the birth of my switch to British rock 'n' roll. I eventually ended up playing with Keith Richards and Ron Wood, New Barbarians, the classic Jeff Beck *"Blow By Blow"* (produced by 'the fifth Beatle', George Martin, and the only rock instrumental in history to supercede 3,000,000 in sales). The Who's *Tommy* with Pete Townshend, Eric Clapton, Richard Bailey, etc. working on Pete's solo.

White City was the start of world tours with Rod Stewart. Four albums later, my bass helped make *"Do Ya Think I'm Sexy"* Rod's biggest monster hit, belting out of the radio worldwide. From the ghetto to the glitter, the 'Bruce Lee of Bass' had finally arrived from the land of mongoose, mangoes, Marley, and Chen.

Written by Phil Chen and edited by Sonia Gordon Scott.

Photographs courtesy of Phil Chen and Colston Chen
Photograph of The Mighty Vikings courtesy of Patrick Lee, from the book
©The Jamaican Chinese Worldwide, One Family - 2004

Patrick Chen
AN ALL-JAMAICAN MODEL AIRPLANE STORY

CHINESE STUDENTS STAND AGAINST
ESTABLISHED AERO-MODELLERS

In the mid-1950s, a couple of decades after the peak in the number of the China-born Chinese in Jamaica, and a decade after the end of WWII, a group of Chinese teenagers became determined to beat the group of older aero-modellers at the model airplane game. (At this time, the Chinese accounted for 1% of the Jamaican population). The teenagers were taking on the established aero-modellers who were working adults, able to buy kits and the best materials. These teenagers, average age about fifteen years old, had to make do and use their ingenuity. How this Goliath and David confrontation turned out is explained by the difference in the approach taken by the youngsters and the adults. Here is the story.

EARLY FLIGHTS OF FANCY

It is difficult for one growing up in tropical Jamaica not to notice birds, small and large. While we hunted the small birds with our sling-shots, the jangkro (vultures called John Crow) was somehow always out of reach and somewhere high up in the sky. I guess flying kites was an attempt to go soaring like the jangkro that seemed to just hang in the air. Flying had always fascinated me and I dreamed of being in the air all the time, sometimes even imagining I was flying while sitting in a chair. After hanging out at the ends of tree branches or on top of the grocery store roof, I began launching paper gliders that then became balsa-wood gliders.

LEARNING ABOUT MODEL PLANES

As a teenager in the mid-1950s I began reading science magazines, such as *Popular Science*, which I received from my mechanical-minded uncle, Ernest Yap Chung, who repaired automobiles and was part-owner of the Betta Cab Company. From these magazines I went on to read model airplane magazines that opened up a whole new world in which I could make and fly planes. Other influences at work were the movies, such as 'The Bridges at Toko-Ri' (1954) with William Holden and Grace Kelly, in which a single-engine fighter jet, the F9F-5 Panther, was featured. One of my first small-scale models was of this plane made from a basic kit, and I spent time making sure the details were scaled accurately. However, it was not a flying model.

DESIRE FOR FLIGHT CONTROL

Not satisfied with just gliding a model plane, or looking at a still model, I became interested in small, foot-long balsa wood gliders to which a small rocket engine, called Jetex, was attached. The engine was an aluminum cylinder with a small, solid rocket propellant (about the size of a thumb), that was ignited by a wick but lasted only a minute. I bought these planes at the Hole-in-the-Wall store, 6 King Street, Kingston, run by the Chen See family. The flight path of the small model was not only short but also very unpredictable. Such short, uncontrolled flights only heightened my interest in wanting to create a model with longer flight but, more importantly, with flight control.

THE CRAZY MODEL AIRPLANE GANG

By this time, there were several of us Chinese teenagers involved in making and flying model planes. There was Colston Chen, son of Chen Kung Yee, Eddie Lim Quee You, Pin Williams and my brother Peter. Randolph Demercado was the most emotional one in the group who, after crashing his plane, would finish the job by jumping on it. We made all types of planes including shorter planes with large wings of about two plus feet for 'combat', flying in a circle. Two persons in the middle would fly their planes, ducking around each other, while holding on to the two fifty-foot long control wires attached to controls inside the planes' bodies. The controls were linked to the tail flaps. Each model had a ten-foot crepe paper streamer attached to its tail. The winner of the contest was the one who successfully cut off the paper streamers of the opponent's plane without damaging the plane.

Above: Colston & Peter with model of the deHavelland DHC-1B-2-S5, April 1959.

Right: Peter Chen at the controls flying model with Patrick Chen bending down to avoid the control wires.

Next: Randolph Demercado having fun finishing off his model which had just crashed. Patrick Chen is holding a typical combat model with large wings and a short body for quick manoeuvres.

FINDING SAFE PLACES TO FLY THE MODELS

In order to have fun flying our planes, the gang looked for open, grassy places as far away from peoples' houses as possible. We went on the weekends, when we would have more time to fly, as it would take us a while to get to these places on our bicycles. Among the places we frequented more often for our flying expeditions were the Chinese Athletic Club field on Molynes Road, the soccer field of St George's School on North Street, Cow Shit Park on Lady Musgrave Road, and the beautifully kept Hope Botanical Gardens at the eastern end of Hope Road. Getting to Hope Gardens was quite a challenge as it was uphill all the way along Hope Road, and we had to carry our models in our hands and balance ourselves for three to four miles on a fixed gear bicycle. We also flew close to home at the empty site by the Odeon Theatre, just north of our store, Speciality Grocery at 5 Constant Spring Road next to the Rainbow Night Club.

Eddie Lim Quee You, Randolph Demercado and a friend flying planes at the St. George's College football field.

THE DANGEROUS CONSEQUENCES OF FLYING

Once we ventured onto the grounds of the Ardenne High School (on Ardenne Road a mile from Half-Way-Tree) one Sunday morning. The model flown was the one we were testing for carrying a given payload. The two-pound lead block slotted into the plane shot out and hit the head of the caretaker who had come out to watch us fly. The caretaker, in retribution, seized the bicycle belonging to Derrick Shaw who had to walk home. The next day, the lawyer father of a student whom we knew, negotiated the return of the bicycle with no further consequences. This was yet another learning event flowing from the potential dangers of a flying object.

A MODEL CLUB JAMAICAN STYLE

Mr. Jim Brown, an American, and a retired Pan American pilot, opened a model shop where we were able to choose from a greater variety of materials. This access to a treasure trove of material expanded our vision and deepened our interest in models. As we took the hobby more seriously, we formed ourselves into the Brown's Balsa Butcher Club. We challenged ourselves further by designing and flying models specifically for speed, combat, stunt, and load-carrying capacities, and scaled models for reflecting, in miniature, the details of a real aircraft. These types of model planes took different approaches in design, building, testing, and flying to achieve the specific goal of the flight. Each one of these challenges required a different technique, and each member of the gang was able to contribute his expertise. It was not necessary that the person who built the plane be the one who made the test flight. Each one had a place in the club. On reflection about the group, girls did not seem interested, although some came to see us fly. My sister, Dorothy, who is only a couple of years younger, reminded me that she was interested but assumed that we may have felt that she was too young. She recalled that when she came into the model room, which was the bakery room behind our grocery shop, she was told to look but not touch any of the models. She did admit that I had given her some small, odd, but menial jobs to do.

The social dynamic of the club was pure Jamaican, from those in the model shop to the hangers-on who were fascinated by our exploits. Mr. Roy Archer, a gentleman of East Indian origin, who had worked for Mr. Brown at his garage on Oxford Road and Half-Way-Tree Road before coming to the model store, was always there to greet us with a joke, such as "What colour dope (model paint) do you want today?" He even told us when not to buy something which was cheaper elsewhere. I am not sure what that has to do with the fact that Roy ended up in the police force. There was a brown Jamaican, Bruce Shaw, a younger boy who was always there to give a helping hand even though he did not have a model plane, and Trevor Julian, a recent English transplant who just hung around, gave us an audience and laughed at our mistakes. The real qualification to be a part of the gang was bicycle ownership because, at a moment's notice, we would have to find a new field in which to fly since the surrounding neighbours would complain of the engine racket.

Balsa Butcher logo.

UNCONSCIOUS DEVELOPMENT OF ADAPTING SKILLS

As I reflected on the triumphs and tragedies of flying planes, I began to realize that what we had learned was much more than how to fly a model plane. We learned to solve problems and how to overcome them with the means at hand. Because we were not able to buy kits with the plans and pre-cut wood and metal parts, we had to do it all ourselves. By copying the designs from the magazines, we learned quickly how to adapt our models to the function we were after, whether it was speed or miniaturization. The major test was: will it take off in a quarter of a circle and fly stably after all that painstaking work, or will it be a 'sudden death' crash? As my brother Peter says, "After a crash, you learned to pick up the pieces right away, work to glue the pieces back, and went flying again!" Learning from our mistakes was sometimes very dramatic indeed. I remember a complete destruction in a quarter circle of my scale model, P-51 Mustang (two foot wingspan) that I had been afraid to fly because I had spent so much time making it!

FULL MIND AND BODY ACTIONS

A combat model plane goes out of control just before impact. This is a common occurrence in flying model planes

Designing and making unique planes teaches you the value of trial and error, the discipline to budget for your model, and the economy of making things for yourselves. It also teaches you how to control your emotions, to keep your cool when flying combat by ducking your adversary-partner, keeping the plane in the air behind the other to cut off his tail-streamer, all the while turning around every five seconds in the centre. Quick thinking and hand-eye coordination, while enough for modern computer games, are not enough for flying combat. While the background blurs as you turn, you also need a full body response to the other moving flyer to avoid tripping over him, which could result in the loss of one or both planes that cost time and money.

A RESEARCH LESSON IN AERODYNAMICS

Building the model to carry weight competitively, and making scale models, demanded different skills. For the model to carry maximum regulated lead weight, we had to design the plane as light and strong as possible. This meant having a large wing area, light skeleton structure, a large area of 'doped' paper surfaces, and the precise location of the weight slot at the balance-point of the plane. Without the use of a slide rule (or, for today, a calculator or computer), we were designing the plane by trial and error somewhat in the way the Wright

An action shot showing a dark blue speed plane just before take off, where the landing gear frame drops off the body providing a minimum of drag for increased speed.

brothers did. (They also rode bicycles.) Wooden propellers were also carved by us just as the Wright Brothers did. Test flights were always traumatic as you watched the plane gather speed, vibrating at the same time. You hoped that there was no big hole on the circular path before the plane took off. This was the point of no return. There was always a great sense of accomplishment as the plane rose above the ground and the 'fans' cheered. This elation was tempered by the

realization that you now held the controls, and that you were responsible for the safety of the flight for a stipulated distance until the fuel ran out, usually a few minutes later.

Planes designed for speed were made small (a one foot wingspan) with a single large engine and stream-lined surfaces, even over the engine head. A fall-away, landing gear wire-frame with three wheels, was used with the speed planes to eliminate the landing gear drag. As the plane took off, the wire-frame would fall out of the slots on the underside of the plane's body. Without this drag, the plane flew about twice the normal speed around the circle with the engine screaming because it had a smaller than usual propeller. No wonder we got kicked out of some neighbourhoods.

RELATED CHINESE AVIATION HISTORY LESSONS

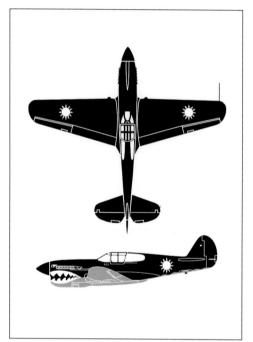

Although we were focused on the airplane's performance, making the scale model plane took us into the real world. Granted, we were not fully aware of the socio-political issues of the aircraft industry and the countries that supported it, but we learned differences that gave us some glimpses of the world at large. The Jamaican Chinese involvement in aviation efforts began in 1940, before I was born, when the Jamaican Chinese Aviation Association was formed to financially help General Chiang Kai-shek in Chungking (Chongqing) in his fight against the Japanese. Although I was not aware of this connection, I did know about the role of the Flying Tigers, used from 1941 to 1942, since I made a scale model of the P-40 Curtiss Warhawks single-prop, fighter plane, with the now famous eye and snarling teeth painted on the front of the aircraft.

I started from scratch to build my largest scale-model with a 46-inch wingspan, by writing to the Douglas Aircraft Company for modelling plans of their B-26 twin-engine bomber plane. The drawing

Top: Elevation and plan of the P-40 Curtiss Warhawk, a single seat fighter. The first one was produced in 1939 and the 10,000th P-40 rolled off the assembly line in 1943.

Left: Model of the P-40 Curtiss Warhawk made by Patrick Chen. The P-40 was used by the Flying Tigers (the American Volunteer Group) to successfully defend China against the Japanese from 1941 - 1942 under General Chennault. Note the eye, mouth and teeth design and the Nationalist Chinese insignia on the wings and on the rear of the fuselage.

only showed the outside dimensions and shape of the aircraft sections. I enlarged the dimensions to full-sized model drawings, and designed the interior structure of balsa wood to ensure that the model engine was hidden as much as possible, while showing the details of the pilot, cockpit, the gunners, and the fold-down exit stairs on the underside of the fuselage. The search for a B-26 with coloured markings that I liked, took me into the history of the countries where the planes were deployed, the role and missions of the aircraft, along with details of the modifications made to the original production model. I can't remember in what theatre of operation the chosen set of red and white-striped tail markings was used in, but it was my favourite.

Trophy from the contest sponsored by the Institute of Jamaica and Pan American World Airways.

SCALING TO WORKING DETAILS ON THE UNDERCARRIAGE

I pushed the realism further by making the undercarriage of the wheels shock absorbing like the real plane. It was always a great pleasure to take off and land the B-26 with the slow, pulsating, near harmonic 'beat' of the twin diesel engines running at almost the same revolution. With the smell of fresh grass and diesel fuel, you pulled back hard on the control handle to keep the heavy plane in the circle on a smooth horizontal flight path while the wheels bounced up and down on the bumpy grass surface. For more realism, I later re-covered the silver-painted surface with aluminum foil. I originally had the model sprayed silver in the backyard of William Wong, Colston's relative. Not satisfied with a painted look, I began to cover the model with the exact outline of the metal panel as in the life-sized plane, risking making the plane too heavy for flight. The B-26 began to look so real that I attempted to take 'realistic photo' angles from ground level of the model with two-inch high people cutout figures. The photographs that I took have now become a bit yellow since I developed and printed my own copies. Along with this search for more realism, I also made a detailed cut-away drawing of the B-26 to show how it worked on the inside. I entered the model and the drawing in the Model Engineering Exhibition Contest, sponsored by the Institute of Jamaica and Pan American World Airways. I won the trophy for the Model Aircraft Section – Class XC in 1961.

Patrick Chen poses with his flying scale model of the B-26 Douglas Invader which had two diesel engines, shock absorbing landing gear and a wingspan of forty-six inches. The body was later covered in aluminium foil over the silver paint and the tail was painted with red and white stripes.

THE PUSH FOR MORE REALISM

Not content with the B-26, I began looking for a sleeker model and settled upon a scale model of a four-engine swept-wing jet bomber, the B-47X. This must have been inspired by the 1955 movie, 'Strategic Air Command' with Jimmy Stewart and June Allyson. Plans were immediately started, with research and drawings, to design a version of the plane that used a propeller instead of a jet. The search turned up an experimental version of the B-47X that had a turbo-prop engine instead of the twinjet on the inside pods of jet engines. This was to be a larger model with a swept-back wing design. Plans were made to have the landing gear retract after take-off and extend before landing by feeding direct current through the two control wires. The worm gears were made at the workshop of Mr. Shaw. Alas, I left Jamaica with the balsa wood body of the B-47 model half-built, and with only the worm gears installed.

ULTIMATE TEST OF THE BALSA BUTCHERS

Although there were other model plane enthusiasts, it so happened that there was a major division between the teenagers and the adults who were at this game for a longer period. While we rode our bicycles to the model store with little money to spend, the adults drove their cars to the store and bought expensive kits, or so it seemed. Among the older aero-modeller adversaries I remember were Garth Drew, a radio announcer, Earl Hollar and John Banks who became an Air Jamaica pilot. Others were: Reid, who died in a crop duster crash, Lyons and Hendricks. These older gentleman considered us young upstarts and did not particularly like us and, as Colston noted, they also looked down on us. We would use English diesel motors while they would use American glow plug engines. This rivalry came to a head when Pan American Airways sponsored a contest in 1958 with the various classes of events. We were experimenting with all types of model aircraft, even planned a vertical-take-off model that was not finished. It was therefore relatively easy for us to join all of the classes, with models from rubber-powered ultra-light models, combat models, speed models, weight-carrying models, to scale models.

VICTORY OF THE LITTLE GUYS AT SABINA PARK

The day of the contest at Sabina Park is just a blur and a feeling of hot sun. Colston remembers some of us stayed up all night to finish working on our planes. Memories consist of the combat event, with our plane in a fight with Mr. Hollar's model, amid the screaming of human voices and the whining of the motors. The winning and losing of each event are long lost in memory. While we did not win all of the events, we cleverly put all of our entries under one name and received the highest total points. Much to our delight, this strategy paid off as we won against the older group. Unless I am wrong, I think that this was the first time that a group of youngsters, Chinese at that, beat the old, established aero-modellers. This was newsworthy enough to be reported in the local *Daily Gleaner* on 25 August 1958. The first prize, a radio control set, gave us the potential to reach the next level of sophistication in model plane control. We could fly beyond the circular dome restriction of the fifty-foot control wires. Radio control meant that we could fly in any pattern we wanted until the fuel ran out. Plans were immediately formulated for a four to five-foot wingspan radio-controlled pulse jet, a model based on the delta wing Convair F-102 Delta Dagger. Although we had the means to implement these plans, they remained only ideas as the members of the group went on to the pursuit of larger goals, having been primed for life.

A SUPPORTIVE FAMILY ENVIRONMENT

To many people, life in a Third World country conjures up visions of poverty and deprivation. Growing up in Jamaica in the '50s was, for the gang, an enriching time. Our parents were supportive of our modelling activities. I remember that because I was always involved in one project or another, usually in science, I was allowed to stay up late to study. My father, Chen Bit Fah, a Hakka shepherd from China, always said that we should study. Following our modelling interest opened many worlds for us. Also listening to the BBC science fiction radio shows, such as Dan Dare, over the Redifussion (cable radio), not only opened our minds to other worlds but helped to develop our imaginations.

ROLE OF TEACHERS AT ST. GEORGE'S COLLEGE

Researching the history of aircraft took us into world politics, and sensitized us to the use of technology for various purposes. I remember the Jesuits at St. George's College saying that the airplane could be used to bomb or to carry supplies to a city. Colston also remembered that if any one of the students brought up the topic of airplanes, Mr. Manning, a teacher, would sometimes spend the rest of the class diverted by the world of airplanes. Even though we were in Jamaica, our interest in airplanes enabled us to visit the *USS Lake Champlain* aircraft carrier in 1959 through a Jesuit connection. (This ship represented the USA at the Jamaica Independence celebrations in 1962, and was the prime ship for the recovery of the first manned space flight with astronaut Alan Sheppard). I did not realize the importance of the ship then, but just being on an aircraft carrier was an awe-inspiring experience. We were also on the British aircraft carrier, *HMS Ark Royal* (1955-58), and even got to touch and look right into the cockpit of a real fighter plane. Although modelling was a large part of our teen years and I thought of becoming an air-craft engineer, only my brother, Peter, went into the aviation profession serv-icing helicopters, operating a wind tunnel for Rockwell Trisonic Wind Tunnel, and teaching at Northrop University in California. My only aviation story is that I started a real flying club while I was at McGill University, Montreal.

LESSONS FOR LIFE FROM HUMBLE ORIGINS

While learning a lot of science and history and how to seek out informa-tion from the outside world, we learned how to apply the information to real life and to deal with real people. Our hobby group experience included deal-ing with individuals and also how to cooperate to have fun. Winning the con-test bolstered our belief that we could tackle any major problem with diligence and painstaking work. Tricky situations that were fraught with danger could be overcome by cunning manoeuvres. We felt invincible.

Unconsciously, we were following in the tradition of our Hakka ancestors who had to learn from the local aborigines how to survive in the upper moun-tain lands in China, and who developed a fierce loyalty among their clan to survive the constant fights against the Cantonese. Our generation benefitted from the sacrifice of our parents who worked to make it better for us, and for that we are indebted to them. Our way of thanking them has been to succeed in our lives. The degree to which this generation has succeeded only enhances our tribute to them and our ancestors. Whatever motivating dreams our ances-tors had on their four-month trip to Jamaica from China, we should attempt out of respect, to create our own motivating visions too.

ACKNOWLEDGEMENTS

Thanks to those who were part of this story: Chen Bit Fah, my father; Yap Yuk Yin, my mother; Peter Chen, my younger brother; Colston Chen, my cousin and partner in the model plane endeavours; the older group of aero-modellers who gave us the opportunity to excel, the teachers and friends who did and did not encourage us, and all those mentioned in our story. For the review of this article, my thanks go to Beverly, my wife; Dorothy, my sister; Franco, my brother; Peter and Colston Chen. Most photos were taken by the author.

Written by ©Patrick Chen and edited by Sonia Gordon Scott.

Down Memory Lane

*Above: In 1945 the **Chee Kung Tung Orchestra** was formed. They performed Cantonese operas and variety
shows for the community at garden parties and at the Ward Theatre.*

L-R, Back: **Lipton HoSang, Buddy Wong Yu Choy, Ivy Lyew (Williams), Ho Fah Sang, Peng Lan Foon
(Jenny Chin Yee), Aston Ho, Wong Yu Ken, Leung Bit Yee (Mrs. Simon Yuen), Wilfred Lue Fook On,
Joseph Lue Den Kee.**
Front: **Chen Tze Pui, Albert Wong Chen Mui, Shim Jin Kee, Chen Geow, Lue Biang Fah.**

Photograph courtesy of Patrick Lee, from the book © 'Canadian Jamaican Chinese 2000'

Down Memory Lane

*Above: Girls from **Chinese Public School** who acted in a Hakka play at the Ward Theatre in 1946.*

*L-R, Back: **Blanche Lee, Verna Lee, Icilda Neon, Helen Lue.***
*Front: **Ivy Lyew, Cynthia Ho Tseung, Elsie Ho Tseung, Milicent Lee.***

Photograph courtesy of Patrick Lee, from the book © 'Canadian Jamaican Chinese 2000'

Annette Hedden (née Chang)
- Miss Chinese Jamaica, 1954
ON BEING MISS CHINESE JAMAICA (1)

WHEN ASKED TO WRITE about my experiences as Miss Chinese Jamaica, my first reaction was a definite "No". However, when forced to think about it, I began to realize that it was in fact the first in a number of important steps which have led me to where I am today.

The year that I was crowned, was the very first year of such an event. At a party attended by a lot of my girlfriends, Lucien Chen argued very persuasively that our help was needed to create interest and support for Miss Chinese Jamaica in the Chinese community. As a result, most of the contestants were recruited at that party.

I had attended a convent school and was a very sheltered and shy teenager. The eldest of five girls, I was barely out of the awkward stage of pimples, and my greatest pleasure was reading books. To my utter surprise, I was chosen Miss Chinese Jamaica and, suddenly, attention was focused on me. I felt very uncomfortable in this new role and not at all like a beauty queen. This forced me to rouse myself, in fact, to rise to the occasion. Throughout the years that followed, many more stressful experiences occurred which forced me to grow – to rise to the occasion – and eventually to go to University and earn a Masters Degree in Fine Art. Each step along the way helped me to gain the self-confidence and self-esteem which I lacked as a young teenager.

After all, when I think about it, as with all things – the first step is always the most important.

Miss Chinese Jamaica 1954 being crowned by Judy Verity.

Written by Annette Hedden (née Chang) and edited by Alex Lee.

Miss Chinese Jamaica 1961 beauty contestants. Left to right:
Norma Shim, the curvaceous little U.C.W.I. Medical Student who gained second place honours: Third place runner-up Lily Chin looking as attractive as ever. The girl who gained a special prize for having the best legs is Gloria Lue Richards, and for having the most beautiful smile a special prize went to pretty Fay Chance. Last but not least, Patsy Pin Chong, the little cutie who the judges awarded a special prize for having the best figure.

Photos by Gil Kong (Hilite)
Sourced by Gloria Chin

Miss Chinese Jamaica 1961 beauty contestants posing in swimwear and evening wear.

Melanie Chang Bitter
ON BEING MISS CHINESE JAMAICA (2)

AS FAR AS I CAN REMEMBER, I had a wonderful experience during the contest as many of the contestants were either schoolmates, a cousin, or friends and, as always, we made new friends. We were shy but competitive, but there was no backstabbing. We were taught how to walk by Rosie DeSouza (I think that's her name) who once had been either a contestant or a Miss Jamaica. Through her we attained poise, learned how to apply makeup, and to combat some of our shyness.

There was much excitement as we prepared for our first appearance in front of the judges. We paraded in cheong sams* for them at a dinner at the Sheraton Hotel, and were interviewed by them individually. The bathing suit parade was also held at the Sheraton, and the final night's coronation was held

at the Chinese Athletic Club on Derrymore Road. I cannot remember the month but I am pretty sure it was 1963.

I was sponsored by Desnoes & Geddes Ltd. and wore the sash of Miss Orange Crush. I was delighted to be crowned by Carol Joan Crawford who had been crowned earlier as the first Jamaican Miss World. All the previous contests had been known as Miss Chinese Jamaica with the exception of my year, which was called Miss Chinese Athletic Club, to facilitate one of the contestants who, although a resident of Jamaica, had been born in Guyana. She was a favourite to win and we did not wish any controversy had she won the crown. There was a dance after I won the contest, and all the young men were vying to dance with me. It was a very heady experience and I had a ball.

I was presented with the Charm Trophy and one of my prizes was a trip to Los Angeles. I took my mom as chaperone and we visited Disneyland, Grauman's Chinese Theatre, and Chinatown. We were also reacquainted with many of our Chinese friends who had relocated there and they treated us royally.

Lucien Chen and Cecil Chuck were the great force behind the Miss Chinese Jamaica contests from the first to the last. Johnny Chuck is now the driving force behind the revival of the contest, and I was delighted to pass on the Charm Trophy to the winner of the revived contest, Miss CBA, held in January 2003.

Annette Chang, my sister, was the first Miss Chinese Jamaica and I was the last. Barbara Chang and Fay Chang also held the title, making four Changs who were title holders. Although Barbara is not related to us, Fay is, and all Changs came from the same village in China, or so I am told. That's quite a feat wouldn't you say?

Written by Melanie Chang Bitter and edited by Alex Lee.

* See Glossary

Down Memory Lane

Enjoying the sun on the pier at Doctors Cave Beach, Montego Bay, St. James
Photograph ©Ray Chen

Vincent Chen

THE CHINESE PUBLIC SCHOOL

IT WAS AT THE END of my sixth year at St. Anthony's Academy Prep. School in Port Antonio, when I was unexpectedly informed by my father that he had decided to enroll me in the Chinese Public School in Kingston, at the start of the next school term. The year was 1940.

I remember greeting the announcement with a great deal of excitement, just anticipating going to the 'Big City'. At the same time I was a little apprehensive about leaving home and being alone for the first time, not knowing what to expect. These fears were somewhat allayed when I learned that I would have as company two other boys whom I knew, and who were going at the same time.

The day came for the journey to Kingston. In the car were Lloyd Phang and Victor Chung, the two I had known for a long time. They picked up my father and me at Snow Hill; at Buff Bay we were joined by Reggie Chin and his father. We arrived at the school in Kingston in the early afternoon that Sunday, and were greeted by the Headmaster, who after showing us around the classrooms and dormitories, led us to his office to be registered. When my turn came, he noted my name and pleasantly remarked that he was from the same village as my father, and in fact we were closely related. He, of course, was the renowned Chen Kung Ngee. If I had entertained any expectations of special treatment because of this relationship, they were soon dispelled. As everyone was to discover in due course, this gentleman was a very strict disciplinarian and brooked no nonsense from anyone, no matter how well connected you were.

Chen Kung Ngee (left), in addition to his job as administrator, also taught the senior class. He was also a fanatic when it came to physical fitness. Every morning he would leave his house next door at dawn, and come over to the school and rouse all the boarders to participate in his fitness exercises. These included the pushups and laps around the football field, stretching and breathing exercises. He also introduced us to calisthenics which, many years later, was introduced to the West by Bruce Lee as Kung Fu. Chen Kung Ngee was an avid proponent and practitioner of this branch of martial arts, and was eager to put it on display whenever the opportunity arose.

The opportunity came about in 1942, on the occasion of the school's Annual Open Day Garden Party. A quartet of us boys (three others and myself) who, in his opinion had progressed well in the discipline, were chosen to give an exhibition of Kung Fu – onstage – to hundreds of people, the majority of whom had never heard the name of this branch of martial arts before. I must say that it was very well received as there was polite applause at the end , but then if there were any mistakes in our performance the audience would not have known the difference.

Boarding conditions at school were spartan but not unbearable. Among the younger boys there was constant need for someone to see to their grooming and personal hygiene. We had an elderly master, Neon Pin Jong, who, to his credit, did his best to make the boarders as comfortable as possible . In the evenings before lights out, he would sit at his station in the main hall of the dorm, and was available to any boy who had a problem. I enjoyed sitting with him on some evenings and listening to his tales of life in China in much the same way as my parents used to relate them. What fascinated me most about this gentleman was his fondness for hard-boiled eggs. I would sit in wonder and watch him consume one dozen at a sitting, and this he would do at least two evenings each week.

If the purpose of my attending The Chinese Public School was to reinforce my exposure to Chinese culture, and to learn the rudiments of reading and writing the language, I must say that I did remarkably well, often being commended on my steady progress. In two years I had risen through the grades from elementary level to Chen Kung Ngee's class. I was able to write to my sister, Gim Fung, in China in simple language and was able to read her letters to me in return.

This stage of my achievement was most satisfying, but the inevitable question, *'What next?'* had to be answered. It was now time to prepare for the world outside the Chinese Public School from which I departed at the end of 1943.

Written by Vincent Chen edited by Sonia Gordon Scott

Photograph courtesy of Clive Chen

Norman Hew-Shue
MEMORIES OF THE CHINESE PUBLIC SCHOOL

The Chinese Public School.

THE CHINESE PUBLIC SCHOOL (called Tong Ngin Huck Gow in our local Hakka dialect), at North and Hanover Streets, was a memorable milestone in my education and Jamaican childhood. Like many of my peers, I was sent there in the '50s to be educated not only in Chinese heritage, but in subjects essential for our future careers. Come with me now back to those memorable and carefree times, as I recall memories both fond and painful.

Central Kingston then was pleasantly residential, with a Chinese grocery (Ham Thwe Poo) at almost every corner. Our farsighted and caring parents scrimped and saved in these for long hours (selling a 100 lb bag of flour yielded a profit of 1 English shilling or 12 pence) in selfless sacrifice, to give us a decent life and education. After pre-schooling in some local private school, we were usually sent to the Chinese Public School, one of the amenities which our farsighted elders – such as Messrs. Albert Chang and C. C. Phang – had made available for us.

On a typical school morning, Hanover Street was like a main artery, collecting all my friends from adjoining streets and lanes, and depositing us at the large front gate of the school at its northern end. At Harbour Street lived Buster; Water Lane – Eugene; Tower Street – Cynthia; Barry Street – Roger; Law Street – Michael; East Queen Street – Maxine, and so on to Sutton, Beeston and Charles Streets (Joan). Come to think of it, we never did pay attention to those street or place-names of colonial legacy. They would roll off our lips in ordinary conversation but later, thanks to this parent-provided education, we would learn that Hanover, for example, was the name of Royal Anglo-Germanic lineage.

The school was dominated by a large concrete courtyard flanked by long buildings, comprising about 6 elevated classrooms with red clay-tiled roofs on each side. The office was at the south-eastern corner of this quadrangle, and had an external flight of stairs leading up to a dormitory. At the northern end was the stage-pavilion with an upright piano, curtains and other theatrical props, where the buildings were interconnected by red concrete walkways. A separate building housed the Albert Chang Hall at the south end, by North Street, named after one of the founding philanthropists of the school. In front of this was a concrete fountain and fish pond.

The old haunted or 'duppy' house, was a wooden structure with sidings on the eastern portion, and served variously as accommodation for the boarders and as a cafeteria at one time. It was beside the old YWCA, before this institution relocated to upper South Camp Road. On the south-eastern side was a second unused gate and driveway, and a small playground with a slide and jungle-gym.

Our playing fields were at the north end, and had a swing and see-saw at the north-eastern corner near to a basketball court. Washrooms at the south-eastern portion of the playing field completed the layout. The northern boundary shared a wooden fence with the Presbyterian church on Lockett Avenue.

Spoiled child that I was, my dear father (bless his soul) would take me to school by mah cha*, or horse drawn buggy, a feasible mode of transport then, for the first few days. After a few tearful partings, I gradually eased into the routine of school life. The classrooms had long, solid wooden benches and desks with lids and inkwells. The blackboards were of real quarried slate that flaked off when damaged, and cleaning them or the dusters (by whacking them outside), was a much coveted assignment. The walls were decorated with running coloured alphabet scripts at the top.

We baby boomers met each other in those first days of school. The girls were memorable in royal-blue skirts and close-fitting, white, Chinese hi-neck blouses with blue piping, side-closed with cloth buttons and loops. We boys looked fittingly drab beside them in khaki shirts and, of course, short pants. Our breath was taken away as we first beheld Lily, Otlee, Eleanor and the other beauties. I sat beside Olive who liked Tyrone Power and would chat away about movies like *Love is a Many Splendoured Thing.* Somehow my name was linked to my childhood friend Cynthia, perhaps because I was also close to her brothers, whom I thank for the friendship and memories they gave me in my early years as an only child. When she won the buttered turkey in a much publicized school raffle, everyone congratulated me as well.

There was a tall lanky chap, descriptively nicknamed 'Donkey La -La', (a title, no doubt bestowed by his fellow boarders, hence the rural flavour). We seldom used his proper name (Richard), preferring this humorous, colourful epithet which he bore with good-nature and silent fortitude. Almost at the time of writing this, I learnt that poor Richard was hit and killed by a motor vehicle in the '60s. May God rest his soul.

School assembly was kept, variously, in the open courtyard, on stage, or in the Albert Chang Hall. In preparation for our going to Anglican or Roman Catholic schools, we might sing hymns like *'All Things Bright and Beautiful....'* or *'Holy, Holy, Holy, Lord God Almighty ...'* .

The Chinese language, spoken and written, was taught as well as history, music and folklore. I was already speaking Hakka as a mother tongue so, for me, it was more a matter of learning the Chinese characters and English. We were admirably prepared for the world, otherwise, with subjects like latin, maths (which wasn't easy, I can tell you, in those days of pounds shillings & pence – 2 shillings and sixpence = one half crown! – and fractions which we were expected to do mentally!). English language and grammar were also drilled into us (remember *First Aid in English*) – 'A pride of lions, a gaggle of geese'; 'feathers are to birds as scales are to fish'. We were even introduced to agriculture by planting corn and vegetables in a plot of land beside the eastern block. Art and craft had us using carved plant stems as printing blocks to stamp various artistic patterns. We would get shiny merit stars in blue, red or gold in our books. Being a dunce I rarely got one.

When I was there, the school was run by Miss Moo Young and then Mr. Chong, who was a strict disciplinarian, and I ran afoul of his swishing cane on several occasions. He would read to us serialized, cliffhanging Chinese stories about ghosts or heroes such as Sam Mow (he had only three hairs on his head), or The Monkey King.

I was an absolute dunce at arithmetic, and I remember a patient, kindly, senior girl sitting down with me and trying hard to show me the principles of division. I recall also dear, lovely Miss Lee who took similar pains to teach me the subject. In one exam, as I was hopelessly floundering, as inspiration or encouragement she told me the answer to the problem, hoping that this would spur me to solve it. Solve it I did – my way. I used all the processes of maths that I knew of, to add, subtract, multiply, and divide the given numbers in an elaborate equation that would confound even Einstein in order to do whatever was necessary to get the correct answer. If the problem required a 5, this would be added from nowhere, then multiplied by one and added to zero in a flourish of 'Normanian Calculus'. I have never seen Miss Lee laugh so hard before, followed by a look of concerned and pitiful affection. Thanks and God bless you, dear Miss Lee, wherever you are.

At lunch time we would line up for tickets at the cafeteria (which was variously in the duppy house or downstairs of the Albert Chang Hall) to get deep fried crabs in batter, show bow*, patties, or rice pudding in the small brown clay bowls, to be cut up with fudge sticks. All these were usually supplied to the school by a well-known gentleman with a deformed hand.

Thankfully it wasn't all school work. Mango trees, three stories high, developed our throwing arm and sense of aim. 'Fruity' would come at the end of the day with her fruit-laden cornucopia in a pram filled with 'stinking toe'*, custard apples, star apples, otaheite apples, etc. Jew plums (Golden apples in the other islands) would be taken with lot of salt, (or is it 'June' or 'Jupe' plums?). As is typical of Jamaican patois, accuracy of pronunciation is not important if it *sounds* close enough. Remember GRASS bottle?

For diversion we had fads such as transfers which were all the craze then. These resembled stamps, were sold in sheets, and came in every conceivable theme e.g. sports, space, cars, planes etc. The ones about Disney's *Alice in Wonderland* were memorable for quality and brilliant colours, for example, the Caterpillar smoking the waterpipe or hookah on the leaf, or the Bread-and-

Butterfly. These were moistened and placed, colour side down, in a favourite text book. The backing was then gently removed at the right time, transferring the intact, colourful image to the page. Difficult ones might require enlisting the aid of a seasoned professional. There was much swapping and bartering of this desirable commodity. Transfers suddenly vanished in the mid-'50s, (for the life of me I can't see why, although they were still used for plastic models) to be replaced decades later with plain direct stick-on decals, which lacked the fun and skill value. This exciting pastime is lost to the younger generations.

We would also press flowers between the pages of our books. The colours usually faded but otherwise they would be preserved in a dried form which appealed to future botanists. I went more for zoology and, to my shame, started a mercifully short-lived craze of killing and similarly preserving butterflies. Water pistols were a fad for a time, the more desirable ones looking like transparent red or green Star Trek phasers with a tiny compass on top. Water was then squirted everywhere, or as far as the punishing cane or featherstick dictated.

The usual childhood games were played, with the boys going for the rowdier ones. Both sexes played chevy chase or softball, using the stage as a base. We would use the fields on weekends to play cricket or football with the associated pleasant memories – some also painful, but comical now. During a Sunday impromptu cricket match, Buster from Johns Lane was at bat, and strode out confidently to clap the ball with an elegant square cut. His bold splayed-legged stride was reduced to a painful slow-motioned roll in the dirt as the hard cork-and-tar ball was suddenly and forcefully blended with portions of his anatomy to make three.

Then there was the strange fascination of all school boys with playing jax or jacks with the girls. Jacks, you might remember, is a game much more suited to a girl's nimble and fine-motored fingers, as it involves rapid and selective scooping up of asterisk-shaped metal pieces during the bounce of a small rubber ball. The girls' tiny fingers and hands could dart in, out, and around to get the required pieces, while the poor muscle-bound boys could only hope to throw the ball high enough to gain the necessary time delay. A more boy-type game, played on the smooth shiny red floor, would be with bottle stoppers which were flicked by the thumb to hit the others. When asked, however, about this fascination with jacks, schoolboys would invariably answer with a grin (boys being boys): "Yes mahn – you coulda get some good 'sites'!"

Another game was marbles, which I wasn't too good at but once, with the help of Bruce Lyn, I devastated the opposition at 'bounce-back'. My desk was full of marbles I had won and I was rich beyond my wildest dreams! Marbles came in all varieties and even included machine iron ball bearings and stone ball valves from kerosene pumps (there must be a few shop-keeping fathers wondering how those suddenly stopped working). They ranged in size from small bearings to veritable shot-putts, depending on its use for defensive or aggressive play respectively.

Gene Chong and I would go through a break in the fence beside the see-saw to explore the adjoining lot which, I think, was owned by the YWCA. We would marvel at the cat's skull or coloured glass unearthed on our juvenile archaeological expeditions.

We had seasonal and random parties and diversions to look forward to. I remember a party in the Albert Chang Hall after school, when music was provided by 16 rpm records on a portable player, and being treated to sandwiches and punch. The Easter Egg Hunt was also a much anticipated event when large, brightly coloured chocolate eggs would be hidden all over the school compound. At the appointed time, we would be released with much shouting and prancing to locate these hidden treasures in the crook of a tree; under the office steps; even the Duppy House was searched!

The Garden Party was another favourite event, with promise of watermelons, train and ferris wheel rides, Moo Kee Lyn unicorn dances and grab bag prizes. We would present a play, skit or recital on stage. I am transported back to those times and Jean Chang reciting "Daffodils" in her clear beautiful voice.

I remember too a Hakka boy-scout leader in blue short pants, lanyarded-whistle, and scarf with the nationalist 12-pointed star. His pack of cubs were peering intently into the heavens as he pointed out the constellations. A Crown and Anchor table was usually present near the rides and we would diligently scour that gravel area of the field for lost coins the next school day.

Once, surprisingly, a rhumba dancer was hired to entertain. This must have been in later times and reflecting the changing mores. Anyway, after the eye-brow raising performance of 'Madam Temptation' or whatever, I was walking along the back of the western classrooms when I saw as many as five schoolmates, driven by curiosity and developing hormones, clinging to a window ledge. I immediately deduced that this was the window to the dancer's impromptu changing room. I resigned myself to bad luck in not getting there earlier as all the space was filled and there was no way anyone else could fit. Or so I thought! As I was passing, a loud gasp went up from the viewers. I tell you, I have often thought long and hard but am still amnesic regarding those split seconds. The next thing I knew, I was up on the window, finding finger-holds on the sheer concrete wall where none previously existed. Bodies flew left and right (I was quite rough in those days) as I just managed to be rewarded with a glimpse of the dancer making crucial adjustments to the lower half of her costume.

Another not so innocent incident happened during another party when Victor, who had a reputation for being a precocious lad, was caught *in flagrante delicto* as it were when Watchie, the caretaker, went to investigate the strange movements of a parked van. I remember the small crowd milling around the protesting Victor and the embarrassed young lady in party dress standing by.

Picnic outings were made to Castleton, Boston Beach, or Flemarie at Yallahs where we were warned of a deep submarine trench. I also remember paying two and sixpence and going in a group to Carib cinema to see Danny Kaye in *Hans Christian Anderson* (*"Thumbelina, Thumbelina tiny little thing..."*) and The Court Jester (*"The Vessel with the Pestle has the Wine that is poisoned, but the Chalice from the Palace has the Brew that is true..."*).

On a more sombre note, there were also the sad memories. We were shocked, one Monday morning, to learn of the tragic death of David, one of our well-liked classmates in the infamous train derailment at Kendal, Manchester, during a church outing the weekend before. I kept a clipping from *The Daily Gleaner* of David's obituary with his photo in my desk thereafter.

In later years, I went to Wolmers High School just up the road, and above what was then the Race Course. I used to pass by the old alma mater after school was over, but by then the school was struggling and enrollment was down. It was being run by Miss May, one of my former teachers, who held on with fortitude in those difficult years. Finally the school was closed but, in later years, I would still visit and walk among the empty dilapidated classrooms and reminisce about the good old days. The stand-up piano that Humphrey's mother used to play so beautifully was gutted, levers and strings exposed. Just a few of the caretaking staff were left over by the old house. In recent years it is heartening to know that our Father Ho Lung is making use of the place in a philanthropic and benevolent way.

In later years, we still used the playing fields for cricket and football as well as the Albert Chang Hall for the occasional party. Some of us Chinese schoolers, such as Gene, Cynthia Otlee and I, went on to the same secondary schools. We would also keep in touch at parties and Joong Sang beach.

In later years, I remember cruising with friends in Trevor's (from Belmont Road) V.W. Beetle. As we were making the corner at Deanery and Langston Roads near Globe theatre, I looked through the rear window and glimpsed a bespectacled Chinese gentleman behind the counter of a shop. Others in the car told me that it was Mr. Chong. Later on I read in the *Star* that he had collapsed and died over the cash register in that shop. To him and those no longer with us, I dedicate this eternally grateful and heartfelt tribute, also to Mrs. Moo Young, Miss Daly, Miss Lee, Mrs. Robinson, Mrs. Ivy Williams, Miss May, Mr. Chen, and all the other teachers, staff and founders of that great institution – The Chinese Public School. I hope that this will keep their names and spirit alive, and I thank them for the love, care, direction and memories they gave us during those early formative years.

Written by Norman Hew Shue and edited by Sonia Gordon Scott.

Photograph of the gate entrance © Ray Chen
Photograph of the school from
'The Chinese in Jamaica, First Edition 1957' ©Lee Tom Yin.

Nikki Lee
THOSE OLD SCHOOL DAYS

I LOVE LISTENING to my Uncle Nathan, Aunt Rita and my father Phillip talk about what it was like growing up and going to school in Jamaica. Especially high school. My family moved away from Jamaica before I was old enough to attend school there but their stories are enchanting enough to put me in the middle of it all. Listening to them takes me back to their tropical playground with dozens of school chums to run around with and classes led by stately nuns who were both feared and admired.

My Aunt Rita was an Alpha girl – a certain excitement comes to my aunt's voice whenever she talks about her upbringing in Jamaica. Carefree and idyllic are the words she uses to describe that period. After the family migrated from Hong Kong to Jamaica in 1952, my aunt and uncle started out at the Chinese School on North Street. When she was six, Aunt Rita moved on to Alpha Preparatory School on South Camp Road. She laughs when describing how some of the teachers would discourage the Chinese girls from speaking in their ancestral tongue, because they were worried about shaky grammar and odd accents. That must have been somewhat of a futile attempt. According to Aunt Rita, an entire *third* of her classroom was Chinese.

Aunt Rita in uniform at Alpha Academy.

After prep school, Aunt Rita moved on to the all-girls high school. Run by Catholic nuns, its official name was Convent of Mercy Academy Alpha, but was referred to then, as it still is, as simply, *Alpha*.

Like most other Catholic-run schools in those days, discipline was law at the South Camp Road campus. The leading lady and principal at that time, Sr. Mary Bernadette, fully expected that her Alpha girls should carry themselves like perfect young ladies. And proper attire and grooming were all a part of the code of conduct.

Every morning the girls had to gather for morning assembly in full uniform. In those days that meant a clean round-collared white cotton shirt, blue pleated tunic, crisp white belt with brown shoes and socks, all topped off by a smart navy beret. And there the tidy collection of girls from all around the country would stand, shoulders back and faces forward, through prayers and general announcements. She still giggles as she remembers the rumours of girls facing the consequences of wearing skirts that were too short.

'I heard that some girls actually got their hems ripped down, or were sent to detention or home!' she says.

An Alpha girl *always* had neat hair – and usually held back in a ponytail or in braids.

Other rules abounded, including one that disallowed the girls from leaving the premises at lunchtime without permission. But according to Aunt Rita, that was not a problem. There was always a delicious hot lunch being served in the cafeteria – like steaming red pea soup, fried chicken, ackee and saltfish and rice and peas. And, as this was Jamaica, flaky hot patties with spicy meat filling were *always* available. After their midday meal, the girls played a game called 'rounders', which is like baseball without a bat. Says Aunt Rita, *'we used our fists and a tennis ball.'*

Unless there was a specialty class like domestic sciences or art on the schedule, the girls generally remained in the same classroom for the entire day, while their teachers rotated and came to them. Aunt Rita's favourite was Mrs. Durrant, who taught her mathematics. Apparently my aunt did very well in that subject. She also had a soft spot for Mrs. Blondel Frances, her English literature teacher who was a Shakespearean actress with a signature flair for drama.

Physical education was also mandatory at Alpha, with every student being required to participate in one sport or the other. I can just see it now. A perfect sea of girls dressed head to toe in sparkling white V-neck shirts, white knee-length skirts with bloomers, white socks and white canvas shoes, running around the huge tropical green field, giggling and trying their hand at volleyball, soccer and cricket.

The most magical part of my Aunt's stories has to do with the large, monkey tamarind tree that has stood witness to generations of young Alpha girls and their fancies. I can almost hear the secrets that have been whispered to this tree as girls carved out their initials, sometimes with the initials of their schoolgirl crushes.

Just down the road and around the corner on North Street, was the neighbouring all-boys school, St. George's College. Run by Jesuit priests, St. George's and Alpha would often have school dances together, properly chaperoned, of course. My aunt would eventually marry Joe, a George's boy she met many years later in Canada. According to my aunt, such unions between Alpha girls and George's boys were quite common back then.

My Uncle Nathan, the eldest, also went to St. George's College and looked smart in his khakis with white and blue epaulettes, while my father, Phillip, boarded at Campion College and sported khakis with red and white epaulettes.

Solid students as they were, my father and his siblings nevertheless counted the days to holiday times. Get them to talk about it, and you'll hear snippets of fun times like Jonkonnu stories at Christmas, balloons from downtown vendors on Boxing Day, and food, red envelopes, stuffed oysters and almond float during Chinese New Year. Listen to them some more, and you can almost see them revelling at a Gunboat beach party on a hot, sunny day, or fishing on a long lazy afternoon by the airport and Gypsum wharf, or catching fat shrimp and land crab in the evening for a home-cooked treat.

I can't ever hear enough stories about my elders as teenagers. These stories are what Jamaica is all about to me, and I am anxious for the day when I will be able to pass along these wonderful tales to my children so that they too can be delighted by the rich history and tradition that means so much to my family. I can't tire of those images of their days in sharp uniforms on sprawling school grounds, and carefree weekends and holidays under the sun …. They had it all. They were Chinese, but *so* Jamaican.

I'd say they had the best of both worlds.

Written by Nikki Lee and edited by Alex Lee.

Down Memory Lane

1

3

2

Sisters of Mercy, Convent of Mercy, Alpha
1. Sacred Heart House
2. Chapel of Christ the King (interior)
3. The statue of the Sacred Heart in front of the former
*   Convent, residence of the Sisters*

Photographs ©Ray Chen

Down Memory Lane

Committee Members of the Kingston Branch of the Get Ming Dong* (National Government of China)

Back Row: **William Wong, Leslie Lue, Moo Kin Leong, Lee Chow Fah, Victor Yap Chung,**
      Chen Kung Ngei, William Chang.
Middle Row: **Lyn Jung Leung, Niki Chang, Fung Sang, Jack Shim.**
Front Row: **Hoo Sin Quee, Vincent Chung, Wong Ah Mook, Vernon Chin, Samuel Chen.**

Photograph courtesy of Clive Chen

Mandison Chin
LADDERS AND BREADFRUIT TREES

I'M NOT SURE how large a family my parents planned on having when they left China as newlyweds in the early 1920s, but I was their 'lucky number seven' of 12 children. I was born in Cambridge, St. James, a little town on the railway line just 15 miles from Montego Bay.

Although my family moved to Montego Bay when I was one year old, to open a wholesale/retail business and a 'rum bar' on Market Street, Cambridge will always remain in my childhood memories as the place where I spent many happy summer holidays with my cousins. My Uncle, Charlie Ah-back*, had a shop opposite the railway station and I had my fair share of fun in those days.... always going somewhere, doing something… It was there that I learned of Jamaican folklore characters - 'Rolling Calf', 'Black-Heart man', 'Brer Anancy' and 'Big Boy'. I also remember the days when bananas from the plantations were brought to the railway station in big carts pulled by bulls with a 'cowboy' running in front, leading the way.

Photo of Edward Chin's family taken in Montego Bay, circa 1945. Mandison is seated left in the centre row.

Growing up in Montego Bay, my siblings and 1 were expected to work in the shop. As soon as you could walk, you started. We were given chores suitable to our ages and these were handed down from older to younger siblings like clothes. The first job was simple - to watch the shop or 'kun poo'.* I was about four when I got that job and I would sit on top of a ladder to get a bird's eye view of the customers. I never caught anyone stealing under my watch, but then I'm pretty sure the customers knew what I was doing.

At seven I was 'promoted' from the ladder to the rum bar, to sell patties and bread, and passed on the 'kun poo' duty to the next in line. I was still so small that I had to stand on a box to reach the counter and the patty pan. My job description was simple enough - cut the bread if someone wanted bread with their patty, and make change from the money collected.

I must have been about ten when my father made a small fortune from a 'Pick-a- Peow' game and bought a building located at 14 Strand

Street, just around the corner and facing the other side of the market. Our wholesale and retail business was moved to Strand Street and a hardware and furnishing business was added there. This meant new tasks for me, like cutting glass and looking after the furniture, but it would prove useful later on in my adult years when I moved up in life and established my own furniture business.

Eventually, I left Montego Bay for a couple years to attend my first school, the Chinese Public School in Kingston. I can't say if it was by design or coincidence but, at the same time, my father was asked to run a friend's wholesale business in Kingston and he was with us when my brother Ben and I went to school in the big city. I don't remember much of my school life, except that we travelled to and fro daily in a big three-seat taxi with a cloth top and two rows of seats. Mind you, we weren't the only passengers. The driver picked up an entire car load of us, all Chinese Public School students.

While I don't remember school, I do remember Barry St. Now that was the place to be. If you wanted to see people and be in the centre of things, you went to Chinatown. A few specific things still stand out clearly in my mind. Like eying the huge blue crab the Yap Sams caught and kept at their Diamond Mineral enterprise. Then there were characters like 'Cook Man', who was a fixture at his shop front in his underwear, complete with merino and board slippers. That was his standard uniform, and all day long he'd patrol and watch you.

After two years we all returned to Montego Bay to the Chinese school there which was djoining my uncle's backyard. Our teacher, who had two girls and a son, was Wan Sen-sang*. I used to like one of his daughters - Pearl, I think, was her name - but I didn't get on with her father. Maybe he just didn't like me, as I always thought he gave me a hard time. Maybe he knew I had my eye on his daughter! Anyway, he used to hit us with a branch from a nearby hedge. One day we're outside in the back doing some class activity. We must have been pretty noisy but he singled me out as the noise maker and whacked me with a fresh branch. Well that just had me seeing red.

Now at the time my uncle's property boasted a very prolific bread-fruit tree. It bore so much breadfruit that many would just be left to ripen on the tree until they turned soft. So I figured, why waste good or bad breadfruit? I got some of them one weekend, found a space between the roof and the wall of the teacher's office, got a good view of my target below, and proceeded to bomb his entire office with ripe breadfruit. My sister Enid was my look out accomplice, so he never found out who did it. In fact, no one ever did.

I tell you, you can't beat memories like these.

Written by Alex Lee as told by Mandison Chin.
Re-edited by Sonia Gordon Scott.

* See Glossary

Derrick Chin
THE GLORY DAYS

SOMETIMES IT'S THE SIMPLEST things that make for the most vivid memories.

Take my school days, for instance. As a kid in the 1950's, Vaz Preparatory School was the hallowed hall of learning for me, my brother and two sisters. Except that the hall was Mrs. Vaz's garage on Dunoon Road in Rollington Town.

Like other schools, we had our routines. As Mr. Vaz reversed his car out in the mornings, we'd stand on the sides, literally waiting to unpack and set up the benches and desks. I'm not sure if we *had* to do this, but we always helped the gardener with this daily task. The school would eventually be upgraded when the Vaz family stopped rearing chickens, and moved a couple of classrooms permanently into the chicken coop. Mrs. Vaz also held many a session under the shady plum, star apple or cashew trees.

Her teaching style, like our little school, was unique and kept us attentive. Sometimes she had us stand back to back in a circle when we did dictation and other subjects. Friday was *spelling* day. I remember that clearly because we'd get hit in the palm of our hand with a sturdy cane for every mistake we made over five.

Top: Vaz Prep School began in a garage that looked like this.

Below: Devotion time at Vaz Prep School.

At first our learning tools were fairly basic, like the slates we used. I assume they were the instrument of choice because they were reusable, and therefore cheaper. They were set in a simple wooden frame and came in two sizes – letter and legal. We used slate or chalky pencils on the $1/16$" thick slates, while our fingers or scrap pieces of cloth served as erasers. The only problem I recall with slates was that when they fell, they pretty much broke.

Eventually we were promoted to exercise books, which we used at our simple wooden desks. Each desk had a ceramic inkwell at the top, looking something like a flower pot with a small hole in the top. Those also changed with the times, the last model I remember being made out of more practical plastic. The ink always came in a powdered form. We'd mix it with water and then carefully fill all the inkwells in each desk. With the ink we used what was called 'common pens'. The common pen was a step up from feather quills, and looked something like a pencil with a nib. So one would have to dip the instrument in the ink and write until the ink on the nib was gone, dip again, write, and so on. The fountain pens of those days were a little more expensive. Expensive and unreliable. They would fail on occasion, forcing you to dip it in the inkwell in order to write. The ink would come back later to haunt us at the end of each term, when we'd have to take razors to the desks to try and scrape out the ink that had spilled on them.

School outings were a must-do for us, and included trips to the many movie theatres to see old favourites like *Robin Hood*. Outdoor treats usually meant Hope Gardens, where we chased armies of iguana lizards, and feasted on mangoes galore when the season arrived. Those days we didn't even bother to pack a lunch. There was also the mini zoo at the Jamaica Institute, which I'd sometimes walk to after visiting my uncle's shop, Henry Chin and Bros, on Beckford Street and Matthews Lane. In the late 1950's, I'd often bicycle to Gunboat Beach with my brother, Loy and a couple of friends from Jackson Road in Rollington Town. Gunboat was a new beach then, and very well kept. Loy would dive for *soldier crabs* and *mussels*, which we'd then use as bait to catch *brim, grunt* and *god bless snapper*. The latter got its name from the two marks on its back, which supposedly represented the thumb and forefinger print left by Jesus the day he fed the multitudes. Sometimes we'd fish all day, and power up on bun and cheese. The energy was necessary for the ride home later, when we'd pedal against the strong breeze on Palisadoes Road, our proud catch in tow.

The many weddings held at Chee Gung Tong on North and East Streets also stand out in my memory bank, and not because I was a sentimental ten-year-old. It had more to do with what was in it for me. When the bride and groom arrived at the East Street gate, they'd light this long string of clappers* and thunder bolts that hung from the mango tree just outside the door on the North Street entrance. After the carnival of explosion and smoke, my brother, cousins and I would go hunt for all the clappers that had not exploded, borrow a lit cigarette from one of the men, and set each one off individually. These weddings were huge with what seemed to be hundreds of people. Basically all the cooking was done on the premises. There was so much food, in fact, that they literally stirred the meat and vegetable pots with a shovel.

When there *wasn't* a wedding going on at Chee Gung Tong*, my brother and I would just hang around while our father played basketball. He also played at Jung San Chinese beach down by Rockfort. That was a nice setting for a basketball court, come to think of it. Not far from the beach. While there, we'd have fun on the two huge swings. They were big enough that you could stand on them. I was told that there were people who could get the swings going so fast and high, that they were able to flip right over the top and back over. *That* I never actually saw for myself. Maybe it was just tall tales. But then even tall tales are all part of great memories. And these are mine.

Written by Derrick Chin and edited by Alex Lee

* See Glossary

Norman Hew-Shue
THOUGHTS OF SCHOOL DAYS IN JAMAICA –
THE EARLY YEARS

IN THIS ARTICLE, I would like to look back at my generation's schooldays, revisiting some fond memories, and sharing our common childhood experiences. I would also like to pay tribute to our parents who had the foresight to realize the value and importance of education. Though memories of names and places stand out indelibly, others might be hazy and I apologize for any errors.

When we lived at Rosemary Lane and Barry Street, beside Seven Stars Bakery, my parents sent me to a private kindergarten at the corner of Tower Street. This was the late '40s or early '50s, and I recall a high classroom built on a stilted foundation, and run by a local black lady. After a short time there my parents nicknamed her 'Meow Tyew Sen-Sang' or 'Puss-Head Teacher',

Front and back covers.

as my only visible accomplishment seemed to be drawing a stylized cat's head, with pointy ears and slanting eyes. I seem to remember getting the idea from the logo on Craven A cigarette boxes.

The book I was given to use then was the *Royal Reader,* and, as is usual in those tender formative years, the texture and odour associated with this book was distinct. It was royal blue, about 4 inches square, and very basic. A whole page might be dedicated to a single letter or word, and, since these were colonial times, was illustrated with a blonde girl in Victorian dress – sort of like Alice in Wonderland. I was fascinated by the teacher's penmanship, e.g. in making a common (British for 'lower case') 'a', she would carefully and slowly make the ascender, followed by a perfect circle, finished off with the descender. This was all carefully done on the blackboard, or on my slate, while she guided my hand. Apart from the cat's head, I was renowned for my '4-foot em's' as the teacher referred to them.

Later, I was sent to a school on Clovelly Road, off East Queen Street. This was two blocks west of the Palace Theatre and Blake Road, with Widows Lane between. Clovelly Road was remarkable for having the most visibly pronounced dip of all the byways of the downtown core, dipping sharply from East Queen Street,

Slate Pencils

and rising to join Blake Road below Kingston College. About three-quarter's of the way down, on the left hand, was the private school run by a Mrs. Huggs (or Booth?). There was a junk or scrap-yard opposite.

The front iron gate opened on to stairs, straight ahead, that led to class-rooms for the higher forms comprised mostly of big girls. Going around the side of this converted house led to the kindergarten and lower forms at the back, where there was a play-yard and a garden with a calabash tree. A zinc fence separated the property from an adjoining terminus for country buses.

The terminus was, at some time, used by the Lindsay Company's fleet, and was visible from beside the gully on East Queen Street. The building, with its imposing white stone façade, served as a landmark for me and countless others, throughout the years of going to and fro in Kingston. Also notable was a clock (which I didn't see working in later years) at the front and top of the building, which seemed to be also made of stone, with red hands and dashes in place of numerals.

The Clovelly Road School served as my introduction to the real, regimented, outside world. To a spoilt only child, this was traumatic, with a lot of crying and carrying-on on the first several days I can tell you. Gradually, I settled into the new surroundings, and eventually couldn't wait to go. I was very small at birth, and my dear mother gave me her special formula of Cow and Gate (infant formula), with one whole egg. Breakfast consisted of modifications of this while listening to Patsy Cline on the Rediffusion *"If you looove... me half as much as I... love youuu... You wouldn't staaaay away...."*

Our slate boards and pencils were replaced or supplemented by exercise books, which came in single or double-lined format. The latter would be used to write the letters within the lines as previously described. The *Royal Reader* gave way to an ABC book, remarkable for the vivid colours of illustrated objects associated with each letter: "A for apple; B for bat; cat; dog; egg ; fan; gun; hat; ink; jug; king; lamp; man; nun; okra; pen; queen; rat; sun; top; van; x-mas; yak; zebra" I remember all except "W". Anybody remember what object was used for that ?

The schoolmates I remember were Bobby; the boys from Hong Kong Grocery; Henry and Edward ; Lola, from across East Queen Street. The big girls found me cute for some reason, and I was regularly treated to hot (in temperature and flavour) patties bought by one of their number.

There was a large bell, which was rung to mark the various periods and breaks by the headmistress or a senior student.

There was a shop at the north-western corner of East Queen Street, where we would stop and buy bubble gum and other necessities. One shilling's (twelve English pence nowadays) lunch money could buy a lot.

Those days also had their share of fads, with associated memorable anecdotes.

Magnifying glasses (solely for focussing the sun's rays) were improvised from eyeglasses, the bottoms of glass bottles etc., and were used to start fires and char paper or skin. Once, during a break, the school's siren, Cherry, was drinking from the stand pipe, while stretching one exposed thigh. This was immediately subjected to the rays of a magnifying glass, with the resultant screams, and intervention and judgment by the teaching staff.

In the days when loud explosions could not be anything but fireworks, there was the fad of the Crackerball, (later called Shh-boom) which was a type of contact firecracker about the size of a pistachio nut, wrapped in brightly coloured glittery paper.

The headmistress was very strict and, although her name may be hazy, her visage is burnt in my mind as being one with East Indian features and a hint of a moustache. Assembly was a serious affair and, once, with every head bent in prayer, I remember peeking through half-closed lids and seeing Neville (the headmistress' big son), flipping a crackerball from hand to hand. Well – you guessed it! The whole solemn proceeding was shattered by a loud 'BLAM!' There was a short pause by the headmistress, who then continued with prayers. The only remaining hint of the incident was a yellowish discoloura-tion on the concrete floor, the smell of sulphur, and an agitated Neville. Afterwards, he was summoned into the inner sanctum from which could be heard the swish of the cane, punctuated by his cries.

Other teachers who I recall were Miss Eloise, with a wide smile and spec-tacles. Once, Cherry, for some reason, was on the receiving end of the cane by Miss Eloise, and wet herself in front of the school. There was also Sam who rode a huge motorbike, and who, I remember, drew a picture of the Earth on the blackboard, coloured in vivid blue, yellow and red, to illustrate the Frigid, Temperate and Torrid Zones respectively,

Residential houses, in those pre-air-conditioning colonial times, were built with high ceilings and a cellar space to aid ventilation and the dissipation of hot air. The cellars would be high enough for us kids to almost be able to stand up straight. Also in vogue were 'oxblood-dyed' concrete verandahs, and steps with solid concrete banisters you could slide down, and glazed French double doors in those safer times.

Sandra was a fair skinned girl living halfway down Clovelly Road, and we sometimes went after school to her house and played under her cellar. Once, we boys were fascinated when she peed in a strange squatting way. Being an only child this was just one of the many feminine mysteries, I was still unravelling.

The boys would use slingshots to shoot the cracker-balls under the cellar, from one side to the other, against the zinc fence, or the legs of the students, or the resident mongrel dogs, who took to dashing this gauntlet only when necessary.

'Gigs' or 'Tops' were also in vogue, and were ingeniously made from cotton thread spools, doorknobs etc. Great expertise was demonstrated in getting these to spin in the palms of one's hands, on other tops etc.

Other memories were of reading about Peter Pan, and memorizing the catechism so that the key phrases stuck in the mind : *No other God before me neither in the Heaven above nor the earth beneath.* What I detested most of all was a book about Jamaica, wrapped in brown paper, describing its history and geography in dry statistical form, which future lawyers or politicians might have enjoyed: *"Jamaica, surface area 4400 sq. mls. divided into the counties of Cornwall, Middlesex and Surrey; Blue Mountain, highest point at 7,402 feet."*

Weekends would sometimes produce the treat of a movie at Gaiety or Palace theatres downtown. A film that stood out indelibly in my mind during this time was "The House of Wax", with Vincent Price. I remember hearing Bobby and the other kids describing the wax figures melting in the fiery climax of the film. For years I was in great fear of all things associated with this film, such as the masks on the cornflakes boxes, or even helicopters, because the film was preceded by a Craven A commercial with one in it. The fact that it was presented in come-out-of-the-screen-at-you-3-D format (with red and green glasses), didn't help matters any. It took years before enlightenment, regarding the pretend world of movies and special effects, finally allayed my fears.

Written by Norman Hew-Shue and edited by Sonia Gordon Scott

Photographs ©Ray Chen

Photo to the right, courtesy of Norman, of his parents and himself.

Norman Hew-Shue
THE CALL OF JAMAICAN WATERS

FOR THOSE OF US who grew up in Jamaica, there is a great bond with the sea, and happy memories from innocent and peaceful times of years past. In the tingling surf, after the initial burning of eyes and nose wore off, we are re-introduced to the home that, it is claimed, our ancestral species left eons ago. My great regret, which I am sure is shared by those of you living far from the sea, is that my kids didn't experience a childhood by the sea which made for a well-rounded life. Unlike land-locked Canadians, we have already experienced Paradise in the tropics, and do not need to spend frequent vacations seeking it.

The sea and its marine life have always fascinated me. I used to ask local boys to go down the lane for sea water, to try and keep oysters and seaweed in a large cookie bottle. Little did I know then that it wasn't that easy, and that nature used breaking waves to aerate the water. The next morning my intended aquarium would be a slimy mess, smelling to high heaven. I would buy Rachel Carson's books e.g. *The Sea Around Us* from Broadway Restaurant (between Whims and Sterling's on the corner of East Street and East Queen Street), at a time when reading paperbacks was one of the few avenues of entertainment available in those pre-TV days. I can still recall the smell of the paper. Later, I worked in the University of the West Indies (UWI) department of Zoology, among sharks, jellyfish and other specimens, learning their Latin names and about marine biology.

My mother would take me down to Hanover Street to The Shell Company (W.I.) Limited's wharf to konn sunn* or watch the ships. A walk up a long concrete ramp led to the wharf with its heavy wooden flooring. I would stand in awe beside the looming ship's hull, anchored to massive iron knobs by huge ropes that seemed to be at least a foot in diameter, and on which were strung large metal plates at intervals. The rolling swell and the rhythmic sound of the pounding surf was hypnotic. It looked as if you could just pull the ship in by hand. Along the ship's side was a mysterious white symbol consisting of a large circle and vertical line with forked tines, ending in cryptic letters such as "FW, NAW or Tropics". Only later did I learn that the plates were to keep rats from climbing the ropes and boarding the ship, and an education in Physics (provided by my dear sacrificing parents), taught me that the strange symbol was the Plimsoll load-line mark. The latter was named after Samuel

Plimsoll, whose British merchant ships carried this mark to indicate safe laden weights under different conditions (e.g. North Atlantic Winters), after unscrupulous owners overloaded insured ships, causing them to sink.

One night a Chinese sea captain came into our shop. My father struck up a conversation with him and was invited, along with other neighbouring families, aboard his ship where I gazed into the gaping cargo hold from the bridge. I wondered at my elders' interest and, later, realized that it was ships after all that had carried our forefathers to a better life.

Beside the Shell wharf was the Hardware and Lumber pier where we downtown kids used to fish all night in our teenage years. The hardier among us used to go bathing in the harbour, along with the locals, from piers like the infamous Gold Street one near to a power station, where, it was rumoured, a large underwater-pipe would 'suck yu in an' drown yu.'

Occasionally we would go to other swimming areas. We had Chinese School outings to Boston Beach and Yallahs. We also went to the river at

Photos above and left: taken at Bournemouth Beach which has a similar look to Joong San Beach.. Below: Myrtle Bank Hotel.

Castleton Gardens which I didn't particularly like, as the bottom was rocky and the running water had a chilling effect. There were also beaches or pools at Bournemouth, Sigarney or Gunboat. Mineral Baths at Rockfort offered private or public areas in water strongly laced with minerals from the surrounding hills. I used to smell the sulphur from the Cement Company kilns from my later home in Mountain View. The Myrtle Bank pool was just down Maiden Lane from me at Harbour Street.

But none of these beaches, rivers, baths or pools had the same allure as Chinese Beach, or Joong San*, which our far-sighted forefathers provided for us to enjoy and socialize in.

Come with me now, down Memory

Lane, for a Sunday outing at Joong San. After returning from mass and meeting as arranged, let's pack a few necessities like bathsuits and shampoo and head for King Street, in front of the courthouse, to take the number 2 JOS bus to Rockfort. While waiting for the bus, we might take a few pictures beside the carriage gun in front of the Government Post Office, with our Brownie camera, using the large red-backed film.

We are soon at the large, open iron gates, near to the end of Windward Road and the start of Rockfort Road. There is a huge poster showing the Coppertone girl's bottom exposed by a puppy. A long, almost straight road takes us down to the sea-side, after passing a concrete courtyard for badminton or basketball and where we sometimes played football. Beside this is a high stage and I remember a hula-hoop competition in which Victor (remember Sukiyaki and 'Vikings'?) Wong shone. Parallel to the road is the boys' changing room on the East, or left, and the girls' on the right. Also on the right is a shop selling showbow, patties, and drinks. A pack of scrawny mongrel dogs are never far away, watching our every move with hungry eyes. We test their skill and awareness by suddenly throwing a tidbit over the shoulder or under-arm, without any warning, causing them all to leap up like basketball players after a loose ball. There is the sound of clamping teeth and it is rare for food to touch the ground.

Above: The view from the upper level of Nathan's Department Store, looking south on King Street at the corner of Barry Street.

Left: Bus stop sign..

We go now to the changing rooms to get into 'bathsuits', usually bought at Nathan's, with the Jantzen logo of the diving girl on them. Girls have one-piece suits, sometimes with french frills on them. We put on suntan lotion, which is nothing more than olive oil straight from the shop shelf. The more sophisticated of us use Coppertone ("mi dear!").

There is a concrete patio area between the changing rooms with almond trees, which is the site for garden parties and other recreations, along with the stage area. Lights and colourful banners would be strung between the buildings and, the place is well planned and maintained.

There is a narrow boardwalk that allows one to walk from the changing rooms out to sea for about 100 yards and around to the the other side without getting wet. There are wooden piling supports that also kept out sharks and probably jelly-fish. I suspect that at one time there used to be netting. At the far end one gets a panoramic view: Springfield yacht club and industrial Kingston to the West, and Rockfort, the Cement Factory, and the Palisadoes to the East. At intervals are about eight steps of iron piping and wood that leads into the sea. Depending on your proficiency, you can launch yourself from these until you are able to dive off the deep end. The deep end side of the boardwalk is also a favourite place for fishing.

Joong San is very good for learning to swim, for there I underwent the transition from wading in the shallows to skin diving with goggles and fins at the far end. Beginners can walk along the sandy front directly into the sea. Flat, tape-like Sea or Turtle Grass is underfoot, with the occasional fallen log or post. Sharp spiny sea-eggs (urchins) are a common recreational hazard.

After mastering floating, the dog paddle and breaststroke, you are ready to launch yourself from off the steps (although in a depth that you could stand up in). As you dive in, you hear the roar of the water in your ears and feel the warm surface water turn suddenly cold as you sink deeper. As you move forward, you get the courage to open your eyes and see the fuzzy outlines of the feet of other swimmers and the turtle grass. You stand up and wipe your burning eyes and clear your nose. After this initial shock, you and the water are one, and you spend most of the day hanging on to the steps, admiring the brightly coloured sponges and other sea-life on the wooden piles. I once found a framed net which I pushed along the bottom and dredged up fascinating marine life, including a bright red seahorse.

Families come regularly, such as the lovely Wongs with mom, dad, Victoria and other siblings. On a sunny day the water is clear and you can see to the bottom, even to 6 feet at the deep end. A day at the beach is advertised by a deep brown tan and glowing feeling. There was of course, the occasional overdone sunburn with peeling skin for days afterwards.

Next door are the wide open beaches frequented by the locals. We sit and watch their antics where a guy somersaults into the water ("tun poopalik") trying to impress the female audience. Also, there is always a grinning 'face-man', teeth goldcapped, "'teaching' the young gal dem fi swim." Occasionally a scantily clad (underwear doubling as beachwear) gal wanders over to our boardwalk, creating great excitement.

The falling sun means choppier colder waters, and time to go home. We go to our respective changing rooms and shower, using the shampoo in the little plastic sachet. We guys used so much gel-like hair oil, that the soap, salt and shampoo would react to make a white paste . After putting on the polyester cotton shirt and fixing up the T.C. (Tony Curtis – film star whose flicked forward hairstyle became all the rage with young men) we pack away the wet bathsuit and head for home.

Then begins the long, tired, but happy walk to the front gate. Before taking the bus home we might stop off at the bar at the front to play skittles, or visit the shops at Club Havana /Adastra to be served by the pretty Chinese girls behind the counter. On the way back, we downtown-core Kingstonians would take the bus along Windward Road past the Rialto theatre; (much, much later

The Ward Theatre located on the north side of Parade

廳 舞 城 灣 亞
CLUB HAVANA

much later called 'Kings' theatre), Palace; Gaiety and Ward theatres, checking the posters to see what's showing to go and see later.

THE END OF PARADISE

In later years, after independence, we had the slow unfortunate downturn of life with increased crime. Attendance at Joong San fell and eventually vanished. The buildings fell into neglect and disrepair; gone were the caretaker and dogs to greener pastures. The boardwalk was dilapidated with dangerous gaps in the planking, and the steps corroded. Even the adjoining public areas were deserted. The whole place was overgrown with prickly weeds, generally called *makka** in patois (and probably another imported African word, like *yabba** for cooking-pot.) The long pricky weed is called thet mah binn* or iron horse whip in Hakka, which my mother used to soak in rum to make a rubbing cure-all.

I would still go to Joong San on Saturdays and would spend the whole day swimming all by myself (something you should avoid doing, but, in those heady high-spirited days, you were invincible). I was content with the solitude and the spirit of times past. I got quite adept at catching the blue crabs, and would go home with about 2 dozen in plastic bags, to share with my dear widowed mother.

At the end of one such day I was taking a shower on the girls' side because the other side was in ruins. Still, the shower was in a bad state, and consisted of three rusted pipe sections, held together and suspended by wire over my head. As I was soaping up my eyes I heard loud banging sounds all around me and was shocked to see the pieces of the sharp-edged, heavy iron pipe sections, laying at my feet.

I couldn't understand how it did not even touch me, except that this was the Creator's (Who took me through many scrapes) way of telling me that it was time to let go and move on. This was further reinforced later by my friend (one of the Chong boys) going there and leaving hastily, after being joined by chanting, drum-beating rastas. We stuck it out to the last, but those were signals of the changing times and the loss, forever, of the glory days and the 'Splendour in the (Sea) Grass'.

Written by Norman Hew-Shue and edited by Sonia Gordon Scott

* See Glossary

Photographs of
Bournemouth Beach from the personal album of ©Kathleen (Kay)Chin
Kingston ©Ray Chen

Vernon Chin
TROPICAL CHINESE

ONE OF MY FIRST ancestors in Jamaica was my granduncle on my mother's side. Tata-San. He was apparently very big and strong. I know from my elders that he started out in tiny Sommerton, St. James, and ended up establishing the first cornmeal factory in Jamaica. Then at some point he came to Montego Bay. I'd say that was a stroke of genius. Montego Bay was a great place to grow up.

Mr & Mrs Henry Chin on their wedding day

Mom was Violet May Hew before she married my dad, Henry R. Chin. She was somewhere between 16 and 18 when she got married. He was 21. Their marriage represented the union of the two main families that made up the Chinese population in Montego Bay.

My parents were an excellent match. She was the thinker, he was the worker bee. Dad had actually come to know hard work from an early age. He was only 13 when his father left him and three other siblings in Jamaica, while he took one son back to China. At that point dad went to work for an aunt of his. After 12 years and some savings, he opened his own shop, built it up over some three or so years, and then took a wife.

Dad (right) would never see the inside of a classroom, but he'd live life long enough to see us own our own hotel, before dying of a heart attack in the 1970s. Mom, the beloved grand matriarch of our family, would pass away at a respectable 82.

There were three of us in our family, all boys, and I was the middle child. The butter between two breads. At that time we owned a small grocery store in what was then the middle class side of Montego Bay. We were one of just three Chinese families there, and while we probably did stick to each other a bit, we also mixed with our neighbours. Those were the days of what I call the 'genteel Jamaican'. The teachers, policemen, taxi drivers… just hard working people who were trying to improve their standard of living. But they had a great dignity about them. In my language, they were class people. I'd say we taught each other respect, because there was hardly a time when we didn't support each other.

Back in our shop, the family pulled together as was expected. When my older brother wanted to go abroad to study, we struggled to send him. It was difficult, but we managed. But my mom's head for business ensured that our situation would improve over time. To her credit, she would take us from small shop to car rental business. At that point we became the first Chinese in Jamaica to venture into tourism.

Looking at my mom, you wouldn't give her a second glance. Violet Chin was tall and slim with short hair, and the picture of pure humility. A very simple, quiet thinker who almost never raised her voice. Really, there was nothing sophisticated about her appearance. But there was a certain dignity about her that you don't often see nowadays. She exuded it. And she was always giving advice from the moral to the practical. She'd say, '*Vernon, never turn away black people. Always help your brothers. Watch how you spend.*' Or the usual staple, '*respect your elders*'. She'd always remind us that whatever she had in this world was for us. You could see it in her eyes that she loved having her children around her.

Mom and I quarrelled a lot because we saw things differently, yet we got along despite the fact that she was very hard on discipline. As a child of six or seven, I couldn't read properly, and would have to practice at nights. And for every mistake I made, I'd get the strap. My parents were like all *tongin** parents. They wanted their children to be professional in whatever they did. Top of the class. The best.

Family life was wonderful when I was a boy. Inside the Chin household, we were happy to be brothers, happy to gather as a family. Life was simple then. My own four corners of the world were within shouting distance of each other, and that was just fine by me. I was even born right on top of the shop. As a matter of fact, Nurse Richardson, our neighbour, delivered all three of us right there. My uncle, when he came to Jamaica, opened a bakery across the road. So I was always running across to him or the other way to the Woons to play with their kids. School was also within walking distance. In fact, everything in Montego Bay back in those days was accessible by foot.

No question about it, despite the fact that we were nowhere near Kingston's Chinatown, I felt Chinese growing up. You were told so. You ate, slept and played it. In the daytime we ate Jamaican. At night, Chinese. Always. While it was dad who did most of the cooking, mom made *suimen** on Sundays. She'd cook this huge pot, and there'd be this great competition to see who ate the most. If there were leftovers, we'd eat it in the mornings. The other Chinese dish she made was a pot-roasted chicken on a bed of cho-cho.

Mealtimes for us meant being properly seated at the table. It was a thing with us Chins that we had to eat together. As my cousins used to live with us, we were usually ten or more around this huge table. The rule was that you had to wait for everyone to be seated before you could start eating. And by the way, you couldn't just eat and leave.

There were other practices that we stuck to. Children were to be seen and not heard, so you mostly heard adult voices at our table. Chopsticks were mandatory, and you must first have a bowl of steaming soup before the main course, which was always served with rice. You took only that piece of food on the serving plate that was closest to you, and you ended your meal with a helping of lychee or other fruit.

I would say we kept to our Chinese roots as best we could. Celebrating Chinese New Year was a good example. Our meals during this time would become strictly vegetarian – like tofu, rice noodle, stir fried cabbage and dried oysters. That was particular to our family, so it must have come from their village. At 3:00 p.m. on the eve of the new year, we'd bathe in bamboo and citrus leaves to wash away the bad luck. Shaddock we placed on the table with the lights on. And all day long on New Year's Day we ate, slept and played mahjong.

As for our Montego Bay playground, the north coast home address was a real treat for us boys. Usually on a Sunday we'd head for the beach after the shop. Other days we'd go early in the morning with dad. But the water would be chilly then, and we'd race to push each other in for that initial cold shock. Weekends also meant being entertained at the movies or Chinese club. Bird season had us manoeuvering through the bushes in the dark and damp of the early mornings. My brother, Junior used to love that. And when that season was over, we always had huge mountain crayfish waiting for us in Barnett River, or juicy black crabs ready for scooping into bags in the Falmouth or Tryall areas.

As we got older, we'd go to parties, but only if they were chaperoned. In those days there was no liquor. But dancing! Now we had lots of *that*. Those were the days of the cha cha, the mambo and waltz. And usually there'd be a live calypso band too. Well, I was an excellent dancer, so I became the envy of every Chinese boy in Montego Bay since all the girls wanted to dance with me.

Family, fun, freedom. What better way to grow up?

Written and edited by Alex Lee as told by Vernon Chin.

* See Glossary

Winnie Chung Devensky
WINNIE'S LIMOUSINE

Winnie

MOST OF MY FRIENDS and acquaintances know that, from age 10, I lived a charmed life in Port Antonio. It was here that I would get frequent glimpses of Errol Flynn and the beautiful people he brought there. His dad taught me biology at Titchfield High School, and I had my first crush on his son, Sean, who died in the Vietnam war working as a journalist. When not in classes at school, my activities were netball and field hockey. At the Chinese club it was basketball and beach all day on Sundays after mass. It was also here that I would play around in Baron Von Thyssen's home as a young teenager after a grocery delivery, unaware of his stature as the German steel magnate, until I came to live in the U.S. Various Chinese clubs from Kingston and Montego Bay also visited frequently, and the small group of Chinese in Port Antonio entertained them regularly.

Winnie

Netball team at Titchfield High School

Life was glorious in a small town. But before Port Antonio, until age 10, I lived in Windsor where I was born. Windsor is half way between Port Antonio and Comfort Castle in Maroon Town on the Rio Grande river. It was so remotely located that there were no schools. My parents supplied the surrounding villages with their every need. Besides their 'ham tier po'* (haberdashery), they even had a butcher shop and raised their own cows. From the view point of a small child, my life was somewhat dull. In the closest town of Riversview, the 2 daughters of the Wong family – Eva and Norma – and I would teach the local children to read and write during the summer. For some excitement, we would even swim in the nude in the Rio Grande occasionally since we had no bathing-suits.

Winnie Chung younger days

We were not wealthy, but I remember acquiring my first 'limousine' when it was time for me to attend elementary school at Fellowship, the closest village that had a school. My parents could not drive and had no car. It was too far to walk, but I had to attend school; education was important. Solution: my parents bought me a donkey. But there was another problem: I was too young to ride this donkey alone to Fellowship.

On his way back home

Solution: they hired an old and gentle black man to walk beside the donkey while I rode. His sole job was to take me to school and return for me after school. My cousin, who would visit from Kingston, remembers the donkey as WINNIE'S LIMOUSINE.

Written by Winnie Chung Devensky and edited by Sonia Gordon Scott.

* See Glossary

Above photograph ©Ray Chen

Down Memory Lane

'Skate' as it was called is a 'bicycle' made from wood with steel bearings for wheels

Photograph ©Ray Chen

Norman Hew-Shue
GETTING FROM POINT A TO B -
TRANSPORTATION IN THE GOOD OLD DAYS

Since our fathers and forefathers came by steamship, Jamaican memories
are embellished by tales of various modes of transport.

THE 'TWO FOOT DEM'

The feet of our youth stood us in good stead in getting around, particularly for those of us growing up in the country. With those legs, or "shanks mare" as the English called them, it was nothing for us Kingstonians to traverse the city areas from Cross Roads to the harbour, or from West Street to Mountain View Avenue.

WHEELS START TURNING

Δ83
Riding bicycles then, required you to have a licence plate. The fee was (£ S D) 4/- (4 shillings or 2 florins).

From foot we graduated to mechanized transport. In our early comic-book reading years, we would make our own scooter skates for yard use, out of lumber, nails, bottle-tops and old car bearings. Later, in the teen years, I remember the exhilarating thrill of borrowing Tony Lee's bicycle, with turn-down handles and twin headlights, to leave our meeting spot near the Institute of Jamaica, and go down East Street, along Harbour Street to Spanish Town Road and back, on streets bereft of traffic and crime. Doing a running springmount on to your bicycle was the cool macho thing to do, especially with an appreciative female audience.

Later, motorbikes like Quicklys or Lambrettas made their appearance, and we would go to the Chinese Public School for football or recreation on these, with up to four of us 'bumming rides' on the Lambretta's pillion seat and running board.

3

4

MAH CHAW (HORSE & BUGGY)

Before the common advent of cars, the horse was a common sight, pulling buggies or dray-carts. At West Parade, near the ever present coconut vendor, was an area called Mah Hyeak Swee ("horse drink water") by our parents, because of the water trough that must have stood there.

My father used to take a horse and buggy, run by two brothers from near Barry Street and Matthews Lane. We would climb into the rocking, black panelled carriage, with plastic windows at rear and sides, the shaky ride punctuated by the clip clop of the horse's shod hooves. In those days one could go east on Barry Street before it became one-way westward. Spoiled child that I was, I used to be taken to Chinatown for goew juu* – flour skin wrapped meatballs on a tooth-pick.

5

PUBLIC TRANSIT / JOS

Tram cars were common when I was a tod-dler, and tramlines might still be visible around Paradise and other Kingston streets. My mother used to take me on trips. I remember the clanking bell and looking through the windows at adver-tisements for Four Ace cigarettes; Sunlight soap etc. painted all along the walls on South Camp Road, or on Windward Road, around Doncaster or Bellevue.

The Jamaica Omnibus Company (JOS) gave us mem-ories of a variety of buses from the "chi chi" or patty-pan types, to automatic diesels with a conductor or conduc-tress. There were often long waits, sometimes ending with two buses flying past the stop. Sometimes the bell didn't ring on pulling the cord, and you had to verbally imitate it to indicate a stop! Route numbers are still indelible etched in my mind – No. 2 to Rockfort and Joong San beach; No. 4 to Cross Roads via Marescaux Road and Wolmers High School; No 13 to Molynes Road, near where a girlfriend used to live on Little Kew Road.

The JOS went out of service to be replaced by free-

6

lancing mini-vans or 'robots'. "Cross Roads, Half Way Tree Mr Chin??", the sideman/conductor would shout, leaning out of an already jam-packed van. Frequently the fare would change mid-trip.

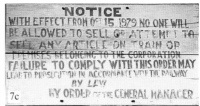

KINGSTON TERMINUS FOR ALL TRAINS
Jamaica Railway Corporation
7b **SERVING YOU SINCE 1845**

NOTICE
WITH EFFECT FROM 0⁵ 15 1979 NO ONE WILL BE ALLOWED TO SELL OR ATTEMPT TO SELL ANY ARTICLE ON TRAIN OR PREMISES BELONGING TO THE CORPORATION FAILURE TO COMPLY WITH THIS ORDER MAY LEAD TO PROSECUTION IN ACCORDANCE WITH THE RAILWAY BY LAW
7c   BY ORDER OF THE GENERAL MANAGER

FOAH CHAW* ("FIRE CAR") THE TRAIN RIDE

My father used to take me on train rides to visit relatives on the north coast in Montego Bay (Johnny Hew) or Green Island (The Williams) and Lucea. We would pack our suitcases (Gap Jonng* – Hakka term derived from "Grip container") and go down to the railway station at the western end of Barry Street. A familiar landmark to us downtowners was the tall water tower, capped by a pointed cone and supported by a tripod of steel beams, which could be seen on looking westward along Water Lane. This most probably was used to fill the locomotives in the train yard. Early trains were coal burning steam locomotives, and I can remember our elders' excitement with the advent of oil burning diesels.

At the train station we waited, seated on the typical Government civil service-type hard, board benches after the tickets were stamped. We heard the train coming into the station in a cacophony of hissing and clanking. The porter opened the gate and we went to a line of green carriages all emblazoned with the letters JGR (Jamaica Government Railway). We embarked in a carriage of our designated ticketed class, with me wanting the window seat.

We would get underway with the rhythmic chugging and hissing, rising to an ever increasing crescendo, until we hit the wide open spaces. I would be enthralled by the changing landscape, punctuated by the stations on the way: Bushy Park, Bog Walk, Christiana, Maggoty, Catadupa... and names commemorating British towns e.g. Cambridge, or events in their history, such as Balaclava of the 1800's Crimean war, and the infamous Charge of the Light Brigade. One name that created feelings of dread was Kendal in Manchester, where a tragic train crash occurred in 1957, on a church outing, taking many lives. Passing it still evoked a noted hush in commuters, years later, when I travelled the line.

The trip would start in the evening about 3 o'clock, when it was still light – except for the occasional dramatic darkness caused by a tunnel, and accompanied by a change in the tone of the clacking wheels. On one trip I remember the emergency cord being pulled by some girls, one of whom had dropped her glasses through the window. The train came to a screeching halt, the girls conferred with the conductor and went back along the track. I remember the train pulling out and leaving them when they did not return promptly.

School outings would see us taking chartered buses for days of carefree fun, to spots like Flemarie beach in Yallahs, Boston Beach in Portland, or Castleton Gardens in St. Mary. Later on we used these same buses for our outings, which became more boisterous, being unsupervised by watchful teachers. The trip usually included a medley of sing-alongs and, invariably, the Doris Day hit "Que sera, sera..." (what ever will be will be...) in which we changed the lyrics to "Kiss me rass; me rass…"

Later when I was in the cadets, huge steel armoured lorries from Up-Park Camp would take us on camping trips to Newcastle or Castleton, or for rifle shooting competitions (in which Wolmer's and Munro excelled), to Twickenham Park's shooting range among the cane fields.

Transportation around the city would be incomplete if I didn't mention the ferry from Victoria Pier on King Street, to Lime Cay or Port Royal.

TAXI CABS

In Kingston in the '60s, there began a business craze with radio-controlled taxi-cabs. Multicoloured fleets of Yellow, Betta, Co-Op, MacCaulay's,

Checker, Diamond, and other cabs, sprung up in quick succession. Most just as quickly disappeared by the law of competition. The survivors, by the time I left in the early '80s, were Yellow, Co-Op (which operated from East Queen Street and John's Lane, opposite the gas station and dry cleaner's), and Checker, owned by Mr. Jones and stationed somewhere near Connolley Avenue, off Marescaux Road and opposite Wolmer's, if memory serves me right.

I remember my father contracting a MacCaulay cab, personally requesting one Mr. Walker as driver, to take us to Royal Flats, a small village somewhere "down de country" near Bog Walk, St. Catherine, to consult a recommended female faith healer, Senn Mah* for some minor ailment of a member of our party. It was more of an outing than of any great faith in her powers.

THE CAR RIDE

Always etched in my mind are the car trips to visit relatives in the country. We would pack up Uncle's BMC Morris station wagon (with the yellow-brown varnished wooden strips along the sides), and leave very early in the morning for Lucea and other areas on the north-coast. Car travel was such a rarity for me that I always got sick, and had to throw-up in the brown paper bag brought specially for me. On the way we would stop at a small village where there was a boy of my age nicknamed Captain. What stuck in my mind was the very strong aroma of Blue Mountain coffee, drunk with slices of hard dough bread, country-man style, while it was still dark outside.

Again, spoilt as I was, and lucky to be given such loving God-sent parents, my father gave me an iron racing car which I pedalled to tong ngin guy* and back on Sunday mornings.

Vauxhall cars seem to have marked milestones throughout my life. When small, my father gave me a toy Vauxhall Velox from Times Store. It was black and chunky as was the style of that era, and used two large D batteries [the only type available then], and would go forward or reverse in circles. I used to run it within the closed shop on Sundays. Later on, I would be given lifts in a Vauxhall Victor or Cresta by my friends, and I used to go partying with Cornell who had a Vauxhall GT Viva at the time.

Those teenage years would find us cruising up Half Way Tree Road in our Sixteen-hundred -E -Gee Tee to the strains of Elizabeth's Serenade/Games that lovers Play from the 8 track cassette, in search of parties to crash, looking for curry goat and a chance to 'locks down' with a mini-skirted, mascara -eyed 'chick' with a Lulu*-style, flipped-up hair-do.

After I got my licence I had a Vauxhall Viva. I doted on that Viva, doing all the repairs and maintenance, even overhauling the engine and changing the

Racing car driven by Wonley Chin Yee at Vernam Field in Clarendon - May 1962.

clutch. I would drive the Viva to Yallahs to visit Margaret, whose family had an assortment of vehicles, including a remarkable full length Land Rover. This was a 'work horse', used to deliver goods to country folk, sometimes across dry river beds with boulders and all, serving as roads, or reversing up steep slopes laden with beer.

One Friday in the '70s, there was a very heavy torrential downpour. I dropped off some of my co-workers from North Street Government Labs at Parade, and continued down Princess Street. Water was up to the

height of the car's floor as I went down Harbour Street, driving wide to avoid a large manhole which I knew was there, and along West Street, going around the western bus terminals. Three black guys under a shop roof ran shouting after the car. They had the advantage of a straight line while I had to turn the corner. I reached over, safety locked both doors (it was a 2-door) and did rapid mental calculations. I must go fast enough without flooding the engine. I had read that human top speed wasn't more than 20 mph so I kept the car at that, with water washing over the guys and the car in big waves. By the grace of God and my waterproofing adaptations, with moulded distributors and air inlet turned sideways, I made it through to the safety of West Queen Street.

On another Sunday, en route to Yallahs in the Nine Mile area on the St Thomas Road, I noticed a black guy on a bike ride into a side road. I went further down and my mind told me to stop at the intersection. I came out and looked at some higgler's fruit – then I saw the guy riding in my direction, but when he saw me he stopped and circled back. A lonely stretch of hilly country road was in front, and I had visions of us jostling on the twisting country roads, trying to push each other off, because I had no intention of stopping. Another thing (I know of) to thank God for.

11

Those experiences were indicative of a Jamaica that was changing from the one I recall with fondness. With the loss of those 'Splendour in the Grass' days, and a view to a better life for my kids I, along with others, finally took the ultimate transport in the shape of Boeing to come to the northern shores of Canada.

Written by Norman Hew-Shue and edited by Sonia Gordon Scott

* See Glossary

© *Photo Credits and captions:*

1.	Kathleen (Kay) Chin	Bicycle rider
2.	Willie Kong	Bicycle liscence plate
3.	National Library of Jamaica	Mah Chaw* in Kingston
4.	National Library of Jamaica	Tram Car in Kingston
5.	The Gleaner Company Ltd.	JOS bus
6.	The Gleaner Company Ltd.	JOS bus conductor
7.	(a,b,c) Ray Chen	Jamaica Railway Station signs and train in station
8.	The Gleaner Company Ltd.	JOS bus in the country
9.	National Library of Jamaica	Taxi cabs on King Street
10.	Linda Chin Yee	Racin car, Vernamfield in Clarendon
11.	Ray Chen	Road sign

Peter Chang
CHINESE SPORTS PERSONALITIES

MANY YOUNG CHINESE Jamaicans today take life for granted. Their integration into today's society seems so natural, yet they are not aware of the history of their people. They know little of the struggles and hardships we had to overcome in early colonial Jamaica to reach where we are today. Later in life I personally experienced some of them by my encounters with racial and social prejudice in Jamaica and Canada.

A lot of good Chinese Jamaicans helped to tear down these barriers for us. I have written about quite a few of them in the field of sports because I consider them trendsetters who contributed significantly to our society and who helped our integration into it. Some were pioneers who made it easier for others to follow. We have come a long way and we must recognize those who showed us the way.

I was fortunate to meet some of the persons about whom I have written, and to find many Chinese Jamaican elders who told me about the difficulties of the early years. We are often stereotyped by those who continue to show their ignorance of other cultures. I have always been very proud of the ordinary Chinese Jamaican who rose above his or her adversities and excelled, not only in sports, but also academically and socially. The sports personalities I have written about exhibit these qualities and we should be proud of their achievements. Many of them are practically unheard of but we must recognize their excellence and achievements.

Peter Chang with George HoSang.

GEORGE HoSANG: Without doubt, the greatest Chinese Jamaican/West Indian athlete ever produced in the Caribbean. Several times champion jockey of Jamaica and twice in Canada, he is very highly respected in the racing industry in both countries and his name and reputation are spoken of with great reverence at Caymanas Park and Woodbine Race Track.

His single season win record in Jamaica stood for almost thirty years; it was recently broken by Trevor Simpson, who did it in almost twice the number of rides.

Alva Anderson, Managing Director of Racing Promotions Limited, (left) makes a presentation of a silver tankard to the champion jockey Emilio Rodriques for reaching the milestone of becoming the first rider at the Caymanas Park to ride 600 winners. Also in the presentation are the former four-time champion George Hosang , who achieved the distinction of riding 600 winners earlier on the race card . -1983. 01. 03

In Jamaica, George paved the way for other Chinese Jamaican jockeys such as Steve Lyn, Michael Lee, Patrick 'White Mice' Lyn and Tensang Chung. In Canada, he paved the way for other Caribbean riders such as Patrick and Simon Husbands, Emile Ramsammy, Ricky and Christopher Griffiths and many others. In his prime George had to overcome a lot of racial prejudice, especially in Canada, but he was successful enough to win over his detractors and critics with his monumental achievements. It should also be noted that his brother-in-law, Patrick 'Deany' Chang, was a former national swimmer and, like George, attended Kingston College. Deany also represented his school with distinction.

HERBERT CHANG: Easily the best Chinese Jamaican cricketer we have produced in this country and the West Indies. A master batsman of the 1970's, he represented Kensington Cricket Club, Jamaica and the West Indies with distinction. He will, unfortunately, be remembered for joining the Lawrence Rowe led rebel tour of South Africa. We should not hold this against him because of the tough economic situation in our country at that time, for he is truly a   great cricketer.

Herbert Chang batting at Sabina Park , Kingston

DOUGLAS SANG HUE: One of the greatest test umpires of all time. He umpired at the highest level for a very long time and was highly praised by all the test playing countries. His decisions were never questioned because this was a man who lived by his principles of honesty and integrity. A true role model.

MAURICE 'DANNY' LYN: Brother of the legendary Noel 'King' Lyn, Danny has been the Technical Director and Head Coach at Constant Spring Football Club for the past twenty years. He has won the major league title three times, the Jackie Bell K.O. Trophy twice, the A League championship, and was a Premier League finalist. He has produced national players in Dean Sewell, Marvin Chin, Chris DaCosta, Ramon 'Rambo' Christian, Fabian Watkins, Gregory Simmonds, Lincoln 'Sixty' Taffe, and Marlon Bennett.

'Danny' Lyn seated right with the players and coach of the Constant Spring Football Club

He has been one of the country's most successful and respected coaches. In 1991 he coached the St. George's College Colts team that eventually won the Manning Cup in 1992. He also coached the 1998 and 1999 Manning Cup teams of which, the 1999 team reached the semi-finals. His captain in 1998 was none other than the Major League Soccer 2003 Rookie of the Year and current national striker, Damani Ralph. Damani has always said that Coach Lyn taught him the finer points of football. A truly great and underrated coach.

DAVID WELLER: David remains the only Jamaican athlete to win an Olympic medal outside of athletics. He won a bronze medal in cycling at the 1980 Moscow Olympics, which still remains an incredible feat.

David Weller

KEESANG 'KIPPY' CHIN: One of the most exciting and explosive players ever to play Manning Cup for St. George's College. Kippy's superb ball-control, dribbling skills and spectacular free-kicks, left spectators with their mouths wide open. A gifted and devastating football player, Kippy's downfall was his religious belief about not tackling his opponents, which cost him a first team All Manning selection and a national selection. He was a player for whom you would travel miles and pay to see him play. He had a fantastic 1968 Manning Cup season and played successfully in Division One for the University of the West Indies, and later with Golden Aces for many years. He still plays Master League football with the same cunning.
He has also contributed greatly to Jamaica's educational system for almost thirty years and is a first rate teacher and educator at Campion College. In addition, he has helped hundreds of students from other schools to pass their CXC and GCE 'O' and 'A' level exams by teaching extra lessons in Chemistry and Mathematics.

RONALD 'RUFUS' CHANG: A hard tackling, no-nonsense player, Rufus was often called 'Ruff House' for his style of play by the boys of St.

George's College. It is believed that in 1942, Rufus was the first Chinese Jamaican to captain a St. George's College Manning Cup team and to win the Cup in that year. Legend has it that he once played through a serious injury with blood soaked bandages on his head, a true testament to his character. In later years, other Chinese Jamaican captains for the school that I can recall were Francis HoLung (1969), Gordon 'Bull' Chin (1970), Dwight Chai Chang (1972), and Chris Zaidie (1983).

STEVIE LEE: A very good Manning Cup player for St. George's College in 1969 and 1970. Stevie was the first Chinese Jamaican, and probably the first Jamaican to play in the North American Soccer League. The NASL is the predecessor to Major League Soccer and had powerful teams such as the New York Cosmos with the legendary Pele. Stevie had a successful College career and was drafted into the NASL. His promising football career was always plagued by knee problems however. While there are several oriental players now in MLS, always remember that Stevie was the first.

(c) The Gleaner Co. Ltd.

An ecstatic Arnette Gardens captain Cornel Chin Sue, races towards his team mates after scoring his teams second goal against VSADC of St. Lucia

CORNEL CHIN SUE: He led Charlie Smith Comprehensive to the 1995 Manning Cup and has always been an industrious and consistent midfielder. Cornel has been with the Premier League Champions, Arnett Gardens, since high school and, subsequently, has toured with the National Senior Team. He has been one of our best locally based players. A true team player who is deceptively strong, I consider him another one of our own whom we have not truly recognized for his brilliant career.

MARVIN CHIN: Probably the best Chinese Jamaican goalkeeper we have produced. Marvin won the Manning Cup with St. Andrew Technical High School, and led Constant Spring Football Club to the finals of the premier league. He was a former All Manning player and played on the National Senior team several times. Honourable mention must also go to Francis HoLung who not only captained St. George's College in 1969, but was the All Manning goalkeeper that year.

MICHAEL TENN: The most talented table tennis player that the Caribbean has ever seen. He represented Jamaica as a very young teenager while at St. George's College. His natural and aggressive style made him the most exciting player we had ever seen. He went on tour to China in the early 1970's where the national coaches proclaimed him a future world champion, if he continued to train and dedicate himself to the hard work ahead. Unfortunately, he experienced some personal problems and was never able to recover his true abilities. Talent-wise, he was way ahead of his time. He was the 'Skill' Cole of table tennis.

BRUCE LYN: A notorious, hard tackling centre-half who was feared for his crunching, physical play, Bruce played on the great 1963 and 1964 St. George's College Manning Cup teams. He represented the All Manning, All Schools and National football teams. Bruce was also an excellent cricketer and has represented Jamaica in golf tournaments. A true born Chinese Jamaican. He wife, Margaret 'Maggie' Lyn has been the best female golfer in the country for the past several years.

St. George's Old Boy 24 year-old Bruce Lyn (Left) receiving an award for the best batting performance from Rev. Don Taylor Headmaster of Kingston College

ANDY CHONG: Probably the best racing car driver ever to come out of Jamaica, Andy was Formula Ford champion in Canada during the mid 1970's. Formula Ford is a level below Formula One racing and Andy was beating the likes of Jacques Villeneuve and Paul Tracy at this level. These drivers went on to achieve major successes in their careers while Andy, being a Landed Immigrant at the time, was unable to secure the big sponsorship necessary to be successful in this expensive sport. He returned to Jamaica in the early 1980's where he was the champion of the single-seater race cars. He dominated this division until he migrated to Florida.

1992 & 1993 MANNING CUP TEAMS: These teams, which were Manning Cup Champions in 1992 and Walker Cup Champions both years, had several Chinese Jamaican players such as Kevin Phillipson, Craig Zaidie, Wayne Chin Sue, Mario Hoo, and the twins, Jason and Johan Chung. All these players were called to the National Under-17 and Under-20 football teams. Mario Hoo and Wayne Chin Sue were also excellent cricketers and both were called to the National Under-17 cricket team. Mario's father, Freddie 'Maddy' Hoo, was also a good pace bowler who captained the St. George's College Sunlight Cup team in 1970. Wayne Chin Sue is, without doubt, the best left-footed player I have seen play for that school. His deadly curling free kicks were a sight to behold. His coach, Neville 'Bertis' Bell, often referred to him as 'the man with the million dollar left foot.' It should also be noted that during this era, Chinese Jamaican Sasha Rhoden, captained the Sunlight Cup team from 1993 to 1995, and was called to the National Under-19 trials. He played against future West Indian players Chris Gayle, Wavell Hinds, Marlon Samuels, Leon Garrick and Gareth Breese.

HAROLD 'HARRY' KONG: An avid tennis player and good golfer, Harry was a role model for the young Chinese Jamaicans. He was a successful businessman and owner of Sunbeam Bakery. He was someone you could seek out for advice and consultation and he was always willing to help his own people. I was often told by several persons, including Harry himself, of an incident that took place about fifty years ago. It happened at Sabina Park, home of the Kingston Cricket Club which, at the time, was a mostly 'white' establishment.

Harry was in his box seat enjoying a tennis tournament when a few white members saw him and asked the usher to have him removed. When approached by the usher Harry objected and showed him the ticket he had purchased. The usher informed him that it did not matter because the other members wanted him removed. Harry stood up for his rights and refused to leave whereupon the police and security were called in to physically remove him. I personally put Harry's defiance on the same level as Rosa Parks who refused to go to the back of the bus in Montgomery, Alabama. Harry took a moral stand which we, as Chinese Jamaicans, should be proud of. Today's generation must recognize that it is incidents like these and people like Harry that helped make it easier for them. We cannot go forward unless we know where we are coming from.

Let us not take our lifestyle today for granted. Always remember our past and be proud of people like Harry who had the courage to stand up for his rights. I am Chinese Jamaican and I am very proud of my heritage and my people.

Written by Peter E. Chang and edited by Sonia Gordon Scott.

Photograph of Peter Chang and George HoSang courtesy of Peter Chang
Photograph of 'Danny' Lyn with team courtesy of 'Danny' Lyn

All other photographs ©The Gleaner Co. Ltd.

Roger Chen
CONTRIBUTION OF THE CHINESE TO JAMAICA

THIS YEAR (2004) marks 150 years since the Chinese came to Jamaica. It is a milestone event for us and a time to reflect on where we came from and where we are heading. It is also a good opportunity for us to reflect on what we have contributed to Jamaican society.

We came here after the emancipation of the slaves in 1834, to fill the labour void on the plantations. This was our first contribution to Jamaica – as indentured labourers when the freed slaves no longer wanted to work on the sugar plantations. We literally took the place of the slaves on the same plantations, under the same working conditions, to escape the conditions existing in China at the time. In our minds, slave labour on a plantation half a world away from home was better than starvation back in China.

The first Chinese arrived in Jamaica on August 17, 1854. Three hundred and ten (310) left Hong Kong 108 days earlier, aboard the *SS Epsom*. They journeyed around India (initially stopping in Java), around the Cape of Good Hope, up the western coast of Africa to St. Helena (79 days), before crossing the Atlantic to Jamaica (29 days). When they reached Kingston, only 267 disembarked; 43 had died. Later that year on November 1, 1854, one hundred and ninety-five (195) Chinese, who had originally been contracted to work on the Panama Railroad, arrived in Kingston aboard the schooner *Vampire,* suffering from opium withdrawal symptoms. They were sent to Jamaica by the Panama Railroad Company with the hope that they could be cared for by the newly arrived Chinese community. Of these, 24 had to be sent to the public hospital in a state of extreme emaciation and 34 were found unfit for agricultural work.

They came to Jamaica under various circumstances. As indentured labourers, they contracted with the Captain of the ship to work on a specified plantation for a period of 5 years, for the sum of £3 per month, at the end of which time they would be given free passage home. Others were forcibly taken off the streets or from prisons, and put on board ship without their consent. Shanghaied! Yet others borrowed monies from their families, or pawned the land that had been in their family for generations, for the passage. They came with the hope of being able to earn enough by the end of their contract to repay their debt and support the family left in China. From the tales they had been told, they envisaged accumulating a fortune in the 5 years they planned to be away.

At the end of their contract, however, many remained in Jamaica because they saw the opportunity for business, or they were unable to return to China because they had gambled away their earnings. Others remained because the turmoil in China had not let up and they felt safer in their new surroundings.

THE "CHINEY SHOP"

Most started small local retail shops. They carried few items and total weekly sales averaged three to six pounds, but they were able to survive. It is in this field that the Chinese made the largest contribution to the Jamaican community. Consider the effect of the 'Chiney Shop' on its community:

- These shops were located in every nook and cranny of the island; all small communities had a 'Chiney shop'. They had set up wherever they were when their contract expired.

- They were pioneers in 24/7 shopping. The customers could knock on the zinc fence and call out to 'missa chin' for groceries on any day, at any time, knowing that they would get service.

- The 'Chiney shop' was the only place where they could get the items they needed in small quantities. It wasn't unusual for a customer to buy "1/2 lb flour, wid a little carn meal inna it; 1/4 lb a salt fish, 1/2 inch salt pork, and 2 Zephyr cigarettes" at 8 o'clock on a Sunday morning.

- Where else could you get food on credit! Some customers had established trust with the shopkeeper and so were able to get groceries on credit for the week, or sometimes for the month. There was a ubiquitous black book into which each item taken was written down with the date, cost and signature. Each week, or period agreed upon, it would be tallied and the monies received entered. No charge card or bank balance needed!

- The shop served as a community centre; more so if it had a bar attached. In the evenings and on pay days, the community would gather to buy their groceries for the week or meal for the day, and would also exchange gossip and news. Oftentimes 'missa chin' would be sought out for personal advice on someone's love life, to settle disputes, or for counselling. (Because of this role, many of the Chinese shopkeepers were appointed local Justices of the Peace by the Government.)

- As a community focal point it was the venue for all political rallies, and all religious gatherings – including pocomania. The preacher would often ask 'fi a hook-up inna de light' (permission to use the shop's electricity) for their 25Watt bulb and 8W amplifier.)

- It was the 'one stop shopping centre' of its time. The 'Chiney shop' would carry all grocery items, down to kerosene oil, and pharmaceuticals – Bayer Asprin, Bay Rum, 'rubbers' (condoms) – while out on the plaza 'Ms Foodie' would have all the locally grown produce – yams, bananas (ripe and green), peppers, pumpkins, 'leggins' (vegetables and seasoning for Saturday soup), peas etc. – and Mr. Green the local shoemaker would tend to the shoes that needed a half sole, or a patch on the uppers where the little toe cut through, or heel taps installed.

This is the legacy of the "Chiney shop". Today they have been replaced by huge supermarkets such as Sovereign, and more recently by the 'Super Plus' conglomerate.

THE BAKERIES

Before the Chinese entered the bakery business on a big scale, there were many small bakeries throughout the island. Each town had its family bakery turning out hard dough bread, bulla cakes and Easter buns. In cities like Kingston and Montego Bay, this industry was dominated by families such as Powells at Cross Roads, Sterrick's and Huntington, and Blake's Bakery of Christiana – all non-Chinese families. (By the way, I can still taste Powell's twin loaf, peg breads, and the bullas – black, heavy and moist with nuff molasses! I just loved them.) Then the Chinese of Hakka heritage got into the bakery business... they knew how to handle wheat flour because they were from north China and they had been making steamed buns, "bow" and "man tow", for centuries.

They started local bakeries, mixed and proofed the dough in open wooden bins, and baked the bread in small brick ovens built at the rear of the premises. When these ovens collapsed, the area would be without bread for several days as it took at least a week for the refractory mortar and concrete to cure. Then they started to deliver further afield using mule drawn bread carts, and then motorized bread vans. Bread was delivered to the shops on consignment, that is, only bread that was sold was paid for. This ensured that only the freshest bread was available to the customer.

What to do with the returned stale bread? Some sliced them up and rebaked them as 'toast'. These 'toasts' had a longer shelf life because, in a dehydrated state, they wouldn't go moldy. Others added molasses to make bulla cake, or bread puddings; still some used the bread crumbs as fillers in the 'patties' they now baked. Soon they were making things like sugar buns and 'mattrass' – a light yellow cake which was called 'spring' if it had icing on top; and toto – a coconut cake. These became staple fare for most school children.

But the biggest change came when National Bakery opened on Half-Way Tree Road and introduced 'sliced bread'. Hundreds of Kingstonians were eating the soft slices without butter for days! "Di best ting since sliced bread!" became the expression of the day.

Then came Consolidated Bakeries, formed out of Purity, Valentine and some other acquired bakeries. Hannah Town Bakery is still baking under a contraction of its name, HTB – hard to beat. Many of the smaller bakeries continued, and eventually specialized in specific products like patties. Bruce's patties were always besting Rainbow's because of their freshness (they never had a chance to cool down – they sold so quickly) and their commitment to using only fresh meats. The king of them now is Tastee, a mammoth machine turning out an endless belt of hot patties along with 'meat loaf'. Not to be outdone, Juici Beef patties that started from one little patty shop in May Pen is now islandwide.

What has this to do with Jamaican society? "Two patty, a coco-bread an' a battle a Ting" was the cry from a hungry belly. Affordable and nutritious, to a point. We survived on that during our school days, only we drank O-So Grape or Cream Soda and had a sugar bun extra. The point is, today, it is the only affordable meal of choice for many Jamaican families, unfortunately.

Long before Ting and Kola Champagne, Diamond Mineral Waters, Liquid Foods and Crescent Waters were putting out drinks like O-So grape, and Cream Soda. Royal Cremo Ice Cream Factory and The Jamaica Ice Cream Factory were also making the favourites of the children – ice cream and icicles.

MUSIC

While Edward Seaga and Chris Blackwell were amongst the first to start recording the artists of Jamaica, it was Leslie Kong's efforts that launched the careers of Jimmy Cliff and Bob Marley. From his office at Beverly's Ice Cream Parlour on Orange Street, he heard the recording potential in the voices of Jimmy Cliff and Bob Marley and distributed their first records. Marley subsequently became the musical icon of Jamaica and his song, "One Love", is the country's unofficial anthem.

One cannot forget Byron Lee and the Dragonaires. Although Jamaican through and through, he is best know for embracing the Trinidadian Soca style of music. His passion for Trinidadian music drove him to bring 'Trini-style Carnival' to Jamaica. Since its introduction in 1990 it has become the premier event at Easter, and the musical activities associated with Jamaica Carnival have been an overwhelming success. He is also credited for bringing the

Trench Town rhythm of 'Ska' uptown, thereby popularising and making it a legitimate Jamaican beat.

No excerpt on the music of Jamaica would be complete without mentioning Phil Chen, Keith Lyn, Ernest Ranglin and Kes Chin. Phil is best known for his work with Rod Stewart, but he has also worked with artists such as Pete Townsend, Eric Clapton, Keith Richards and Jeff Beck on the classic "Blow By Blow" (produced by the 'fifth Beatle', George Martin, and the only rock instrumental in history to supercede 3,000,000 in sales). Phil got his start in Jamaica playing with the Vikings and the Vagabonds (led by Colston Chen). Keith Lyn is the prodigal son who has returned home, bringing with him his signature song, "Empty Chair".

Ernest Ranglin – yes, he's half-Chinese – received the Order of Distinction for his contribution to Jamaica's music. He is renowned for his guitar work and was voted the number-one jazz guitarist of London in 1964. He was the one who arranged Jamaica's first million-seller, "My Boy Lollipop", by Millie Small.

Kes Chin and the Souvenirs were Jamaica's Latin band of choice. Kes and his band were regular featured at Club Havana on Windward Road.

THE ARTS

The Chinese are seldom known for their contribution to the Arts, but this is not the case here in Jamaica. Two who immediately come to mind are my brothers, Ray and Washington.

Look everywhere around you and you will see the images of photographer Ray Chen. They are the first to greet you and the last to send you off at both international airports. They are in pharmacies and souvenir shops all across the island; even some 'bend-down plaza' entrepreneurs carry them. His coffee-table pictorial books of Jamaica are given as gifts to visiting dignitaries, as well as being taken home by people who visited and fell in love with the island. His award of the Order of Distinction is well earned.

Washington Chen might not be a household name here in his homeland, but he was respected as a performer and ballet master of classical ballet and jazz-dance in Switzerland and Germany. Washington received his initial ballet training as a student of Madame Soohih, whose studio was above Rainbow's ice cream parlour at Half Way Tree. Ken Mock Yen (now Monsignor Kenneth Joseph Mock Yen, pastor of Sts. Peter & Paul Church) was a fellow student. Madame Soohih was a Chinese lady married to a Russian dancer, and she opened her dance studio to bring ballet to enthusiasts of the art. After completing his training at the Legat School in Tunbridge Wells, England, Washington returned home for a visit to choreograph the ballet, "Faust", in which he performed with the students of Madame Soohih.

In my early teens in Jamaica the first entertainment centre we had was a Telefunken radio bought by my brother Wellington. Just a plain AM/SW radio; no record player. That would come much later as Welli bought his classical records. So our entertainment was surfing the airwaves for stations in Miami. But our Sunday favourite was to listen to Joe Pinchin reading his prose and poetry over the radio. My mother loved it even though she didn't understand much of what he said. She just loved his intonations and, I suspect, because he was Chinese. Today you listen to Easton Lee the radio personality, author and preacher. Although I have never heard his program I'm sure he evokes the same memories for many of you as Joe Pinchin did for me. I know Easton from our days in Allman Town.

RELIGIOUS MINISTRIES

And speaking of preachers, one has to recognize the work done by Father HoLung, Sister Benedict and Sister Grace in Kingston.

Father Ho Lung founded the Missionaries of the Poor in Kingston to minister to the homeless and poor — mostly the very young, elderly, disabled, deformed, mentally handicapped, or seriously ill who had lost their families, or who were turned out of their homes because their families could not support them or cope. The Missionaries run four residences: a men's and boys' residence (The Good Shepherd), a women's and girls' residence (Jacob's Well), a children's residence and (separate) AIDS patient residence (The Lord's Place), in what is probably the poorest area of Kingston. He is known affectionately as the 'ghetto priest' and is recognized for the religious musical plays he frequently puts on, and for which he writes most of the songs.

Sister Benedict Chung hails from Troy, Trelawny and found her calling as a nun because of the inspiration of Sr. Marie Therese at the Alpha Convent. She's now involved with two projects that occupy all her time. First is the Holy Family school. Under her guidance, it grew from 600 students to its present enrolment of over 1200. They have acquired the surrounding properties and the total property now includes additional classrooms, hall, staff room and caretaker's cottage. The other project is the Laws Street Trade Training Centre that grew out of the training program of the school where children receive skills in baking and garment-making. Her graduates are always in high demand because of the skills they leave with and the strong work ethic that has been instilled into them at the Centre.

Sister Grace works in the heart of Trench Town and was instrumental in setting up the Trench Town Cultural Yard which was opened by HRH Prince Charles five years ago. The Cultural Yard's main feature is one of its native sons – Bob Marley. There is a fledgling library with a few computers, a photo exhibition by Star Travel writer, Susan Pigg, a small intimate restaurant serving local fare, a medical/eye clinic, feeding assistance to the poor, and child care programme.

Sister Grace also runs a co-op programme with Mount Allison University in New Brunswick, Canada called YPJ – Youth Partnership with Jamaica. On this programme each year, about ten students volunteer their Reading Week to come to Jamaica to participate in a variety of volunteer activities such as working on flood relief, performing cultural awareness activities, working on sustainable development projects, assisting the staff at an orphanage, and installing computers at various Jamaican schools.

As mentioned earlier, Kenneth Mock Yen has ministered so effectively to the Catholics of Jamaica that he was invested as Monsignor in 1991.

Many of our sisters and brothers also entered the religious orders. Many of them returned to do community work, like Fr. Ho Lung; many also stayed with their order to teach at the academies like Alpha, Immaculate, St. George's and Holy Childhood. At these institutions they helped to shape the character of many students and pointed them to a future role in Jamaican society – an invaluable contribution.

PROFESSIONALS

As far as professionals are concerned, there are so many lawyers, doctors, engineers, nurses, teachers, ophthalmologists etc., that it would be impossible to name all of them here. Suffice it to say that together, they have raised the level of professional service in Jamaica by several degrees. Some that come to mind are Dr. Victor Chen See, dentist, Arthur Lyew and Clifton Yap, architects, and Tommy Lyew, engineer.

There are also numerous professionals who stayed abroad but nevertheless have contributed to the good name of Jamaica. My eldest brother, Wellington Paul, comes to mind. He represented the US Nuclear Regulatory Commission on all matters dealing with pressure vessels for the Nuclear Power Industry. Also noteworthy is Glen Chin's contribution to the Space Shuttle Program as NASA Mission Manager at the Kennedy Space Centre, and John Lodenquai's contribution as a Research Physicist for NASA. Still in the area of flight, Larry Tenn has worked for Lockheed and contributed to their aviation program.

FINANCIAL/INDUSTRIAL: RAY CHANG, MICHAEL LEE CHIN, PAUL CHEN-YOUNG, LASCELLES CHIN, KARL HENDRICKSON

In the past year the names of Ray Chang, Michael Lee Chin and Paul Chen Young have been in the Jamaican and international press. Through the sound education they received in their formative years in Jamaica, they have gone abroad, made their fortunes, and returned to Jamaica to invest and, in a way, to say 'thank you'. They have set an example that other nationalities in Jamaica would do well to emulate.

Ray Chang is Chairman of CI Fund Management Inc. He came to Canada in 1966 to study engineering, but switched to accounting and became a

Chartered Accountant. He joined Coopers & Lybrand as a financial consultant and gained experience in helping small businesses to straighten out their problems. At the end of 2003 Ray, together with Grace Kennedy, introduced The Funds to Jamaica... a means of investing in mutual funds. Ray is an active member of the St. George's Old Boys Association, where he has held the position of Treasurer for some time. He was awarded Jamaica's Order of Merit.

Michael Lee-Chin: In 1971 Michael Lee Chin boldly returned to Jamaica to ask then Prime Minister, the Hon. Hugh Shearer, for a student loan to com-

plete his engineering education in Canada. Prime Minister Shearer saw enough spunk and vision in Michael to grant him a Cdn$15,000 scholarship. Lee Chin did not forget. As the CEO of AIC Limited, he has donated much of his wealth to charitable and cultural institutions. In gratitude for the help Shearer gave him, Lee Chin has returned to invest heavily in Jamaica. He started with the purchase of the troubled National Commercial Bank (NCB) and, in a span of 2 years, turned his investment of J$2.65B into a net worth of J$26B. He has since established J$22M worth of university scholarships for students in Jamaica, donated J$60 million to the Entrepreneurial Centre at the University of Technology (Utech); J$50 million for a new police station in Grants Pen, and millions more to cover CXC registration fees for every Jamaican child sitting a business subject.

Among other investments he has made in Jamaica are: Radio Jamaica, Desnoes and Geddes (D&G), Cable and Wireless, Life of Jamaica (LoJ), and the 160,000 square foot Mutual Life twin towers on Oxford Road.

Paul Chen Young was one of the first Chinese financial investors in Jamaica. Starting with Crown Eagle Life Insurance Company, the company expanded into the banking sector with the Eagle Financial Network. Between 1990 and 1997 the Jamaican economy had grown only 0.3% and all businesses had a hard time servicing their debts. Rapid devaluation of the Jamaican dollar caused great concern to the banks and, in order to earn the US dollars needed to protect themselves against inflation, they invested heavily in tourism and real estate (hotels). These investments proved to be the downfall of Paul Chen Young's empire. Although he lost his compa-

nies, Paul's vision of the potential of banking and commercial institutions in Jamaica paved the way for people like Ray Chang and Michael Lee Chin.

Honourable Lascelles Chin O.J., C.D. grew up with us in the Molynes Four Roads area. When his family moved he would stop often on his way home to the foot of Red Hills as he passed by on his bicycle. My dad had always admired Lascelles for he saw in him attributes of hard work, determination, perseverance, clarity of vision and the ability to see obstacles as challenges. Starting with the importation of blackpepper and peas, Lascelles eventually partnered with Henkel Chemicals (Caribbean) Ltd. to become a significant player in the supply of adhesives and chemicals in Jamaica.

Today, Lascelles is Chairman and CEO of his own business, the LASCO Group of Companies. On his way to this pinnacle he has garnered many awards and recognition from the industry he's in as well as from the Jamaican Government. He has been awarded the Order of Jamaica and the Order of Distinction for his contribution to industry; he has been the past Chairman of many corporations – Jamaica Industrial Development Corporation (JIDC), National Productivity Council, and the Jamaica Exporters Association (JEA), as well as a Director of a few banks.

The Honourable Karl Reginald M. Hendrickson, OJ, CD, while studying at McGill University in Montreal, Canada, took a job at Steinberg's, a large wholesale bakery where he was introduced to soft breads. It changed the course of his life. He left McGill to return home and seized the opportunity to revolutionize the bread making industry in Jamaica by introducing soft, sliced bread. National Continental Corporation (NCC) on Half Way Tree Road was the result. From baking he branched out into packaging for consumer goods (National Packaging), furniture making, Caribbean Broilers and Feed Mills, and hotels – the Courtleigh and Knutsford Court Hotels in Kingston, The Ruins in Ocho

Rios, Sunset Beach Resort and Spa in Montego Bay, and Sunset At The Palms in Negril. Also set to open in Winter 2004/5, is the Coconut Bay Resort & Spa. He was also extremely active in the public sector and was, concurrently, Chairman of Jamaica Merchant Marine and Jamaica Public Service; he has also been director of Air Jamaica and Vice-Chairman of Jampro. In the late '80's he was appointed Ambassador-at-Large by Prime Minister, Michael Manley, in acknowledgement of his role as a valued advisor. In 2003, the Government of Jamaica conferred on him the honour of the Order of Jamaica, 'for his outstanding contribution in the field of Commerce.' He is currently Entrepreneur-in-Residence at the Mona School of Business.

He retired from active operations in 1995/96, but continues in acquisitions, planning and development. His four children each have responsibility for different areas of the empire he built. Two years ago, at age 72, he was asked what he considers to have been his greatest success. Without a moment's hesitation he replied: 'My wife, Nell, and my children. To raise a family, that's my greatest success. My wife has stayed with me, that's a success in itself! My greatest pleasure in life has been that.'

GAMBLING

Here's another 'financial' institution that was introduced by the Chinese. In the '40s and up to the early '60s there were two popular forms of gambling: Peaka Peow and Drop Pan.

Peaka Peow: This game takes its name from the manner by which the tickets, wagers and winning numbers were exchanged between the players and the betting houses. These 'houses' were usually located in the lofts of established businesses (because they provided more anonymity and a buffer from the law), and pigeons were used to carry the tickets and wagers between the outlying 'distributors' and the head office. Thus

the name 'pigeon ticket'. In Canada we play a game called 6/49 that's similar, but instead of selecting 6 numbers from a set of 49, here you had to select 10 from a set of 80.

I'll digress here to explain this game since it is now just part of Jamaica's Chinese history.

A picture of the ticket is shown at right. It consists of the first 80 characters (8 rows x 10 columns) of the *Ts'in tsz'man*, or Thousand Character Classic. Since no two of these characters are alike, they are used as a substitute for numbers to avoid any suspicion of cheating.

The object of the game was to match as many of the twenty characters/numbers that were selected. Drawings were usually done each night.

All the tickets were identical – every day, every draw. It was a nightmare for agents to keep track of valid tickets. Each had their system and trusted customers to avoid any disagreement. A player would mark their ticket by blotting out the characters they were betting on. A minimum of ten spots had to be purchased. The wager was not in proportion with the number of spots wagered on, because your chances of winning increased as you increased the number of spots marked. Also, what you won depended on the number of matching characters you had.

A player prepared his tickets by dotting the characters he selected with black ink, and this ticket was handed to the house manager, with the money wagered. The house kept a bound book of blank tickets into which the corresponding characters, the player's name, and the amount wagered was recorded.

To start the drawing of the game, the set of eighty official stamps were brought out. These eighty stamps were identical to each of the characters on the ticket. A set of eighty individual characters were printed on to eighty pieces of virgin stock. These were then rolled into identical balls, indistinguishable from each other, and placed into a pan.

After thoroughly mixing them, they were separated into four bowls of 20 pellets each. One of the players was then asked to select the winning bowl. The pellets were then opened and marked onto a master ticket and posted. Every move was watched by the players present so fixing a game was very difficult, which is why it received such wide acceptance.

Based on a wager of $1 for a ticket of ten markings, the winnings were in this range:

- For 5 winning numbers..... $2
- For 6 winning numbers..... $20
- For 7 winning numbers..... $200
- For 8 winning numbers.....$1,000
- For 9 winning numbers.....$1,500
- For 10 winning numbers...$3,000

There have been occasions when the House was 'broken' by excessive losses.

The players would often ask Chinese children to 'give them a read' – that is, select 10 characters that may mean something and may be the winning combination.

Drop Pan: A very basic game of chance. You had to select the winning number drawn from a set of 36 numbers. After all the wagers were in, the house manager dropped all the numbers (previously all 36 were stamped on to a square of paper and rolled up into a ball) into a pan and, after a good mixing, selected the winning number from the pan. Today in Jamaica it is called Cash Pot, and is sanctioned by the Government.

MIXED MARRIAGES – OUT OF MANY ONE PEOPLE

Because of government restrictions prohibiting the immigration of their wives, the Chinese men married or lived in common-law relationships with many local girls – Africans, Indians, Germans, and British. We have to acknowledge that a lot of beautiful people have come about from this cross breeding. Just look around at all the beautiful half-Chinese girls and boys. Let's admit it: chop suey not only eat nice, it looks nice. We have added the creamy complexion, the almond shaped face, reduced the 'trunk', straightened the hair, and brightened those 'ackee seed' eyes. On the other hand, the other races have given them some waves and curls, a tint in the hair and, in the girls, a 'toosh' and 'heavy weights' upstairs. No doubt the beautiful blends of colour, texture and shape, in both men and women, from the co-mingling of the Chinese is true to Jamaica's motto: Out of Many One People.

CONCLUSION

I believe the most important values the Chinese have left Jamaica's society are their tolerance, fairness, compassion, hard work, dedication, honesty, strong sense of community, and support for each other. The Buddhist and Confucian beliefs they brought with them are reflected in their care and nurturing of children and the emphasis they place on education and family life. These are examples for the Jamaican society to emulate. Like the African cultures, the Chinese have the tradition of the extended family i.e. all members of the village are family and deserve the same respect as those of the immediate family. So you treat all members of your generation as siblings and, in the Confucian tradition, have respect for age, whether it is to a member of the immediate family or others. In the Buddhist tradition, the Chinese do not like violence; they prefer to compromise and to talk things out. Only when this fails do they stand their ground. These are the contributions of the Chinese to the Jamaican society.

Written by ©Roger Chen and edited by Sonia Gordon Scott.

Norman Hew-Shue

JAMAICAN LIFE AROUND THE PEAKA PEOW SHOP

MANY OF MY FONDEST memories of growing up in Kingston, Jamaica, are associated with friends who lived on Tower Street. Their residence was part of a complex comprised of a large yard dominated by a huge venerable almond tree, an adjoining grocery, and a Peaka Peow* shop.

For the uninitiated, Peaka Peow was, and is, a Chinese betting game similar to the Canadian 6/49 (six-forty-nine) lottery, using Chinese characters rather than numbers. Another similar numbers-based game was 'Drop-Pan', resembling the New York State lottery. From what I can gather, these games were brought from China practically unchanged, with imagery, omens and dreams playing a more paramount role than in other lotteries.

Peaka Peow form

In Peaka Peow, bets are made on a date and time-stamped form with 120 characters (in China the game is called (Yit) Bak Ngi-Sip Sue Peow* – or One 'Hundred & Twenty Character Lottery'). Eight brush marks are made with green ink. These might be random (analogous to 'quick-pick' in 6/49), or derived from some dream or object specified by the 'bettor'. Bets are made in any number of 'banks' (up to a dozen in its heyday) or betting-houses such as Fook Sang, Tai Hing, or WB. Result forms with 30 red-inked marks are posted later in the day. Matching five or more marks pays according to the amount in the pot or number of persons winning. My friend's father worked for one of these banks and, before the days of practical photocopying, he and his brother would help make result-copies for distribution. I would watch, fascinated, as they made these very important copies with quick, deft brush strokes.

Betting was done twice daily and, before fax machines, this elaborate system was orchestrated by 'runners' on bicycles and limited, therefore, to the city core. The term Peaka Peow is said to have been derived from Pak Hap* or pigeon (or literally 'white duck') Peow* (ticket or lottery), and one can imagine pigeonhole-type shelving being used to store the result forms.

I remember back then in my rebellious youth when I would, during vacations and on (rare) occasions, 'scull' (skip) school to spend the day in said friend's yard. This supplemented my education in ways that High School could never do, as many an eye-opening hour was spent behind the 'peow' shop counter, watching the microcosm of humanity passing by.

These shops ran afoul of the law, I think, because the revenue was not in government control as was the 'home-grown' Irish sweepstakes or Football betting pool in those colonial times. There might well have been unfair betting practices but I am not here to judge, rather to recall the fond memories associated with the shop.

The rich and poor would frequent the shop, the handcart man rubbing shoulders with the customs broker from T. Geddes Grant. Even the local policemen played, but some would come seeking protection money, as otherwise, occasionally, the shop would be raided. This happened one day when I – fortunately – was at school.

These shops were almost universally alike, their walls festooned with results from the various banks, and 'bettors' checking these in the dim light, reacting either in grinning jubilation or 'teeth-kissing' disgust. At the counter sat the marker-cashier with his stamp-pad, finger moistening wet sponge, brush and ink, and paper forms held by bulldog clips or impaled on a wire stand. Our shop had an old, yellow, metal oscillating fan going in the corner, and strains of Ernie Freeman's *"Dark at the Top of the Stairs"* might be heard playing on the Jukebox from the bar next door. These shops were usually manned not only by Chinese, but also by local chaps, who would pick up and adopt the Hakka speech and customs. They would even hold the brush in the traditional Chinese way – vertically with palm facing forward.

'Lloydie' was the lanky half-Chinese operator of said shop who did small appliance repairs in his free time. I remember him working on a 35mm camera needing a special gear with three curved cogs. With great patience and old time improvisation, I saw him fashion at least three old silver six-penny coins by first punching the middle with a file handle to get a square hole, then laboriously filing out the three curved arms until the film could wind evenly.

Operators like Lloydie could transcribe all thoughts into the eight marks (the precision and accuracy of these between shops would make an interesting study). Certain common marks, however, would be stalwart mainstays; for example, Good Luck or Money marks. Frequently, ladies of ill-repute with sultry eyes and flimsy dresses from the *Big Apple Club* (an adjoining 'sporthouse') would come in asking for 'White Man', 'Long Tone' or 'Big Wood' marks, or some similar graphic descriptions of experiences, or attributes of their clients. Lloydie, with a serious heard-it-all blasé face, would make the appropriate entries with a graceful flourish of the brush.

Dreams were another main source for Peow marks, as illustrated by the following story reputed to be true: One of two friends was bemoaning his winless streak. The other, who was terminally ill, promised to 'dream him' with a winning mark after he passed on, which he did soon after. One… Two… dreamless months passed, and the impatient friend went to the gravesite at the Chinese Cemetery late at night where he sprinkled white rum and jumped around. The caretaker, in his hut near the gate, noticed these nightly movements near the back wall and sent word to the deceased's next of kin about this lively duppy. The kinsman hired a horse and buggy (mah cha*) and, accompanied by the caretaker, drove near to the spot and lobbed a string of lit firecrackers over the wall. On seeing the figure of the startled supplicant suddenly running towards them, the kinsman and the caretaker turned and bolted towards the waiting carriage. The episode ended with the friend chasing the galloping buggy (drawn by the white-eyed, spooked horse) while shouting "wait fi mi! wait fi mi!" all the way down Waltham Park Road.

The shop invariably attracted shady characters selling back door deals of lighters, cigarettes or cameras, etc. Usually, these were from sailors looking for local spending cash. It was during that time that the miracle invention of transistors was taking place, resulting in a fascinating parade of miniature radios passing through the shop in different styles. I saw one looking like a bottle. Previous to this, a 'portable' tube radio would require about 10 large D batteries and was slow to start and shut off. 'Small' tape recorders had 6-inch diameter spools. Lloydie had a transistor radio constantly playing and he would listen eagerly in the morning, at about 8 o'clock, to hear the latest Sparrow song on Calypso Corner.

When not in the shop, we would be occupied with BB-gun target practice on the almond tree or the ladies' negligees hanging next door at the *Big Apple*. One Christmas, during the '50s when fireworks were freely available, one of the landlord's sons was said to have filled up an Ovaltine tin with all the explosive powder he could find, including that from 'thunderbolts', squibs, cracker balls and even matches. When the tin was full, he banged the lid shut, forgetting about the contact-sensitive powders and the need for a vent hole. He spent that Christmas in hospital.

We once found a large dagger blade without a handle grip. We polished and sharpened the knife and named it Suzy Wong – after the contemporary

Nancy Kwan movie – and probably a girl from the *Big Apple Club*, so nick-named because of her trademark thigh-high slit dresses.

One day, a fuss broke out between Tony and a local chap named Philip (the son of the Institute of Jamaica Museum's caretaker) over Tony's bicycle. Tony took the knife and threw it between the legs of the running Philip, who picked it up and ran straight up George's Lane to the Central Police Station.

Later, we decided to go to the station to clarify things. About six of us marched up George's Lane past Tower, Barry, and Law Streets to East Queen Street where the lane ended almost in line with the front entrance. While there, our friend, who spent a lot of his time marking results, had a wad of marked 'peow' papers fall from his pocket on to the station floor. Luckily, the desk sergeant did not notice.

Drop Pan was another game of chance using numbers as well as imagery, in which the diehard punter would be well versed, for example, number 4 is 'Death' in typical Chinese custom. There is a catch in these games in that one could almost always find excuses for the outcome. For example, if the peow 'monkey' mark was answered by a 'tree' mark, this would elicit the response: "Lawd, how ah didn't see dat monkey live in a tree?" There was also the additional dimension of numbers in Drop Pan so that a 5 result to a number 10 might be rationalized as being half of that. And don't for an instant imagine that higher learning or education makes one immune to this gambling craze. All that results is a more learned rationale for losing: "Dear me – seven is obviously the square root of forty-nine."

There is a joke about the futility of hoping to win at Peaka Peow. A man 'dreaming' schoolboy, bought "Boy going to school" mark, only to have this answered by 'Boy coming from school'. Undeterred, he bought 'Boy coming from school' which played 'Boy going to...'. Infuriated, he stormed to the shop-counter with his jaws tight and 'him nek-string tan up' and demanded, 'BOY, GIRL OR TEACHER going TO AND coming FROM school' marks in ALL BANKS. The result played SCHOOL ON HOLIDAY.

Thanks to those contributing information for this article.

Written by Norman Hew-Shue and edited by Sonia Gordon Scott

* See Glossary

Norman Hew-Shue
THE NIGHT DUPPY BRUK UP DI 21 GAME

KINGSTON, 1960s.

One windy Jamaican night, I was hanging out with friends on East Queen Street in a home near to the Wildman Street corner and Hill's ballet shoe establishment. We had all congregated in the Chung brothers' home above a drugstore. The pharmaceutical odour from below permeated all the way to their second storey lodgings.

This gathering of party-crashing, fried-chicken connoisseurs consisted of myself, Michael, Clifton, Victor, Clarence, Tony and other members of the *Wolf Pack,* as we liked to call ourselves. There we were, all revelling in youthful, male-bonding camaraderie, playing cards, some sitting with their chairs turned around, using the backs as arm rests. Others just hanging around, watching the game or reading comics.

We were playing 21, otherwise known as Blackjack *'ovah in farrin'.* The card game had by then graduated from being a childhood diversion between siblings or friends, to one in which lunch money was being bet after school. As a result, I ended up with several lunch-less days.

So there we were, all gathered around a circular wooden table in a spacious front room, which served as kitchen, dining and recreational area. An adjoining bedroom offered a view of East Queen Street and the large Dairy Farmers ice-cream parlour on the opposite side. The single entrance door opened on to a narrow verandah-walkway with banister railing. A few steps to the right took you to a landing and to the top of a steep, wooden, double-banister staircase, with 20 or so steps. This led down to a concrete courtyard with tenements, to the drugstore, and to the street which lay just beyond a big green door.

Inside, a single shaded light bulb hung from the ceiling. That night it was swinging gently with the breeze that whispered from the north. From Dairy Farmers, faint music escaped the juke box and wandered up to the room where we were gathered. It was The Prophet, a song by Chuck (Any Day Now) Jackson. The lyrics, based on the writings of Middle-Eastern sage, Khalil Gibran, was a favourite of mine, and held me captive as I sat daydreaming to the strains of its haunting half-sung /half-spoken lyrics:

Live for to...day;
and love for To... morrow
Dah..dah daa
On another... day....
These...are the words of the prophet

Meanwhile the game was settling into a routine, with the banker shuffling and offering the cards for cutting. It was all about drama, of course. After two cards were dealt, the second would be flipped face-up to increase the tension. The recipients of a picture card, ten or ace, would anxiously wonder if they had an instant 21 or possible five horses. They'd reshuffle their two cards, holding them close to their faces, and slowly squeeze one across the other to reveal the hidden card, and their good or bad luck.

And so the evening sauntered on, with joyous bantering and chit-chat, when a surprise gust of wind shifted the cards in a mild flurry. The banker, who was busy trying to assess each hand, called out exasperated for someone to *'shut de door, nuh man!'* at which one of the spectators, Tony, who was seated nearest to the door, gave the door a kick with the sole of his foot. But the door, which had begun to close, slowly swung open again. The banker scoffed while others heckled Tony. *'Push harder, man – yuh mus' be hungry!'*

Indignant at the fact that his strength was being challenged, Tony complied with a firmer kick. Again the door swung almost to the point of closing but this time it sprang open more briskly. Suddenly, what had initially been treated with casual indifference became the focus of attention. All eyes shifted to the door and stayed riveted.

Another bystander kissed his teeth, Jamaican style, and with a *'Chuh man! Watch out, Tony,'* he lifted his leg and booted the door forcefully. To everyone's horror, the door flew open just as forcefully, this time even wider than before!

The room went silent momentarily, as the proverbial hair at the back of our necks began to stand, while we digested this occurrence. Thoughts of *Duppy, Rolling calf,* May Pen burial ground, obeah, *sighants*,* and other local horror folkloric tales mingled with Hollywood images of body snatchers and zombies in our collective minds. The fact that our hosts' father had not too long passed away didn't assuage our growing panic. What occurred to us, simultaneously, was the realization: *If the door can open on its own... then it might close on its own... which means that...*

Suddenly, there was a scraping and overturning of chairs, and a thundering of feet on the wooden floor as we were all galvanized into a stampede out of the room. Cards, money and comic books were abandoned as the dozen or so terrified card players and spectators used their youthful energy to accomplish impressive feats of athleticism.

We bolted straight out the door and vaulted over the railing, foregoing the formality of going around the landing and taking the upper five or so superfluous steps. Our rapid descent was accomplished with flamboyance and in various styles worthy of the Olympics. Yours truly grabbed the banisters with both hands and made the descent in only three leaping bounds, despite the throng. With winged heels, we flew down the stairs, along the passage, and dashed through the big green door to the safety of East Queen Street.

After a few minutes of audible panting, some decided to call it a night, and headed breathlessly home. The rest of us regrouped over at Dairy Farmers to sit and rationalize the startling incident. Feeling somewhat secure in our distance from the scene of our fears, we cast frequent apprehensive glances at the upstairs window, back-lit by the swinging light bulb which was casting eerie shadows on the curtains.

The problem, of course, lay with the ones among us who actually lived there. They, poor souls, had to return. We eventually accompanied the Chung brothers back upstairs, this time tip-toeing in great trepidation, our bodies half-turned and readied for instant flight. Relief and shame gradually turned into laughter when we finally discovered that our 'duppy' was the long wooden handle of one of those locally-made brooms, which had apparently fallen between the door and its jamb, thereby acting as a mischievous spring.

That night went down indelibly in our collective memories as *de nite wen duppy run out de Wolf Pack.*

Written by Norman Hew-Shue and edited by Alex Lee & Sonia Gordon Scott.

Photograph ©Ray Chen

Glossary

A

abeng	– Maroon horn
Ah back	– an uncle older than your father
Ah gung	– grandfather (father's father)
Ah goo	– an aunt younger than your father
Ah neung	– an aunt older than your father
An yong	
Ah qui	– an uncle younger than your mother
Ah shuk	– an uncle younger than your father
ashook	
Ah po	– grandmother (father's mother)
Ah yee	– an aunt younger than your mother
Anansi	– name given to a spider in
Anancy	Jamaican folklore
annatto	– small tree from which an orange dye is obtained
archie bombo	– a type of fried dumpling

B

baddoe	– a root vegetable like yam
ban-tong-fah	– half chinese born
barsoap	– soap, usually in the solid form about 18 inches long, sliced and sold
bat sen	– a large fan
bissy	– kola nut, used as tea, or an antidote for some poisons
bok choy	– see pak choy
Booby	– sea bird
bow chung	– fire crackers
bow gai	– boiled chicken
bow gye	
bulla	– a round, flat molasses cake

C

calisthenics	– martial arts exercises
cha	– Chinese tea
Chang Gin Sang	– Chinese name
Chee Gung Tong	– Chinese Freemason Society
Chee Kung Tong	
cheong sam	– close fitting, high necked dress with diagonal, buttoned, shoulder opening and side split on skirt
chung sam	
chi chi bus	– first buses to use air brakes; named for the sighing sound ('chi-chiii') made by air released by the brakes
chim pee moi	– plums preserved with orange peel and licorice
chan pi moi	
chan pi moy	
chan pui mui	
chim pee muy	
chin pi moy	
chun pee moy	
chun pee muy	

chow choy	– stir fried vegetables
chow gow	– to quarrel
chow mein	– stir fried noodles with an assortment of meats and vegetables
clappers	– fire crackers
clawt	– broad pronunciation of 'cloth, used with other words, e.g. 'blood', as an expletive
crinoline	– circular half-slip, usually made of cotton and/or lace, starched very stiffly and worn under a skirt/dress to make it stand away from the body, similar to ballet dancers skirts;several would be worn to achieve this effect
crocus bag	– a burlap bag
Cupping	– a technique that is especially useful in the treatment of problems of local qi, or blood stagnation in the channels; usually performed as an alternative to acupuncture. Small cups are warmed with a burning taper, held for a very short period of time inside the cup which is then quickly placed over the selected acupuncture area.

D

Day Jump	– day party
Decoction	– boiling or simmering the roots, bark, seeds, or rhizomes of any herb. Boiling is a quick and simple way to use herbs. The disadvantage is that many volatile oils are lost in the process in certain plants.
dow mah	– a cleaver
drop pan	– a Chinese gambling game
Dung-goo	– Chinese mushroom
doongu	
Dung-goo Tong	– Chinese mushroom soup
Dunga Tung	
Dung-gwa tong	– a 'winter melon soup'
duppy	– Jamaican word for spirit or ghost

E

e-e-yu	– Also known as U-I-Oil. For cuts, insect bites, liniment for bruises

F

fah-chung	– Chinese sausage
fah-chong	
Fah Keow	– name given to the Chinese diaspora
Hua Keow	
farthing	– quarter of one penny (old British currency)

fee fee	– small tin whistle
flit gun	– apparatus used to spray insects
foah chaw	– train
foo-gah	– also known as bitter melon; used as a vegetable
fook shook	– Uncle Fook
fudge-man	– the ice-cream man ('fudge' is ice cream on a stick)
fui	– monetary partnership (to 'join a partner')
fung bow fum bow	– a red envelope with a small monetary token

G

Gah San	– ceremony of cleaning the graves of ancestors and making food offerings during the Ching Ming festival.
gai mow sow gai mow sao	– feathered stick duster
gam-fo-cha	– a bitter herbal tea; a treatment for fevers to induce sweating.
Gap Jonng	– Hakka term derived from 'Grip container'
gat chuk gah chuk gah chok	– to rap someone in the head with one's knuckles
gaw tsiu	– dried, roasted watermelon seeds
gawn	– Jamaican patois for 'gone'
gee pai gee pye ghi-pi	– Chinese playing cards, about 2 x 8 cm.
Gim San	– Gold Mountain; common name for American west and Canada
gimbelin	– a small tart fruit, usually served pickled
gin choy	– preserved vegetables used as a condiment in soups and steamed dishes
Gleaner	– a Jamaican daily newspaper
go pee	– dried mandarin orange peel
goew juu	– flour skin wrapped meatballs served on a toothpick
gong tong wah	– to speak the Chinese language
gow jew	– steamed pork wrapped in pasta
gow tsui	– to teach
gui gee	– red grains, good for eyes
gui-jai	– local chap or coloured person, usually any male other than Chinese
guimah gweema gweemah	– a local female helper
Gung Gung	– paternal grand-father
gweesi	– same as gui-jai
gymkhanas	– children's riding competitions (horseback)

H

ha'penny	– two farthings or half a penny; aka 'a'penny'
haa gung ban haw gung ban	– a fritter made with minced shrimp
Hakka	– clan of the Han people
ham choy	– salted preserved vegetable
ham-lam	– salted Chinese dates
ham saa-li	– pickled Chinese apricots
ham tdiu poo	– grocery shop or 'saltfish shop' in Hakka
ham teaw poo ham tew poo ham thew poo ham thwe poo ham tier poo	
higgler	– a peddlar or vendor

I

J

jacks	– a child's game played with star shaped metal pieces and a small ball
jackass corn	– probably got its name because like the donkey or jackass, it is tough and durable; a hard biscuit made of coconut, flour and sugar
Jah gung	– maternal grandfather
Jah gung tai	– maternal great grandfather
Jah po	– maternal grandmother
Jah po tai Japo tai	– maternal great grandmother
janga	– a river shrimp
Jippy jappa	– a straw hat; the material from which it is made
jiu nyuk	– pork
jong niu jung nu	– a young boy that looks after the cows (literally to watch the cow)
Jung San Joon San Joong San	– name of the Chinese beach in Kingston

K

keun choy quin choy	– Chinese parsley
konn sunn	– to watch the ships
kun poo cun poo kun foo	– to watch the shop
kyak	– wooden slippers

L

labrishing	– chatting or gossiping
lam	– sugared Chinese dates
lap hap	– preserved duck

lau-gung   – husband
   lowgoong
lau-po   – wife
   lopo
len tai   – smart
Leung   – 'cool' energy or Yin
li jai   – pickled Chinese sour plums
lignum vitae   – Jamaica's National Tree
Lo   – old Cantonese spelling, while Luo is
   Lowe   the Mandarin spelling
   Luo
loi sue   – rice vermicelli
   loy sue
longan   – a Chinese fruit similar to guinep
lopet   – daicon, a vegetable
lopet ban   – a steamed bun made of rice flour and
            filled with shredded seasoned daicon;
            sometimes also filled with turnip and
            dried shrimps
Lulu style   – flipped-up hairdo

M

macca   – thorn or prickle; prickly weeds
   makka
mah cha   – a horse drawn buggy or carriage
   mahchah
mah jong   – a Chinese game played with tiles
mattress   – a type of cake baked in a large
            rectangular pan, then cut into squares
mawga   – very slim; skinny
mi lau po   – my wife
Montego Bay   – capital city of St. James, Jamaica's
   Mo Bay   second city
   Moxibustion   – A technique in which a stick or cone
            of mugwort, *artemesia vulgaris,* is
            placed over an affected area of the
            body. The cone is placed on an
            acupuncture point and burned for a
            specific period of time.
mn-peow   – fish mah, used in some soups
   impeow
muk-nee   – dried fungus

N

Nam Yang   – the Hakkas in some South Eastern
            nations e.g. Malaysia and Burma
   Lam Yong
Neijing   – The Yellow Emperor's Classic of
            Medicine
Nyet hee   – 'hot' energy or too much Yang

O

P

Pa Kua   – Yin Yang

pac ap   – pigeon
   pak hap
pacquee   – White person or White man
pai que   – Chinese card game
pak choy   – a Chinese vegetable with big green
            leaves
pak-fah-yu   – remedy good for stubborn sore
            muscles
pak jam gai   – a whole chicken boiled slowly in a
   pak-jam-guy   soup of dried dates and fish maw,
            served with soy-sauce or a mixture of
            minced ginger, spring onions or
            escallion and salt in hot oil.
peaka peow   – a Chinese betting game, based on the
   pick a peow   selection of 8 winning characters out
            of 81
peow   – ticket or lottery
Phang Shee   – Chinese name
pickney   – Jamaican word for child
pie que (e)   – a Chinese game of chance
Po-Po   – paternal grandmother
pocomania   – literally a 'little madness'; Jamaican
            religious cult
poopalik   – somersault
pork and muknee   – a Chinese dish with pork and
            mushrooms

Q

Qi   – aka Chi, the life energy that flows
            through our bodies
Qi Gong   – A system of exercise that includes
            healing postures, movement, self-
            massage, breathing techniques, and
            meditation.
quattie   – one and a half pence
            (old British currency)
quin choy   – a vegetable

R

rass lick   – Jamaican colloquialism for a very
            painful blow
Rema   – an inner city community in Kingston
rolling calf   – believed to be the 'duppy' of a
            wicked person which appears
            (at night, usually in a cemetery)
            as a calf with red fiery eyes, wearing
            clanking chains

S

saa-li   – pickled Chinese apricots and sour
            plums
Savanna-La-Mar   – capital of or main city in
            Westmoreland, a parish in Jamaica
sighants   – science
Senn Mah   – recommended female faith healer
Sen-sang   – teacher, to show respect...Mr.
seow yah   – midnight snack

shao bow
  chow bow
  show bow
  sow bow
	– a steamed bun with a variety of fillings

shi-yu seeyu	– Chinese Black Bean sauce
shift	– straight, tube-like dress, fitted closely at the hips
ship chit goo	– aunt number 17
ship yin dan	– Chinese medicine a.k.a. Saplingtan, forerunner of aspirin. A white powder for headaches and general pain.
ship yit diam ship-it-dam	– local born Chinese
shookmay	– wife of uncle that's younger than father
shut pan	– a metal container used to carry food
sighants	– sigh ants, science
Ska	– musical genre which originated in Jamaica
skull	– (from British 'skulk') to avoid going to classes; to goof off.
son pan	– abacus, a Chinese calculating board made up of rows of beads.
sore foot so foot	– children's treat, money given to children by someone who has won at mah-jong
sour sop	– large green fruit with soft prickles on the skin; the white pulp makes a delicious and refreshing drink
stinking toe	– a type of fruit grown in a very hard brown shell; proper name is locust
suimen	– a steaming bowl of noodles in a soup combined with various meats and vegetables.

T

Tai-chi	– prescribed martial arts movements of defence and attack, designed to induce flexibility and strength to the muscles and joints.
tai-que	– an older brother of your mother
tai-yee	– an older aunt of your mother
tang wah	– to listen to parents
teaw dungsee	– to steal from the shop
teef out	– to leave without consent or knowledge
thet mah binn	– long prickly weeds; Hakka for 'iron horse whip'
tie-que	– see pie-que; Chinese game of chance
tiki tiki	– small fish; minnows
tong ngin guy	– China Town or Chinese Street
tong-nyin tongin	– a Chinese person
trupence	– three pence, (old British currency)

U

V

W

wah moy
  wah moi
  wah mui
	– salted dried prunes or salted preserved plums

wait fi mi	– Jamaican patois meaning "wait for me"
wash	– colloquialism for limeade, called 'lemonade' in Jamaica
won ban	– a steamed cake made from rice flour and sugar
wonton	– a Chinese dumpling stuffed with minced pork or shrimp
woon choy	– water convolvulus; a hollow stemmed vegetable aka 'hung choi'
wu-gui	– Chinese for a local or Jamaican

X

Y

yabba	– African word for a clay cooking-pot
Yi Yee Tong	– another community organisation formed within the CBA by some of their members who disagreed with the policies taken by the President.
yim cha	– to drink tea
Yit Bak Ngi-Sip Sue Peow	– 'One hundred and twenty lottery' (peaka peow)
yu-nan-pak-yuk	– A white powder, used for serious injuries, deep cuts or wounds
Yuk choi	– a kind of medicinal soup

Z

Zsa Gung	– an elderly gentlemen (see Jahgung)
Zsa Po	– an elderly lady (see Jahpo)

Contributors' Biographies

Bitter, Melanie Semi-retired from housework, orchid hobbyist, does volunteer work in the gardens for Stella Maris Church and St. Joseph's Hospital, plays mah jong once a week. (387)

Chang, Gladstone 'Ray' is Chair of CI Fund Management Inc., which headquarters in Toronto, Canada. With over 600 team members across the country and investment management subsidiaries in New York, San Francisco and Orlando, they manage in excess of C$25 billion. He is a 2003 recipient of The Prime Minister's Medal of Appreciation for Service to Jamaica – both in Jamaica and Canada. (141)

Chang, Peter (425)

Chang-Allen, Fay Alison, businessperson married to Tony Allen… two children, Christopher Michael and Anna Alicia. Fundraising Chairperson for the Restoration of the Chinese Cemetery in Jamaica. (305)

Charlton, Stephanie moved to Toronto, Canada in 1995 where she attended York University and Centennial College. She is now a public relations consultant and event planner for Jesson Artmont Communications. (184)

Chen, E. Muriel retired businesswoman and active CBA member, lives in Jamaica. She and her late husband G. A. Chen have one son. (219)

Chen, Lillian like her mother, Lillian is also the only daughter and the youngest of five children. She is sister to Wellington (deceased), Washington, Ray and Roger. She is mother to Sebastian, and lives in Vancouver. (93)

Chen, Minnie, eldest daughter of Ship Chit Goo, a registered nurse and a certified midwife, graduated in the United Kingdom, worked in England and Canada, is presently semi retired. (131)

Chen, Monica (329)

Chen, Patrick lives in Ottawa, Canada with his wife Beverly and both their children, Lisa and Tyson are attending university. Patrick has written a book, The Peoples of the Caribbean Commonwealth, An Illustrated History of their Origins, Migration and Self-determination. (373)

Chen, Phil musician extraordinaire, learned his skill in Jamaica playing mento and ska. In England, a fortunate circumstance led him to become the Bassist in demand. He is the musician that comes to mind when one thinks of Fender Bass Guitars. Phil is an advocate for Macrobiotics lifestyle. (365)

Chen, Ray (332)

Chen, Roger a retired Structural Engineer, he now builds bridges between generations. Roger is the youngest son of Samuel and Violet Chen. With his wife, Barbara Kong, they have 3 sons and 3 grandchildren. (125, 302, 315, 431)

Chen, Rudy born Kingston, Jamaica is the youngest of 3 children of James Chen (Chen, Kee Onn) and Lily Hugh. Retired Air Canada employee now living in Toronto, Ontario, Canada. (359)

Chen, Vincent is retired and enjoying life. (389)

Chen-Young, Paul was the founder of many financial entities in Jamaica and Miami, the most notable being Eagle Group and the stock broking company, Paul Chen Young and Company. He was married to the late Michele Pauyo from Haiti. He has three boys, Phillip, Gerald and Michael and one daughter, Claudine. Since 1983, Paul and Dorit Hutson have shared their lives together. (137)

Chin, Derrick born and raised in Rollington Town. Migrated to Toronto, Canada in 1969. Returned to Jamaica in 1991 with wife Sandy, now deceased, to start Vision Plus Optical. (403)

Chin, Grace having lived in Toronto for the past 30 years, Grace has adjusted to the North American lifestyle. Each season has something different to offer but summer is still her favourite. It never comes early enough and doesn't last long enough. She will always cherish the memories and years she lived in Jamaica. (249)

Chin, Mandison was born in Cambridge, Jamaica on March 22, 1935. The 7th child of Edward and Rhoda Chin (nee Wong). Migrated to Canada 1976. Electro Mechanical Designer at Littons System. Retired 1990. Children: Glenn, Tracey, Kathryn and grandfather of 7. (401)

Chin, Reggie is a Director and Vice Chairman of United Petroleum Jamaica Limited (UNIPET). (147)

Chin, Rose (nee Lim), born in Kingston. Attended Holy Family Prep School and Alpha Academy High School. Mother of 4 girls and 1 boy. Emigrated to Canada in 1976. Occupation: Owner Uniglobe Bon Voyage Travel, Toronto. Goal: that one day everyone who walks into my office will purchase only First Class travel! (266, 328)

Chin, Sing tireless businessman, father of four and grandfather of five, Sing now lives in Kingston, Jamaica where he happily works alongside his brother and children. (355)

Chin, Vernon residing in sunny Montego Bay where he has lived all his life, Vernon's work is still focused on the tourist industry. To this day he dances whenever he hears good music. (414)

Chin, Yvonne born in Montego Bay, Jamaica to Frederick and Sybil Lee Hing (nee Ho, formerly, Hew Wing). Educated at MoBay High and Ryerson. Retired Bank Manager (RBC). Children: Jeffrey and Monique Guthrie; Granddaughter: Jade. (109)

Chin-Loy, Donette M. has created and managed successful communications strategies and government relations programmes for corporate, government and institutional clients. Ms. Chin-Loy was part of the groundbreaking Innoversity team and is a partner in La Grassa Chin-Loy Communications. She has worked extensively in sports and entertainment marketing, on major events. (155)

Chin-Quee, Karis is a PhD student in Physiology at Tulane University in New Orleans. She is fascinated with cultures of the world generally and especially with their myths and folk tales. (167)

Chong-Young, Charles is a 'George's boy' who studied in the States and migrated to Canada in 1976. He is in the performance improvement business, helping client companies develop and implement employee training, process improvement, and technology tools. (79)

Chung, Sister Benedict (288)

Chung, Joyce youngest daughter of Levi and Marion Lee spent her childhood in Old Harbour Bay. Married to Donald Chung. Two children, Kevin and Donna. Emigrated to Canada in 1976. Currently retired. Three grandchildren: Alex, Patricia Joy and Jacob. (263)

Chung-Groves, Simone (111)

Chung, Osbert (152)

Chung Fah, Winston Jamaican and international football personality, music enthusiast, father, grandfather, coach and friend, Winston ('Chungy') continues to focus his energies on talented youth wherever he lays his hat. (357)

Devensky, Winnie - separated and living in Boca Raton, Florida, for the past 31 years. Has 2 daughters; first daughter Lara, married with 2 children and living in North Carolina while second daughter, Nikki, lives and works in Shanghai. (417)

Fong Yee, Leopold (187)

Fung, Clive rebellious, controversial, provocative. The epitome of endurance with an inordinate passion for pleasure. (343)

Gordon Scott, Sonia is a freelance writer with a background in public relations and marketing. She has authored a Jamaican travel guide, contributed to others, and her articles have appeared in several Caribbean and international publications.

Hedden, Annette resides in Ft. Myers, Florida, and has lived in the U.S. for 38 years. She has four children and four grandchildren. Besides being a professional artist, her hobbies are duplicate bridge, golf and reading. (385)

Hew-Shue, Norman was born and raised in Kingston by loving parents and with warm memories. Married with two sons, he loves to share his reminiscences of those good old days in his well-known articles. (195, 245, 391, 405, 409, 419, 443, 447)

Ho, Cecil one of the founding elders of the Swallowfield Church. He is the oldest of four children. His siblings, David (now in Glory), Ray (USA) and Len (USA) were all or still are involved in full time ministry. He has been married to Inez since 1956 and has three children. Richard and Andrew, both Swallows, and Melody, who now resides in the USA. (299)

Hoo, Everard is a retired credit manager and former insurance broker/salesman and bank manager and one of the Toronto, Ontario editors of the Chinese Jamaican website. He and his wife, Nolia (nee D'Oyen) have three children and five grandchildren. Hobbies are grandparenting, reading, photography, gardening and sports. (177)

Kong, Phyllis (294)

Lee, Alexandra a graduate of York University in Toronto, is a French /English translator and business and technical writer by profession. The principal writer for Pro-Writing Services Limited based in Kingston, Jamaica, she has in recent years written extensively for the International Chinese -Jamaican community.

Lee, Basil Austin was born in Montego Bay. Son of Johnson Lee and Daisy Ho Sang. Married to the late Gloria Wisdom and has four sons and one daughter. Presently living in Scarborough, Ontario, Canada. (116)

Lee, Donna lives in Montego Bay and operates yacht cruises and tours. (133)

Lee, Easton broadcaster, public relations professional, playwright, published author and Anglican priest. Married to supportive wife, Jean for over 50 blessed years, he is the happy father of four and grandfather of eight. (84)

Lee, Nikki lives and works in sunny Los Angeles, California. She fondly remembers many childhood vacations in Jamaica and loves to browse through old photo albums and listen to family stories about island living. (397)

Lee, Patrick A. (Li Zitung) is the son of Lee Tom Yin and his wife Theresa. Patrick is also the author and publisher of *Canadian Jamaican Chinese (2000)*, and *Jamaican Chinese Worldwide (2004)* along with his wife, Loraine (Chin). They have 2 children, Christina and Robert. (144, 163)

Lee, Robert chartered quantity surveyor, badminton enthusiast and active CBA member, Robert Lee lives in Kingston, Jamaica with wife Emilia. The couple have two children and two grandchildren. (181)

Lee, Tiffany was born in St. Andrew, raised in South Florida, and currently works in clinical research in the Cincinnati area (and misses South Florida dearly!). Her story is dedicated in loving memory to her grandparents on both sides who strived for a better life and taught them about courage and love. (107)

Lee Sang, Sister Josette M., O.S.F. retired from teaching in the classroom after thirty seven years, but is still actively involved in Education, Church and Religious Community Ministries. (222)

Lim Shue, Albert and his wife Corine live in Toronto with their 2 children, Albert John and Catherine. He is the founder of Universal Marketing Agencies. (362)

Lodenquai, Blanche Retired from business and lives in Kingston with Felix and Paul. (87)

Lodenquai, Raymond, born in Jamaica and migrated to Canada in 1976. He is married to Beverley (Chin) and has 2 daughters. Raymond currently works for McCormick as the Technical Development Manager and has accepted a position with his company as the Regional Technical Director of R & D for the Asia Pacific Zone. (77)

Lowe, Maxine certified court reporter in Vancouver, B.C., Canada. Married to Paul Wu; son, Shaun, 22; daughter, Alyssa, 15. Left Jamaica in 1978 for Taiwan with parents and siblings; acquired vast experience of the best of both worlds while remaining a true, patois-speaking, irie, dawta from yard. (203)

Lowe Ching, Sister Theresa (283)

Lue, Aston and wife, Michelle (nee Chan) live in Florida, and are the proud parents of Benjamin, Jeannette, Celena and Kathy. He's been in the international foods import and distribution business since 1987. (207)

Lue, Constance Beverly (nee Chung): was born in Darlingston, Westmoreland. 3rd of 6 children of Jena and Edward Chong. Married to Franklin Lue, with three children, Tracey, Frances and David. (340)

Lue, Franklin A. was born in Hong Kong and migrated to Jamaica as an infant. Very active member of St. Peter & Paul Parish Church. Migrated to Canada in 1974. Research scientist career; contributed to the development of literature for Sleep Medicine. Currently a Group Leader at Defence R&D Canada. (215)

Lue, Hubert : Retired and living in Toronto where he enjoys spending time with the grandchildren. (53)

Lyn, Gloria Helena was born in Springfield, St. Elizabeth, Jamaica. Her parents were John and Ada Chen-See who immigrated to Jamaica from mainland China. In 1951 she was married to Basil E Lyn, Chem. Eng. MSc (MIT) and had four children. Her husband died in 1982. She taught at the University of the West Indies, retired in 1992 and now resides in Canada. (257)

Mills, Sonia is a Jamaican who has worked in print and audio-visual media for the past forty years, principally as a writer. She has written news, features, radio and television scripts and for the stage. (119)

Moses, Joan is the daughter of Sylvia (nee Lue Tenn) and Kingsley Lee. She is married to Paul Moses and has two daughters – Michelle and Lisa. (90)

Palomino, Gloria, Senior Justice of the Peace, Founder of the Police Civic Committees, consummate charity worker, environmentalist, avid gardener and tennis player, Gloria lives in Kingston with companion, Tino Calarelli and has two daughters, one son and four grandchildren. (98)

Pinchin, Joseph He lives in Kingston, Jamaica with his wonderful wife of over 50 years. He and Maria have five children and many grand and great-grand children. (268)

Russell, Peggi lives in Mandeville. She was married to Richard Russell (the Graphic Artist - not the Tennis Player!) for 26 years. Now widowed. Mother of two sons - Mark and Matthew Russell. Loves to bake and read. (271)

Simpson, Joy migrated to Canada in 1974 and lives in Toronto with her 5 children. She occasionally works in a beauty salon but works at a department store. (135)

Tai, Kennedy and wife Dorothy have two sons and three grandchildren. They have lived in Calgary and now call Toronto home. (276)

Tenn, Maurice born in Bog Walk, St. Catherine, 26th January 1934. He has 3 children and 3 grandchildren. (279)

Weston Jakob, Melanie was repeatedly told by her family that she was 'found under a rock.' Melanie is sure of only a few things regarding her personal story; she was born and raised in Kingston and now living in New York City. (175)

Williams, Penny, an Alpha Academy graduate, was educated at McGill U. in Montreal. She has lived in Toronto since 1976 but has been teaching English in China for the last two years. Penny has two sons, Andrew and Cary, who are living in Jamaica. (209)

Williams, Dr. Samuel I, son of James & Ida Williams, Shopkeepers. Educated at Cornwall College and Edinburgh University. Married Mavis Chin in 1953, daughter of Edward & Rhoda Chin of Montego Bay. Mavis passed on in 1999. Sam and Mavis have 3 children; Hilary, Andrew & David. Remarried in 2002 to Patricia Luck (widow of Dr. Isaac Luck). Retired in 1998 in Whitby after 42 years of medical practice. (113)

Williams, Stanford place of birth is Green Island, Hanover. Married Ivy Lyew in 1951, has four children. Migrated to Canada 1975. Worked with Sears Canada until retirement 1991. (159)

Wong, Carol Mearle (nee Williams) born in Williamsfield district and grew up in Petersfield district, Westmoreland, Jamaica. Married to Edward Wong formerly of Montego Bay. Blessed with three sons - Brian, Gordon and Jason; two grandchildren - Mitchell and Amelie Wong. Presently living in Unionville, Ontario, Canada. (226)

Wong, D. Tony is a keen amateur photographer and golfer residing in Kingston with family. (169)

Wong, Earle, is a retiree. Current Activities: – Church Work. Vice President – North York Soccer Association, President - North York Community Soccer League, President – Flemingdon Park Sports Club. (191)

Wong, Stanford G. born in Kingston Jamaica and now resides in Markham, Ontario, Canada. Married to Joyce with 2 sons and a daughter. (239)

Wong, Tony was born in Montego Bay. He is a senior reporter with the Toronto Star, Canada's largest circulation newspaper. Tony is married to Sharon Lem, a senior reporter with the Toronto Sun. One day they hope to retire in Jamaica and open their own grocery store. (101)

Young, Karlene (deceased) popular cake decorator and caterer, enjoyed her role as mother of five, grandmother of seven and wife of Hubert, to whom she was married for 48 years. Those close to her remember her for her spirit of kindness. (171)

Young, Mavis is a writer of short stories and biographies. (217)

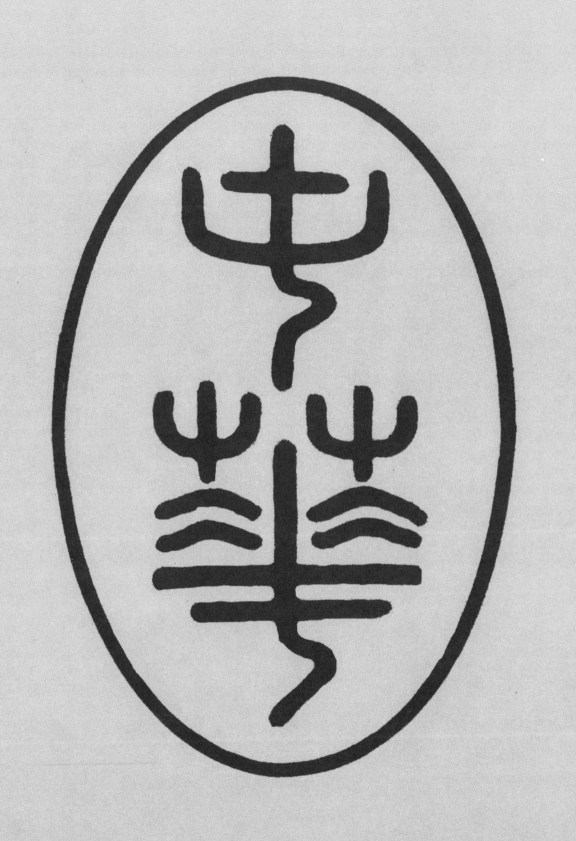